CROSSCURRENTS IN
INDIGENOUS SPIRITUALITY

STUDIES IN CHRISTIAN MISSION

VOLUME 18

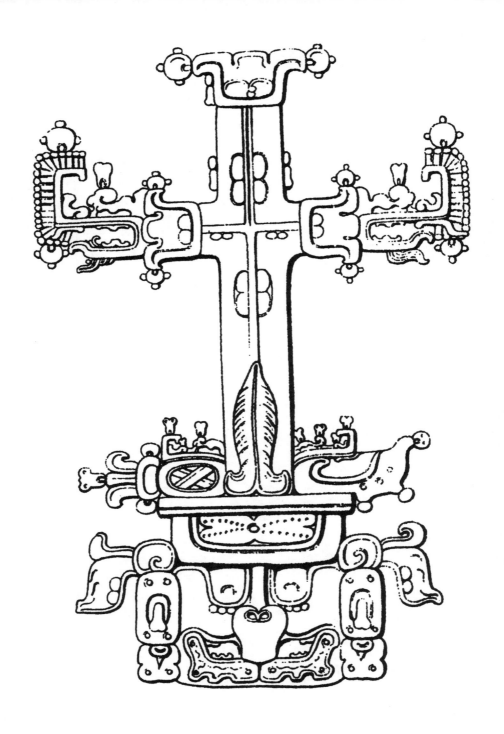

The "Foliated Cross", Temple of the Cross Palenque,
Chiapas, Mexico

CROSSCURRENTS IN INDIGENOUS SPIRITUALITY

Interface of Maya, Catholic and Protestant Worldviews

EDITED BY

GUILLERMO COOK

E.J. BRILL
LEIDEN • NEW YORK • KÖLN
1997

This series offers a forum for scholarship on the history of Christian missionary movements world-wide, the dynamics of Christian witness and service in new surrounds, the transition from movements to churches, and the areas of cultural initiative or involvement of Christian bodies and individuals, such as education, health, community development, press, literature and art. Special attention is given to local initiative and leadership and to Christian missions from the Third World. Studies in the theories and paradigms of mission in their respective contexts and contributions to missiology as a theological discipline are a second focus of the series. Occasionally volumes will contain selected papers from outstanding missiologists and proceedings of significant conferences related to the themes of the series.

Enquiries and proposals for the publication of works in the series should be addressed to the Administrative Editor, Studies in Christian Mission, E.J. Brill N.V., P.O. Box 9000, 2300 PA Leiden, The Netherlands.

The paper in this book meets the guidelines for permanence and durability of the Committee on Production Guidelines for Book Longevity of the Council on Library Resources.

Library of Congress Cataloging-in-Publication Data

Cook, Guillermo.
   Crosscurrents in indigenous spirituality : interface of Maya, Catholic, and Protestant worldviews / by Guillermo Cook.
      p.   cm. — (Studies in Christian mission, ISSN 0924-9389 ; v. 18)
   Includes bibliographical references and index.
   ISBN 9004106227 (alk. paper)
   1. Mayas—Religion.   2. Maya philosophy.   3. Christianity and culture—Latin America.   4. Spiritual life—Latin America.
5. Catholic Church.   6. Protestantism.   I. Title.   II. Series.
F1435.3.R3C66   1997
200'.89'97415—dc21   96-49379
                                                                                          CIP

Die Deutsche Bibliothek - CIP-Einheitsaufnahme

Crosscurrents in indigenous spirituality : interface of Maya, catholic and protestant worldviews / by Guillermo Cook. -
Leiden ; New York ; Köln : Brill, 1997
   (Studies in Christian mission ; Vol. 18)
   ISBN 90-04-10622-7
NE: Cook, Guillermo; GT

ISSN   0924-9389
ISBN   90 04 10622 7

PRINTED IN THE NETHERLANDS

CONTENTS

Table of contents vii
Foreword: Personal notes ix
Preface xi
Glossary xv
Map xvii
Introduction: Brief History of the Maya Peoples
                 Guillermo Cook 1

PART I
CLASH OF CULTURES AND WORLDVIEWS 33

1. The Invasion of Christianity into the World of the Mayas
    Vitalino Similox Salazar 35
2. Christianity and Aboriginal Religions in Abia Yala
    Goyo Cutimanco 49
3. Invisible Converts to Protestantism in Highland Guatemala
    Liliana R. Goldin and Brent Metz 61

PART TWO
MAYA CULTURE AND STRATEGIES OF RESISTANCE . . 81

4. The *Pop Vuh*: The Sacred History of the Mayas
    Edgar Cabrera 83
5. Ethnic Resistance and the Maya Calendar in Guatemala
    Jesús García Ruiz 91
6. The Social Role of Maya Women
    Dalila C. Nayap-Pot 101
7. Anchored Communities:
    Identity and History of the Maya Q'eqchi'
    Richard A. Wilson 113

PART THREE
THE RISE OF INDIGENOUS THEOLOGY 137

8.   *Teutlatolli*: Speaking about God -
     Indigenous Theology and Roman Catholicism
     Eleazar López Hernández 139
9.   Birth of Latin American Indigenous Theology
     Edward L. Cleary 171
10. Indigenous Theology: A Reformed Protestant Perspective
     Facundo Ku Canché and team 189
11. Is Christ being Resurrected Among the Indigenous People?
     Moisés Colop 199

PART FOUR
ISSUES IN DIALOGUE AND EVANGELIZATION . . . 205

12. Inculturation and indigenous theology
     Jesús Espeja 207
13. The Old Face of the New Evangelization
     Pop Cal 217
14. The Evangelization of Culture
     Pablo Richard 225
15. Political Aspects of Guatemalan Reality:
     Mayan Widows Speak Out
     Rosalina Tuyub 233
16. Understanding Mayan Spirituality:
     A Proposed Methodology for Dialogue with Christians
     Wuqub' Iq' 241
17. Traditional Values and Christian Ethics:
     A Maya-Protestant Spirituality
     Antonio Otzoy . . . . : 261
18. "A Nation Where Everyone has a Place":
     The Chiapas Uprising
     Ofelia Ortega 271
Conclusion
     Guillermo Cook and Dalila Nayap-Pot 293
Index of Subjects 323
Essential Bibliography 327

FOREWORD AND ACKNOWLEDGEMENTS

Writing books for me has never been an academic pursuit. It is a road into the unknown and a way of sharing what I have learned with as many people as are willing to embark on a pilgrimage of discovery, which is not without risks.

A Community Endeavor

I've been on this road for more than six decades. As a child, I played with Quichua children in the Bolivian village where I lived with my missionary parents. Like most small children, I learned to communicate with my peers in a mixture of Quichua and Spanish. Years later, as a young missionary teacher in Guatemala, I spent memorable vacations in highland Mayan villages. Several decades later I became a promoter of non-formal theological education.[1] I was privileged to sit at the feet of Guatemalan and Yucatán Maya, of the Peruvian Quechua and the Bri-Bri of Costa Rica. In recent years I have participated in Protestant conferences where indigenous peoples have been prominent. I have reflected on Christology in México with Catholic Totonacas from Puebla, insurgent Tzeltales from Chiapas and Presbyterian Maya from Yucatán. Several of my closest and dearest friends are indigenous women and men into whose community I have sometimes been privileged to enter.

In a word, my pilgrimage has made it possible for me to observe the Maya and other indigenous persons in various stages of their process of self-awareness. I have sat with them, argued with them, and absorbed their criticism. I have consulted with them about my personal observations and reflections on their religion and culture, and gained the blessing of those who have contributed to this book for the great responsibility of setting down their story in a language of domination: English. The only thing that I have been required to do is to share my thoughts with them, and receive their correction whenever necessary. Copies of their translated papers were sent to them in advance; they also shared in the modest "honoraria fund" that was made possible by a small grant from Christian Aid of the United Kingdom. To them, and to other contributors, my heartfelt thanks. Funding for the initial stages of this research project came from Evangelisches

---

[1] With the Centro Evangélico Latinoamericano de Estudios Pastorales (CELEP).

Missionswerk of Stuttgart. A William Paton Fellowship from Selly Oak Colleges, Birmingham, UK. (1994-95), provided the time needed for much of the writing and translation. The final work has been done late at night and on weekends in the midst of my involvement in a much larger task.

Structure of the book

The chapters in this book deal with specifically Maya concerns as well as those of the broad Mesoamerican region. Three chapters (2, 9 and 12) address wider indigenous issues throughout Abia Yala. They may help to relate the Maya struggles and contributions to a much wider context. It is hoped that the perspective of "informed outsiders"—anthropologists, ethnologists, theologians (almost half of the total)—will provide a significant counterpoint to the candid reflections of indigenous thinkers.

Though confessional balance was not necessarily a goal, it has been maintained—except in the case of Maya religionists, of which we have only two, who unwittingly allow us glimpses of their Christian formation. We have been favored, as well, with four chapters by women, two of whom are Maya.

The four main sections of the book are laid out in more or less logical order. The chapter distributions do also follow a certain logic, although, admittedly, they could well have been organized in a different way. The authors are introduced at the beginning of each chapter.

A Word about Terminology

While Spanish words and expressions are placed between quotation marks (inverted comas), indigenous words, except for place and tribal names, are italicized. Inasmuch as possible, I have tried to maintain Spanish spelling and accents in order to accustom my readers to Spanish pronunciation. The spelling of Maya words and tribal names, follows, as much as possible, the unified alphabet of the Mayan Academy of Guatemalan Languages, which does not use accents.[2] The apostrophe in Maya words is meant to indicate glotal stops and vowel emphasis.

---

[2] This has wrought havoc with the SIL spelling that had been used for years by Protestant missionary linguists. It is a clear sign that the Maya are determined to take control of their own history.

PREFACE

An American tourist was visiting the ruins of Palenque in the jungles of Chiapas, México. Marvelling at the haunting beauty of its empty ruins, he asked: "Where did all the people go?" To which his guide replied, "But we are still here, Señor!"

The Maya have remained close to their land, and are today very much in evidence throughout Mesoamérica. There is today a Liga Maya Internacional, with headquarters in Costa Rican exile and representatives in Europe and North America, which is dedicated to communicating Mayan culture, values and religion.

The Maya are not alone. Indigenous self-awareness has exploded since 1992, the date that symbolizes the 500th anniversary of the "conquista" of the inhabitants of Abia Yala by the European empires. Learned men and women, tribal leaders, priests from all over the region meet together in international and regional conferences to celebrate together, compare notes, learn from each other, and establish a unified strategy for asserting their place in the sun. What we know as "America", North, Central and South, is being called by them *Abia Yala*. It is what the Kuna people of Panama call their world: "land of the sun", and hence, "land of light" or "the ripe land".

Change and Continuity

Reflecting upon the amazing accomplishments of the Maya, a renowned archeologist observes: "Creators of one of the most spectacular civilizations the world has ever known, the Maya today have been reduced to... a 'folk culture' with little or no voice in their destinies... No imperial conquest has ever been so total or a great people shattered... But it has not always been this way". Most certainly. And one objective of this book is to demonstrate this point.

The same Mesoamerican scholar laments that among the "demands of oppressed nationalities for their place in the sun... little or nothing is heard from the millions upon millions of indigenous... people in Latin America. "Has any native American language", he asks, "been heard in the halls of the United Nations?" "None", is his own reply to this rhetorical question.[1]

---

[1] Michael Coe, *Breaking the Maya Code* (New York: Thames and Hudson, 1992), p. 47.

Subsequent events have modified these categorical affirmations. But, barely two years after this statement was made, indigenous languages began to be heard in the corridors of the United Nations, their presence made possible by the proclamation of the Internationa Decade of the World Indigenous Peoples.

But the most stunning act of all, with Mayas at the forefront, took place on January 1, 1994. On that date the North American Free Trade Act (NAFTA) went into effect and all México was supposed to rejoice. Instead, an indigenous rebellion broke out in the Maya state of Chiapas, México, which "transfixed" the world. Thanks to wide popular support of its demands for far reaching constitutional changes that would benefit every marginalized Mexican citizen—and to the canny use of the Internet from the heart of the jungle—the Zapatista revolution, if nothing else, has managed to make the signatories of NAFTA edgy. Yes, the Mayas are still here, and making their voices heard.

Indigenous peoples all over the world are speaking up for their rights. Emboldened by the commemoration of the "five hundred years", vast masses of "first nations" peoples have marched on the parliaments of several Latin American countries. In Guatemala, as well as Chiapas, Maya civic associations proliferate for the first time in centuries, and Maya academics and politicians of every political stripe are joining together to challenge their nation to a new social order based on love of land and family, respect for personal and collective rights and holistic spirituality—values that have been practiced by the Maya peoples for thousands of years. The social and cultural awakening of the indigenous peoples of Abia Yala is inseparable from the evolution of their age-old spirituality. Hopefully, this will become clear in the indigenous contributions to this book.

Objectives and Parameters

1. To understand the world-view—history, culture and religion—of the Mesoamerican indigenous peoples, and in particular of the Maya. Other Indoamerican peoples shall be touched upon only by way of comparison and clarification of our basic theses.

2. To raise issues of inter-religious dialogue, mission and evangelization for all Christians. Evangelical Protestants in Latin America have, heretofore, dodged the problem, when we haven't rejected it outright, hiding

behind timeworn labels and stereotypes. Our purpose is not so much to convince as to increase awareness of the challenges and opportunities.

3. To evaluate, with a critical eye, the evangelization of Abia Yala, by European missionaries, during the Spanish "conquista" and Protestant missionary expansion from North America. Present failures in cultural awareness will also be faced with frankness.

4. To understand and interpret the reasons for the resurgence of indigenous spirituality and evaluate its essential beliefs in its own right, and in the light of the Christian faith. Our purpose is not apologetic but irenic.

5. To explore the use of images in Mesoamerican and Christian spirituality, with a view to establishing bridges for communication between them. To look critically at the representations of divinity in both Christianity and indigenous spirituality for evidences of explicit or implicit idolatry, while avoiding culturally defined value judgments.

6. To analyze, perceptively and receptively, the implications of the Maya resurgence for Christian life and mission, as well as for a society that has lost its fundamental values and beliefs. Does the resurgence of Maya spirituality have anything to say to the Christian worldview?

7. Last, but not at all least, we want to pose the question of the activity and self-revelation of Yahwe, the Creator God of the Judeo-Christian Bible, in a region of the world that was totally cut off from Eurasia and Biblical revelation for thousands of years. How can we interpret God's unique revelation through Jesus Christ, in the New Testament in this context?

May this book make a significant contribution to the world-wide discussion on Gospel and Cultures that is taking place within Christian churches around the world. My hope is that it will become a catalyst, also, for discussion among my evangelical sisters and brothers whose commendable zeal for sharing the Good News becomes bad news when it is not tempered with a spirit of dialogue and tolerance of alien beliefs and practices.

May we become both bridges and bridge-builders.

Bridges only fulfill their purpose when they are firmly anchored *on both sides of a deep divide*. If people are forced to jump from where they are onto "our" bridge we have not been communicating the Gospel of Jesus Christ. If we are unable to extend our bridges all the way to the "other side"—or to make the jump onto the other side when the bridge is not complete, then we do not understand the Incarnation, nor the mission of Jesus the Son of God. "Pontifex", the Latin word for bridge-builders (eng.: pontiff) as been assumed as a privileged title by some religious leaders, or derided as a dubious religious vocation by others. All the same, far too many of us today would rather "pontificate" than to build genuine bridges. To complete the metaphor, bridges are made to be walked upon; whoever wants to be a bridge, must be willing to be trampled upon—a painful exercise for all of us and for most human institutions.

Guillermo Cook, Consultant
Conference on World Mission and Evangelism (CWME)
World Council of Churches
Geneva, Switzerland
Pentecost 1996

GLOSSARY OF TERMS

Abia Yala — a Kuna (Panamá) term meaning "land of the sun," or "ripe land" which indigenous leaders use to refer to the Americas.

CELAM — Latin American Episcopal Conference.

Cofradía — Catholic brotherhoods who paid for the privilege of handling the affairs of particular saints on their feast days.

Conquista — the "conquest" of Abia Yala by the Spaniards.

Conquistadores — the Spanish adventurers who did this to the "pueblos oririginarios" of Abia Yala.

Costumbre (custom) — Guatemalan term for indigenous rituals.

Indígena — generic term that, until recently, was preferred over the more pejorative "indio" to refer to aboriginal, native or autochthonous peoples. Of more recent vintage is "pueblos originarios", original (first nations) peoples.

Indigenismo and *indigenista*, when used by indigenous peoples, refers to a paternalistic approach to their evangelization, liberation and development.

Ladino — a pejorative originally applied to Moors and Jews who forcibly converted to christianity in sixteenth century Spain. Indigenous use it today in place of *mestizo*.

Mestizo — the mixed Hispanic and indigenous race that dominates the indigenous peoples of Latin America.

Milpa — the cultivation of the staple maize and the culture surrounding it.

Pastoral can be either an adjective or a noun, as in "indigenous pastoral". It expresses the church's active pastoral concern for marginalized sectors of society.

Pop Vuh — the sacred book of the Ki'che' Maya peoples, mistakenly called "Popol Vuh". It signifies "the Council Book", or the Council Mat ("Pop) Book ("vuh").

Teutlatolli — "Speaking about God", in the Nahual or Aztec language.

Zapatistas — Armed Mayas who have risen up in the jungles of Chiapas under the banner of a past Mexican peasant revolutionary hero, Emiliano Zapata.

Mesoamerica (5'000 BCE – 1:400 CE)

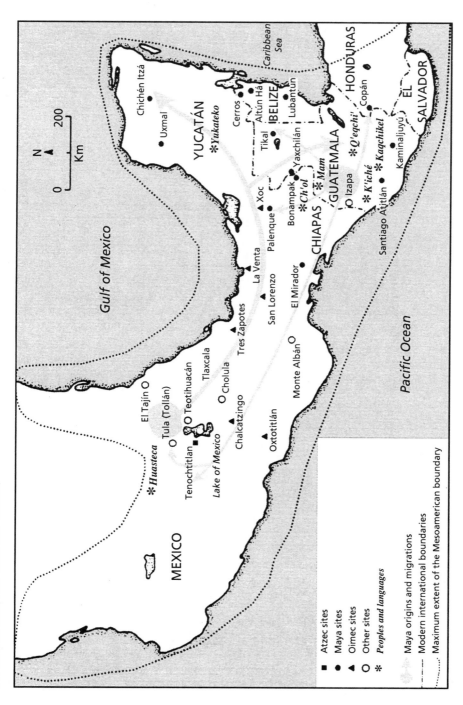

Gulf of Mexico

MEXICO

- El Tajín ○
- Tula (Tollán) ○
- ✱ *Huasteca*
- Teotihuacán ○
- Tenochtitlan ■
- Lake of Mexico
- Tlaxcala ▲
- Cholula ○
- Chalcatzingo ▲
- Oxtotitlán ▲
- Tres Zapotes ▲
- Monte Albán ○
- San Lorenzo ●
- La Venta ▲
- El Mirador ●
- Chichén Itzá ●
- Uxmal ●

YUCATÁN

- ✱ *Yukateko*
- Cerros ●
- Altún Ha ●
- Tikal ●
- Lubantún ●

Caribbean Sea

BELIZE

- Xoc ▲
- Palenque ●
- Bonampak ●
- Yaxchilán ●
- ✱ *Ch'ol*

CHIAPAS

- Izapa ○
- ✱ *Mam*
- ✱ *K'iché*
- ✱ *Q'eqchi'*
- ✱ *Kaqchikel*
- Santiago Atitlán ●
- Kaminaljuyú ●

GUATEMALA

HONDURAS
- Copán ●

EL SALVADOR

Pacific Ocean

N

| 0 | 200 |
Km

Legend

- ■ Atzec sites
- ● Maya sites
- ▲ Oimec sites
- ○ Other sites
- ✱ *Peoples and languages*

— Maya origins and migrations
—·—· Modern international boundaries
········· Maximum extent of the Mesoamerican boundary

INTRODUCTION

BRIEF HISTORY OF THE MAYA PEOPLES

Guillermo Cook

Between ten and fifteen thousand years ago,[1] when the Indoeuropean peoples were just beginning to fan out from the steppes of Central Asia into India, Anatolia, the Aegean and Europe, a unique culture began to develop on the Pacific watershed of Central America. At about the time when Abram, Sarai and other *habiru* peoples were migrating southwestward from the Fertile Crescent, the culture which we today call *Maya* began to move into the Guatemalan highlands and jungle lowlands—today's Chiapas, Petén, Belize and Yucatán—over a period of many centuries.[2] Around the time of the birth of the Buddha in Nepal, and of the return of the Jewish exiles from Persia, a sophisticated civilization of towering temple pyramids was at the height of its development in the jungles of Petén, Guatemala.

Traces of this culture beyond the boundaries of what is generally recognized as Maya-land strongly hint that the movement of people spread northeastward toward the central Mexican plateau and the legendary Toltec capital of Tulán interacting with many other peoples on their way.[3] This is also attested in their Council Book, the *Pop Vuh*[4], which also tells of a

---

[1] Between 50.000 and 6.500 BCE, "groups of peoples from northeast Asia entered the Americas through Bering Strait land bridge bringing hunting cultures, shamanism, and animal ceremonialism". They "migrated southward and eventually reached the Basin of Mexico by 20.000 BCE... Various... physical types speaking many languages migrated into North America and Mesoamerica" (David Carrasco, *Religions of Mesoamerica*. San Francisco: Harper and Row, 1990, xxi, 27).

[2] Coe 1993, 23,24.

[3] The sacred book of the Mayas, tells how the K'iche' or Maya people "multiplied there in the East", and lists the names of several tribes which scholars have tried to relate to known peoples. The Yaqui-Tepeu were a people "of Toltec origin who emigrated together with the Quiché" before they arrived in "Tulán" (*Popol Vuh: The Sacred Book of the Ancient Quiché Maya*. English version by Delia Goetz and Sylvanus G. Morley, from the translation of Adrián Recinos (Norman and London: University of Oklahoma Press, 1950), 170,174.

[4] Editor's note: It has been demonstrated more recently that the correct name is *Pop Vuh*. "If *pop* signifies 'time', and *Vuh*, 'book', the document's name then signifies 'The Book of Time' or 'The Book of Events'". Cf. Edgar Cabrera in chapter Four. But *pop* also means the "mat" upon which the council of elders sits to deliberate, suggesting yet another name: "The Council Book". See the translation

return mass journey of "mexicanized Maya",[5] after several generations of servitude,[6] to the Yucatán peninsula and the Guatemalan highlands,[7] where they subjugated their brethren and founded new kingdoms. Judging from the archeological evidence, this probably took place in the twelfth century C.E., about the same when the Roman papacy had attained the pinacle of power in Europe. These Maya kingdoms had run their course by the time of the arrival of the Spaniards in the early sixteenth century.

The sheer scope of the time and space that this civilization has encompassed is staggering. To put it into a more familiar perspective, the beginings of the Classic Era of Mesoamerican[8] civilization is contemporary with the close of the New Testament period. It ended, in the ninth century, not long after Charlemagne was crowned Holy Roman Emperor by the pope. All over the region thriving urban centres collapsed suddenly in the ninth century CE, within a few years of each other. What happened? Many theories have been put forward. Recent discoveries suggest that the great Maya civilization came to an end as the result of a concatenation of causes that sound very familiar to us today: overpopulation and urbanization, deforestation, climatic changes, draught, famine, plagues, crisis of faith, loss of confidence in authority and social unrest.[9] But this was not the end of the Maya. Revitalized by cultural infusions, they achieved new glory in the Yucatán lasting until the twelfth century. Their last kingdom was subjugated in 1697. And they are still very much with us.

The Mesoamerican Civilization

> After that they began to talk about the creation and the making of our first
> mother and father;
> of yellow corn and white corn they made their flesh;
> of corn meal dough they made
> the arms and the legs of man.[10]

---

by Munro S. Edmonson, *The Book of Counsel: The Popol Vuh of the Quiche Maya of Guatemala* (New Orleans: Middle American Research Institute, 1971).

[5] Coe 1993, 24.

[6] Ibid, 206-218ff.

[7] The Yucatecos called this military and commercial invadores Itzas'. The resident Mayas of Guatemala referred to them simply as Toltecs.

[8] Mesoamérica is a geographical and cultural region that encompasses the southern two thirds of México and most of Central America.

[9] Schele and Freidel, 334-336,343-345,379-386ff.

[10] *Pop Vuh*, 167.

Perhaps it is no accident that a culture that has lasted for perhaps twenty thousand years developed such an all consuming interest in time. The very name "Maya" may derive from the Yukatek word *may*, denoting a cycle of time in their complex calendar.[11] In every aspect of their lives, the Maya people of old tied together earthly life with spatial and temporal dimensions within a total cosmic worldview. Within unlimited infinity "they adjusted themselves patiently over countless generations until now". Their calendar, based upon rigorous astronomical observations, is an outcome of this worldview,[12] which, in turn, led to amazing mathematical discoveries centuries before they were known in Europe, and perhaps even in China.[13]

The Mesoamerican civilization may have been the first to discover the use of numbers and the place notation system. They did all of their mathematical calculations with just three symbols: a dot for 1, a bar for 5 and an eye-shaped zero.[14] In fact, it was Mesoamericans who discovered the concept of zero—but not as the equivalent of nothingness, but of totality.[15] Their patient observation of astronomical phenomena and acute

---

[11] Cf. Ronald Wright, *Stolen Continents: The Indian Story* (London: John Murray, 1992), 166,255. A *may* consists of a full cycle of 13 *katuns* (roughly 20 year periods) in the modified Itza', chronology.

[12] Vitalino Similox, 37,38.

[13] Elisabeth P. Benson (*The Maya World*. New York: Thomas Y. Crowell Co., 1967, 11,12), argues that "migrations by boat across the Pacific" may have brought more developed cultures than those of the people who had wondered down the Pacific coast from Alaska". Some physical evidence of contacts with Asian traders or off-course navigators has been found on the west coast of South America. A few cultural traits and words are shared with Asia hint at this, but nothing more. Paul Arnold (*El libro Maya de los muertos*. México: Editorial Diana, 1990) shows apparent similarities between a number of primitive Maya glyphs and archaic Chinese characters with like meanings. This leads him to suggest that, at some prehistoric time, Mesoamerica had some contact with Chinese voyagers. However, Carrasco (1990, 26,27) cautions, that "although it appears that limited contact between Asian cultures and the peoples of Mesoamerica took place... [the] indigenous cultures developed their own cultural processes independent of significant contributions from outside civilizations".

[14] Indigenous scholars observe that their dot and bar system has been "rediscovered" in our time by computer scientists.

[15] Whereas today we use the decimal system, based upon the fingers of both hands, their system was vigesimal, including also the toes. Unlike our horizontal place notation, theirs was built vertically, line upon line, with each line worth 20 times the one below it. After counting to 19 (three dashes and four superimposed dots), they moved up a line and placed a zero for 20. The next place up was 400 and the next 16.000, etc, to infinity. Their most common symbol for zero was shaped like a seed, pointing, perhaps, to the mythical origin of life, maize.

knowledge of mathematical principles allowed them to calculate time far back into the past[16] and to predict with amazing accuracy astronomical phenomena far into the future.[17] The Maya were the only indoamerican people to use a complete dating system on their monuments. Their hieroglyphic writing was unique in pre-colombian America.[18]

The Mesoamerican concept of time is undoubtedly a factor in the Maya' continued resistance to invasion and attempted cultural destruction.

> The Maya were determined to engineer their own survival. Aware of the immensity of time and that their own history was measured in thousands, not hundreds of years, they prepared to outlive the Spaniards as they had outlived... others... From the sixteenth century to the twentieth, they have ignored the European when possible, accommodated him only when unavoidable, taken from him what they could use, and fought him tenaciously whenever he has threatened to break the stalemate between his civilization and theirs...[19]

Chapter 5 documents the importance in colonial times—and even today—of the sacred calendar as mechanism of ethnic resistance and organizing principle for life. Knowledge of time was a function of the Maya's need to ensure the continuance of their civilization in a hostile environment. In order to provide for their livelihood and make room for their burgeoning population, the Maya tamed hostile jungles and drained steamy swamps. As they gradually organized themselves into small farming communities they learned how to domesticate the foods that became their staples until today: beans, squash, avocados, cotton, chili peppers, and most importantly, corn or maize. Over thousands of years, Mesoamericans "engineered" the transformation of a grass-like weed with small edible seeds ("teosinte" or *tripsacum*) into the tall graceful plant with succulent golden grains that has

---

[16] "The highest number found anywhere in Maya writings, [is] equivalent to about 5.000.000 years". Sylvanus Griswold Morley, *An Introduction to the Study of Maya Hieroglyphs* (New York: Dover Publications, 1975), 114-116.

[17] Maya calculations of the length of a solar year are off only fractions of a second from the exact measurement of today's atomic clocks.

[18] Cf. Linda Schele and David Freidel, *A Forest of Kings: The Untold Story of the Ancient Maya* (New York: William Morrow and Company, 1990), 77-84. See also Rafael Girard, *Los Mayas* (Mexico City: Libro Mex, 1966) 303. Cf. Michael D. Coe, *Breaking the Maya Code* (New York: Thames and Hudson, 1992), 61,62.

[19] Wright, 150,161,175-187.

become the staple of millions all over the world.[20] So important was maize
to them that Mesoamericans, in their creation myths, identified it with the
substance of their own human bodies. Indeed, their entire life -until
today—has revolved around the "milpa" system of agriculture with maize
as its center.[21]

But it is the Mesoamerican urban culture which so enthralls archaeologists and visitors today. At its height, the Maya world encompassed more
than 100.000 square miles. During the early Classic Period of
Mesomaerican civilization (300 to 900 C.E.), city states erected ceremonial
centres ruled by priest kings in the Petén and Palenque in the Chiapas
foothills.[22] After their rather sudden demise, other cities arose in Yucatán,
revitalized by Itza' invaders, who may have been displaced by the collapse
of Tula (Tulán) in central México.[23]

But long before this, great civilizations had thrived in Mesoammerica.
Witness the giant basalt heads of Olmec rulers along the Gulf of México
(900-300 BCE);[24] Monte Albán near Oaxaca and the gigantic four
quartered city of Teotihuacán, an imperial capital which thrived in the
Central Mexican plateau from 100 to 700 CE. and was mysteriously
abandoned.[25] Was this part of an overarching Maya culture, or something
different?

The world of the Maya

Although it might seem to some readers as a technicality of merely
academic interest, it is important for the purposes of this study to pause for
a moment to discuss the extent in time and space of the world of the Maya.
Wherever dialogue between peoples of different faiths is accepted, the
concept is almost always applied to the "world-class" religions of Eurasian

---

[20] Girard 1966, 313-316,322-330. While in general agreement with the Guatemalan highlands source of some earliest forms of maize, Coe summarizes the debate on its origins (1993, 33).

[21] Cf. S. Annis, *God and Production in a Guatemalan Town* (Austin: University of Texas Press, 1987).

[22] At Tikal, Yaxchilán, Uaxactún, Caracol, Naranjo, Piedras Negras, Ceibal, Cedros, Altún Ha, and countless other places that are yet being uncovered.

[23] Chichen Itza', Uxmal, and Dzibilchaltún, etc.

[24] Cf. Carrasco, 30-37.

[25] At its peak, around 500 C.E., Teotihuacán was populated by over 200.000 people (Carrasco, 40-43). It ruled over most of Mesoamérica for over a century and a half (Coe 1992, 72).

provenance that have millions of followers, cover vast extensions of the earth's land mass, and—as an added though not idispensable qualification—can boast of a very long history. It is important to realize that the spirituality of the "New World", which the indigenous call Abia Yala, meets most, if not all of these qualifications. Indeed, it is at least as old as Judaism and Buddhism, and older by far than Christianity and Islam. Of the world religions, only Hinduism has existed as long. It lacks only a recognizable name, and that because the Europeans took it away from them, or forced them to hide it. The fact that indigenous spirituality was unknown and unsuspected for millenia, supressed for five hundred years and only now is begining to find a new identity, is not a reason for ignoring it or writing it off as a "folk religion". We can do this only at our own peril. Our oversight may come back to haunt us.

I am using "Maya" and "Mesoamerican" as loosely synonymous terms that refer to a broad geographical area whose peoples shared similar cultural traits and a common cosmogony over thousands of years. The fact that Maya are known today as a specific race of people who inhabit a particular region of Mesoamérica, should not obscure the above fact. Nor is it meant to imply Maya hegemony over the whole of Mesoamérica at any time. I use "Maya" as a short-hand way of speaking of Mesoamerican culture and spirituality until the begining of its recorded history on stone and bark paper.

Scholars agree that the Maya culture that has been uncovered by archeologists and deciphered by epigraphers represents the apex of a multiethnic and multilingual cultural region called Mesoamérica. They also admit to not knowing where it all began. One of the best known authorities on the subject, Michael Coe, comments: "Given the similarities among the diverse cultures of Mesoamerica, one can only conclude that its peoples must have shared a common origin, so far back in time that it may never be brought into light by archeology", and that "there must have been an active interchange of ideas and things among the Mesomaerican elite over many centuries".[26] He and his colleagues have long been convinced of the hypothesis of a central Mexico origin for all Mesoamerican culture. "The fact is that the Maya of both highlands and lowlands have never been isolated from the rest of Mesoamerica, and that Mexican influences have sporadically guided de course of Maya cultural history since very early times". Yet they have gradually come to realize "that the reverse was also

---

[26] Michael Coe, *The Maya*. London: Thames and Hudson, 1993, 12.

the case: strong Maya influence can be detected in Central Mexico and the Gulf Coast of Veracruz.[27]

A fair number of North American scholars have long believed that,"begining about 3.000 years ago" the Olmec of southern Mexico—at least what is known about them[28]—had elaborated many of the cultural traits of Mesoamerica. was the "Mother culture of later Mesoamerican civilizations".[29] It was, they argue, "the template of worldview and governance that the Maya would inherit a thousand years later".[30] The Maya, it is asumed, were the inheritors, but not necessarily the originators of some of the key elements of Maya culture.[31]

Latin American scholars, such as Edgar Cabrera, the author of Chapter Four, disagree with this Western "compartmentalized" approach. He and other Central American ethonologists argue for a more integrated and interactive interpretation of Mayan/Mesoamerican culture from the very beginning of its history.[32] By whatever name or names they called

---

[27] Ibid, 47.

[28] Olmec is "a name given them by archaeologists - we don't know what they called themselves". Coe had argued that this "far earlier civilization" knew the art of writing as well as the "Maya" calendar during the latter part of their development (1992, 60-62). However, more recently, while continuing to lean toward the Olmec hypothesis, he confesses that the "Mayacentric" outlook set forth by epigrapher Sylvanus Morley, that the Maya were "*the* great innovators and culture-givers to the rest of the peoples of Mexico and Central America... may have been more right than wrong" (Coe 1993, 11,12).

[29] Carrasco, 30-35.

[30] Schele and Freidel, 38.

[31] Cf. Coe, 61, 70-72; Schele and Freidel, 162,164,442-444. According to this reasoning, not part of the "Maya" civilization was the enormous and misterious city of Teotihuacán in the valley of Mexico. Nor was Izapa (300 B.C.E.-200 C.E.)—with its more than 75 pyramid mounds and numerous stone stelae—although it is recognized as "major transition point between the Olmec style and the Maya achievement" (Carrasco, 37).

[32] Cabrera points to a study by Guatemalan archeologist Miguel Orrego (*Investigaciones arqueológicas en Abak Takalik*, Reporte Número 1. Instituto de Historia y Antropología de Guatemala, El Asintal, 1988) that strongly suggests that this evidently Maya ceremonial centre in South Western Guatemala may be centuries older than heretofore dated. Cabrera argues that recent archeological discoveries in México indicate that "the Olmeca thesis has collapsed. Today it is said that 'Olmeca' was not a culture, not even a language, nor an ethnic group, but only an artistic style that existed in México at different times ", from which variants emerged which today are called "Olmec" and "Maya" (Edgar Cabrera, *El calendario Maya: Su origen y su filosofía*, 1995,28,29,210; cf. Cabrera's *La cosmogonía Maya*, 1992, 26; both published by Liga Maya Internacional: San José, Costa Rica. See also Girard 1966, 378-380). For a more recent contrary view, see

themselves or were known to others, indisputably the Maya that we study today were for a very long time a key component of a vast interrelated cultural world which could aptly be called "Maya" because of its common understanding of time and the universe.[33] The indigenous argument for an integrated Mesoamerican culture is based as much upon philosophical grounds as it is on an understandable sense of cultural pride.

> Our culture has always accepted the principle that we are not alone, nor are we the centre of the universe. Very much to the contrary, we realize that we are part of families and in turn of larger and larger communities. Similarly, while our religion is monotheistic, we believe that God expresses himself in many forms and cosmic energies... Our culture is, then, multifaceted... as polychromatic as our 'huipiles' (cloths). We are a unity in the midst of plurality...[34]

The unity of the Mesoamerican religion, of its symbols and myths also testifies to the vital interaction of its peoples over thousands of years. The task of uncovering this has fallen to ethnologists, who patiently record the stories retold by living Maya and delve into the extant literature of the Maya.[35] Whoever may have developed the complex calendars that all Mesoamericans used,[36] it was indisputably the Maya who fine tuned it and

---

"Mystery of the Olmec", *Time Magazine*, July 1, 1996, 44,45.

[33] As already noted, the name "Maya", derives from the Yukateko word "may" which, according to one source (Wright, 166,255), denotes a cycle of time. Another source suggests that "may" ("to count or divine") derives from the Mixe-Zoquean language that the ancient Zapotecs and perhaps the Olmecs used (cf. Coe 1993, 28). There is evidence that the Maya may have also identified themselves as "Chan", after their snake deity (cf. Rafael Girard, *Los Mayas eternos*. México, Antigua Librería Robredo, 1962, 2).

[34] Cabrera 1995, 24-26.

[35] See chapters four and ten for commentaries on portions of several of these documents.

[36] The Mayas used three calendars. The most important of these was the 260-day, "sacred round" ("tzolkin") or lunar calendar, which kept track of sacred days with their celebrations. Shared by all the peoples of Mesoamérica, it was composed of thirteen numbers consecutively combining with twenty day names. A second cycle, which kept track of the seasons, consisted of 365 days divided into eighteen months of 20 days, with a month of five days left over at the end of the year. These calendars are kept today "by scores of indigenous Guatemalan communities" (Barbara Tedlock, *Time and the Highland Maya*. Albuquerque: University of Mexico Press, 1992, 1). Both calendars functioned in tandem to form the famous 52-year cycle of the Mesoamerican calendric system, or "Calendar Round", which repeats itself every 18,890 (52 X 365) days. The third system of recording time is called today the "Long Count" calendar. "Unlike the dates of the Calendar Round, which are fixed only within a never-ending—and recurring—cycle of 52 years, Long

integrated it into a masterful whole. Three ancient ceremonial centres have been proposed as originators of the Long Count calendar: the Zapotec city of Monte Albán near Oaxaca, México (600 B.C.E.-900 C.E.),[37] and two Maya centres: Copán (900 B.C.E.-827 C.E.) in western Honduras,[38] and Izapa (600 B.C.E. to 200 C.E.) on the Pacific coast of Chiapas (México).-[39] The location of the two Maya centres in relation to the placement of the celestial bodies when the initial calendar date was set may be an argument in their favor.

Count days are given in a day-to-day count", which started on 4 Ahau 8 Cumku of the Calendar Round, or August 11, 3114 BCE (Coe 1992, 62; Schele and Freidel, 79-82).

[37] In an early work, Coe suggests that the inventors of the Mayan mathematical system and of the calendar were neither the Olmecs nor the Mayas but the Zapotecs of Monte Albán (Coe 1962, 61; citing Joyce Marcus, "The first appearance of Zapotec writing and calendrics, in *The Cloud People*, ed. K.V. Flannery and J. Marcus. New York and London: Academic Press, 1983, 91-96). Cabrera counters that the estimated 500 B.C.E. dating of the Zapotec calendar is exceeded by the 800 year old date on stela number one in Abaj Takalik, the 1.000 year plus date of structures in Nakb'e, a Maya city in the North of Petén, Guatemala, and the 2.000 to 1.000 year dates ascribed to the Cuello site in Belize (1995, 123-125, 146-148).

[38] Girard has calculated the location of the planets back on August 11, 3114 BCE (4 Ahau 8 Cumku). He postulates that the location from which this date could be most accurately determined at that time was at latitude 14° 15', about the location of Copán (in Western Honduras), which had an advanced culture very early in Maya history (1966, 304-311).

[39] Mexican archeologist Beatriz Barba (*Buscando raíces de mitos Mayas en Izapa*, Universidad de Sudoeste, México, 1988) postulates that this is where the Ceremonial Calendar of 260 days and Solar Calendar of 365 days were fixed. She bases this conjecture upon the city's location: 15° latitude north—a position which slices the yearly revolution of the earth into two segments: 260 days south of Izapa and 105 days north of it (260 +105=365). She hypothesizes that Izapa may have been the birthplace of the advanced Maya civilization. In any case, several Izapa stellae do recount myths that replicate the creation epics in the *Pop Vuh* of the K'iche' Maya. These myths—which survive today also in the oral traditions of other Maya peoples—Barba suggests, may be as old as the starting date of the Maya calendar (3314 B.C.E.), which is also recorded on these stellae (Cabrera 1992, 25-27f). Maya civilization may be even older, suggests Cabrera (1995, 199). On stella three in Quiriguá, Guatemala and on the Temple of the Cross in Palenque, Chiapas, there is recorded the initial date of 4 Ahau 8 Zotz, which corresponds to the year 8238 B.C.E. (Cf. S.G. Morley, *An Introduction to the Study of the Maya Hieroglyphs*. New York, Dover Publications, 1975, 207).

Mesoamerican languages

> The speech of all was the same.
> They did not invoke wood nor stone,
> and they remembered the word of the Creator and the Maker,
> the Heart of Heaven, the Heart of Earth...
> And there it was that the speech of the tribes changed,
> that their tongues became different.
> They could no longer understand each other clearly
> after arriving at Tulán...
> We have given up our speech!...
> We had only one speech when we arrived there at Tulán,
> we were created and educated in the same way.[40]

Comparative linguistics, collated with some clues in the ancient Maya writings, may throw some light on the question of the diffusion of Maya culture in Mesoamerica.[41] This may also provide a helpful introduction to the various Maya groups that we shall be meeting in the chapters of this book.

Thirty Maya languages are spoken today in Guatemala, México, Belize and Honduras. They can all be traced back to a common proto-Mayan source which, linguists estimate, existed about 4100 years ago, before the long process of separation, over time and space, into languages and dialects began. Perhaps significantly, the closer to the mythical source of Maya origins in the south-western Guatemalan highlands, the older the language. Mam, which continues to be spoken in this region, is the most ancient (3.400 years old) and its people conserve in their traditions the memory of

---

[40] *Pop Vuh*, Part. iii, chaps. 3,4,5, in Goetz, 172,176,177.

[41] In the 1970s, Terence Kaufman, an authority on Mesoamerican languages, proposed a way of dating the Maya languages by using statistical analysis of language development. Using his criteria, it is possible to establish broadly the time of separation of kindred dialects as they evolve into distinct - and mutually unintelligible—languages. Concrete data on which these calculations are based is knowledge concerning archaic forms of Maya, together with the discovery that the glyphs on eight and ninth century monuments were based upon the Ch'olti' (Ch'ol) and Yukateko languages. Documentation from the colonial period shows how the principal Maya languages of today—K'iche', Kaqchikel, Yukateko and Ch'olti'—were pronounced in the sixteenth century. Cf. Nora C. England, *Autonomía de los idiomas Mayas: Historia e identidad* (Guatemala: Editorial Cholsamaj, 1992), 20,21f. Cf. Nora England, et.al., *Maya' Chii': Los idiomas mayas the Guatemala* (Cholsamaj, 1993).

being the "original people".[42] The most recent fully developed languages are the tribes that, according to the *Pop Vuh* epic, returned to their ancestral lands after years of sojourn in Tolán in central México[43]—the Ki'che' family—[44]or emigrated to the Yucatán peninsula, after the breakup of the Toltec empire,[45] to build great cities and thriving kingdoms.[46] Both southward migrations brought with them cultural, religious, architectural and linguistic innovations from the Toltec kingdom.[47] The migrating tribes

---

[42] Girard (1966, 313f) writes that "both the *Pop-Vuh* and the *Annals of the Caqchikels* state independently that maize was discovered in Paxil, and highlight the extraordinary fertility of that land. In this regard, one should mention the existence of a place called Paxil, in the heart of the territory that is today inhabited by the Mams, who maintain the tradition that it is where 'maize was born'... The triple coincidence between the myths, the living traditions of a people and botanical evidence regarding the location of the primary source of the domestication of maize is quite significant". In addition to his own field-work in the area (western Guatemala), Girard acknowledges his indebtedness to the work of Suzana Miles ("Mam Residence and the Maize myth" in *Culture and History*. New York, Brandeis University/Columbia University Press, 1960), 430-436. He also refers to León A. Valladares, "Lugar mítico de los orígenes del maíz y de la cultura", in *Revista Artis*, Guatemala, 1960, 63-74. See also Coe 1993, 26).

[43] The *Pop Vuh* states that the Mayas who arrived at Tullán "could no longer undestand each other clearly" (Pt. iii, chp. 4, Gortz, 176).

[44] The *Pop Vuh* relates the epic of three brothers and their tribes—today's K'iche', Kaqchikel and Tz'utuhiil—who spoke one language and worshipped one creator god when they arrived in Tollán. When, on their return journey, they turned to separate gods, their languages were divided (Prt. iii, Chp. 4, Goetz, 172,175,17-7,).

[45] The *Pop Vuh* speaks of a segment of the people "who had to go East" (to Yucatán, Gortz, 176, n8). It later relates that, once the K'iche' federation had arrived at their final destination, their leaders travelled East to receive the insignias of authority from Nacxit—the abbreviated name of Topiltzin Acxitl Quetzacoatl, Toltec ruler of Yucatán (Goetz, 207, n. 3). The destruction of Tula (Tulán) took place in either 1156 or 1168 C.E. Historical sources in the Yucatán speak of the arrival from the west of a chieftan calling himself Kukulcán, feathered serpent during the same period. (Coe 1993, 142,143).

[46] After this Post-Classic renaissance had run its course, bands of still another group of Mexicanized Mayas, the Itzás, uncouth merchant warriors led by yet another Kukulcán, moved into the vacuum and revived a proud city, Ucil-abnal, to which they gave the name of Chichén Itzá, the "cenote" or well of the Itzás. The Itzás also founded Mayapán and, after being finally evicted from northern Yucatán, they established a new capital, Tayasal at the sight of the present town of Flores, Petén. It was the last Maya bastion to fall to the Spaniards, in 1697 (Coe 1993, 157,158).

[47] Nahual, the language of the Toltecs and Aztecs, has left many place names in Central America. However, the fact that the K'iches', during their northern sojourn, evidently continued to speak a Maya language, leads one to surmise that

lamented that some of their brethren (the Tepeu Oliman, Olmecans) were left behind in (central México).[48] Today, separated from the majority of Maya speaking people behind tribes of Nahual, Totonaca and other native languages, live the Maya speaking Huasteka people.[49]

A shared worldview

Whether or not the successive "empires" and city states spoke a Mayan language or a totally unrelated idiom is less important than the cultural and religious worldview that they held in common all over the region. It is certainly of some significance that the flora and fauna depicted on the stonework of mysterious Teotihuacán—which is located in the chilly highlands near Mexico City—is not native to that arid region. It can be found far away, in the Pacific lowlands. This is not without significance. They are the same animals and plants that inhabit the birthplace of the Maya,[50] as related in the *Pop Vuh* and the *Annals of the Caqchikels*[51] and which the Méxican myths remembered as *Tamoanchán*—place of the flying serpent.[52] Quetzalcoatl, the flying serpent[53]—prominently displayed on

------

a form of Maya was spoken at least in some parts of central México, in the heart of the Toltec kingdom.

[48] "In Tulán we were lost, we were separated, and there our older and younger brothers stayed... in the land which today is called México. Part of the people remained there in the East, those called Tepeu Olimán, who stayed there... (*Pop Vuh*, 189).

[49] Whether the Huastekas emigrated to northeastern México not long after 2000 B.C.E. (Coe 1993, 24), or were part of ninth century C.E. migrations which "may have played a formative role in what was to become the Toltec state"—to judge from Maya-style bas-reliefs found in central México (Coe 1993, 129,130), or are the groups who remained behind, as recounted in the *Pop Vuh* (189), is still unresolved.

[50] From tropical rain forests to smoking volcanoes and lush mountain valleys: this fits the description of their original paradisiacal home, according to their myths of origin (Cf. Girard 1966, 391,392).

[51] The K'iche' an Kaqchikel traditions place the earthly paradise in Paxil, a village that still exists in Mam territory in Western Guatemala. Mexican myths place paradise in Tamoanchán (*Pop Vuh*, Prt iii, chp. 1, in Goetz, 166).

[52] "Tamoanchán, land of flowers, of rain and cloud forests, was the original homeland of the gods and of civilization". Though the term is found in the traditions of central México, it only has meaning in Maya (*ta* = locative particle, *moan* = bird and *chan* = serpent) - the place of the bird-serpent... Tamoanchán is the place where human beings were created from corn mixed with serpent blood which had been brought by a hawk (Girard 1966, 391).

the giant pyramids of Teotihuacán, was translated *Ku'kulkan'* in Yucateco and *Gucumatz* in K'iche'. Several of the chapters in this book will deal with aspects of this worldview and its manifestations today.

The European Invasion

On that day, dust possesses the earth;
On that day, a blight is on the face of the earth;
On that day, a cloud rises; on that day, a mountain rises;
On that day, a strong man seizes the land;
On that day, things fall to ruin;
On that day, the tender leaf is destroyed;
On that day, the dying eyes are closed.[54]

The Spanish "conquistadores" were dazzled by the splendor of *Tenochtitlán*. The people that we call Aztecs (the Mexicas) saw themselves as heirs to the glories of a mythic Toltec civilization—they were unaware of the thousands of years of cultural development that had preceded these fairly recent interlopers on the Mesoamerican scene.[55] But the fierce Aztecs were

---

[53] Scholarly research into the myths and legends about Quetzalcoatl suggests that there were several heroic figures that went by that name. The Creator God Quetzalcoatl of the Aztecs is associated (or confused) in the myths with the ruler of Tula, Ce Acatl Topiltzin Quetzalcoatl (One Reed, Our Young Prince the Plumed Serpent), who brought the Toltec kingdom to the summit of power and prestige. A priest warrior, he attempted a religious revolution against human sacrifice. Fierce opposition from his enemies forced him to abdicate. One strand of the legend has him embarking on a journey across the seas, promising to return in One Read (*Ce Acatl*, 1519), the year in which Cortéz did indeed arrive. This was an important factor in Aztec emperor Moctezuma's deferential treatment of the Spaniards when they first arrived from across the seas (Carrasco, 44,45; Wright, 21). Another legend has Quetzalcoatl reappearing in Yucatán to found the kingdom of Chichén Itzá. The warlike conduct and sanguinary religious practices that this king introduced might indicate that this was an entirely different chieftain who had taken the name of the mythic Toltec ruler.

[54] Ralph D. Rooys, *The Book of C hilam Balam of Chumayel* (Norman: University of Oklahoma Press, 1967), 186n.

[55] For the same reason, the Maya records tend to conflate their mythical paradise in highland Guatemala with a golden age that the myths located in Tulán in central México.

conquered very quickly by disease—the European's "secret weap-
on"[56]—and a handful of gold-crazed Spanish warriors with muskets.[57]

The search for greater wealth was on. But, as the Spaniards moved
southward they found impressive citadels, many of them in ruins, but very
little gold. Only in the Yucatán did the invaders find small warring
kingdoms, but they were soon subdued. Meanwhile, in the Guatemalan
highlands, the Ki'che' empire was breaking up.[58] When Pedro de
Alvarado—the most cruel of the "conquistadores"—came on the scene he
found the K'iches' fruitlessly attempting to subdue their kinsmen and one-
time allies. Making an alliance with the Kaqchikels, Alvarado defeated the
Ki'ches', then turned upon his allies, setting fire to their capital, when they
began to chafe under the brutality of their new overlords. More remote
peoples, such as the Q'ekchis', continued to resist for some time.[59]

The Maya elite, however, did not take matters lying down. The list of
their uprisings is long. Rumors of revolt were never lacking.[60] Emboldened by memories of initial victories against the Spanish, and energized by
their religious fervor, Yucatán "caciques" (chiefs) rose up in 1546-47 in
what is known as "the Great Maya Revolt".[61] A "resurgence of paganism",

---

[56] At the time of the "discovery" there were as high as 100 million people in the
New World—a fifth, more or less, of the human race, "representing, at least, 133
independent linguistic families. During the next 150 years it is estimated that the
population was reduced to 10 million—a drop from 25 million to 1 million in
México alone (Rivera Pagán, *A Violent Evangelism: The Political and Religious
Conquest of the Americas.* Westminster: John Knox Press, 1992, 22). An
estimated 2.5 million people lived in pre-conquest Guatemala. They were conquered
by 600 men. Disease did away with between 80 and 90% of the population (Cf.
Nelson Amaro, *Guatemala: Historia despierta.* Guatemala: IDESAC, 1992, 32,33).
"Old World plagues killed at least half the population of the Aztec, Maya and Inca
civilizations just before their overthrow. The sheer loss of people was devastating...
but disease was also a political assassination squad, removing kings, generals, and
seasoned advisors at the very time they were needed most". Mayas have since
bounced back. "Altogether, there are about 6 million Maya speakers today, perhaps
the same number that existed when Columbus reached America" (Wright, 14;22-
25,48).

[57] Cp. Wright, 19-21,27-47.

[58] At the height of their civilization, the K'iche' people may have numbered as
many as one million people. Cf. Amaro, 32.

[59] Ibid.

[60] Inga Clendinnen, *Ambivalent Conquests: Maya and Spaniards in Yucatán,
1517-1570.* Cambridge University Press, 1987, 53,54.

[61] Cf. Robert S. Chamberlain, *The Conquest and Colonization of Yucatán*
(Washington: Carnegie Institute, 1948), 237-252.

in 1562, the extent and depth of which may have been much exaggerated, was brutally suppressed.[62] In 1761, the Maya rebelled again under the leadership of a charismatic leader named Jacinto Can Ek. He "crowned himself king in the local church and declared that the time had come to drive the white invaders into the sea". Within weeks the rebellion was crushed and the leader's body dismembered.[63] Twenty years after the Spanish finally withdrew from the Yucatán—at a time when the province was debating the matter of independence from México—the Maya rose up again in the Great Caste War. This was "without question the most successful Indian revolt in world history".[64] It lasted from 1847 till 1891. Indigenous uprisings have continued into the presente century: El Salvador (1932),[65] Guatemala (throughout the 1980s) and the revolt in Chiapas which began January 1, 1994 and is still unresolved.

Christianization and cultural genocide

Spanish friars, following on the heels of the "conquistadores", provided the ideological support for the European invasion. Their goal was to Christianize the natives and their "pagan" culture. For some, this meant eradicating all vestiges of indigenous culture and religion. The role of others was more benevolent, defending the indians from the excesses of the Spanish overlords. During the first years of the colonial era, a handful of Dominicans friars (Pedro de Córdoba, Antonio de Montesinos, Francisco de Vitoria and Bartolomé de las Casas) were among the few persons to seriously question the practice of slavery and the right of the colonizers to impose their culture and religion. On the Fourth Sunday of Advent, 1511,

---

[62] Clendinnen, 72,92. "More than 4.500 Indians were put to the torture during the three months of the Inquisition, and an official enquiry later established that 158 had died during or as a direct result of the interrogations. At least thirteen people were known to have committed suicide to escape the torture, while eighteen others, who had disappeared, were thought to have killed themselves. Many more had been crippled, their shoulder muscles irreparably torn, their hands paralysed 'like hooks'" (Clendinnen, 76).

[63] Wright, 176.

[64] Victoria R. Bricker, *The Indian Christ, the Indian King: The Historical Substrate of Maya Myth and Ritual* (Austin: University of Texas Press, 1981), 87. Cf. Wright, 254-263. See also Paul Sullivan, *Unfinished Conversations: Mayas and Foreigners Between Two Wars* (New York: Knopf, 1989).

[65] When Pipil indian peasants rose up in protest against a military dictator, the government responded to a violent by massacring 30.000 of them. This is still refered to as the "Matanza" (killing).

Fr. Montesinos preached a fiery sermon (which had been signed by all of the Dominicans in the house) to all of the notables, including Admiral Diego Colón, in the cathedral church of Santo Domingo. It was like a voice crying in the wilderness.

> You are all in mortal sin!... because of the cruelty and tyranny you use with these innocent people. Tell me, with what right, with what justice, do you hold these indians in such cruel and horrible servitude? On what authority have you waged such detestable wars on these people, in their mild, peaceful lands, where you have consumed such infinitudes of them...? How is it that you hold them so crushed and exhausted, giving them nothing to eat, nor any treatment for their diseases, which you caused them to be infected... And what care do you take that anyone catechize them, so that they may come to know their God and Creator... Are they not human beings? Have they not rational souls? Are you not obligated to love them as you love yourselves?... Know for a certainty that in the state in which you are you can no more be saved than Moors or Turks who have not, nor wish to have, the faith of Jesus Christ.[66]

Siting in the audience was a wealthy slave owner, Bartolomé de las Casas, who was converted to the cause of the indians and, as a Dominican friar, dedicated his life to defending them. Much later, Bishop de las Casas, the "apostle to the indians", wrote that "no submission, no servitude, no burden can be imposed upon the people without the people's freely consenting to this imposition".[67]

In Yucatán, four decades later. Franciscan friars were instrumental in having the Spanish governor removed because of his cruel treatment of the natives. In 1550, head of mission Friar Luis de Villalpando "wrote a long letter to the Crown in which he named and listed the delinquencies of ten 'encomenderos'".[68] But there was also a darker side to the role of Catholic missioners. After arriving in Yucatán, a young friar named Diego de Landa

---

[66] Cf. Gustavo Gutiérrez, *Las Casas: In Search of the Poor of Jesus Christ*. Maryknoll: Orbis Books, 1993, 29. Translated from Las Casas, *Historia de las Indias*, bk.3, ch.4 and *Obras Escogidas*. Madrid: Ed. J. Pérez de Tudela, 1957-58, vol. ii, 176.

[67] Las Casas, *Regia potestate* (Madrid: Alianza Editorial, 1990), 33. Las Casas freed his own Carib slaves in Santo Domingo and, later, as a Dominican monk, defended the rights of indians in Perú. In Guatemala he was granted permission to set up a reservation (Verapaz) where the native Americans were protected from the "conquistadores". They were taught Christianity and western techniques of cultivation, cooking, etc.—which may not have been as good as those the Mayas had practiced for centuries.

[68] Clendinnen, 55.

expended considerable effort in learning the Maya language and culture.[69] He won the trust of Maya chiefs, who showed him their sacred book, which he later burned along with many other documents.[70] The "resurgent paganism" mentioned above—alleged secret worship of "idols" and crucifixions in the dead of night—may, according to Clendennin, "reveal more of the shaping power of Landa's imagination than the actual behavior of Indians".[71]

At the very least, the unhappy events surrounding bishop Landa suggest that the christianization of the original inhabitants was, at best, superficial. This is recognized today by most serious Catholic thinkers. The secret practice of indigenous religion was a form of cultural self-defense. So was the popular catholicism which developed throughout the indigenous regions of Latin America. Once one has been able to appreciate the richness of indigenous spirituality, it is possible to perceive in popular religiosity a creative synthesis between Medieval Christianity and the autochthonous traditions of Mesoamerica (the issue of "synchretism" shall be discussed at some length in my closing chapter).

All over Mesoamérica, the Maya realized that they would have to bow their heads and wait out the storm. They had in their favor centuries, perhaps even millenia, of adapting to passing conquerors.[72] Their lords were careful to dress like Spaniards and to seek permission to ride on

---

[69] Somewhat nostalgically, while in forced exile for excess of zeal, Landa wrote about his adopted land in *Relación de las Cosas de Yucatán* (México: Editorial Porrúa, 1959 edition). But there was a darker side to this dedicated Catholic missionary. In his memoirs, he confessed that he wanted to "penetrate the body of Maya culture and drive a stake in its demonic heart" (quoted in Wright, p. 163).

[70] With the characteristic hospitality of indigenous people, the Mayan lords had listened to Fr. Landa "with a spirit of encounter and told him whatever he wished to learn. They taught him Maya", recounted their history and achievements and even let him see their precious manuscripts. "The Mayas, who valued knowledge, did not yet suspect that this man of knowledge from another world would try to murder their past" (Wright, 163,164). Evidencing the contradictions that can be found in zealous missionaries, Fr. Diego shows in his writings a great admiration for the social qualities of the Mayas (Clendinnen, 68-70, cf. 119,123).

[71] Ibid, 121,122,123.

[72] "The Spaniards were identified with the Itza', those earlier, ambivalent invaders and their destructive, fructifying presence". They had endured their intrusion "and survived through calculated accomodation. It time the strangers would withdraw, as had some of the Itza', or be absorbed has had the rest, or would be driven out: in time the native lords would rule again" (Clendinnen, 157,158). The Itzá, it will be remembered, were probably Maya related people from central México, who invaded Yucatán in the ninth century C.E.

horseback like "caballeros".[73] Meanwhile, their priests went underground, content to be written off as mere "brujos" (witch doctors), their sacred icons buried under Catholic altars and imbeded in church walls. Only the cross, the sacred Maya symbol of cosmic equilibrium, could be worshipped openly, because it seemed to be, for all intents and purposes, the Christian cross. "At some point in time it seems a crucial decision had been made: certain Christian teachings were true. Therefore they must be accepted, and so incorporated into a Maya scheme of things".[74]

Protestantism in Maya Lands

> The Indian's religion is a strange mixture of the worst forms of Roman-ism, nature worship and spiritism. Witch doctors are ten times more numerous than priests and both combine to take away the Indian's money, giving him nothing in return. What between opression, vices and false religion, which only sinks him deeper in the throes of his sin, the indian is without hope. But praise God! no!...[75]

The zeal of the Spanish inquisitors kept protestantism out of Latin America until after the various provinces became independent nations during the first half of the nineteenth century—three centuries after the beginning of Catholic christianization.[76] The first Protestants to settle in Central America were British businessmen who exacted the right to worship in

---

[73] This appears to have been "a Maya strategy to bring their authority structures into parallel with (and so alternative to) the Spanish system, which requires some adjustment and some innovation in those traditional forms. Yet the meaning... remained obdurately Mayan" (Ibid).

[74] "The Maya had responded easily to the spare, simple, quadrilateral shape of the great crosses raised in the church patios and cemeteries, accepting them as markers for their own sacred locations, and as sacred objects themselves... The association was almost certainly with their own stylised 'Great Tree of the World' with its Four Directions... The great cross came to be identified with the 'Lord Dios', the supreme deity of the new order" (Ibid, 174,182-186).

[75] William Cameron Townsend, "Among Guatemala's Indians" in *Christian Herald* (21 January, 1922).

[76] The most notable exceptions were shipwrecked English pirates and privateers who were marooned on Spanish soil. Every pirate "ship had its Bible on which the Oath of Brotherhood was sworn" in their "Holy War against the greed of the 'conquistadores' and the cruelty of the Inquisition". Wilton M. Nelson, *Protes-tantism in Central America* (Grand Rapids: Eerdmans, 1984), 3,4; cf. 7,8. He is quoting Anglican priest Stephen Caiger, *Honduras Ahoy* (London: SPCK, 1949), 13, as well as other missionary documents.

private and in English. The Miskitos on the Caribbean coast of Nicaragua, whose harwood forests were much coveted by European traders, were the first indigenous peoples in Central America to be evangelized by Protestants—Anglican and Moravian missionaries—during this period.[77]

Guatemala: Protestant missions and Liberal agenda

The arrival of Protestants to evangelize the general population of Latin America was facilitated by the need of Liberal[78] politicians to break the strangle-hold of Roman clericalism. Free-lance Bible colporteurs were allowed to propagate their faith. A "Liberal" president of Guatemala, General Justo Rufino Barrios (1835-1885), invited U.S. Presbyterian missionaries to set up schools and churches. Establishing a secular state, he promulgated lay education and confiscated Church property.[79] However, when Barrios nationalized Church owned lands, he exposed the native peoples to the rapacity of uncaring profiteers.[80]

The second wave of Protestants to arrive in Central America were from the United States—the Presbyterian Board (Guatemala, 1882) and the independent Central American Mission (now CAM International) of Dallas, Texas.[81] Of interest to our study is the fact that both mission societies in the 1930s produced versions of the New Testament in three of the four

---

[77] Nelson, 4,18-19, citing Caiger, 13,14. British loggers turned the Miskito natives against the Spanish, and crowned a Miskito chieftain king, in 1845. Moravian missionaries arrived in 1849. Kenneth Hamilton, *Meet Nicaragua* (Bethlehem: Commenius Press, 1939), 15.

[78] Liberal "mestizos" wanted to modernize their nations after the style of Northern Europe and the U.S.A. Conservatives, dominated by the aristocratic and devoutly Catholic landholding class, were intent upon maintaining the status quo.

[79] Nelson, 12-18ff.

[80] Paradoxically, the land-grabbing and anti-clerical Liberals, many of whom were "mestizos", were far less concerned about the welfare of their indentured indigenous charges than the Spanish colonial regime and post-Independence Conservative parties.

[81] The CAM arrived in Guatemala in 1989 and founded an Indian Bible Institute in Chimaltenango a quarter of a century later. The Primitive Methodists, who arrived in 1921, teamed up with the Presbyterians to found the Quiché Bible Institute, near Quetzaltenango, which is now run by the Presbyterian K'iches' themselves (Ibid, 29-35,39,40). Other missions to lowland and coastal natives in Costa Rica and the Caribbean coast of Central America were attempted in the 1890s (Ibid, 36).

major Maya languages of Guatemala. The Kaqchikel Scriptures were
translated by CAM missionary Cameron Townsend, who would later found
Wycliff Bible Translators. Two Presbyterian couples translated the K'iche'
and Mam New Testament. The Scriptures in the vernacular and basic Bible
education provided a stimulus for the gradual spread of Protestant
congregations in the western highlands of Guatemala.

Mission and the evangelical agenda

But, was the gospel, as proclaimed by Protestants, ultimately any more
liberating than Catholic evangelization? Facundo Ku Canché (chapter ten),
judges not. Speaking in general about Protestant missions to indigenous
peoples, at least one well-known evangelical Protestant missiologist would
seem to agree.

> Protestant missions only *appeared* to be different; instead of subordinating
> the expression of the faith to magisterial authority, as in catholicism,
> Protestants unwittingly subordinated it to the presuppositions of Euro-
> American culture. Protestants were, on the whole, even more suspicious
> of "non-Christian" cultures than Catholics, not least because of their
> emphasis on humankind's total depravity. They allowed some freedom but
> in the main worked for an exact reproduction of European models. This
> could even be seen in cases where they deliberately set out to encourage
> indigenization...[82]

During the decades of the forties and fifties a number of evangelical mission
societies from the U.S.A., "planted churches" in Guatemala. The fact that
over sixty percent of the population is aboriginal, made it inevitable that the
majority of these bodies made their presence felt among the indigenous
population.[83] However, the story of North American missionary work
among the native population of Central America is general subsumed under
the larger history of continued Protestant growth in Central America and
requires considerable digging in mission periodicals to uncover.[84] By the

---

[82] David J. Bosch, *Transforming Mission: Paradigm Shifts in Theology of
Mission* (Maryknoll, Orbis Books, 1992), 450.

[83] Ibid, 38-40f. A case in point, the Church of the Nazarene, headquartered in
Kansas City, United States, established churches and a training institute among the
Q'ekchis' in the partly inaccessible north of Guatemala.

[84] For example, W.R. Read, V.M. Monterroso and H. A. Johnson, *Latin
American Church Growth* (Grand Rapids: Eerdmans, 1969), 157-163, do not mention native American churches in their description of Protestantism in Guatemala.

mid-century—during the decade that it was this writer's good fortune to reside in Guatemala—two Pentecostal churches, the Church of God (1935-) and the Príncipe de Paz (a schism in the Assemblies of God) had large numbers of converts among Maya seasonal workers on the Pacific coast plantations. Today, all over the Guatemalan highlands, dozens of Protestant groups vie for the attention and loyalty of Maya Christians.[85] Several chapters in this book speak to this issue. The research by Goldin and Metz (chapter three) in a fairly prosperous K'iche' village reflects this situation. Dalila Nayap-Pot (chapter six) speaks about the success of pentecostalism with highland Maya women in Guatemala.

Missionary paternalism and ideological imperialism

Mainline church missionary societies and independent "faith missions" alike have been involved during a major portion of this century in evangelism to the indigenous peoples of Central America. One agency—the Wycliff Bible Translators/Summer Institute of Linguistics (WBT/SIL)—focused almost entirely upon the linguistic dimension of evangelism: reducing the many languages and dialects of the region to written form and and translating the Scriptures into these languages. What was initially seen as positive, came in time to be perceived—particularly by the ideological left and increasingly threatened Catholic hierarchy—as an attempt at cultural and political domination. WBT/SIL's use of state of the art technology to accomplish this goal and its conservative political slant left it open to the suspicion of being a tool of U.S. imperialism.[86] An overly sensationalist treatment of the negative aspects of WBT/SIL's approach to the indigenous people has been

---

[85] Cf. Roland Ebel and David Scotchmer, "When Protestants Take Power: Change and Continuity in a Predominantly Indian Community". SECOLAS Meetings, Antigua, Guatemala (Feb., 1993). See Rubén Reina & Edward Schwartz, "The Structural Context of Religious Conversion in Petén, Guatemala: Status, Community and Multicommunity", *American Ethnologist*, vol i:1 (Feb. 1974), 157-191. Cf. Benjamin D. Paul, "Fifty Years of Religious Change in San Pedro de la Laguna, a Mayan Community in Highland Guatemala", American Anthropological Association, Chicago (Nov. 18-22, 1987).

[86] For years, this agency was held up by fellow Evangelicals as a paragon of missionary enterprise. It was also respected by a nuember of North American anthropologists and Third World governments for its expertise in linguistics and indigenous literacy methods. But in the '70s, it began to be accused of duplicity and paternalism, and suspect of being a tool of U.S. foreign policy.

questioned even by critics of the agency and of Protestant missionary approaches to the indigenous people.[87]

Whatever the case, WBT/SIL should be made accountable for the purposeful ambiguity of its goals and strategies which is inherent in its double name.[88] WBT/SIL purported to be a non-partisan "faith mission", while its hi-tech equipment—computers, transceivers and light planes based in isolated and strategic areas seemed to belie this fact. Is it then surprising that WBT/SIL's critics in the '70s and '80s were eager to buy into conspiracy theories?

WBT/SIL policies, while by no means attributable to every Protestant mission among Mesoamerican indians, does provide clues into the forceful critique that a new generation of indigenous Protestant leaders level against the Protestant missions of the first six decades of this century.[89] Approaches such as Wycliff's and that of the New Tribes Mission—another U.S. based mission—cast a broad shadow of suspicion upon al Protestant mission work to indigenous peoples, no matter how exemplary and dedicated it may have been. For some, it raises the question whether the Bible portions that have been translated by Protestants into the various tribal languages were

---

[87] Cf. Martin 1990, 98,99. See also David Stoll, *Fishers of Men or Founders of Empire? The Wycliff Bible Translators in Latin America* (London: Zed Press, 1982). Stoll, is careful to avoid inculpating WBT/SIL outright. He does make the valid point that WBT/SIL has had to pay the price for the disingenuous strategy, which he considers a consequence of its millenialist theology. He nonetheless argues that, while WBT/SIL bought into U.S. ultra-nationalism anti-Communist phobia, it should not be made a scapegoat for U.S. policy in Guatemala in recent decades.

[88] WBT/SIL attempted, at one and the same time, to be a non-sectarian agency that was fulfilling contracts with national governments while at the same time servicing Protestant church "planting" missions among indigenous tribes, a fact which it also used as a source of Evangelical financial support in the North. There is also a deceptive tension in a religious organization with a conservative evangelical bias that is also an "objective" scientific team of linguists.

[89] Cameron Townsend, who translated the New Testament into Kaqchikel, seems to have been doubly motivated when he founded WBT/SIL, says Stoll. He wanted to provide indigenous peoples with direct access to the Word of God in order to help free them from "ladino" bondage. However, he and his colleagues seem to have been more shaken by the Pipil indian uprising in neighbouring El Salvador—which they believed to be Communist inspired—than they were shocked at the military's "matanza" which followed. None of this has inhibitted WBT/SIL from signing contracts with local "ladino" autocracies and military dictatorships in order to achieve its goals of "freeing the idingenous" (Cf. Stoll 1982, 9, 10,11,12,14, 36,49,50 249,259f).

an instrument of liberation,[90] or, as enemies of conservative christianity are often quick to believe, was this a form of domination?[91]

We need to avoid simplistic reactions which usually reflect our ideological biases. The changes in personal and community life that the chapter by Goldin and Metz document, and Nayap-Pot refers to, give a positive response to the question of the transformation of persons, families and entire villages from harmful conduct. This has also been documented by numerous impartial studies.[92] Evidently, the Christian message, proclaimed today, not only by Protestants but by Catholic missioners and catechists as well, is producing numerous evidences of profound personal transformations as well as shifting community allegiances. The problem is not with the Bible, but with its communicators who were incapable—as we still are today, no matter what our theological stance—to distinguish between its message and our own cultural and ideological baggage.

Political liberation from the economic and cultural bondage of the "ladinos" (ironically, from the same Liberal class who had granted WBC/SIL permission to work in Guatemala) was also a goal of Cameron Townsend and his early band of linguists. But the strategy was not direct confrontation with opression but "indigenismo". They set themselves up as protectors of the indians by interposing themselves between the Maya and the "ladinos", at both the social and religious levels.[93] This approach was

---

[90] "...and not *Das Kapital*". Cf. *Christianity Today* (September 4, 1981), 58.

[91] The theory and methods of the WBT/SIL literacy programs came under fire for their apparent "inefficiency" and lack of effective results. Over the years, Wycliff has had to experiment with new theoretical models, until in the 1970s, fifty years after it all began, the solution was found: to allow olliterates and semi-literates to "produce their own literature on paper or through tape recordings" (Stoll 1982, 249-257f).

[92] Cf. Donna Birdwell-Pheasant, "The Power of Pentecostalism in a Belizean Village, in *Perspectives on Pentecostalism: Case Studies from the Caribbean and Latin America*, Stephen D. Glazier, ed. (Lanham, MD: University Press of America, 1960), 95-109, and June Nash, "Protestantism in an Indian Village in the Western Highlands of Guatemala", in *The Social Anthropology of Middle America*, C.M. Leslie Editor. Alpha Kappa Deltan, vol.xxx, no. 1, 1980, 49-58. Cf. Sheldon Annis, *God and Production in a Guatemalan Town* (Austin: University of Texas Press, 1987), and Linda Green, "Shifting Affiliations: Mayan Widows and *Evangélicos* in Guatemala", in Virginia Garrard-Burnett and David Stoll, eds., *Rethinking Protestantism in Latin America* (Philadelphia: Temple University Press, 1993), 159-179. Cf. Reina and Schwartz, and also Benjamin.

[93] The Protestant "indigenismo", by means of which North American missionaries retained effective control of the indigenous congregations within the national churches, might be likened to Fr. las Casas' dream of setting up a region in

highly paternalistic. It was distrustful of the indians' capacity to properly interpret Scripture, despairing of their leadership capabilities, and totally negative in their appreciation of traditional Maya religiosity.[94] This "triangular struggle" to maintain good relationships with oppressed indians and their "ladino" oppressors satisfied no one.[95]

In truth, not all evangelical Protestant missions to the indians were associated with the Wycliff methods. But they did display what indigenous people consider to be a paternalistic attitude toward them. This is a lesser criticism than the charge of racism which is levelled against the "mestizo" churches by indigenous leaders who have a strong suspicion that they are being used by conservative Protestant missions and "mestizo" churches for public relations purposes and material advantage. This suspicion is sometimes extended to churches and agencies that are related to the ecumenical movement. In sum, for many indigenous leaders, protestantism has been just as colonialist as their Catholic predecessors from Spain.

Protestantism and the awakening of Maya identity

To the superficial observer, the various Maya peoples were devout Roman Catholics. Their popular religiosity was perceived by outsiders, and particularly by zealous Protestants as merely an extension of Spanish Catholicism. The fact that priests (from Spain, Italy and Belgium) were even more zealous in the defense of their flocks and tolerant of indigenous catholicism, only served to prove this point. It has taken several decades of relatively objective ethnological analysis to uncover the deep undercurrent of Maya religiosity in the beliefs and practices of the native peoples of Guatemala and the neighboring lands of Belize, Western Honduras and

---

Northern Guatemala (the Verapaces) where indians could be evangelized without fear of the intervention of the "conquistadores". Unlike las Casas, however, the evangelical missionary approach lacked a coherent theology in defense of the personhood of the indians, including, ultimately, the freedom to choose between Christianity and their ancestral religion. (Cf. Las Casas, *Regia potestate*, p. 33. See also Rivera 1992, 141-144,229-234).

[94] Ibid, 31,35,36. The original sources are: Townsend, "Among Guatemalan Indians", *Christian Herald* (January 21, 1922) and *Central American Bulletin* (July 15, 1924), 25; *CAB* (January 15), 1925, 3. Albert Julian Lloret, "The Mayan Evangelical Church in Guatemala". Th.D. dissertation, Dallas Theological Seminary, 1976, 276.

[95] Stoll 1982, 48.

Yucatán.[96] Some of the chapters in this book (by Ku-Canché, Colop and Otzoy) will demonstrate the same phenomenon taking place among some indigenous Protestants.

In the process, indigenous spokespersons have demanded the right to control their own languages and non-missionary linguists have helped them to set up their own institutions to regulate spelling and maintain the integrity of indigenous languages.[97] "Dynamic equivalence"[98] of the Biblical text, in which the missionary brings the content and the indian provides the form of expression is gradually giving way to "shared equivalence" structure, in which both sides bring their own understanding to a shared framework. This has enabled indigenous students to begin to relate the Bible to their own ancestral beliefs.

During this period profound changes were taking place in Mayan religious attitudes (if not necessarily in their underlying beliefs). In Chapter Seven, British anthropologist Richard Wilson deals with some of the political and religious causes of these changes during the violent decade of the '70s and '80s. When Catholic parishes and Protestant mission stations were forcibly abandoned during the violent decade of the '80s, indigenous Christians of all confessions were, for the first time in 500 years, in a position to make their own life and death decisions.

Although, Wilson does not mention the role of protestantism, other studies that focus upon Q'ekchi' Protestants help to confirm his findings and fill in the picture.[99] In another article, Wilson alludes to the ideological

---

[96] Cf. the late Presbyterian missionary David George Scotchmer, *Symbols of Salvation: Interpreting Highland Maya Protestantism in Context*. Ph.D. disertation, State University of New York at Albany, 1991. By the same author "Convergence of the Gods: Comparing Traditional Maya and Christian Maya Cosmologies". Bibliographical data not included.

[97] Indians have been critical of the "hispanization" of their language spelling which was developed by WBT/SIL and government indigenist organizations. The are also alarmed that their major languages are being fragmented into too many small local dialects through the efforts of these organizations. (cf. Stoll 1982, 257).

[98] The concept of "dynamic equivalence" was developed by missionary linguist Eugene Nida and his United Bible Society team. Technically, in dynamic equivalence Scripture translation meaning takes precedence over form.

[99] Cf. Luis E. Samandú, "La Iglesia del Nazareno en Alta Verapaz, su historia y presencia en el Mundo Kekchí" (San José, Costa Rica: CSUCA, 1987. By the same author, "Estrategias evangélicas hacia la población indígena de Guatemala" (San José, Costa Rica: CSUCA, 1988). See also by Mario Higueros, "Entrevistas en Carchá: Apuntes de entrevistas sobre las creencias de hoy", in *La Revelación de Dios en las culturas: Antología* (Guatemala: Editora Semilla, 1994), 33-42. Of interest is Higueros' verification of the involvement at some level of Q'eqchi'

support of the military that some Protestant groups provided during the brutal uprooting of the Q'ekchi' community and their herding into "strategic villages".[100]   A lot has been written about the complicity of certain specialized Protestant agencies during this tragic period in Guatemalan history. Simply put, Evangelical Protestants all over the region were much polarized during this violent period. The highly publicized involvement of right wing Protestant movements from the U.S.A. must be balanced by the low key and often clandestine efforts of Christian men and women in mainline and independent churches to defend the rights of the indigenous and other oppressed peoples.[101]

México: Seeds of today's revolution

January 1, 1994 was supposed to have been a red letter day for the president of México and his Partido Revolucionario Institucional (PRI) which has "won" every national election since it came to power on a wave of peasant revolt more than half a century ago. This was the day in which the North American Free Trade Association (NAFTA) was to kick in. Instead, the entire Mexican establishment—and their uneasy partners in the U.S.A.—was rudely kicked out of bed by the news of an indigenous insurgency in the far southern and backward state of Chiapas.

Mexicans glory in their revolutionary past. But revolutions were long ago institutionalized by the ruling party. What made this revolution so

---

evangelical Protestants in the *Tzuultaq'a* cult.

[100] Richard Wilson, "Machine Guns and Mountain Spirits: The cultural effects of state repression among the Q'eqchi' of Guatemala", *Critique of Anthropology*, vol xi(1), 1991, pp. 33-61. His dissertation—*Maya Resurgence in Guatemala: Q'eqchi' Experiences*—was published by Norman/London: University of Oklahoma Press, 1995.

[101] David Stoll (*Is Latin America Turning Protestant? The Politics of Evangelical Growth*. Berkeley: University of California Press, 1990, 180-217) provides a synthesized overview of the dynamics of right wing intervention in Guatemala during the 1980s. In 1994, '95 and '96, the lives of activist indigenous Protestants have been in danger. Two indigenous presbyterian leaders have been assassinated and others have been threatened, including authors of three of this book's essays—Similox, Otzoy (both Kaqchikels), Colop (Ki'che') and their respective families—have been threatened by a secret band of paramilitary assassins called Jaguar Justiciero (Vengeful Jaguars). Cf. Antonio Otzoy, "Guatemala: The struggle for Maya unity", June 12, 1996, "hrnet.indigenous@Germany. EU.net" and "New threats against María Ventura de Saquic", June 25, 1996, Julia_Ann_Moffett.parti.-@ecunet.

unusual was its magisterial use of the media. A rag-tag band of Maya peasants, armed mostly with wooden guns, were able to destabilize a well entrenched institution, thanks to the wry wit and inspired use of the Internet by its "sub-commander" Marcos.[102] These same Maya, with vast national support and considerable international goodwill, have forced the PRI to begin opening up the democratic process and turning the country back to the people. Who would have expected that a rag-tag band of Maya peasants would be able to make even the government and business of the United States nervous enough to bring pressure upon its Mexican partner to put a stop to the uprising, by force if necessary?

When we remember the continuing history of Mayan uprisings in Mesoamérica, this latest and more sophisticated event comes less of a surprise. However, it is the dynamics of the revolution that are surprising, at least when we compare them to the indigenous revolt across the border. Guatemalan "mestizos" either turned a blind eye, or acquiesced in the genocide of the highland Maya. In México there have been large mass demonstrations of "mestizo" support for the Chiapas insurgents in front of the presidential palace. México has been able to maintain its "indian heart" far better than Guatemala, where the "mestizos" opted for the white man's world and turned upon their own blood. Protestants, both indigenous and mestizos, have been sympathetic to the revolutionaries, largely because they include some of their own co-religionists. The issues are complex. Don Samuel Ruiz, the courageous Catholic bishop of San Cristobal las Casas—a Nobel peace nominee, has evenhandedly defended Protestant peasants from the oppression of Catholic and Maya landlords.

The participation of indigenous Protestants in the Chiapas uprising is the latest installment of a long history of Protestant involvement in southern México. A 1969 study of Protestantism in Latin America comments that "the greatest concentration of Presbyterian members is found in southern Mexico". This is said to be in large part due to "people movements" or mass conversions among the Yucatecos, and particularly among the Ch'ols

---

[102] The military title at first gave rise to the supposition that he was under orders from some mysterious Marxist command structure. It turns out that the real commanders of the Chiapas insurgency are the indigenous peasants. The author of this chapter, who has himself received messages diseminated by electronic mail from Sub-commander Marcos, finds considerable irony in the fact that people whose culture has been minutely analized and stored on SIL computer banks in Dallas, Texas have leaped into the computer age and are creatively adapting it to their own aims.

and Tzeltals in Chiapas.[103] Presbyterian missionaries were present during a widespread turning to Evangelical Protestantism in Tabasco state, in the decade of the 1950s.[104] Even today, hundreds of Presbyterian congregations dot the ancient Maya lands of southern México. In fact, one can find in many a small Yucateco village "First" and even "Fourth" Presbyterian churches, along with even more numerous Evangelical groups—Baptists, Nazarenes, Pentecostals, etc.—of more recent vintage.[105]

Social conflict is not new to Chiapas. In the 1940s there was conflict between Ch'ol and Tzeltal Maya peasants and encroaching cattle ranchers and coffee planters. The rapid growth of protestant churches signified that they soon became involved in the land disputes. In one village, half the population, now Protestant, ousted the town government of "ladino" Catholics. New, alcohol free lifestyles and social economic prosperity brought conflict. In this and in similar instances, SIL agronomists—that had moved into the region in the 1940s—advised non-confrontation, and helped indigenous Protstants to open up new lands in the Lancandón Forest. The present conflict, which focuses around the Tzotzil municipality of San Juan Chamula, has been simmering for years. The town has been ruled for several decades by indigenous "caciques" who made their fortunes as government labor agents, bilingual teachers, liquor smugglers, usurers and so forth". Protestants have been murdered and run off their lands.[106] This is part of the dynamics that has caused Protestant churches in the state, sometimes with the support of their national church leaderships, to be

---

[103] Cf. Read, Monterroso and Johnson, 169. See also Charles Bennet, "The Evangelical Church in Chiapas: A Preliminary Survey" (Pasadena, CA.: Fuller Theological Seminary, 1967). Unpublished research.

[104] Cf. Charles Bennett, *Tinder in Tabasco* (Grand Rapids: Eerdmans, 1968).

[105] Although there is a sizeable "mestizo" population in Yucatán, the culture is very self-consciously Maya, to the point where, in the interior of the state, Yucateko is used as a daily medium of communication across class divisions. To varying degrees, Maya culture remains strong also in Protestant congregations. Cf. David Martin, *Tongues of Fire: The Explosion of Protestantism in Latin America* (Oxford: Blackwell, 1990), 171-175, 186-191.

[106] Stoll 1982, 51-53. Sources: John Beekman and James C. Hefley, *Peril by Choice* (Grand Rapids: Zondervan, 1974), 226-37. Henning Siverts, *Oxchuc* México, DF, Instituto Lingüístico de Verano, 1969, 171-184. Jan Russ and Robert Wasserstrom, "Evangelization and political control: The SIL in Mexico", in Peter Aaby and Sore Hvalkof (eds), *Is God an American? An Anthropological Perspective on the Missionary Work of the Summer Institute of Linguistics* (Copenhagen: International Work Group for Indigenous Affairs and London: Survival International, 1981), 166,170. Cp. Martin, 211-214.

sympathetic to the Zapatista revolution. Chapter eighteen by Ofelia Ortega presents the role of world Christians in promoting peace in Chiapas.

The Maya Challenge for Today

> If we judge the Maya by our own definition of progress, they had few technological wonders... If the Maya did not invent an advanced scientific technology... what then did they invent? They invented ideas that harnessed social energy... The invented political symbols that transformed and coordinated such age-old institutions as the extended family, the village, the shaman, and patriarch into the stuff of civilized life.[107]

As the time approached for the "celebration/lamentation" of the 500 years since Columbus "discovered America", indigenous leaders all over Abia Yala decided that it was time to come down from their mountain fastness and emerge from their secret places of worship in the dwindling forests of Mesoamérica and tell their story to the world. It is perhaps not a coincidence that, according to the Maya calendar, this present world cycle will come to an end on December 23, 2012.[108] Indeed, one wanders whether the Maya sages of old could have foreseen the demise of their civilization and eventual resurection poenix-like in the twenty first century.

Maya theologians and intellectuals today believe that they have fundamental values to offer (in ecology, family and community lifestyle) to a contemporary world that is self-destructing. What they have suffered for centuries from "conquistadores" and priests, "criollos" and "mestizos", old and new world orders, has not left in them a spirit of fatalism nor of revenge. While most of them do not idealize their culture, they are convinced that they have much of value to contribute to the new world that of necessity must rise from the ashes of our current self-destruction.

The challenge to a "new world order"

> In an age when the word "invention" has become synonymous with technological progress, it is difficult for us to imagine any other kind of invention... We in the West see ourselves as the

---

[107] Schele and Freidel, 96.

[108] December 23, 2012 (4 Ahau 3 Kankin) concides with the completion of thirteen 400 year cycles, or 5200 years of 360 days, after which a new (and fifth) creation will begin (Schele and Freidel, 82).

> inheritors of a great hope—the tradition that technology and
> scientific discovery will be the salvation of human kind.
> However, another and more fundamental form of invention ex-
> ists...[109]

The fundamental worldview of the Maya still centers upon community life
and land. With comparatively little arable land in their rugged mountains,
swamps and jungles, the Maya—like the Incas in the high Andes—created
a thriving civilization. More important for us is their holistic world view.
The countries of the North today emphasize alienating values such as
economic progress, the expectation of material prosperity, personal security,
law and order and might makes right. Through years of struggling with
some of the same issues, the ancient Maya codified their concept of
development through religion and ritual rather than macro-economics.

> It never occurred to eurocentric historians that plows and wheels
> are not much use without draft animals, such as oxen and
> horses, neither of which existed in the Americas before Colum-
> bus. Far from marvelling that civilizations arose despite these
> "handicaps," historians took the absence of plow and wheel as
> proof that ancient Americans could not truly have been civi-
> lized. In the same spirit they concluded that Maya hieroglyphs
> were not real writing—though they looked like writing—because
> no white man had been able to decipher them.[110]

The basic life concerns of the Maya had to do with the origin of humanity,
the purpose of human life on earth, and the interrelationship of the
individual with family, community and the supernatural world. Despite the
difference in our cultures and worldviews, Maya spirituality can speak to
central and enduring problems of "civilized" human beings: nature and the
land, nationhood and power, justice and equality, individual purpose and
social destiny. Even the sudden demise, at different periods and in different
places, of the kingdoms of Mesoamerican civilization serves as a warning
to us today to turn back from our destructive ways so that history will not
repeat itself. Does this have significance for "modern civilization" and for
the Christian faith?

---

[109] Schele and Freidel, 96,97.
[110] Wright, 6.

A challenge to christianity?

For the first time in our 500 year history, Latin American Christians are having to take seriously the phenomenon of religious pluralism and to accept the challenge of dialogue with non-Christian religions. The Maya resurgence challenges the Christian faith at the level of its practice. There are significant parallels between Maya cosmology and the Judeo-Christian tradition—an earth-centered cosmology, a cyclical/linear experience of time, a holistic understanding of reality, respect for the whole of life and for family values, a unique sense of history—which need to be seriously faced. Indeed, a growing number of young indigenous—and some non-indigenous—Christians find the Maya world view very attractive. The challenge for them, and perhaps for us, is to discover how to relate their Christian faith to their ancestral cultural beliefs and values. Particularly are they attempting to integrate Jesus Christ and his absolute claims upon us into their history. The challenge of Christ to indigenous theology shall be considered in the closing chapter, after we have had an opportunity to listen to our Maya sisters and brothers speak to us from their unique viewpoint.

PART I
CLASH OF CULTURES AND WORLDVIEWS

CHAPTER ONE

THE INVASION OF CHRISTIANITY
INTO THE WORLD OF THE MAYAS

Vitalino Similox Salazar

"From the time of the Spanish invasion, the Maya peoples have
been forced to relinquish their culture and to remain silent...
There has been a systematic practice of demeaning, marginalizing and exploiting us. The time has now come for my people to
become critical subjects of our own history; we need to practice
a faith that is as free as possible from foreign influences". The
author is a leader in the Kaqchikel presbytery of the National
Evangelical Presbyterian Church of Guatemala and Executive
Secretary of CIEDEG (Confederation of Evangelical Churches
of Guatemala). This chapter is an approved summary and
adaptation of the first part of the Rev. Similox' thesis.[1]

The spirituality of the Maya peoples, their values—objective (morals,
ethics, conduct) and subjective (history, language, technology, and so
on)—are the starting point of their theology today. At this moment in time
these values are particularly important in view of the social and religious
situation of the Maya peoples in Guatemala and southern México (Chiapas).
They also have something to say to the Christian "evangelization and
mission" projects in their various forms after 500 years of European
domination.

The commemoration of this fact in 1992 covered up harmful religious
ideas and conduct. The notion still persists that any religious practice that
is not "Christian," that is, of the religion that was brought to us half a
millennium ago, is, ipso facto, "pagan." Mayan spirituality and theology
arouses a consensus of suspicions that pronounces it "idolatrous." This is
even more the case when we begin to systematize the ideas that flow out of
the religiosity of the Maya.

The suspicions are not new, and they work both ways. King Atahualpa
of Tahuantitsuyo, along the Andes range, was equally suspicious of Fr.
Valverde's indoctrination on the one true God, which to the Inca emperor,

---

[1] Vitalino Similox, *La expresión y metodología del pensamiento Maya
contemporáneo en Guatemala (Ri nat'oj Mayab chi iximulew, ri ru'bixik ri rukemik)*,
in partial fulfillment of the requirements for the Licentiate in Theology degree at
Mariano Gálvez University in Guatemala City.

seemed incoherent. Garcilaso de la Vega, a descendant of the Incas has recorded Atahualpa's reply. "He would seem to be the same God that we call Pachacamac and Viracocha." Other pre-Colombian peoples also had a monotheistic religion, to which even some of their conquerors testified. An early chronicler, Clavijero, has this to say about the Aztecs:

> The Mexicans had an idea, albeit imperfectly, of a supreme being, absolute and independent, whom they professed to worship, respect and fear. They did not represent him in any way because they considered him to be invisible. Neither did they call him by any name except the common name of God, which in their language is *Teotl*, more similar in meaning than in pronunciation to the Greek Theos. They did, however, address him by many titles which expressed the grandeur and power which they ascribed to him. The called him *Ipalnemoani*—"Him Through Whom We Live"—and *Tloque Nahuaque*—"He Who Contains Everything in Himself".[2]

The Maya had the same understanding and knowledge of God as the Incas and Aztecs. For the Maya—according to their sacred book, the *Pop Vuh*—the supreme God is called "Heart of Heaven" and *Q'uq'umatz*, in my own K'aqchikel language. It is he, and only he, who fixes the bounds and movement of the universe. He is both plurality and unity. All of this, however, was overlooked by "christianity", and is not taken very seriously today.

Protestantism penetrated the Maya region of Mesoamerica dressed in the ideological garb of liberalism. It was infused by un underlying racism; materialistic and individualistic values informed its concept of the salvation of humankind. As a result, the Maya view of God was undervalued. Protestantism, without understanding Maya religion and theology, wrote it off as pagan, idolatrous and polytheistic, along with the religiosity of the catholic "cofradías" which tended to imitate some of the central aspects of pre-colombian Mayan religion. What they failed to perceive is that this was, in fact, a form of resistance to Western attempts at acculturation.

Nevertheless, after 500 years of "evangelization," it is possible today to look for alternatives by means of which Christians can evaluate the Maya worldview within an ecumenical perspective of mutual respect. We can search within our respective religions and worldviews to find points of convergence between them.

---

[2] Miguel León Portilla, *Antología de Teotihuacán de los Aztecas, Fuentes e interpretaciones históricas*. México, UNAM, 1983, p. 526.

Objectives of this Study

From the time of the Spanish invasion, the Maya peoples have been forced to relinquish their culture and to remain silent. This is not because the Maya do not know how to express their ideas and have no collective memory, but because there haš been a systematic practice of demeaning, marginalizing and exploiting us. The time has now come for my people to become aware of our own history, to be critical subjects of it; we need to practice a faith that is as free as possible from foreign influences.

With this in mind, this essay seeks to rediscover Maya Theology, with particular attention to its understanding of God, Nature, Salvation, and the Family. It hopes to establish a basis for a theological methodology that is suitable to the challenges that the Maya are facing today. I seek to demonstrate that Maya Theology is not a thing of the past, but that it has relevance for today, as it is expressed in the twenty Maya languages in Guatemala and numerous other idioms in neighboring countries. While Maya Theology may not have all of the scientific presuppositions and epistemological foundations of christianity, it possesses its own complex of meanings, methodology, and sources. These derive from the questions that the Maya ask about the cause and reason for their vital problems. In seeking answers, Maya wish to make use of their own rationale, moral judgments, and principles of knowledge, which has been conferred upon every human culture in order to discover and know God. Unfortunately, we are just beginning our search, so we have very little formal material on which to base our theology.

In our approach to christianity, we wish to present the truth, as objectively as possible, about the way the Maya were treated by christianity, without entering into polemics. What we want is to create the conditions for an open dialogue. The basis for this dialogue, we believe, should be the following:

1. *The first manifestation of the God of the Bible and Creator of the Universe among the Maya peoples did not take place at the arrival of the Spanish priests.* The faith of the Maya was neither nonexistent nor primitive, even in earliest times, despite their lack of knowledge about the God of the Christians. To affirm the contrary is tantamount to declaring that God is historically limited and circumscribed to an European context.

2. *Even while the various Christian traditions—Roman Catholic and Protestant—maintain their unique theological positions, they are not static,*

but dynamic, as their varied expressions and practices testify. Despite their differences, all these traditions conclude that every culture finds meaning in life, develops ethical systems and expresses its spirituality as an echo of the divine voice that speaks to all human beings, both personally and in their social relations. These are conduits of divine revelation to humankind, in particular time, space, and cultural modalities. Once this point is recognized, we can understand the second theological reference point: the possibility that the Bible can be read and interpreted in the light of different cultures, as is the case with the oral or written "Bible" of the indigenous peoples of the Americas.

3. *The Christian Bible declares that God's presence and works shall be known among all peoples (Ps. 19:14).* Jesus is surprised by the faith of non-Jewish people (Lk. 7:10 and Mr. 7:24-30). Paul is the most emphatic of all New Testament writers. He states that God's general revelation is for every human being, and not just for Jews, who limited the divine action to the fulfillment of the law and circumcision. The works and divinity of God have been manifest from Creation (Ro. 1:17-25). Every human being has the capacity to perceive God by means of the intelligence that we have received from the Creator (Ro. 1:20). Every human being of every culture has within his or her reach the capability of doing good (Ro. 7:18). When people find it impossible to do good, it is because sin has taken hold of them, of their environment and society. Faith is above the Jewish law. Faith and the true knowledge of God are demonstrated through the practice of human beings, and not through keeping the law or circumcision (Gl. 5:6). This is why Paul asked the Romans to rise above the norms of the religion of his time (Ro. 12).

The Importance of the Maya Perspective

This topic has been dealt with by various people, but not necessarily from a Maya point of view. Maya theology has not developed necessarily along the formal academic lines of European theology. This is a millennia long process during which our religious self-awareness has grown, along with the development of our collective memory.

A theological response needs urgently to be given, in Maya categories, to the problems of our people. The Maya are not isolated from the rest of the population of our ancient heartland (Southern México, most of Guatemala, and nearby areas in Belize, Honduras, and El Salvador). We are part of it. Our problems are also the problems of the wider society to which we belong. Consequently, solutions to our problems are solutions that effect everybody in the region. We Maya will contribute out of our own culture and based upon our own needs to find solutions to our problems, and in so doing we believe we are contributing, as well, to resolving major problems of our global society.

It is important to note that, until now, Latin American Theology stands in need of our kind of reflection. In Latin America there are other Amerindian peoples that live in the same circumstances as the Maya. Their theology is an expression of their struggle and hope, and should become a challenge to students of theology, particularly in Central America.

1992 was widely viewed in Catholic circles as the Fifth Century of Evangelization in Latin America. There have been five hundred years of Catholic evangelization and a century or more of Protestant evangelization. For the Maya, it is a remembrance of five centuries of genocide and exploitation. It is not possible to wipe out the historical memory of the massacres and violations that have been committed against the Amerindian peoples. This is why a social process was set in motion to strengthen the Amerindian national identity as a counterbalance to the celebration of the "evangelization of Latin America."

At this moment in time, we Protestants cannot remain aloof from reflecting upon the "commemoration"of the 500 years. Protestants should help open the way for their Maya sisters and
brothers to do their own reflecting. They must help create the theological conditions for us to develop our own theological thinking, in the context of what remains of our own culture, values, worldview, and centuries old resistance. Yes, and we have the right to analyze and reflect upon the role played by "christianity" in the European invasion and the ensuing pillaging and exploitation of our indigenous peoples, even until now.

A study of Maya theology will make it necessary for us to read the Bible in the light of the "oral and written Bible" of the Amerindian peoples. It is possible that some of the miraculous and inspiring acts of Judeo-Christianity (e.g., the liberation from Egypt, the assistance of Yaweh in wars of conquest, miraculous healings, etc.) might have taken place likewise in Mayan history, as a clear manifestation of God in the history of all humanity.

Various Approaches to Maya Theology

There are several responses to the resurgence of Maya theology.

Polarization between Maya spirituality and christianity

Even in the twentieth century there has been inquisitorial persecution by some conservative clergy, at times with encouragement from "official" religion. Faced with this antagonism, some representatives of the Maya religion have preferred to remain anonymous, secluded in the highest mountains and densest jungles of our countries.

Suspicion of Maya syncretism

Synchretism is wrongly evaluated as negative. There are many forms of syncretism, including very positive aspects in both the Christian and Maya religions. In any case, judaism and christianity are much more syncretic, having assimilated elements of the Canaanite religion, and from Greek, Roman, and other European cultures.

Outright rejection of indigenous spirituality

Christianity rejects indigenous spirituality out of hand because of a religious dualism that does not allow for the presence of God in the aboriginal cultures. In this view, those who do not know the Bible have the devil in their hearts. The only truth, the only absolutes, and the only logic belongs alone to the Christian religion. These kind of Christians are convinced that no other religion has any knowledge of God.

Recognition of commonalities

A holistic and conciliatory attitude will recognize that, while different cultures know God by different names, there are certain common theological axis such as divine revelation in other religions. God was already here before the Europeans arrived. They did not bring God to us. In the words of the Santo Domingo Declaration:

...God the Creator of life, was already in our lands thousands of years ago, acting as the vital force in our cultures... the Spirit, giver of life and health and the Sustainer of all our peoples, manifest in mother earth.[3]

All of this is by way of demonstrating the difficulties that the Maya peoples have had to overcome in order to live, develop, and express themselves within a colonialist system during five hundred years. It is not easy to maintain a theology when there has been a practice of extermination, from the most crass genocide to more sophisticated practices, which have produced the same results—assimilation and integration, rooted in indigenist, ethnicist, racist, and "economicista" theories and rationale.[4] None of these ideas belong to the Maya peoples. Despite these discriminatory practices, and the ideologically based attempts at exterminating us, the Maya are still very much alive. We maintain our historical memory, our religious awareness, and theological reflection.

Brief History of the European Invasion

There are those who have called Spain (in the fifteenth through eighteenth centuries) a kingdom that, despite its apparent similarities with other absolute European monarchies, should probably be grouped with Asiatic modes of governing.[5]

Invasion and christianization were one and the same thing for Spain. Church, State, and the Invader would seem to have been part and parcel of the same mission: to conquer our peoples. Mires develops the thesis that these three components gradually became separated as a fourth component was introduced, the Amerindians. Whatever the case, what developed was a kind of theocracy. Temporal interests were fused with spiritual goals. As Mires observes, quoting José Ingenieros:

> The divine right of the old regime and the intolerance of Spanish fanaticism are symbolically represented in that unique agreement between Charles V and the pope Alexander VI to dominate the new world at the

---

[3] "Declaración de Santo Domingo", unpublished paper. CEHILA 1989, 3.

[4] Editor's note: "Indigenist," from "indigenista", refers to "white-man-knows best" approaches to indigenous problems. "Ethnicist" and "economicist" speak of an academic and utilitarian approach to ethnic studies and development programs.

[5] Cp. Fernando Mires, *La colonización de las almas*. San José, Costa Rica, DEI, 1987, p. 15.

exclusive service of a two-headed monarchy, which was simultaneously
seated in El Escorial and the Vatican.[6]

The author is, of course, referring to the concession of "discovered" lands
to the Spanish crown by the papal Bull of 1493.[7] We can add to this the
fact that the Spanish had just recently defeated and expelled the Moors—a
triumph of "christianity" over the Muslim religion! Underlying the Spanish
worldview was the Aristotelian philosophy that some people have been born
to be masters and others to be slaves. This mix of philosophical worldview,
history, and religion is the background for the Spanish invasion of the
peoples of Mesoamérica, and among them my people, the Maya.

   The Invader needed to believe that he was in charge in order to be able
to christianize; he therefore had to find theological justifications. For
example, the humanist Ginés de Sepúlveda (in the sixteenth century)
justified the massacre of the indigenous peoples on theological grounds. A
consultation of indigenous peoples and blacks in Costa Rica (in 1985)
declared that

> the humiliation of our people reached its limit; they were treated as beasts
> of burden. Some writers said that the aborigines were not worthy of being
> considered human beings. Our lands were irrigated with aboriginal blood
> while the pope in Rome was resolving the problem of whether or not we
> had souls.[8]

In this way "christianity" was the theological, juridical, and moral,
foundation for the invasion. Each step of this invasion was legitimated by
an ideology which turned lies, distortions, and deceit into good, correct, and
acceptable ideas. At the same time, and at great odds, there were clerics
that defended the cause of the Maya. There was, for example, Fr. Las
Casas who summarized the pejorative attitudes of his contemporaries
concerning the aborigines in the following terms:

> What kind of doctrine could such men offer—earthy idiots who barely
> know how to cross themselves; infidels with many languages so different
> from Castilian; people who have never learned to speak more than three
> words?[9]

---

[6] Ibid, p. 19.

[7] Ibid, p. 40.

[8] *Pastoralia: "Racismo y marginalidad en América Latina"*. Vol. vii, no. 4 (July
14, 1985). San José, Costa Rica, Centro Evangélico Latinoamericano de Estudios
Pastorales (CELEP), 56,64.

[9] Quoted in ibid, p. 53.

Besides Bartolomé de las Casas, there were other defenders of the Maya peoples who fought to change the colonial status quo. Yet, even the fact clergymen defended us is an expression of our dependence and subordination, because the Maya people themselves were never heard from. Even in this way, "christianity" demonstrated its way of acting and thinking.

When liberal governments took power, Protestants arrived, as was the case in Guatemala under Gen. Justo Rufino Barrios and president Benito Juárez in México. It was a period in the history of Latin America when Protestants were attempting to counteract the domination of the Catholic Church and its alliance with power groups.[10] Roger Bastide comments on the influence of protestantism in Latin America. "Racial prejudice seems to be stronger and more pernicious in Protestant countries than it is in Catholic lands." He goes on to say that "religion can become a factor which permits and encourages the creation and strengthening of these prejudices".[11]

Protestantism, therefore can be as subtle and effective as catholicism in fostering the extinction of the Amerindians.[12] The extinction of the Maya people took the form of radical changes and transformations which resulted from the imposition of a religion that was developed within other systems of production upon the Maya that practiced an "asymmetrical mode of production." Protestantism brought its own class structure and other social aspects which were unique to it, not to mention the heavy ideological overtones in the message that it proclaimed. Other fundamentalist sects, such as the Jehovah's Witnesses and Mormons, can be charged with being more prejudicial to the Maya and the problems that we face. The following assessment is by a Guatemalan daily.

> The 542 Protestant sects which operate in the country, the majority of which come from the United States, cause this country problems of identity, as well as of apolitical and economic nature... Liberal groups in México have accused such sects as being instruments of ideological penetration, under the auspices of the government of the United States. These sects, most of the time, alter the cultural patterns of the population.[13]

---

[10] Guido Girardi, *La Conquista de América Latina, ¿Con qué derecho?*. San José, Costa Rica, DEI, 1988, p. 40.

[11] Quoted in ibid, p. 41.

[12] Ibid, p. 50.

[13] Taken from the journal *Siglo XXI*, Guatemala City, September, 1990, p. 25.

This secular point of view emphasizes the fact that non-Maya and Christians cannot blame our critical attitude simply upon reverse racism, or to a desire by Maya to extract their historical revenge. Rather, it must be understood as the perspective of the vanquished—the Amerindian peoples—now that we are becoming aware of the facts and reality of our history. This understanding is uniquely indigenous, as can be seen in the various documents that have come out of important events. A case in point is the gathering in Santo Domingo that was organized by CEHILA. Among other important things, its final document states:

> The European culture... in spite of its structures of domination, also gave to us, in a complex racial mix, its positive cultural and religious values, including its own christianity of the poor. These values have been integrated into the religious and cultural tradition of the oppressed, which has enabled a popular culture of resistance and struggle against domination to evolve. It is here that a new way of being the church was being born, as a sign of hope for all peoples.[14]

The above declaration makes clear that certain positive elements in christianity have been assimilated by the Amerindian peoples, who today have a very high respect for the Christ of the poor. We cannot deny that Amerindian religiosity, in various parts of Latin America, is subtly expressed through a kind of imitation of Christian religiosity. The unpublished document of the Sicuani (Cuzco, Perú) Bible Institute states, quoting Luis Varcarcel:

> When the unavoidable foreign domination came, the indigenous peoples astutely put their best attempts at simulation to work. Unable to openly and proudly reject the imposition of the predominant values, they pretended to accept them. The Amerindians became Catholic and were baptized; they were assiduous in their practice, taking part in rites and holy days. Nonetheless, they continued to be firmly attached to their old gods. Surreptitiously and clandestinely, they incorporated their own into the Church's liturgy. While priests and lay congregations believed that they had triumphed in their policies, indigenous peoples rejoiced in worshipping their divinities on the traditional dates. Priests and missionaries often found indigenous symbols hidden inside the altars, sacred objects that bore the marks of recent use.[15]

---

[14] CEHILA, p. 4.

[15] Jean-Daniel Kaestli, *El protestantismo latinoamericano y el cambio social.* San José, 1970, Costa Rica: SEBILA, 10.

We are aware of similar experiences in Guatemala, both in Catholic and Protestant churches. Idealizing a jewish Christ, a popular church, including among the Maya, express their cultural resistance through the Christian religion. This resistance is evidenced by many Maya who pretend to be Catholics or Protestants in order to avoid being molested, or even persecuted. This phenomenon has occurred repeatedly in our country. An example: in 1980, many Catholics in the Mayan highlands—particularly in Quiché and Chimaltenango—became Evangelicals in order to avoid the political repression, while continuing to practice the Maya religion. A Presbyterian minister, during one of his pastoral visits, found a local church elder, waving incense over his maize crop. He was told that he had been taught to do this by his parents, grandparents, and all of his ancestors. This is only one of many other similar cases. Anthropologist R.M. Carmack comments that

> taking into account the many forces that were at work to exploit and control the indigenous peoples during the colonial period— Church, State, plantation owners, "ladinos"—it is amazing that they have been capable of retaining even a vestige of the Maya culture. Nonetheless, they have done so. Even today it is possible to visit certain places in the highlands where people continue to live fundamentally as Maya. The spirit of resistance was somehow kept alive through the political organization of the indigenous peoples during the colonial period.[16]

This can be explained in part through the syncretic culture which the Maya developed, which should be seen as a passive or ideological form of resistance in the face of alien forces that were pushing for change. Yet, the Maya did not simply adopt Spanish culture in a passive way. They carefully wove into their culture a texture whose visible patterns were Spanish, but the warp and woof were Maya. This process began early and continued throughout the colonial period. Let us listen to a friar in sixteenth century Guatemala.

> When the elders are on their deathbeds, they pass on their idols to other old men. They receive, care for, honor, and venerate them, because they and those who follow their law will continue to be... because the Spaniards are presumptuous and will someday meet their end. So when they have died, these gods will send a new sun that will illuminate all who

---

[16] Robert M. Carmack, ed. *Harvest of Violence: The Maya Indians and the Guatemalan Crisis*. Norman and London, University of Oklahoma Press.

follow them, and that generation will recover its lands and shall possess them in tranquillity and peace.[17]

Over the years and centuries the ancestral truths are upheld. The physical and spiritual cohesion of the Mayan peoples is maintained, sometimes out of a sheer will to survive. Whatever the reason, the Maya peoples and their culture have remained until today. This endeavor has been threatened time and time again. The most serious threat came from the church, although there were villages where Catholic priests were more lenient in enforcing attendance to mass and matters of politics, morals, and village economy.

Although the Maya were baptized as Christians, they resourcefully managed to transform the rituals and beliefs so that they were closer to their own Maya religion than to the catholicism of the priests. In almost every town the Catholic saints came to be associated with the "pagan" gods of rain and fertility. The worship of saints became associated with the Maya religious calendar, to the point that catholic priests were surprised by churches that overflowed on the "good" days of the 260 day Maya calendar. The Maya continue to burn "copal" and to act out their ceremonial dances and dramas. The ethical criteria of the villagers continues to be Mayan. The first duty for everyone is to sow their "milpa" an to invoke the gods of nature, of water and land that have sustained them with the necessities of life. They believe that the gods who are not given offerings by negligent individuals or communities may punish them with disease, drought, and other calamities. Their rituals were further transformed as the catholic lay brotherhoods were coopted by the same clans and lineages that had overseen the ritual life in the Maya temples before the coming of the Spaniards.

This "syncretism" generally enabled the Maya to channel and reduce Spanish influence over their lives. In the smaller villages, the "principales" and the "Consejo" dealt with the foreigners in representation of the people, giving the impression of doing things the Spanish way. But village life continued much the same as it had for generations. Wherever the Spanish became aware of the pagan manifestations, the village elders did nothing to destroy the social world of their people, but chose instead to protect them from the worst aspects of colonial society. As long as the Maya continued to pay tribute, provide manual labor, and did not rebel against Spanish

---

[17] Ibid.

authority, they were mostly left alone by the Crown and their colonial representatives, including Catholic priests.[18]

During the nineteenth century the Catholic Church was a bastion of conservatism, with links to the "cofradías" with their partially Amerindian beliefs and rites. The Maya held both civil and religious posts in the villages, ascending gradually along the established route to power and prestige in order to become "principales".

During the past fifty years, the Protestant presence among the Maya has followed a different route. Protestantism evolved forms that, in the majority of cases, resulted in practices that were contrary to Mayan culture. The services took place in an individualistic way: each person singing and praying to his personal God, and reflecting upon him as an individual. There was no manifestation of community. Dialogue was unknown. Throughout, this elitist practice separated and divided the participants. Preaching condemned specific sins—laziness, alcoholism, sloth, witchcraft, paganism — but hoarding, low wage, exploitation and ill gotten gains were not preached against. There was no mention of social sins, much less in denunciation of what is behind the social and economic structures that oppress human beings, and the Maya people in particular. Even until today the emphasis is upon the virtues of work, frugality, non-membership in labor unions and non-political involvement, etc. It seems obvious that this Protestant practice is foreign to the gospel. It belongs rather under the rubric of "evangelism," that which was brought to us by a few missionaries and continues to be preached by Protestant pastors who present an ideological, political and culturally alienating gospel.

All of this was contrary to the life of the Maya who do not separate their religious and daily lives. It is all of a piece. Everything that indigenous people do, think as a family, and carry out in their daily work, contains a practical understanding of religion. When protestantism arrived, it compartmentalized the Christian life, which was usually identified with Sundays, and with sacred church space. Religious practice became isolated

---

[18] Editor's Note: This was the case in Guatemala during the seventeenth century, but the earlier experience of the Yucatán Mayas under the inflexible hand of Fr. Diego de Landa, is an entirely different story. (Cp. Inga Clendinnen, *Ambivalent Conquests: Maya and Spaniard in Yucatán, 1517-1570.* London and New York: Cambridge University Press, 1987. See also Diego de Landa, *Relación de las cosas de Yucatán.* Edición de Miguel Rivera, Madrid: Historia 16). Serie Crónicas de América 7, 1985. Cp. Robert S. Chamberlain, *The Conquest and Colonization of Yucatán: 1517-1550.* Washington: Carnegie Institution, 1948).

from life in general. This caused a dichotomy between spiritual and material existence, which disrupted the essential unity of human beings, within themselves and in their community relations. Ethical values were taught that reduced transgression to the areas of food, drink, and dress. Nothing was said of those sins that transcend individuals, moving into the social, economic, and political realms.

It is only been during the past few years that these practices have begun to change. Today we can find Mayan Protestants who worship, share and practice their religion generally within their own cultural values.

CHAPTER TWO

CHRISTIANITY AND ABORIGINAL RELIGIONS
IN ABIA YALA

Goyo Cutimanco

"We understand 'indigenism' to be the efforts in favour of the
aborigines by non-indigenous persons. The exact opposite is a
romantic 'indianism' that holds that indians alone can reflect
upon and analyze their situation. Either extreme can be harmful
because they can all too easily become polarized by a narrow
minded approach". The author of this essay, Goyo de la Cruz
Cutimanco, is a young Quechua Protestant theologian from
Perú. He is a founder-leader of the Coordenadora de Pastoral
Aborigen (COOPA/IETSAY), a grassroots indigenous organization which seeks to establish dialogue between traditional
christianity and aboriginal culture and spirituality. This chapter
is used with permission.

Among the salient factors in the present religious situation of the aboriginal
people of Abia Yala is the way in which indigenous religions are treated by
institutional christianity, and its various projects of "evangelism-mission".
All the Christian confessions target resurgent indigenous spirituality for
condemnation with pejoratives such as "pagan" and "idolatrous". They can
only view with suspicion any religious practice that is not "christian". We
shall address this issue—and the rights of the indigenous religions of Abia
Yala by way of a brief incursion into the history of the insertion of foreign
creeds into this continent.

The Incursion of Christianity into Abia Yala

Roman Catholicism

To conquer and to christianize were synonymous terms for Spain. Church
and State and the "conquistador" were at first part and parcel of the same
mission. Fernando Mires develops the thesis that these three components
gradually became more differentiated as a fourth indigenous element was

introduced.[1] What is certain is that a kind of theocracy ensued in which temporal interests were joined to spiritual ends. We must keep in mind that the Eurospanish arrived straight from a victory of christianity over the Muslim religion, having expelled the Moors from Iberia after 500 years of occupation. Also, the Aristotelian philosophy which was in vogue at the time taught that some people were born to be masters and others servants. These interrelated factors religious, historical and philosophical—are part of the background of the Spanish conquest.

The "conquistadores" needed to believe that they were conquering in order to christianize, which meant that they needed to find theological justifications. One of the faithful representatives of the "theology of death" was the humanist Ginés de Sepúlveda, who, without ever having set foot on the soil of Abia Yala elaborated a macabre apologetic of the "just massacre" of the aboriginal peoples of this continent.

It was upon this kind of theological, juridical and moral framework that the European invasion and conquest were gradually legitimized. At the same time, although against great odds, there were clerics who defended the indigenous cause, such as Montesinos and Las Casas. It should be said, though, that Las Casas did not go so far as to question the essential objectives of the "conquistores", that is, the evangelization of the "infidels" and the implantation of christendom.[2]

The question as to the attitude of Catholic christianity regarding indigenous peoples is still with us. And the "enlightened" response seems to be that mission should be, for the most part, conciliatory, in the style of Fr. Las Casas. A "peaceful" method of colonizing and integrating the aborigines within the present day nation state.

Protestantism

When, in the nineteenth century, liberal oligarchies took over the governments of Latin America, the Protestant form of christianity arrived, closely allied to these power groups. Halfway through the present century, the Summer Institute of Linguistics (SIL) penetrated our aboriginal communities. This "evangelistic" project continues to cause harmful repercussions

---

[1] Fernando Mires, *La colonización de las almas*. San José, Costa Rica: DEI, 1987, passim.

[2] Giulio Girardi, *La conquista de América: ¿Con qué derecho?*. San José, Costa Rica, DEI, 1988, 40.

in our midst. For example, in México, what neither the Spanish colonizers nor the present administrations were able to do in more than four hundred years, SIL has managed to accomplish in 50 years of penetration of our indigenous communities. On the pretext of translating the Bible into the autochthonous languages, it has managed to make of our people passive and hostile to their own culture. Religion can actually generate and heighten prejudices (in Protestant countries racial prejudices seem to be more malignant than in Catholic countries). In particular, fundamentalist and sectarian protestantism, we suspect, is much more subtle and effective in fomenting the extinction of the indigenous peoples than catholicism.

Five hundred years of resistance

During the celebration and counter-celebration of the five hundred years of colonization, many programs have been created—some long lasting, others short lived, and various social actors have come to the fore. Even among those sectors that are most indifferent to the indigenous people, there are those who took the time to express an opinion regarding the nefarious "celebration" and indigenous resistance. The Latin American Episcopal Conference (CELAM) held an Assembly (in October of 1992) in which five hundred years of Evangelization were celebrated. Meanwhile, there are Protestants who do not consider Christopher Columbus to have been an adventurer, but a successful entrepreneur who, with God's help and trusting in the promises of Holy Scripture, was able to accomplish the great feat of "discovering the new world".

In stark contrast, there is a sector of both Catholicism and protestantism that is deeply concerned about how to face the indigenous problems and counter the deadly effects upon our peoples of their contact between Europe and Abia Yala. Among these groups can be counted CENAMI, CEHILA, COOPA, CIMI, and CLAI.[3]

---

[3] Editor's note: CENAMI is the Roman Catholic Centro Nacional de Ayuda a Misiones Indígenas, located in México. CEHILA is the Comisión de Estudios Históricos sobre la Iglesia en Latino América, with research focci throughout Latin America. COOPA is the protestant Coordinadora de Pastoral Aborigen, with headquarters in Costa Rica. CIMI is the Centro de Investigación de Missiones Indígenas; CLAI is the protestant Latin American Council of Churches, with offices in Ecuador.

Movements in Civil Society

World-wide indigenous networking

In 1974 the World Council of Indigenous Peoples (CMPI) was officially
created. This organism brings together people from several countries in
Abia Yala, Australia, Finland, Norway and Sweden. This fourth level
consultative organization to the United Nations does not have much impact
upon grassroots organizations and has very little contact with them. More
important is the "Continental Campaign of the Five Hundred Years" which
was orchestrated by the Confederation of Indigenous Nations of Ecuador
(CONAI) and its Colombian counterpart (ONIC). It also brought in the
popular sectors which eventually became more influential than the
indigenous sector.

The ecological movement

The change in Western lifestyles after the despoliation of our continent that
followed the "conquest" has brought about an "ecological backlash". The
irreversible destruction of our planet's ecological balance has created some
sympathy for indigenous causes and brought about a somewhat idealistic
attraction to the indigenous land and community based society.

Christian Missiology and Indigenous Peoples—A Typology

Indigenism or paternalism

It is the imposition of a North Atlantic Christian mould, at least in the
Protestant context.

   Inculturation is the indigenist Catholic perspective that was present
at CELAM in Santo Domingo (1992). It recognizes "seeds of the kingdom"
in the indigenous peoples, with some awareness of what is really a
"caricature of our autochthonous faith".

   Transculturation is an approach that is used today in Protestant
missiology. Elements of indigenous culture are evangelized in order to
"purify them".

   Liberation is what some Latin American theologians are recognizing in the autochthonous religions.

"Indigenism" or "indianism"

We understand "indigenism" to be the efforts in favour of the aborigines by non-indigenous persons. The exact opposite is a romantic "indianism" that holds that indians alone can reflect upon and analyze their situation. Which is like saying: "indians, with the indians and for the indians". Either extreme can be harmful because they can all too easily become polarized by a narrow minded approach. This study accepts the fact that we do not dare fall into a manipulative indigenism which takes advantage of indigenous problems for selfish purposes. Nor can we fall into a romanticized "indianism", self sufficient, manichean and unrelated to the modern world. In essence, we want to take advantage of the serious contributions of non-indigenous people, as well as the popular wisdom of our aboriginal peoples.

Some anthropologists have now become aware of indigenist and indianist theologies. The first represents non-indigenous theologians who live off of what they write, professional intellectuals who speak—always in the third person—about the "faith of the native peoples of Abia Yala". On the other hand, indianist theologies are those somewhat fossilized currents of thought that dream about the past, are unable to dialogue with christianity, and prefer to argue in favour of the "de-christianization" of the indigenes.

Religious Pluralism and the Native Religions of Abia Yala

Another typology takes into account the current responses to indigenous religiosity in today's pluralistic environments.

Indian/indian theology

It is the autochthonous and millenarian religion of our ancestors. Although "pure" indians are said to no longer exist, precolumbian religions[4] do exist within the aboriginal cultures. Especially in the Amazon region and in the tropical forests of South America there are today religious practices that have not been touched by European culture. Some indigenous priests have clung with great fervour to the religious practices of their ancestors, reacting against the numerous Christian groups whose preaching is not

---

[4] Christianity is, of course, also a pre-columbian religion.

coherent with their practice.

Indigenous/Christian theology

To one degree or another, the essence of the gospel has been sown in the hearts of many indigenous sisters and brothers. This seed will soon spring forth in a unique way. Judged primarily on "Western" terms, it cannot claim to be "authentically Christian". But, this theology will discover its own unique values which will enrich the form of christianity that was presented to us in alien cultic clothes. This process will require a certain re-working of the faith. And there is another cultural limitation. To varying degrees, the cultural vehicle through which the gospel was received in Abia Yala has left marks which keep indigenous christians from fully appreciating their own culture. In this sense, we can speak today of a certain degree of the "mestisaje" of the aboriginal religions.

Indian theology of liberation

This happens when non-fundamentalist white Christians do indigenous theology. It involves those whites and "mestizos" who are concerned about the situation of extreme poverty and racial marginalization of our peoples. Notwithstanding, the context in which these intellectuals were trained will make them, in one way or another, want to impose their worldview and criteria for the liberation of indian peoples. The experience of the liberation theologies that fall into this category has not been rooted in indigenous reality. The tend to be more European, such as the theologies of captivity, hope, death, etc.

White fundamentalist judeo-christian approach

It is the closed minded attitude of those groups whose values are in opposition to those of indigenous religiosity.

Non-Christian religions attempting indigenous theology

Religions that are rooted in Asian and other cultural religions—they are usually practitioners of vegetarianism and transcendental meditation—are trying to identify with the indigenous religions of Abia Yala. Despite their openness, they are also very prone to proselytism. In this regard another phenomenon is also worthy of mention: the young "mestizos" who, in search of their roots, gather in the Zócalo in México City to be near to their Aztec ancestors. They have chosen the esoteric path of yoga and dancing.

The orthodox marxist approach

It is based upon a conservative class analysis that does not take into account ethnic and cultural factors which bring their own values to society. A case in point, one of Lenin's tracts was entitled "The role of labour in transforming monkeys into men".

The Churches: Practices and Attitudes

Syncretism

A better term for this phenomenon would be simulation or reenactment. Many of our indigenous sisters and brothers maintain their religiosity beneath the umbrella of the Catholic "cofradías" or of popular protestantism. Guatemala is an example of both. This mimiking (of indigenous meanings in Christian forms) is a kind of cultural resistance and of identity preservation.

Religious assimilation

This is particularly observable in the urban "belts of misery" which (in the Andean region, México and Guatemala) is made up of migrant aborigines. The impact of urban modernity, the abandonment of the social pressure of feasts and traditions, etc. cause the indigenes to lose their religiosity. This kind of religiosity could perhaps be called a kind of "malinchismo".[5]

One can observe, particularly in indigenous communities, the sad "folkloric spectacle" of indians who try to become assimilated into the christianity and culture of the white missionaries. In an attempt to become "little missionaries", they put on coats and ties—and wear the same sandals made from old tires. Or they mangle an un familiar Spanish language to acquire a status that is a cut above their people; or sing anglo-saxon hymns

---

[5] Editor's note: "La Malinche" is the derisive name by which Mexicans refer to the indigenous mistress who helped Hernán Cortés conquer the Aztecs.

badly in a pitiful attempt to master an alien liturgy.

Popular religiosity

It is very much a white and mestizo phenomenon; of those who conceive of
a poor Christ, aboriginal, poor and exploited—a liberating Christ who
brings justice to the dispossessed. Popular religion appropriates the positive
elements of christianity, together with a high regard for religious and
cultural elements from the indigenous peoples.

Crucial Biblical-Theological Themes

Let me suggest at least three axis of reflection on which the dialogue
between the Judeo-Christian scriptures and the indigenous religions might
turn.

Divine revelation

God has revealed himself in both religious streams. He was already here
when the europeans arrived. They did not bring God to us.

> ... God the Creator of life was here for thousands of years in our own
> lands, acting as the vital and spiritual force within cultures... It was the
> Spirit, the mother of this earth, who gave life, health and support to all
> peoples.[6]

Salvation and the law

As the Bible states in Romans 2:13-15:

> For it is not those who hear the law who are righteous in God's sight, but
> it is those who obey... Those who are not Jews, who do not have the
> law... show that the requirements of the law are written on their hearts,
> their consciences also bearing witness, and their thoughts now accusing,
> now even defending them... on the day when God will judge men's
> secrets...

---

[6] "Declaration of Santo Domingo", an event that was organized by CEHILA (5 -
12 October, 1989), 3. Unpublished document.

The pretensions to exclusivity of the Christian religion are qualified here by Saint Paul, who opens the possibility of salvation for those who, without embracing christianity, have fulfilled God's Law.

The Bible and race

There are an abundance of Biblical passages which oppose racial exclusiveness, as well as the xenophobia of the Hebrews. Four examples should suffice.

1. When Moses married a black woman from Cush (Ethiopia), his sister and brother, Miriam and Aaron, criticized him. God punished their infamy with leprosy.

2. Among the ancestors of Jesus was a pagan woman who was also a prostitute, Rahab.

3. In response to Jonah's xenophobia, God taught him a lesson of love and universal compassion.

4. In the New Testament, Paul (who loved non-Jews) quarrelled with Peter (who represented traditional chauvinism). Reason finally prevailed in the first Christian Council in Jerusalem. Other biblical examples are: Jesus and the Syrophoenician woman, the miracles of Jesus and the apostles which were directed to the "ethne". Last but not least, Cornelius and Peter.

There are, however, seeming contradictions. In the Old Testament, God used the term 'am (my people) for Israel and go'im (pagan) for non-Jews. In the New Testament, St. Paul is sent to proclaim the Good News to the non-Jewish ethnos (a discriminatory term?) who are not called "my people".

Opportunities for Interreligious Dialogue

After five hundred years, one would think that nothing remains of our ancestral forms of worship. But, as part of the excitement of indigenous revindications, the thesis of some researchers is being corroborated: forms of worship that have resisted five centuries of foreign imposition exist today within our cultures. These have been maintained through simulation and reenactment, even within Christian worship, that have defied time and continuous persecution. To a great degree, this attributable to the stoic preservation of our traditions by our wise men and women—to their daily enactment of the cultic forms that have been passed on, primarily, by indigenous women. In a word, women have been the pillars of resistance of the more than fifty million indigenes that populate the continent of Abia Yala.

On the other hand, we cannot deny that aboriginal religiosity is still partially covered over, in some places, by a kind of reenactment of ancient rites in Catholic and Protestant garb.

Inculturation

What we have said in this essay should not be interpreted as a kind of reverse racism—a perverse desire for "historical revenge". We cannot propose a dualistic polarization between the indigenous religions which survive today and christianity. There may be another way of perceiving religions that are different from christianity. The vision of the "vanquished"—the indoamerican peoples—is beginning to be expressed in the documents that have been produced at important events, such as the one in Santo Domingo, which was organized by CEHILA. It makes the following statement:

> The European culture... in spite of its structures of domination, was able to give us, within complex "mestizo" forms, its positive cultural and religious values and its own christianity of the poor. These values have been integrated in the religious and cultural tradition of the oppressed, from which has been born a religion and culture of resistance against domination. Out of this is being born a new way of being the church, as a sign of hope for all peoples.[7]

We see in this declaration how christianity and its positive values are being assimilated by our aboriginal communities who today feel a profound respect for the Christ of the poor. Christian churches today have the great opportunity of becoming enculturated in order to accompany the aboriginal peoples in their via crucis and slow development. But they must not make the mistake of satanizing the faith of our ancestors. We must develop an atmosphere of mutual respect.

---

[7] Ibid.

Conclusions

1. Spain and its descendants, the "criollos" and "mestizos" of Latin America, celebrated in October of 1992 the "Fifth Centenary of the Discovery of America". Many voices were raised to express their opposition to celebrating the shameful massacre and violations perpetrated against our aboriginal communities.

2. The great armed conflicts, as well as the invasion of Abia Yala by the Europeans and Spaniards, demonstrate the extent of the supremacy and imposition of one religion upon others.

3. The subtlety and arrogance of "official" christianity, to the detriment of aboriginal culture and religion, is still practised today, a fact which requires serious and realistic analysis.

4. It is important that the Judeo-Christian Bible be interpreted in the light of the oral and written bible of the indigenous peoples of Abia Yala.

5. Aboriginal religions have always been judged as syncretistic, pagan, animist, etc., with no recognition of God's presence within cultures in general, however imperfect they might be.

6. We urgently need a respectful systematizing of the Sacred Traditions of Abia Yala in order to preserve our oral indigenous Bible. We must publish and transmit it to future generations, as a way of defending the cultural and religious heritage that we have received from our ancestors.

7. We urgently need to face up to the collapse of our cosmic equilibrium. We must find solutions from within the indigenous worldview to reverse the imminent destruction of our planet.

CHAPTER THREE

INVISIBLE CONVERTS TO PROTESTANTISM IN HIGHLAND GUATEMALA

Liliana R. Goldin and Brent Metz

"This case study provides additional evidence to the complex and intriguing fuzziness of ethnicity as category of identification. Religious linkages, values, and apparently indelible beliefs may be removed or transformed, but the social self continues to re-define itself as an enduring but different entity". A social anthropologist, Liliana Goldin, who is Associate Professor of Anthropology (Latin American and Caribbean Studies), State University of New York, has done field work in Guatemala since 1980. Brent Metz, fluent on Ki'Che' Maya, is Assistant Professor of Anthropology, Central Connecticut State University,. Both authors have contributed numerous articles on indigenous people in Guatemala to books and specialized journals. Their article—which appeared in *Ethnology*, No. 30, vol. 4, 1991 pp. 325-338—is used with the permission of the authors and publisher.

Introduction

The process of religious conversions to protestantism is widespread and rapid in the underdeveloped world, and the numbers in Latin America are especially significant.[1] It affects urban and rural peoples of varied cultural and ecological backgrounds. Often, major economic changes are either attributed or related to the significant ideological shift associated with religious conversion. The nature of the changes taking place as individuals or families convert is complex. In Latin America, and particularly in Guatemala, people convert for reasons as varied as the popularity of a Protestant political leader (president Rios Mont), an earthquake, and the ongoing violence.[2] Nash found alcoholism to be one of the major reasons for conversions, and refers to protestantism as the Alcoholic Anonymous of

---

[1] D. Stoll, *Is Latin America Turning Protestant? The Politics of Evangelical Growth* (Berkeley: University of California Press, 1990).

[2] S. Annis, *God and Production in a Guatemalan Town.* University of Texas Press, Austin, 1987.

Maya indians.[3] Economic, political, and social reasons have been cited as the basis for conversion to protestantism in the area.[4]

Some scholars have pointed to the tendency of studies to provide limited attention to experience, discourse analysis, and other processes of identity change within which conversion may be understood.[5] Historical accounts of protestantism's introduction to Latin American countries elaborate on the type of discourse that different denominations use in their missionary enterprises, often through development or education projects.[6] The association of economic development through progress and modernization with protestantism has been explicit in the teachings of Protestant missionaries and writers[7] and the social and economic benefits of associating with Protestants is emphasized by numerous recent studies.[8]

In the case of western Guatemala which we shall discuss below, the

[3] J. Nash, "Protestantism in an Indian Village in the Western Highlands of Guatemala". In *The Social Anthropology of Middle America*. C.M. Leslie Editor. Alpha Kappa Deltan, Vol.xxx(1) 1960, pp.49-58.

[4] Cf. R. Redfield, *A Village that Chose Progress: Chan Kom Revisited* (Chicago: University of Chicago Press, 1962); see also R. Wasserstrom, "Revolution in Guatemala: Peasants and Politics Under the Arbenz Government", *Comparative Studies of Society and History* Vol. xviii, 1976, pp. 443-478; D. Brintnall, *Revolt Against the Dead. The Modernization of a Mayan Community in the Highlands of Guatemala* (Gordon and Breach: New York, 1979); cf. R. Falla, *Quiche Rebelde* (Guatemala: Editorial Universitaria, 1980); see also R. Reina and N. Schwartz, "The Structural Context of Religious Conversion in Peten, Guatemala: Status, Community, and Multicommunity", in *American Ethnologist* Vol. i:(1), 1974, pp. 157-191.

[5] Cf. M. Heirich, "Change of Heart: A Test of Some Widely Held Theories About Religious Conversion", *American Journal of Sociology* No. 83, 1977, pp. 653-680; see also R. Snow, and R. Machalek, "The Sociology of Conversion", *Annual Review of Sociology* No. 10, 1984, pp. 67-90; and B. Taylor, "Conversion and Cognition: An Area for the Empirical Study in the Microsociology of Religious Knowledge", in *Social Compass* Vol. xxiii(1), 1976, pp. 5-22.

[6] Cf. V. Garrard Burnett, "Positivismo, Liberalismo e Impulso Misionero: Misiones Protestantes en Guatemala 1880-1920" in *Mesoamerica* No. 11, pp. 1990, 13-31; Stoll, 1990; and S. D. Rose and S. Brower, "The Export of Fundamentalist Americanism" in *Latin American Perspectives* Vol. xvii(4), 1990, pp. 42-56.

[7] J. Dennis, *Christian Missions and Social Progress: a Sociological Study of Foreign Missions* (New York: Fleming H. Revell, 1906).

[8] Cf. N. Tapp, "The Impact of Missionary Christianity upon Marginalized Ethnic Minorities: The Case of the Hmong, *Journal of Southeast Asian Studies* Vol. xx(1), 1989, pp. 70-95; see F. Manning, "Pentecostalism: Christianity and Reputation", in *Perspectives on Pentecostalism: Case Studies from the Caribbean and Latin America*, Stephen D. Glazier, ed. (Lanham, MD: University Press of America, 1980), pp.177-87; cf. E. C. Green, "Winti and Christianity: A Study in Religious Change, in *Ethnohistory* Vol. xxv(3), 1978, pp. 251-276.

connections of trade, capitalization, and conversion are apparent. As suggested, the reasons for conversion are complex, and while their identification is important, so are the implications of the rapid change and the way in which it is taking place.[9] The rate of religious change highlights the deeper changes that are taking place at all levels of society and may indirectly affect further changes. The impressive showing of Protestant candidates in the national elections of 1990 is significant, as it reflects the continuation of conservative trends within a framework of North American, free market, and modernization discourse in the midst of repression. The new political alliances often overlap with religious and economic interests that presently serve the interests of relatively few Maya indians. However, conversions and the seemingly corresponding conservative ideology arise from all sectors of the same population. Maya who were long repressed call now for "order" with the infamous implications that this may have in Guatemala. People who are changing occupations, are experiencing a redefinition of values and priorities.[10] Ethnic identities and new class formations are forcing people to question themselves and their neighbors. The study of conversion seems to be one way of elucidating profound social and economic transformations.[11]

Here, we consider religious change as one variable in a gamut of related cultural changes. By analyzing the value statements of both Catholics and Protestants, we are able to identify a substantial group of Maya that have experienced important ideolo-gical/cultural changes often associated with protestantism and the Protestant Ethic. This is further revealed in the analysis of people's discussions of their decisions to convert or to remain Catholic as they assessed their own lives. We explore the possibility that

---

[9] D. Scotchmer, "Convergence of the Gods: Comparing Traditional Maya and Christian Maya Cosmologies", in Gary H. Gossen ed. *Symbol and Meaning Beyond the Closed Community. Essays in Mesoamerican Ideas* (Albany: Institute for Mesoamerican Studies, 1986).

[10] L. Golding, "The 'Peace of the Market' in the Midst of Violence: a Symbolic Analysis of Markets and Exchange in the Western highlands of Guatemala", in *Ethnos*, Vol. No. 52, 1987, pp. 368-383.

[11] Some of the specific mechanisms that we identified as potentially relevant to the conversion process and that, in some cases, have only been indirectly discussed in the conversion literature include (1) group solidarity and support, (2) responsive and empathic religious leaders, (3) providing specific behavioral codes and guidance in everyday life, (4) linking everyday behavior to higher moral codes, (5) working towards common goals, (6) the role of public commitment, (7) the strategy of appealing to both men and women in the family unit, and (8) responsiveness to economic, social, and political constraints.

many non-converts who hold positive views of Protestants have "accepted" (in the language of Protestants) the new moral code, and have reshaped their world views to coincide with those of Protestants. However, these individuals have not formally converted, as this would imply a public commitment to a lifestyle with which it is difficult to comply. In this sense, *declared* religious affiliation may mean little when examining the relation between social practice and world view. These perceptions are a commentary on the process of social and cultural change, reflecting concurrent processes of accommodation and friction.

Issues of religious change in the community or personal conversion arose in the context of eliciting life histories. It is in this framework that people chose to talk about change, "economic improvement", the favorable position of the town with respect to others in the region, and the changes the town has undergone in the last fifty years. Religious change summarizes for many the overall rationalization of a broader, more profound cultural change which people are in the process of experiencing.

Research Setting and Methodology

The data for this study were collected between 1988 and the summer of 1990 in Almolonga,[12] where Goldin began research in 1980. Based on categories extracted from qualitative fieldwork, a questionnaire was administered to a random sample of 10 percent of the population of Almolonga in 1988. The survey covered economic and ideological issues

---

[12] With a population of approximately 12,000 people, of whom 99 per cent are *K'iche'* Maya dedicated to horticulture and trade, Almolonga is conveniently located about 5 kilometers south of Quetzaltenango, the second largest city in Guatemala (approximate population: 100,000). The road between Almolonga and Quetzaltenango was paved in 1983, making communication with the rest of the region easier and more frequent. Almolonga holds its weekly market on Saturdays when large wholesale of vegetables takes place just outside the local market. The people of Almolonga had been known to trade and produce some vegetables throughout the colonial years. However, at the beginning of this century they were dedicated to the growing of alfalfa as fodder and to the provision of grazing fields for animals taken from the north to the south coast. Their vegetable production today, one of the largest in the country (Goldin 1989), is totally oriented towards sale in the markets. Several professional traders have little land but have been able to accumulate considerable capital from their commercial enterprises. As a whole, Almolongueños are considered to be quite progressive and better off than other people in the region.

to provide a general framework for the analysis of socio-cultural and economic change. Questions addressing people's views of their own religion and ethnicity, and those of others, were included. Catholic and Protestant local interviewers, were employed to conduct the survey in the native language (*K'iche'*). Goldin conducted more intensive interviews with a subset of heads of households previously identified in the survey. The families represented households that, while having comparable economic backgrounds in their grandparent's generation, were economically differentiated in 1990. All life-histories collected in the summer of 1990 addressed religion in the context of discussing people's lifestyles, major life changes, or the problems they had or continue to have at the time of our research.[13] Most respondents who had experienced what they considered beneficial economic changes in their lives had also converted to protestantism.

The results of our survey suggest that approximately 52 per cent of the population of Almolonga is Catholic and 48 per cent Protestant.[14] This contrasts with the finding that during the generation of the parents of the present heads of household, only approximately 13 per cent of the population was Protestant, and the remaining 87 per cent Catholic. Of the present generation's grandparents, only about 3 per cent were Protestant. This recent and rapid rate of conversion is associated with a decrease in "cofradía" (civic and religious hierarchy) participation from approximately 42 per cent during the sample's parents' generation to approximately 26 per cent during the present generation, and a major decrease in the practice of traditional "costumbre', from approximately 82 per cent during their parents' generation to approximately 42 per cent for the current generation. The decrease of Catholics (both traditional and orthodox) is coupled with the loss of a permanent resident priest in the community. Since 1988, a priest has shared his obligations in Almolonga with two other townships.

---

[13] The collection of life-histories was not intended to assess informants' answers to specific questions about religion or religious change, but to allow them to place each significant life event in the context they felt most comfortable. The context in which discussions about religion arose provided clues for the understanding of peoples perceptions, the process of religious change, and the implications for cultural change.

[14] Many Protestants seem to have converted from orthodox catholicism rather than from traditional catholicism, as if the former were a stage towards protestantism. The distinctions between orthodox and traditional catholicism were elicited through qualitative research. In the formal survey, people identified themselves as either Protestant or Catholic.

The context in which religion appears in people's discourse is suggestive. There are slight differences between men and women which I will discuss below, but almost without exception, male heads of household talk about religion in the context of their youth and how their parents were very poor, had little or no land, and also drank too much. Often the informant himself would refer to his own drinking but proudly emphasize his life change as he converted to protestantism.

Religious Change in People's Discourse

Alcohol consumption

Nash has suggested that many indians convert to protestantism as a means of dealing with alcoholism,[15] and indeed the theme of drinking problems was raised in numerous accounts. Sometimes the problem concerned the drinking behavior of the individual and other times it focused on the drinking of family members. In one case, an informant said that his father drank too much, and the informant went to the church looking for relief. Women's accounts of religious conversion often appear in the context of discussing their husband's, father's, or brother's drinking. The fact that within the Evangelical church men do not drink was particularly attractive to women who have been subjected to abuse from their drunken male relatives. This important incentive prompts many women to try to convince their spouses or other relatives to convert after the women and their children have begun to attend the new church.[16] For both women and men, it was not drinking *per se* that initially was objectionable, but rather the suffering that drinking directly brought to the household through its negative impact on family relations and family economics. However, with the formal adoption of a Protestant moral code that prohibits drinking and links sobriety to God and religion, the act of drinking itself has become a vice to be avoided. The following testimony is illuminating:

> My mother had died, I was alone with my father and he drank a lot and we suffered a lot... my father drank, my father in law, and we also drank, and nobody told us anything; my mother in law also drank... I stopped drinking eight years ago and then six years ago I changed religions. I

---

[15] Nash, 1960.
[16] L. Bossen, *The Redivision of Labor* (Albany: SUNY Press, 1984), pp. 24-26.

changed religions because I suffered a lot, I had nothing. I realized that I could not get out of the situation I was in. Then maybe God touched me. Before I did not have this house the way it is now (it was smaller). I tell my children they have to work hard, not to go towards the vice, that I would be dead if I hadn't stopped drinking... Because I accepted the word of God, God gave me a miracle so that my things ("cuentas") would work out.

In this account, the informant stopped drinking two years before formally becoming a Protestant. Yet, he claims his life did not change significantly until after he formally converted. He clearly labels drinking as a problem source. However, it was not until he formally embraced the Protestant belief system that God rewarded him by changing his life.

The view that religious conversion merely is a means of coping and obtaining support for drinking problems fails to capture many of the dynamics underlying the drinking-conversion dynamics. Alcoholism can have an adverse economic and social impact on the family unit and lead individuals to seek new sources of help. However, protestantism links sobriety to a broader religious code, thereby promoting more fundamental cultural changes. Acceptance of sobriety in this context fosters acceptance of other aspects of the belief system and vice versa. The importance of these broader links is underscored by the following account:

[things that I used to do] like drinking, having fun, according to the tradition, but I had problems with that, with alcohol. Then I said enough! Because I read the Bible and there is a God, and he is powerful and can make one change. There are groups like Alcoholic Anonymous that can help us, but I think it has to come from someone superior. And since I accepted the new religion I felt a life change.

Economic considerations

Poverty and poor economic conditions were other factors mentioned in accounts of religious conversion. However, as with alcoholism, the underlying mechanisms are more complex than the behavioral translation of a desire for economic improvement. With the growing scarcity of land in the region,[17] many Almolongueños were forced to seek alternative means of support relative to traditional "milpa" production. The result was an increased emphasis on trade, diversification, and participation in the broader market system. The need for constant dedication to this work was in conflict with the maintenance of traditional ritual cycles. Traditional

---

[17] Cf. Goldin, 1989, pp. 45-48.

catholicism was associated with "cofradía" activities, patron saint celebrations and other festivities that served as significant symbolic spaces in the
agricultural cycle. The "traditional life" had room for these times of joy
and celebration, even when alcohol consumption extended the period beyond
the time of the Fiesta itself. The new occupation, professional trade, was
guided by a different set of temporal and spatial assumptions.[18] In this
framework converts see traditional activities as "interruptions" of productive
time, a "waste of time". They are proud to emphasize that they do not take
much time to rest, Saturdays and Sundays, and use the time of the patron
saint celebration to go on business trips:

> I don't miss the fiestas because for example last year the patron saint day
> I left for my trip to Petén, to work. I was only interested in God and the
> things that most help me in my life.

The "miracle" that God gave people so that they could improve economically was the enforcement of a code of behavior already considered appropriate, but contradictory to the traditional lifestyle. This code was not
necessarily new; it was gradually acquired through significant occupational
changes brought about by the scarcity of land.[19] However, the broader
Protestant belief system served to validate the behavioral code and link it
to a higher moral system.

Many of the informants discuss the importance of good and bad
investments. For example, some state that the "big changes" in Almolonga
are due, in part, to the fact that those who do not drink can now invest their
money better:

> Things changed in Almolonga because there is much trade. Because of
> the religion, people stopped drinking and now they only think of work and
> business. Before, many people had vices and many had to sell their land
> for that reason, but now they are taking good care of it.

Another informant states:

> You invest money in beneficial things... one does not waste money to
> have fun in places that are not good (healthy), then one can see economic
> progress... I think that the basis of development is the change in reli-
> gion... because I have seen, and felt that you earn it and invest it in good
> things to improve the home, the education of the family, and all that...

---

[18] Cf. Goldin, 1987, 1989.
[19] L. Goldin, 1992, pp. 103-123.

> When one does not have that principle one always thinks in having fiestas, and you know that the fiestas are lost investments... what Catholics earn they invest wrongly.

A "good investment" in this view, is one associated with material gains. Profit is a measure of success. A "bad investment" (food and liquor in a traditional fiesta) is one that may generate social, political, and other rewards, but not economic ones. These definitions represent a significant cultural shift from earlier views of fiestas and the "cofradías". People insist that you do not become Protestant to become rich, but that as you convert you start investing your money better and then you improve your economic situation. Investing well also implies "multiple" investments and "diversification". Again, these notions depart from "milpa" agriculture and traditional lifestyles[20] and emphasize the need for alternative means of subsistence.

Moral commitment

An interesting concept that arose frequently in people's accounts was that of commitment. Converting or remaining Catholic is, in the words of the informants, a "commitment" to comply with a larger set of moral standards; a public statement. Specifically, conversion means a commitment to sobriety, to honesty, to monogamy, and to refrain from traditional celebrations. Many of the informants proudly emphasize commitment. At the same time, there were some who, even though they converted, expressed nervousness about the nature of the commitment:

> We have to set an example, a different attitude. We have to be positive. Of course there is a risk that I might not fulfill everything I said I would when converting. I have to be good, but one is human and can make mistakes, but we try not to follow the old traditions. It is a commitment with God.

The act of making a public commitment through conversion serves to increase pressure on new converts to obey the new moral code. Just as

---

[20] This does not imply, of course, that this lifestyle did not involve any other activity outside milpa agriculture; peasants often sold the excess of their production at the market and occasionally produced complementary crops, among other activities. It is the emphasis on the diversification of investments and multiple businesses which is here noted.

important, this commitment enhances the adoption of the broader Protestant belief system. Studies have shown that the act of public commitment is sufficient to bring about fundamental changes in individuals' beliefs so as to make those beliefs consistent with the commitment.[21] Such a process may be operative here.

Solidarity and support

Another motivation often discussed when reflecting on conversion is the need for community solidarity to help and support other people in the town, and the lack of it. Many individuals who converted indicated that they were not interested in participating in "cofradías" or in other traditional communal activities. Where could people get help, advice, and guidance when having problems? The Protestant church meets these needs with its frequent weekly meetings in which the minister addresses people's lives and problems in his sermons. Members of the church, become "brothers" and "sisters", terms of address that reinforce closeness and trust. The church becomes a large extended family, leveling all members, including "ladinos", to fairly egalitarian terms.

> I felt a need to live together ("convivir") with the people of my town, because when I was Catholic it was as if I was more isolated from society; because I saw Christians to be more united, to work together. In case of problems, there were all the people.

Solidarity is also an important theme of catholicism in Almolonga. However, the different strategies used to promote solidarity in the respective religions are striking. Traditional Catholics tend to rely more on social activities and fiestas whereas Protestants emphasize the promotion of unity by working on common goals and problems.

Empathy and relevance

The themes of relevance and understanding were also raised. Not only is it important to people that the minister advises them on general life matters, it is important that the ministers are local people who speak the same language, in this case *K'iche'*, and share the same cultural framework. The minister is not an outsider, as the Catholic priest often is, but someone from

---

[21] Cf. R. Cialdini, *Social Influence* (New York: Basic Books, 1985).

the town. He knows the people, their "suffering and the backwardness" resulting from constant "cofradía" participation and deeply understands his congregations' interpretations of his sermons and Bible readings. Unlike the outsider, he is said to have the profound power of translation in its larger, more holistic sense.

Ministers try to relate the doctrine with people's everyday experiences and cite examples to which most people can relate when explaining the Bible. They talk about family feuds over land, environmental problems, poverty and limited resources, and do so in informal and simple terms. The Catholic church, someone said, "did not provide us with teachings. (The teachings) contribute to a good life, a life with guidance and orientation". Another informant states:

> The minister, besides religion, he gives you advice on how to improve your socioeconomic situation. Such as: "avoid fiestas, dress better, invest money, buy a car, enjoy development..." Because it would be useless to obtain money if one will continue living like before, you have to get a modern lifestyle.

Specific and general codes of life

Many of our informants discussed the importance of having specific behavioral codes for knowing how to act that are grounded in a more general moral code for life and salvation. For example, the "new" moral code discusses the love and respect for one's spouse and family (as does the old), but it is the strict behavioral regulations which, especially from the perspective offered by women, imply an improvement in their own lives. Studies report the positive effects that conversion seems to have on women, either by allowing them access to literacy,[22] compensating for loss of prestige, as with Navajo women,[23] providing advice, and, as in our case, by restricting alcohol consumption and polygyny in Guatemala.[24] The apparent freedom of Catholics "to do whatever one wants" often translates into freedom to drink, to womanize, to misbehave, according to Protestants.

---

[22] Cf. S. S. Sered, "Women, Religion, and Modernization: Tradition and Transformation among Elderly Jews in Israel" in *American Anthropologist* Vol. icii(2), 1990, pp. 306-318.

[23] Cf. K. Blanchard, "Changing Sex Roles and Protestantism among the Navajo Women in Ramah" in *Journal for the Scientific Study of Religion* No. 14, 1975, pp. 43-50.

[24] Cf. Bossen, 1984.

In other words, this freedom is perceived as leading to excess.

Religious change is regarded as an "improvement" of the person and the group and an acceptance of a new, broad moral code. The change is major and facilitated by "God's help". Salvation itself constitutes an ultimate statement, the proof of total achievement. Salvation of the soul corresponds to salvation in daily life. In fact, discussions of religion primarily appear in the context of change and progress in life rather than spiritual, cosmological, or theological concerns:

> The truth is that since I accepted the Gospel I felt a change in my life. I felt more responsible, more dedicated to my work, my home. I stopped all traditions and fiestas because most of what you see there is liquor (at weddings, marimbas, "cofradías").

Mutual Perceptions

With the rapid increase in religious conversions and the fundamental shifts in culture and ideology occurring concomitantly, we expected polarization between existing religious groups within Almolonga. As Catholics have seen their numbers diminish and others adopt a lifestyle that is at odds with tradition, we expected a growing hostility and negative view towards Protestants. Similarly, as Protestants leave behind their past identities and associate with a new lifestyle, people who retain their old ways would be viewed with some disdain. Our analysis of life histories and our recent survey suggest, however, that this is not the case.

Our questionnaire asked people (180 heads of households) to comment about and describe both Protestants and Catholics, among other groups of people. The questions were open-ended so that people were free to choose the style and categories of answers. Interviewers were both Protestant and Catholic. We expected the religion of the interviewer would bias people's responses, but our results revealed that answers did not differ appreciably as a function of the religious affiliation of the interviewer. This was probably due to the fact that the questions were asked in the context of a broader set of questions about the individual's current life and that of his family as a whole.

The kinds of categories supplied by respondents in their characterizations of Catholics include "go to mass, like fiestas, get drunk, believe in idols, are kind and good, practice "costumbre", have not changed, have vices, are backward, have no fear of God, are careless, believe in several gods, are changing, and like to attend processions". The major categories used to describe Protestants included "they like to go to service, are kind and good, are affectionate, have changed their lives, are different, do not like fiestas, have no vices, set good examples, are true Christians, have fear of God, do not drink, and have the truth".

There were several noteworthy trends in these data. First, as we expected, Protestants were somewhat critical of Catholics. In addition to simple descriptors such as "goes to mass" and "likes fiestas", Protestant characterizations of Catholics tended more frequently to emphasize concepts such as "having vices, getting drunk, believing in idols, and not having a fear of God". By the same token, Protestants were generally self-praiseworthy, mentioning few negative attributes for Protestants as a group. In addition to statements about "goes to service" and "doesn't like fiestas", Protestants tended to characterize themselves as being kind and good, setting good examples, respecting God, and representing change and progress.

Surprisingly, Catholics were also generally praiseworthy of Protestants. In addition to the general statements such as "goes to service" and "doesn't like fiestas", Catholics also tended to describe Protestants as kind, good, and setting good examples. In fact, the only clearly negative attribute mentioned by a few Catholics was that Protestants speak negatively of Catholics. Catholics tended to describe themselves as "going to mass" and "liking fiestas". However, nearly one out of five Catholics were critical of other Catholics' vices and beliefs in idols.

The results suggest that Protestants are generally well viewed by Catholics, even by Catholics who are relatively traditional (i.e., who practice costumbre and participate in the "cofradía"). In addition, there are some self-identified Catholics who are critical of Catholics as a whole, whereas this is a relatively rare occurrence for Protestants. The negative views that Protestants hold of Catholics probably represent disillusionment with the traditional religion and an incompatibility of the religion with emerging lifestyles resulting from other fundamental changes in the township (e.g., land loss). Similarly, as Protestants identify with a new group and experience renewed levels of empathy, solidarity, support, and guidance, their conceptions of Protestants will be generally positive. Of greater interest is the somewhat negative characterizations of Catholics by Catholics. One source of such characterizations may be formal divisions among Catholics themselves, such as members of Catholic Action.

However, our life histories suggest another mechanism, namely that *a significant proportion of self-identified Catholics have essentially converted to protestantism, if not formally, then ideologically.* This conversion is internal and personal; the "acceptance" of a new belief system. Some Catholics are critical of their own behaviors and traditional practices, but may not be ready to make a formal commitment to the new religion. If they formally converted, they would have to be held accountable by others, both Catholic and Protestants, for their actions. Conversion itself is less a spiritual than a public announcement of a new lifestyle.

If this interpretation is correct, these "invisible converts" would reflect in their views those positive attributes they themselves are trying to emulate. Several of the people we talked to in our collection of life histories seem to fit into this group. They identify themselves as Catholics who changed much of their lifestyle, are becoming economically successful through the practice of trade and diversification of both crops and activities, and claim to go to Church only "when they have the time". They stopped drinking years ago because they realized it was hurting them and say they would rather not convert to protestantism because they had "made a commitment to God", or that "this is not a toy, we'd better leave it the way it is". A recent convert says: "I just changed religions, but I wasn't one hundred percent Catholic. I only went to church for fiestas..." Many of the recent converts, and probably many future converts, are people who feel isolated. As the communal system is disintegrating, the participation in the "cofradías" is diminishing, the Catholic church is losing power, and the number of priests is low.[25]

While the Catholic church thought that by conducting mass in Spanish it was getting closer to their people, the Maya view Spanish as the language of power and domination. The message of the Catholic church is said to be foreign and obscure. People are turning to protestantism, in part, to replace some of their lost sources of solidarity, for support and as a tool to enhance their self-esteem. In fact, "building up of self-esteem" is often found in the Protestant discourse.

In sum, the positive perceptions that many Catholics have of Protestants result from the fact that they probably have already undergone some change in their own general attitudes about life, i.e., good citizenship, obligations towards family and community, and overall morality. The number of

---

[25] On the disillusionment of people with the Catholic Church, see J. Sexton, *Campesino: The Diary of a Guatemalan Indian* (Tucson: University of Arizona Press, 1985).

"invisible converts" is probably substantial. It is evident, however, that public affiliation with a religious group, particularly Catholics, does not necessarily correspond to one's deeper, internal self-identification. Those Catholics not formally converted may be "functional converts" in as much as their models of reality have changed.

The Process of Cultural Change

The fundamental cultural changes that are rapidly occurring in Almolonga are fostered by many of the mechanisms discussed above in the context of religious change: new leadership by responsive and empathic ministers who speak the language of the people; specific guidance as to proper behavior as well as more general moral guidance; the promotion of solidarity and togetherness by the formation of clearly identifiable networks (e.g., addressing each other as "brother" and "sister") and working towards common, newly established goals; the linking of everyday behavior to broader religious salvation (and achievement of earthly success); public commitment as a means of inducing behavioral conformity and belief consistency; a responsiveness to the changing needs of the community as a result of land loss and occupational changes; and a responsiveness to the problems of both men and women in the context of the family unit.

There are several cultural changes associated with the new ethic, shared by most converts and many non-converts alike.

First: there is a greater emphasis on competition. Numerous informants' accounts stressed the importance of bettering oneself and using other individuals as a standard for comparison. For example, in the context of material change, people are told that they should dress better and have a better house. "Competition with your neighbor" is now viewed as a positive trait, reflecting a desire to prosper in life: if my neighbor is dressing better, if my neighbors live better, then I tend to do the same thing, that (strategy) was for me very beneficial.

Second: there is the stress on individualism and the bettering of oneself by relying on one's own efforts and hard work. This theme has been noted by other researchers and is apparent in this study. However, we also found that such individualism is fostered by an appeal to community support and solidarity. Thus, shared community ideals, in the past fulfilled through "cofradía" activities, are now being fulfilled through the participation in the new community of "brothers and sisters" who work towards the common goal of self betterment.

It is paradoxical that while the new ideology emphasizes individualism, competition, personal improvement, and social and economic progress, among other values, it does so by appealing to fundamental Maya values associated with community solidarity, support, and guidance.

Third: the shifting criteria that people use to define success in life, is another important change. The individual's world is increasingly viewed in terms of "good" and "bad" investments, where material gain and personal wealth become a measure by which individuals determine their personal and communal progress.

Fourth: shifts in social activities. New occupational trends (professional trade) are in harmony with the new religion.[26] There is no time for celebrations that last several days and interrupt the commercial calendar. The agricultural calendar had time and space for ritual and social drinking, and prolonged, intense fiestas. The pace of the merchant is the pace of the new market society that has led more and more individuals away from the cultural heritage of the celebrations and fiestas.

Related changes concerning leisure activities and the cultural traditions that are communicated in the context of leisure. With the elimination of fiestas and other ritual celebrations, and with the absence of alcohol, a whole new type of activities associated with relaxation and "healthier" recreation has been created. This has resulted in an increase in the practice of sports, games, travel to visit nearby sights, or time spent with the family.

Discussions of religious conversion in the literature address the issue of determining whether changes are behavioral or ideological;[27] i.e., whether they are based on conviction or belief rather than on action.[28] The case of Almolonga suggests that conversion and overall ideological change has to do with what Cuchiari's analysis of pentecostalism in Sicily described as

---

[26] Cf. B. Paul, "Five Years of Religious Change in San Pedro La Laguna: A Mayan Community in Highland Guatemala. Paper presented at the American Anthropological Association Meeting (November 1987), pp. 18-22.

[27] Cf. Blanchard, 1975, p. 46.

[28] C. A. Kammerer, "Customs and Christian Conversion among Akha Highlanders of Burma and Thailand", in *American Ethnologist* Vol. xvii(2), 1990, pp. 277-91.

a "transformation directed toward more integrative systems of meaning, personal autonomy and moral responsibility".[29] This transformation, as suggested by Jules-Rosette is constantly relived and ratified, and activates an inner struggle between competing representations of the world.[30]

The ideological transformations may reflect less on cosmological and spiritual domains than on political spheres of power and control; e.g., new commercial elites ally with conservative factions, as is the case in Brazil,[31] Belize,[32] Ethiopia,[33] and currently in Guatemala. In fact, conversions in Guatemala are closely related to ideology introduced by North American missionaries after the reforms of Justo Rufino Barrios in 1870. These were accompanied by the introduction of the American model of life promoted by The Central American Mission since 1896.[34] The encouragement to develop commerce, to become wealthy or wealthier than others as a reward from God rather than a cause for supernatural and social punishment (envy, disease), and to improve the traditional standard of life, are all principles that underlie the change.

Conclusions

Protestantism offers individuals a set of specific codes about proper behavior that directly address situations that have led to economic and familial stress (e.g., drinking, polygyny). These codes are linked to a broader belief system rooted in God's word. Formal adoption of the codes fosters acceptance of the broader belief system and reassures individuals with the promise of religious salvation. The codes have favorable

---

[29] S. Cuchiari, "Adapted from Heaven: Conversion and Culture in Western Sicily" in *American Ethnologist* No. 15, p. 418.

[30] B. Jules-Rosette, "The Conversion Experience: The Apostles of John Maranke", in *Journal of Religion in Africa* No. 7, 1976, pp. 132, 164.

[31] J. C. Hoffnagel, "Pentecostalism: A Revolutionary or Conservative Movement?", in *Perspectives on Pentecostalism: Case Studies from the Caribbean and Latin America*. Stephen D. Glazier, ed. (Lanham, MD: University Press of America, 1980), p. 118.

[32] D. Birdwell-Pheasant, "The Power of Pentecostalism in a Belizean Village", in *Perspectives*, Glazier, ed. pp.95-109.

[33] J. Hammer, "Practice and Change: An Episode of Structural Disjunction and Conjunction among the Sadama of Ethiopia", in *Anthropological Quarterly* No. 2, 1985, pp. 63-73.

[34] Cf. Garrard Burnett, 1989.

implications for all members of the family, thereby engendering family support. Adoption of the belief systems and codes of conduct require a public commitment on the part of the convert. Although this commitment is viewed with trepidation by some, once made, it opens the door to a strong source of solidarity and support. Solidarity is developed not so much through social mechanisms (as is traditionally the case) but rather from working towards the common goals of economic, social, and familial betterment through individual betterment. Public commitment not only serves to engender support, but further fosters the entrenchment of the belief system within the individual. The codes and belief systems also are influenced by other major forces affecting the community.

Recent land loss coupled with the need to explore alternative occupations have forced new lifestyles on many individuals. The belief systems advocated by Protestants are ones that help validate these lifestyles and give them a moral context. In addition, there is a strong practical focus of the new religion. Ministers speak the language of the Maya and are a source of advice and authority on everyday problems that must be confronted.

A new ideology is being assumed through practice and thought by a large sector of the population of Almolonga. This set of beliefs corresponds with those espoused by protestantism, but it goes beyond Protestants and represents approximately 60 percent of the population of the town. Historical and socioeconomic information suggests that the new religion is indirectly tied to ongoing cultural change. More encompassing social and economic changes which relate to incorporation in the capitalist system through new activities and degrees of involvement in the market have paved the way for the acceptance of the religion and the values consistent with it. The fact that converts share the ideology of the new religion with many non-converts suggests that protestantism is only partially responsible for general cultural changes. People may choose to discuss change in the context of religion because it is framed in a system of norms and ideas that provides justification and rationality for the more apparent changes the township is experiencing. As always, religion is a source of explanation and argument, but the values it represents exceed the religious realm.

Our study identified several cultural changes that reflect economic and religious transformations. A growing number of individuals are using competition as a means of judging their position in life. Competition is viewed as a healthy process. An increased emphasis on individualism and the bettering of oneself as a means for bettering the community is also evident. Interestingly, this is fostered in the context of a system of support and solidarity that appeals to traditional Mayan values. Success in life is increasingly defined in economic terms and in judgments of "good and bad investments", interpreted broadly. Social and leisure activities also are being affected. With less emphasis on fiestas and traditional celebrations, new forms of leisure activity are developing that are congruent with the broader belief system.

These values and ideals extend beyond formal converts to protestantism, but also directly affect Catholics who retain traditional affiliations. Thus, there are "hidden converts" who have adopted many aspects of the Protestant philosophy but who choose not to publicly commit to membership in the Protestant community. This suggestion has important implications for researchers who study the relationship between stated religious affiliation and various political and economic phenomena. The presence of "hidden converts" may obscure the relationship between conversion variables and other variables when conversion is defined strictly in terms of self-stated affiliation. Indeed, in a previous analysis of the relationship between religion and economic beliefs in Almolonga,[35] we observed few significant ideological differences as a function of Catholic versus Protestant affiliation. Part of the reason underlying this was that a significant number of Catholics (about 20%) were espousing non-traditional economic beliefs more consistent with a Protestant perspective than a Catholic one.

Just as there are self-identified Catholics who are functionally Protestants, there are also probably some Protestants who retain reluctance about giving up aspects of their previous religious heritage. Our research suggests the importance of distinguishing between public and private religious affiliation and the distinctions between religious belief systems and religious affiliation.

Profound sociocultural change permeates large elements of Maya society. While committed to being "naturales" (natives) through the expression of pride in their ethnic affiliation, the widespread use of their native language, the wearing of traditional women's clothes, and many other cultural traits, they have changed many other beliefs related to nature, the supernatural, work, accumulation, and other features that used to be identified with Maya traits that are associated with the ideology of corn production.[36] This case study provides additional evidence to the complex and intriguing fuzziness of ethnicity as category of identification. Religious linkages,

---

[35] Cf. Goldin, 1992.
[36] Referred to by S. Annis (1987) as "milpa ideology".

values, and apparently indelible beliefs may be removed or transformed, but the social self continues to re-define itself as an enduring but different entity.

PART TWO
MAYA CULTURE AND STRATEGIES
OF RESISTANCE

CHAPTER FOUR

THE *POP VUH*:
THE SACRED HISTORY OF THE MAYAS

Edgar Cabrera

"The Sacred Book describes clearly the basic norms of conduct,
of morals and ethics, at the individual and corporate levels... it
describes the various stages of the evolution of the Maya
people". Prof. Cabrera lectures in anthropology at the University of Costa Rica. He has dedicated many years to tracing the
migrations of the Ki'Che' Maya peoples from the legendary
Tula (Tulán), in the heart of México to the Guatemalan highlands, as recorded in the *Pop Vuh*, the "council book" of the
Ki'Che' and kindred Maya peoples.[1]

The *Pop Vuh* is doubtless a book that has multiple meanings—as many as
the early Maya Ki'Che' community needed to maintain its identity and
cohesion. It was their sacred book, the repository of the worldview of an
organized and persistent group of people. The book, then, conveys diverse
messages because of the different situations in which the life of the
community developed over a very long period of time. These multiple
messages are capable of a wide range of possible understandings, depending
upon the level of each reader. In other words, although the *Pop Vuh* was
in general usage and accesible to all, the number of images and representations that each reader could comprehend depended upon the level in which
they found themselves in the community—and in particular, their degree of
understanding and recognition of the values of the Maya culture.

Esoteric and exoteric

The *Pop Vuh* is at one and the same time an esoteric and an "exoteric" text.
This double characteristic becomes very evident in the description by Fr.
Ximénez (see below). He observed that Ki'Che' infants suckled the doctrine
of their Sacred Book with their mothers' milk and learned it by heart from
early childhood. The Spanish friar went on to say that large quantities of
these books were kept by the communities.

---

[1] This chapter is adapted from the Introduction to Prof. Cabrera's book
La Cosmogonía Maya, Costa Rica, Liga Maya Internacional, 1992. It is used with
permission.

And the unknown Ki'Che' person who transcribed the *Pop Vuh* into Latin characters probably refered to the same fact when he affirmed that he was re-writing the book because it was no longer to be found. That is, to his knowledge it no longer existed—not in large quantitites, in any case. By implication, he had seen copies (of the book in Maya glyphs), at some earlier time in the communities.

The book was doubtless hidden away by the Ki'Che' wise men during the Spanish invasion. The following paragraph from the Pop Vuh gives us the reason: "We shall write this within the law of God, within Christianity; we will bring it to light because the *Popol Wuh*, so called, can no longer be seen".

Clearly, the Sacred Book, and most other aspects of Maya knowledge and culture, took on a clandestine character during the Castilian invasion of 1524. They were secreted away to preserve them from the first onslaught of the invading horde. With the total occupation of the land of the Sun in mind and bent upon putting down any resistance, whether physical or spiritual, the Spanish destroyed artifacts, books, stelae, and sacred images. And they assassinated those who owned such objects, or knew of them. The Ki'Che' people responded by sending all of their wise men and sacred objects into hiding. It was a desperate measure, based upon the hope of better times for their race and culture.

Who wrote the Pop Vuh?

We can surmise, then, that the author of the *Pop Vuh* version in Latin script was among those who gave in—at least partially—to the invadors. He was willing to learn their language straight away and to imbibe their ideology, that is, he became an instrument of Spanish cultural penetration. Because the Maya sages had hidden their cultural treasures from the invador's eyes—and from their collaborators—the person who transcribed the *Pop Vuh* into Latin script did not have access to it in its original version. This strange personage, however, must have belonged to the Ki'Che' intellectual elite, because he knew the book practically by heart, or at least its most important chapters and primary message. Thus armed, he sat down and wrote down the philosophy of his people, using the alphabet which he had learned from the Spanish friars. Might it not have been an act of repentance: his attempt to preserve for posterity the principal precepts and traits of Maya culture?

Theology, philosopy, history, and much more

It should be stated at this point that oral tradition was not the only way that the Maya had of preserving their wisdom, until the Spanish invasion. Over centuries, the Mayas had developed the art of writing with glyphs that they engraved on paper, stone, bone, cloth, etc. However, Maya writing was probably lost with the mass assassination of priests and scientists by the invading troops. Unfortunately for us, at that moment in time our writing was considered to be something esoteric.

As many researchers have described, the *Pop Vuh* does, in fact, communicate messages that are theological, philosophical, ceremonial, agricultural, calendric, historical, and more. The book is a guide for the community. For whomever can understand it, the Sacred Book describes clearly the basic norms of conduct, of morals and ethics, at the individual and corporate levels. There is an obvious civilizing discourse in the *Pop Vuh*: it describes the various stages of the evolution of the Maya people, their technology, science, philosophy, all of which had reached very high levels of competence.

The historical discourse is also fundamental. It begins with the creation of the world by cosmic energies who are the executors of the Central Deity. It goes on to tell of man's creation from maize and eventually the creation of the sun—the dawn. Western scientists call this "historical mythology".

Ideological penetration

All of this cosmology needed to be destroyed after the military defeat of the Mayas. In order to strengthen their hold upon these lands and to impose the Iberian ideology of the day, the invaders called upon the church to destroy the culture and break the back of the beliefs of the native population. One of the first measures was to create a small intellectual elite among the indigenous that could serve the interests of the conquerors. Schools were started in the parishes and classes were put in motion in order to attract young representatives of the indigenous ruling class. The purpose was to facilitate the *ideological conquest*. The one who later would dedicate himself to remembering the *Pop Vuh* and to transcribing it in the Latin alfabet studied in one of these small schools.

Friar Francisco Ximénez of the Dominican order was a part of this same approach to domination. He arrived in Guatemala in 1668, over a century after the begining of the invasion. The confrontation, while now more overtly ideological, was not so much different than in the early days of the arrival of the Castilians. The Maya communities had set up ways of cultural resistance which have, in fact, continued in force for five hundred years. It was Francisco Ximénez's good fortune to discover the above mentioned manuscript while he was parish priest in Siguan Tinamit, called Santo Tomás Chuila by the Spaniards, and known today as Chichicastenango ("the place of the thistle", in the Nahuatl language). Local people have told me that the manuscript was kept under a stone which, luckily for him, the Spanish priest happened to lift up, and found the document which made him famous.

Ximénez was able to produce a Spanish translation of the *Pop Vuh*. Over the years, he had become proficient in the Ki'Che' tongue, which he used for the purpose of introducing his ideas into the indigenous communities. Francisco Ximénez gave to his work a title which is as long as it is revealing of his real intentions: *The begining of the stories about the origin of the indians of this province of Guatemala, translated from the Quiché tongue into Castilian, for the greater benefit of the Ministers of the Holy Gospel, by the Rev. Fr. Franzisco Ximénez, Indoctrinating Curate to the Royal Patronage Town of Santo Tomás Chuila.*

Francisco Ximénez was soon disatisfied with this first translation and set himself to improve it. He prepared a second manuscript on the history of Central America in which he included the *Pop Vuh*. This new document bears the name of *History of the Province of San Vicente de Chiapa and Guatemala*.

Increasing his efforts, Ximénez continued to study the native languages until he was able to master them satisfactorily, in particular Ki'Che', Kaqchikel and Tzutuhil. Convinced that the Crown's representatives should master these languages, he then dedicated himself to preparing a dictionary and a gramar in all three related languages. It bears the title of *Treasures of the Kaqchiquel, Quiché and Tzutuhil Languages*. This work lies at present at Newberry University in Chicago, together with Ximénez' first version of the *Pop Vuh*.

Scholarly research and confusion

These works by Ximénez were for a long time in the archives of the Convent of Santo Domingo in Guatemala City. They later passed into the hands of the University of San Carlos, where they were found by European scholars who translated them into their own languages. One of these scholars, a Frenchman, seems to have been the one who coined the phrase "Popol Vuh", which is the title by which the book became internationally known.

The Ki'Che' word "pop"—literally the woven cane (rattan) mat or "petate" as well as a metaphor for "time"—was twice altered to please European phonetic sensibilities. "Pop" became "popo" when Ximénez added a vowel to achieve a more Spanish sounding effect. Later, the French translator added a final consonant to preserve the sound of Ximénez' Spanish term, since final vowels are often silent in French. In this way, "pop" became "popol", a word which, as Ki'Che' scholar Adrián Inés Chávez points out, has no meaning whatsoever. Other translators have complicated matters further by calling our book "Popol Buj", which, they argue, is better adapted to the Spanish language in the Americas.

All of these efforts, doubtless well intentioned, have produced a lot of confusion. If "pop" signifies "time" and "vuh" means "book", then the document's name is "The Book of Time", or better still, "The Book of Events". It later came to be called "The Council Book" by Prof. Adrián Recinos and many others, on the basis of the symbolical use of the rush mat.[2]

External validation of the Pop Vuh

A certain inferiority complex regarding indigenous values, exacerbated by a colonialist mentality which disparages the real level that Maya civilization attained, has led some mestizo Latinamericans to deny the legitimacy of the Ki'Che' document. In contrast, many Western scholars from developed countries, without colonialist ideals and—needless to say, without an inferiority complex!—have gradually come to recognize the validity of the Pop Vuh. It is, they agree, a legitimate Maya document which has a rightful place among universal literature. It goes without saying that enlightened Latin American scholars have participated in this effort.[3]

The Pop Vuh is not the tale of only one group of people. Many of its

---

[2] Editor's note: The various meanings of "pop" (rush mat), derive, perhaps, from its criss-cross pattern (the warp and woof of time?). They became symbols of authority. Kings and high priests sat on them when addressing their subjects. Later on, councils of elders sat cross-legged on "council mats" mats during their deliberations.

[3] Editor's note: The remaining paragraphs of this chapter summarize a quite lengthy disertation.

stories can be found in the traditions of a variety of Maya communities. The cultural traits that are evident in this work are scattered throughout all of Mesoamérica. The Maya city of Izapa, which stands on the Pacific coast of México, hard by the present Guatemalan border, remains in a remarkably good state of preservation.[4] Stellae which were engraved probably before the time of Jesus Christ clearly retell scenes that are related in the *Pop Vuh*. The most recent investigations in the ruins of Tikal in the Petén region of Guatemala—especially in that part known by archeologists as "the lost world"—have unearthed carvings and ceremonial objects that parallel some that are mentioned in the sacred book of the Ki'Ches'.

Rafael Girard relates the results of his many years of research among the Chorti' Mayas who still inhabit eastern Guatemala.[5] He arrives at the conclusion that the worldview and ceremonies of the Chorti' priests who, presumably, have never read the Council Book which is written in Ki'Che'—a language which belongs to a different branch of the Maya

---

[4] Editor's note: On several pages of his work, Cabrera cites Mexican anthropologist Beatriz Barba's book *Buscando raíces de mitos Mayas en Izapa*, an account of her search for the source myths of the Mayas. She argues that Izapa, a large ceremonial center which flourished between 300 B.C.E. and 200 A.C.E., in southern Chiapas (México), could have been the birthplace of the advanced Maya civilization. Izapa is located at 15 degrees latitude north, a position which slices the yearly revolution of the earth into two segments: 260 days south of Izapa and 105 days north of it. Prof. Barba hypothesizes that this location may account for the fact that the Maya Ceremonial Calendar has 260 days, while the Solar Calendar consists of 365 (260 + 105) days. This and other calendric and linguistic data have led her and other anthropologists to hypothesize that Izapa was a very ancient center of Maya astronomical research and priestly knowledge. Whatever the case, there is growing consensus that the Maya peoples first appeared on the Pacific coast of Chiapas, Guatemala and Salvador, from where they slowly migrated northwest to Central Mexico, either to found or be assimilated into great city states (Tolán, Teotiuacán). Centuries later they travelled again southward to the Yucatán peninsula and the Guatemalan highlands. This would account for the similarity of epic myths found throughout the Maya region. If this is true, then the foundation myths and migration stories in the *Pop Wuj*, and in the oral traditions, may be as old as the starting date of the Maya calendar, 3314 B.C.E., which is recorded on their stellae.

[5] Girard, 1966. An earlier investigation by the French ethnologist locates the origins of the Maya calendar between latitudes 14° 15' and 15°, i.e. in the same general area as does Prof. Barba. He does this after comparing the geographical, climatic and botanical clues that appear in the *Pop Wuh*. However, his conclusion, after examining astronomical data, is that the source of the calendar may well have been the city of Copán, in western Honduras. He argues that it was the closest to the stellar conjunctions at 4 Ahau 8 Cumku (August 11, 3114 B.C.E. (Rafael Girard, *Los Mayas*. Mexico City, Libro Mex, 1966, pp. 304-311).

family tree—coincides in every respect with that of the *Pop Vuh*.[6] There can be no doubt that, after their military defeat by the Spaniards, the Chorti' and countless other communities have preserved a common worldview, thanks largely to their oral tradition. This process has been buttressed by the large number of symbols that the Mayas still use. Who knows how many pre-Conquest manuscripts may still be kept zealously hidden in isolated indigenous communities? Ironically, also, a shared heritage has been maintained through the use of the Spanish idiom of the conquerors.

Other texts uphold the genuiness of the *Pop Vuh* and demonstrate the widespread nature of its theology[7]—by using the same religious terminology, mentioning the same place names and numerology, presenting identical cosmologies, and many more similarities. Historians of the second century of Spanish rule in Mesoamerica—such as Friars Bartolomé de las Casas (Guatemala) and Diego de Landa (Yucatán) relate elements of the Maya beliefs which coincide with stories in the Sacred Book of the Ki'Che' people.

The message of the Sacred Book

In the *Pop Vuh*, the creative Trinity clearly bespeaks of elemental energy. In this mythology, which may reflect the proto-Mayan experience at the dawn of time, volcanic fire and water produced life. Cosmic forces generated father heaven and mother earth. But creation does not cease. Man and woman were created and given the task of continuing to create. Creation begins each time a baby is born, and when an elder teaches a growing child the secret tribal lore. Creation begins anew with every sunrise, just as it is shown, near the end of the *Pop Vuh* over the Ki'Che' nation as they began the great migration back to the land of their origins in Guatemala.

Today, the Maya communities rejoice every time a woman finishes weaving a brightly coloured *huipil*. Every time the Lord *Huhnahpu'* rises on the eastern horizon their hearts soar, because he brings them hope of

---

[6] Ibid, pp. 268-277.

[7] Editor's note: Some of the post Conquest Maya documents which Prof. Cabrera cites are the Motul (Yucatán) Diccionary, and the books of Chilam Balam, the "Titles of the Lords of Yucatán" and "Annals of the Caq'chikels". Five pre-Conquest codices, one recently rediscovered, that survived the holocaust of Spanish destruction, also reflect the *Pop Wuj*'s worldview.

renewed life, of a better life for them and their families, and for humanity in general. Creation continues its endless march.

CHAPTER FIVE

ETHNIC RESISTANCE AND SOCIAL REPRODUCTION IN GUATEMALA

Jesús García Ruiz

"A key personage among the indigenous authorities who does not figure as a leader outside of the community... is called *Ah kin* ('he of the sun'). These were the true leaders of the resistance". The focus of this study are the Mam people who occupy the territory in southwestern and western Guatemala proximate to México.[1] This essay has been extracted from *Tradiciones de Guatemala*, No. 15, Centro de Estudios Folklóricos, University of Guatemala, 1981. It is used with the publisher's permission.

Throughout their history, indigenous communities have learned to structure various mechanisms that are capable of resisting foreign aggressions and internal dissensions that could, at one time or another, endanger their unity and coherence. This realization makes it necessary to single out some of the mechanisms that have contributed to the situation that ethnologists find today in Central America.

Mechanisms of Ethnic Resistance

Structures of Authority

The way in which authority is structured is, we believe, historically one of the basic elements in resistance. Communities where one and everyone has ongoing and specific responsibilities, to which they have been appointed according to social status and age, are able to maintain group integrity and to strengthen the allegiance of their members. These values are also effectively transmitted from generation to generation as their meanings are developed in everyday situations.

---

[1] The Mam peoples are thought to have descended from one of the original Maya tribes which may have occupied a larger area in the Guatemalan highlands than they do today. Perhaps five centuries before the arrival of the Spaniards, they and kindred tribes were displaced by the Ki'che' confederation of peoples who were returning to the Maya heartland, after the fall of Tolán and the Toltec empire in central México. This is related in their Council Book, the *Pop Wuh*.

The principal role of authority is to become an integrating and reproductive factor that will insure the transmission of values and religious
beliefs that have come down from the ancestors through generations.
Expressed in other terms, authority structures have the responsibility of
regulating the conflicts that occur within their groups.

This regulatory function has its own history in the Guatemalan communities that we have studied and we have gathered enough data to allow
us to understand something of how this works. Although we do not purport
to analyze the mechanisms of ethno-resistance, its is important to outline the
main thrust of the process in order to undergird the conclusions of this
study. The direction of our work is determined by certain presuppositions.
That the present structure of indigenous communities is grounded in a
particular history. That—before studying the genesis of people—we need to
dig deeper into the present structure in order to find meaning for the present
in the depths of time. The original intention, to focus the topic of this study
upon the present situation of the communities, has forced us to take a new
look at the historical significance of the Maya calendar as an important
element in social control.

Indigenous authority in the colonial era

The various lineages of the indigenous peoples, who had been relatively
powerful in pre-hispanic times, were integrated into colonial society, being
entrusted with specific functions of government and administration in a
hierarchical relationship with their own communities. The lineages—having
been restructured within the new order—seemingly accepted and submitted
to Spanish rule, which allowed them to acquire a number of privileges.[2]
At the same time, this arrangement made possible an in-depth control of the
indigenous communities which, while it sometimes implied abuses and

---

[2] These privileges were at times the cause of deep internal tensions, particularly
between the indigenous administrators (governors, justices, chieftains, etc.). One
special decree granted them the right of direct appeal to the king ("Recopilación de
Indias de 1680", book IV, title 7, law 12), as well as tax exemptions (Ibid, law 18).
They were granted the right to bear arms, for personal adornment or self-defense
("Gobernación, laws 258, 159,263,164). They were also granted special debentures,
the possession of land, etc. ("Archivo General de las Indias - Archivo de
Guatemala", file 393, book 2, folios 203 and 192).

tensions,[3] also helped maintain community cohesion and avoided disintegration.[4]

On the other hand, there is a key personage among the indigenous "authorities" who does not figure as a leader outside of the community. He is, nonetheless, fundamental to the internal structure of the community, because he is the repository of tradition—knowledge, meaning, and effective ritual. Depending upon the situation, he is called *Ah kin* ("he of the sun"), *Chuchakau* ("he who searches for a favorable day")[5] or *Ictunal*, which is the generic name for a wise priest.

These were the true leaders of the resistance. Beholden to no one, their actions were much more tenacious and untiring than that of the other indigenous authorities. In contrast to the pre-hispanic type of indigenous political leadership which in some measure recovered its authority in colonial Guatemala, it is a fact that the role of the *Ah Kin* was never accepted by colonial society. To the contrary, they were the object of missionary persecution, being perceived as prime representatives of "the world of the devil", whom they stood accused of serving and in whose "kingdom they were ministers".[6] Speaking of the *Ah Kin* or *Chuchakau*, we are told that "this is a very secretive indian species".[7] On the other hand, this group of wise men-priests enjoyed great prestige and influence

---

[3] The abuse of authority by indigenous chieftains took the form of occasional land appropriation and the use of indigenous labor - intended as a form of tax payment - for personal gain. The more blatant abuses forced the Spanish authorities to formulate specific prohibitions such as: "that the chieftains pay daily wages to the indians who work on their fields" ("Gobernación", book iii, title vi, law 10 of 8 July, 1577).

[4] It should be said that this authority structure was explicitly judged by the Catholic missioners to be totally negative, even in the eighteenth century. This is evident in the complaint by Cortés y Larraz, bishop of Guatemala, that the indians submitted blindly - with neither will nor understanding—to the whims of a handful of leaders. This same bishop sent a questionnaire to each one of his Spanish parishioners before a pastoral visit, and many of the replies reiterated the argument, in essence that the indians should be ruled directly by the Spanish "ayuntamientos" for their own spiritual benefit (Cortés y Larraz, "Descripción Geográfico Moral", vol. i, p. 173; cp. vol. ii, p. 91. "Testimonio de las cartas", file 948, ii, folio 139).

[5] Ramón Zamora, "República de Indias", p. 350. Cp. "Testimonio...", fol. 154-155.

[6] Bishop Cortés y Larras, vol. ii, p. 156. Cp. Fuentes y Guzmán, Recordación florida", vol. ii, p. 44, and A. Remesal, "Historia general de las Indias", vol, i, p. 203, vol. ii, p. 212. See also F. Vásquez, "Crónica de la Provincia de Guatemala", vol. i, pp. 39,40, vol. ii, p. 227, vol. iv, pp. 110, 389.

[7] *"Testimonio de las Cartas", vol. ii, folio 125.*

and were "greatly praised" within the communities.[8]

One of the mechanisms that was most frequently used by *Ictunal* to defend themselves from the incessant searches and attacks by the missionaries was to present themselves as "healers" or "witch-doctors". This strategy worked because the Spaniards perceived medicine and religion to be of a different kind and therefore autonomous. But for pre-hispanic people, medicine and religion were intimately related since sickness and disease came, they believed, from the gods, the *tahawic* or *ahwa iwic*, and from the ancestors. This fundamental difference in understanding allowed the wise men-priests to present themselves as witch-doctors without the Spanish ever suspecting what their real role was.

Thus presenting themselves to the outside world as healers, their activities could continue efficiently under the noses of the missionaries', allowing the *Ah Kin* to extend every effort to control and repress any sign of a turning away from their ancestral religion. Fuentes y Guzmán, among others, lists the punishments which were inflicted upon those who transgressed the secret community practices.

> Great punishments fall upon the prevaricators of sacred things—those who dare to profane their oratories, or to disrespect their ministers. The punishment was to hurl culprits over a cliff and to put a curse on their families, who would loose all rights and become slaves in perpetuity. If the irreverence was slight, the perpetrator and his family were enslaved, and if he persisted, the entire lineage was so punished, with death being the fate of a third time offender.[9]

These punishments continued into the eighteenth century. This partially explains how the indigenous communities have maintained their identity. If missionaries discovered one of these ritual centres or one of the *Ah Kin*, it was usually by pure chance, since "accusations were virtually impossible".[10]

Other authority structures

Along the same lines, the patrilineal and patrilocal structure of the lineage groups played an important role. The missionaries realized this.[11] Because

---

[8] Cortés and Larraz, vol. ii, p. 272.

[9] Fuentes y Guzmán, vol. i, p. 321.

[10] "Testimonios", vol. ii, folio 125.

[11] Cortés y Larraz, 1958, vol. ii, p. 31.

fathers controlled the means of production until their death, their children remained under his control. They were able, even to cut them off from their share of the inheritance. One father disinherited his son for having revealed that he had hidden his idols in the pedestal of a crucifix.

The missionaries attempted to correct those that were found out, severely and in public.[12] They sometimes forced them to appear before the community with a candle in their hands, and with a rope around their necks. After they had humiliated them, they were made to attend catechism with the children.[13] In other cases, in spite of having caught the "witch doctors" red handed, the missionaries were obligated to free them without punishment, such was the community outcry and unrest.

The Maya Calendar and Ethno-resistance

One of the most interesting, and at the same time most secret aspects of Mayan resistance was, without a doubt, their knowledge of the ancient Mesoamerican calendar and its relationship to everyday life. The object of strict and efficient prescriptions, the calendar is the nexus and organizing principle of their productive—as well as ritual—activity. The testimonies to this fact are numerous.

Despite the imposition of the Western calendar, indigenous Guatemalans continued to depend in the depths of their being upon the rhythm of the pre-Hispanic calendar. Bishop Cortés and Larraz was aware of the complaint that the *Ah Kin* "continue to guide, every day of the year, the activities of the indians, both good and bad, such as sowing, travel, idolatries and other dishonesties that they perform to animals as well as to the devil, who is the highest object of their worship".[14] The calendar continued to regulate activities and conduct throughout the indigenous communities, to the chagrin and puzzlement of the missionaries, for whom the indigenous concept of time vis a vis their own practice, was incomprehensible.

The testimonies in the correspondence to which we have alluded explicitly state that

the natives differ totally in their reckoning from us. Their year has fewer

---

[12] "Testimonios", vol. 2, folio 167.
[13] Ibid, folio 166.
[14] Fuentes y Guzmán, ii, p. 156.

months and their weeks more days than ours. Giving them peculiar names such as the fruits of their sowing and of their various trades and offices, they look to those who have the knowledge to interpret their meaning in order to assure success for their crops and other endeavours.[15]

This witness seems to us to be of prime importance, because it confirms that the Maya calendar was used, and with identical meanings, throughout the various indigenous communities.[16] It explains the social relevance of "those who have the knowledge to interpret" calendric numbers. They were the organizers of community life and, as such, the mediators between symbols, concrete knowledge and productive activity.

As an integral part of the communities' authority system, the *Ah Kines* are today responsible for the complex ritual activity, with its individual and collective coded practices. As "administrators of uncertainty", they have in their hands the power to structure and shape the precarious equilibrium of the community, by constantly reenacting its rituals. The ritualization of the communities allows these religious leaders to mediate the agricultural production on which the people depend both physically and symbolically to reproduce their own kind.

The missionaries were surprised and discomfited with a conduct that they could not explain. On the one hand, they had to resort to overt repression[17] to make de indigenous population attend church and fulfill the stipulated prescriptions of the Catholic religion. On the other hand, they noted that on certain days that had nothing to do with prescribed christianity these same indians would ask them to officiate the mass, to be on hand in the church, and to pray before certain saints. Or they would simply come all of them in a body to express their faith through particular rituals.

Fr. Gerónimo Real details this perturbing contrast. "On the eve of these days (that were favorable according to the *chuchakau*), at midnight, they explode firecrackers at the homes of all the faithful. Many of them will fill the churches, which they light up with an excessive number of candles, and spend the rest of the night in prayers. On the following day, from early

---

[15] Editor's note: I have omitted a detailed explanation of the "confusing way"—for Spaniards—in which the natives discerned favorable days. "Testimonio de las cartas", ii, folio 78, vs. 109f.

[16] Ibid, ii, folio 149, states the following: "This is the calendar that is used in all of the Kaq chikel, Ki Che' and Mam parishes, and I am convinced that it is the same one that they had when they were gentiles (i.e. pagans)".

[17] "Testimonio de las cartas", ii, folio 108, 183f. Cortés y Larraz, ii, p. 174, etc.

morning, the women repeat the same ceremony". The same missionary adds, not totally convinced in spite of himself, "that he was unable to notice any irreverent act, except for the improper, painful and strange way of expressing their devotion.[18]

As we have already indicated, missionaries saw in everything indigenous an expression and perpetuation of the "devil's world". The calendar and its social effects they judged to be "necromancy that the devil has taught them",[19] and for this reason they hunted it down for punishment. By every means possible, the missionaries tried to acquire information on these practices, but they were hardly successful. Despite the fact that they were on more than one occasion thoroughly convinced that these practices existed, and accounted for the indian's conduct, they were unable to find anything that they could put their finger on. A kind of nameless ambiguity floated in the air, but it was never easy to identify any of the culprits. Occasionally, missionaries were known to use overt pressure upon the consciences of the people during the sacrament of confession. In the solitude of the confessional, priestly pressures can be quite effective. However, when they asked about "this sin", "everyone would deny it".[20]

The only way for the indigenous people to survive was to maintain a common front, both implicitly and explicitly, about their secret. Secrecy, the principal arm of their resistance, enabled them to preserve their identity.

Function and Structure of the Maya Calendar

In the course of our field research among the Mam Maya of Guatemala, we have both sensed and verified the formidable influence that the calendar exerts upon individual and community conduct. This becomes evident in the way they choose planting and harvest days, plan their journeys and select marriage dates; it can be seen in their offerings to the mountain divinities, and in their ceremonies to mark the birth of a first born child. All of these events are difficult to adequately describe and yet do justice to their intricate interrelationships. We would need to reconstruct complex situations, events and motivations, which would be to exceed our present purposes. So we

---

[18] "Testimonios de las cartas", ii, folio 154f.

[19] Fuentes y Guzmán, ii, p. 45; cp. i, p. 400. See also "Testimonios...., ii, folio, 26f.

[20] Cortéz y Larraz, ii, p. 120.

shall limit ourselves to systematizing various data which will set forth in a
linear fashion. Although this methodology will, admittedly, obscure the way
in which the Maya calendar fits into daily life, it will allow us to elucidate
the function of the calendric structure. We shall have to live with this
contradiction.

Our interest in the calendar, we repeat, derives from our conviction that
it is one of the privileged loci in which to analyze specific communities. It
is possibly the key intermediary between the productive cycle, the system
of representations and beliefs, and social reproduction in Maya culture.

It is a truism that human life takes place in time. Temporality implies
that we are personally making every single moment of every day our own.
Now then, this abstract fact expresses itself systematically by means of a
particular calendar which allows us to substitute lineal time—that is
homogeneous and continuous time—for time that is heterogeneous and
discontinuous. Calendars are also referential, because they are the social
context where the relationships of individuals and their groups become
concrete and significant. The heterogeneous factor in calendric time
introduces points and moments of reference and identity in which appropriate functions develop that enable groups and individuals to interact with
nature, with their own history and with the world of the sacred.[21]

However, the representations and practices that make time meaningful
to us are neither casual nor sporadic. They have a lineal history in space-
time which is the result of the "practices of successive generations within
a specific type of living conditions".[22] The strict ordering of time—which
is especially the case in the complicated pre-hispanic calendars—is neither
coincidental nor sporadic. Without a doubt it is the product of a minutely
programmed determination to leave no fundamental aspect of life to the
whims of individuals. In other words, the organization of time has as its
purpose to restrain and suppress, insofar as possible, any failures,
uncertainties and weaknesses of individual actors. Instead, explicit
prescriptions and codified references are set up in relation to fundamental
moments of the physical and climatic cycles.

Even as calendars organize cyclical time, they clarify and regulate our

---

[21] Cp. M. Auge, *La construction du Monde*. Paris, Maspero. Cp. P. Bourdieu,
"Genèse et structure du champ religieux" in *Revue Français de Sociologie*, No. xii,
1971. By the same author, *Esquise d'une théorie de la pratique*. Genève-Paris,
Droz, and "Le sens pratique" in: *Actes de la Recherche en Sciences Sociales*. Fev.,
1976, No. 1.

[22] Bourdieu, "Le sens pratique", p. 51.

daily knowledge of our place in time, and the role of physical and symbolical reproduction. While anomalies stand out in cyclical time, it also makes possible self-identification, because groups of people get to know each other when processes are reiterated—key events such as sowing, ritual acts—and thus learn to depend upon each other. Cyclical time regulates the process of identity appropriation by synchronizing the past and the present through ritual acts. The calendar, we insist, orchestrates community life by determining, throughout the process, referential and identifying moments. The when, the how and the why find their place and meaning in cyclical time.

On the other hand, this way of programming time allows the communities to constantly update their collective memories, with a wide range of meanings. Practices then attain the level of historically significant models that give substance to beliefs and rituals—to the ultimate meaning of human existence. By affirming the nature of the reference points of their specific identity, individuals and groups interiorize patterns of conduct which provide reason and order to their daily lives.

What truth can be more convincing, what belief more efficacious than one which allows me to subsist by providing rain for my corn and giving life to my body? And if the life of my body is corn, what is more convincing than my own life and existence? At this point, reproduction becomes most rooted. Calendars structure my relationship to my ancestors whom I invoke and evoke. Placing me squarely in my community's history, a calendar makes me the object of future invocation and evocation. By reaffirming the depths of my identity, the calendar places me within an identity in which my descendants will recognize themselves.

CHAPTER SIX

THE SOCIAL ROLE OF MAYA WOMEN

Dalila C. Nayap-Pot

"Maya women have remained close to their men in their
struggles, yet not in a passive and subordinate way. And when
their men have been silenced or wiped out, they have taken up
the struggle themselves, but without loosing their social and
cultural location". Ms Nayap-Pot, a native Belizian of Maya-
Nahuatl descent, lives in San José, Costa Rica, where she
coordinates Base Research in Indigenous Development, Gender,
and Evangelical Spirituality (BRIDGES) and is a volunteer
worker with the Coordinadora de Pastoral Aborigen (COOPA).
She worships in a small Pentecostal congregation.[1]

Introduction

Historically, the perception of the role of women in Latin American society
has been limited to *reproduction* and *production*. Their main function is
defined in terms of work, family, and domestic labor. In marital relations
(which the Catholic tradition upholds as a divine sacrament), sex is not
defined so much in terms of personhood as of division of labor (an obligation). This limiting perception has framed the social context of women until
today—their social position, access to resources, homemaking responsibilities, division of labor, work-space, working hours, individual rights,
political participation, government and civil services—the list is long.
Women became the cultural metaphors of social property rights.

Because of the key role that women fulfil in our society, we can say that
social oppression is somehow related to the oppression of women.[2]

---

[1] Ms Nayap-Pot has a Licenciate from the Seminario Nazareno de las Américas
(SENDAS) of Costa Rica, an M.Th. from New College, Edinburgh and is currently
researching her disertation for the Doctor of Ministry degree (Womens' Studies) at
San Francisco Presbyterian Seminary. This chapter is extracted, with permission,
from the author's Masters' thesis: *The Spirituality of Maya Women and Grassroots
Protestantism: Sources for Dialogue and Development* (1992).

[2] A U.N. study finds that 'Women are the largest "excluded group in the world,
lagging behind men in earning power, political influence, literacy and recognition
as contributors to the global economy. No country treats its women as well as it
treats men..." The report called women "the nonparticipating majority. They make
up more than half the world's population and work longer hours than men, but hold

Throughout history, the reality of women has been framed by the way we
have been perceived. Latin America and the Caribbean are no exception
to the rule.[3]

Women's Liberation and Development

Admittedly, this situation has been changing in a number of places and
situations. Many women, such as the "First World" feminist elite, have
acquired a certain freedom and even a degree of social authority. This has
given them the right to speak of liberation, as well as to work toward the
freedom of their fellow oppressed women. Many such women have an
understanding of "womens' liberation" which reflects their own experiences
in an elitist environment. This can lead even to an elitist interpretation of
Scripture passages that have to do with women which may be different than
that of grassroots women.[4]

After sharing with a number of women and then reading material on
womens' liberation, I find that two basic areas of oppression stand out in
the thinking of "First World" women liberationists: male paternalism and
authoritarian society. Tereza Cavalcanti, a Latin American theologian, is
an example. Dealing with methodological issues, she argues:

---

just 10% of parliamentary positions and fewer than 4 percent of cabinet level
government posts. The report went on to say that, "in the developing world there
are... gender discriminations in nutrition, education and health care... Maternal
mortality rates... are more than 15 times higher than in the industrial countries".
But most forms of sex discrimination exist in most countries, rich and poor...
"Women are often invisible in statistics... If women's unpaid housework were
counted as productive output in national income accounts, global output would
increase by 20 to 30 %" (*Baltimore Evening Sun*, May 24, 1993).

[3] Despite the growing awareness of their role in society, the full participation
of women has been greatly hindered, even worsened in recent years, mainly because
of the impact of economic factors in our countries. Women are suffering the
combined weight of many forces: the external debts of our nations, the population
explosion, the massive migration from country to city (and thus the accelerated
growth of the cities), the increase in the number of women as heads of households,
and the decrease in public services for all, both in the cities and the countryside.

[4] In the Bible, women have also paid special attention to the oppression and
liberation of their context. Yet, like the Maya women, they have taken several steps
that at first sight seem as that of "silence" and "perpetuating male dominance". Both
women in the Bible and Maya women pay particular attention to their context and
social relations. This has determined their method of action.

Since the biblical texts were written in the context of a patriarchal society, materials related to our themes are few and far between. This limitation has been reinforced by the fact that women have for so long been considered inferior to men, both in the church and in society. Theological reflection has mirrored this reality, both in what is spoken, and what remains unsaid.[5]

However, even while this perception mirrors a particular (elitist?) understanding of reality, not all societies think in this way. In fact, not a few think differently—particularly those who find their roots in closely knit ethnic groups. Here I must add my voice to that of Delores S. Williams, an Afro-American woman. In commenting on Latin American female voices that claim that their liberation struggle is inextricably linked to the struggle of their poor and oppressed community (male and female) for social, political and economic liberation, she says:

> There is, however, some uneasiness Afro-American women may experience as they encounter these essays by Latin American (female) Liberation Theologians. In a few of the essays brief mention is made of the need for women to deal with the issue of racial oppression in Latin America. Yet no article gives serious attention to the effects of racial oppression upon Latin American women's lives. Since the U.S. press has given attention to the issue of oppression against blacks in Brazil, North American black women are apt to have considerable interest in learning how, and to what extent, Latin American women will deal with the problem.[6]

I cannot but agree. Indigenous women focus their liberation approach upon a different perspective, which I believe is more biblical. Take Ruth, for example, who submitted to male paternalism to obtain liberation for herself and Naomi. She is also a paradigm of mission in exile, about the possibility of hope in a "strange land".

Scripture has been used and abused in order to justify or criticize paternalism and patriarcalism. But it should also be said that the Bible contains important passages that illustrate different cultural perceptions of the divine will in matters of human sexuality and conduct. Patriarchal societies resolve social conflicts in ways that may seem unjust in "more enlightened" cultures. Abraham allowed Sarah to mistreat Haggai his concubine (Gen. 16:6). In Pharaoh's court he lied to save his own skin, and

---

[5] Elsa Támez, ed. *Through Her Eyes, Women's Theology from Latin America* (Orbis Press: Maryknoll, NY, 1989), 118.

[6] Ibid, viii.

perhaps even Sarah's (Gen. 12:10-20). But, in spite of this glaring fault, he is venerated by both Jews and Christians as "father of the faithful". Patriarchal societies can also be just to women. When the virginity of a woman was questioned by a husband who wished to reject her, the entire family and community came to her defense. In important matters women were equally benefitted and equally responsible before the law, in patriarchal Israel. Both parties in adultery deserved equal punishment, but in cases of sexual violation, only the man was punished (Dt. 22:13-25). Among other things, dowry was also a way of protecting women from male sexual abuse and subsequent abandonment. In Biblical times, women had property rights (Num. 27:1-11; 36:1-4), and, the same as men, had to make restitution when they had sinned against a neighbor (Num. 5:1-10). A woman taken into slavery was given the liberty to mourn her family for a month before being joined in marriage. And her master could not sell her if she did not satisfy him (Dt. 21:10-14). Finally, certain women seem to have exercised a priestly ministry that few churches practice today. God spoke equally to Miriam, Moses and Aaron (Num. 12:1-12).

Maya Women and Liberation

What do Maya women have in common with peasant women in other parts of the world? They live in rural areas where illiteracy, ignorance of their rights, and the weight of home and family tasks and responsibilities add to their burdens. Do they have anything theologically significant to contribute? Yes, they do, because, as has often been remarked, indigenous women in Latin America are triply oppressed: by men throughout history, by the racism of whites and "mestizos" and by the unjust social structures of today. And all too many Amerindian men have, unfortunately, picked up the "machismo" values of their oppressors. This is the context of the theological reflection of indigenous women.

Indigenous women have been known more for their silence than for their outward resistance. Yet, in spite of all their oppression and hardships, they do have development goals. They are struggling to be the owners of their own time. As portrayers of life, they take advantage of every opportunity to maintain the cultural values of their ancient race. This is not a weakness, but precisely the source of their strength. Throughout history they have managed to survive by "obeying" their masters. One example is sufficient. Bearing lots of children by many different Spanish men was not their choice nor their will, nonetheless they often had the will and stamina to outlive the men who abused them, and thus perpetuate their race. With this "submission" the indigenous women seemed to affirm male domination, but they did it for survival purposes.[7] Julia Esquivel, a Guatemalan woman of Mayan descent, says about indian women: "Conquest and domination by the Spaniards increased their defenselessness because, like the land and the gold, they became the property of the victors. Their bodies became land to be conquered because they became the property of the men who waged the war".[8]

Alternative Perceptions of Liberation

This oppressive situation also became a religious imposition, because women have been taught that this is the will of God and "thus saith the Lord". This raises important questions. Are Maya women, then, mere victims of their circumstances and do they, by insisting on maintaining their tradition, perpetuate oppression? Or have their motives been misunderstood? If the latter is the case, then perceptions about indigenous women may be a case of shortsightedness on the part of those who claim to be liberating their sisters from male oppression.

Pablo Richard, a well-known liberation theologian, recognizes that the ideological Left, in unquestioningly accepting the contradictions of the marxist view of man/woman, race and culture as subordinate to economic factors, has made a grave mistake. The marxist perspective of development has not helped to strengthen the role of women in oppressed cultures. Instead it has strengthened male "machismo". Fr. Richard further points out that "a man who is unable to have a relationship with a woman is never going to be able to leave behind his attitude of control and his pride".[9]

Perhaps we can learn something from the way in which Maya women and men relate to each other in their own context. Here is where the Maya women have tried to tell their men, and other men and women as well, that it is more important to build on the basis of healthy relations than speak of

---

[7] Sylvanus Griswold Morley, *The Ancient Maya* (London: Oxford University Press, 1946), 69,73.

[8] Julia Esquivel, "Conquered and Violated Women", in *Concilium - 1492-1992: The Voice of the Victims* (London: SCM Press, 1990), 69.

[9] Quoted in Támez 1987, 106ff,112.

liberation at the cost of bloodshed and enmity. That talking about liberation, or even seeking it through violent actions, may not be nearly as effective as "prayerful silence", alongside of "prayerful protest" when necessary. Maya women have remained close to their men in their struggles, but not in a passive and subordinate way. And when their men have been silenced or wiped out, they have taken up the struggle themselves, yet without loosing their social and cultural location. How have they managed to do this? Has Christianity helped or hindered them, and in what ways?

The Spirituality of Maya Women

In the Guatemalan highlands, we find no stellae or pyramids with inscriptions, as in the jungles and plains of the Yucatán peninsula. But we have a transcription of the sacred scriptures of the Ki'Che' tribes (the *Pop Vuh*), the *Annals of the Kaqchikel* tribe (written after the Conquest), several documents of land entitlement (with local histories and genealogies), as well as many of the oral traditions of the highland Maya which help to explain their present customs.[10] The Maya have come from yesterday as a living symbol that informs our present and inspires hope for a better future.

The fundamental question, should economic development frame the life of a society, needs to be considered from a Maya perspective. An affirmative answer is implicit in many of the discussions on development, including within church-related agencies. It has to do with the orientation of development projects and also with their theological and ideological presuppositions. From a Maya perspective, holistic development comes from full community participation, and adequate management of those few resources that God has given them and which their oppressors have not managed to take away from them. Let us consider some of the liberating contributions that the Maya have made to the development of their communities. For the Maya, these are existential development issues that go far and beyond economic development. Maybe it will answer the question I've heard many times concerning the "poor". How can they be so "happy" and full of hope?

Maya feminine spirituality begins with the liberation and reproduction

---

[10] Barbara Tedlock, *Time and the Highland Maya* (Albuquerque: University of New Mexico Press, 1992), 1.

of life. Life is sacred to them since it stems from the Giver of Life and then from us, women, as portrayers of life. As sexual partners and guides, mothers and midwives,[11] Maya women count their role a special privilege and blessing. Like the Jewish women of old, they celebrate the birth of a new life as a gift from God. Loving their children from before birth is part of their "duty"; they feel that whatever that child becomes in the future will be part of their own their success or failure. During the "conquista", the Maya women were able to resist the Spanish oppression by bearing children—multiplying their race in order to avoid extinction. Their reproductive role also had religious implications which were intimately related to the cycles of nature.

A liberating affirmation of identity

The resistance of Maya women begins with self-affirmation, which is inseparable from their ethnic affirmation. This is part of their recognition of who they are. A first step in this resistance in recent times has been the redefinition and acceptance of the pejorative word "indio"; Maya men and women begun to feel proud of being indians and to wear their native clothes with dignity.[12]

Liberating family relationships

Maya families have very strong ties. Although they do not often show their affection for each other outwardly and outspokenly, they have their own ways of getting the message across. In traditional societies, children are rarely punished physically. They are "trained more by their own desire to conform with established social practices than by disciplinary measures". Respect is seen as a virtue rather than something to fear. Older children take care of the younger ones and have authority over them. Respect for the old by the young is a law. "The father is the undisputed head of his

---

[11] Ibid, 74.

[12] Lydia Hernández, "Even Today What Began 500 Years Ago", in *Church and Society* (January/February, 1992), Lousville, KY.,
Presbyterian Church, USA. 1992, 71.

family and nothing is done without his approval, though respect for the mother is almost equally pronounced".[13]

A liberating acceptance of authority

Though men are the "priests" of the household, the hunters, farmers, and wage earners, the women don't seem to resent this, since the division of labor is culturally defined and every family member works towards common goals. The women cook and work in their garden plots. They are not only part of the community and key figures in it, but they are also the cultural life-force of Maya society. They would not think of overthrowing their husbands to attain power. Freedom and rights for them does not stem from competing for positions of power. Their rights and freedom from oppression and exploitation will be the result of the efforts of the entire community. Maya women cannot talk of rights and freedom when their men are also oppressed and exploited. It is significant that Maya women have equal access to the priesthood, and to positions in public life.

A liberating approach to social relations

Although the values of many urban Maya have been perverted, as a people they have a strong respect for law and a keen sense of justice. They are not naturally quarrelsome, even when they get drunk. Until recently, their disputes were chiefly over domestic troubles and damage to a man's crops by the livestock of another. Honesty and self-reliance is one of their central causes for pride. Until recent times, petty thieving among them was almost unknown, and houses were left unlocked most of the time. Originally, houses were constructed without doors. Everything could be used by everyone. Because of ancient taboos against stealing, it was unheard of for a highland Maya to steal corn from his neighbor. Even today, it is unusual to find a Maya begging. For many years, they would insist on paying even for the free medical services of non-governmental aid agencies.

Liberating culture and community

Yet other cultural traits of the Maya, which have endured for generations speak of their common life. These reveal certain similarities to Old

---

[13] Tedlock, 31-33.

Testament values, particularly their strong sense of community solidarity. Peasants still share many of their belongings with each other, and especially with those that are in need. They love their neighbors as they love themselves. This they do with an extraordinary skill and generosity, in spite of being counted among the "have nots". As persons living in community, they maintain in tension their spirit of community and their individuality. They are extremely independent. From childhood they learn not to compete but to work together toward common goals.

While Maya women are by nature very modest with strangers, within the extended family they are remarkably liberated.[14] Sexual promiscuity among married and single women, while not acceptable, is not totally absent in Maya culture and unwed mothers are not marginalized as in Northern societies. Despite the inroads of "modernity", prostitution is still fairly uncommon because the Maya have developed culturally acceptable ways to direct the sex drive. In the past, older women and widows usually had the function of introducing young boys to sex, "while young girls have their first sex experience with their youthful lover".[15]

A liberating approach to religion

Resistance to domination is a fundamental part of being a traditional Maya. Their theological development is not limited by denominational and ecclesiastical impositions. It is mingled with their own context of a hermeneutical community which does not separate political, economic, and social issues. Maya men and women feel that their boundaries have been invaded. That "modern ways" threaten their values, customs, and beliefs. For them, understanding and reconciling sensitivity among themselves, as well as to others is essential.[16]

They possess a concept of Christianity, and of the relation of Jesus with the poor, which while it may seem theologically deficient, can be liberating.

---

[14] Paul Sullivan, *Unfinished Conversations: Mayas and Foreigners Between Two Wars* (New York: Knopf, 1989), 40,41,112-114, n. 19.

[15] Morley, 34.

[16] Recent studies show that highland indigenous peoples in Latin America, the Maya women included, have a unique capacity to pick and chose among the various religious options that which best fits their needs at different moments in their lives. This is not opportunism but a survival strategy. Cp. Virginia Garrard-Burnett and David Stoll, eds., *Rethinking Protestantism in Latin America* (Philadelphia: Temple Uiversity Press, 1993), 174,181.

Many Maya women have embraced Christianity identifying with many aspects of Jesus' life and social context. They sense that he accompanies them in their daily lives. They understand that the life of our Redeemer was filled with tensions and human dilemmas similar to their own. He was born in a cave (a sacred place in Maya religion); his family was poor and had few social options. His conception and birth were embarrassing and his earthly father was considering a quiet separation—experiences which are not unknown to them today. A ruthless king—likened to military rulers today—resorted to infanticide to get rid of the newborn child. So Jesus spent his early childhood as a refugee in a strange culture, then returned to a homeland that remained hostile and dangerous. Like the Maya, Jesus was a stranger in his own land. According to Mt. 2:16, Jesus spent at least some of his formative years in Egypt, displaced from his homeland. His family, instead of remaining in exile, returned to settle in rural and impoverished Galilee (2:22-23).

Catholic Maya, encouraged by the Catholic Action movement, also identify with Mary, the Mother of our Lord. To the men she is the ideal mother figure, and to the women she is the peasant girl who suffered many of the same sorrows that they have in recent years. She gave birth out of wedlock, surrounded by cattle; she fled with her family into exile; she saw her son go. away to the Big City and eventually die there for a just cause. As refugees themselves from violence and war, the highland Maya of Guatemala see in Jesus a motivation for being agents of change in their situation.

Due to the crisis among the inhabitants of Guatemalan highland villages, the Catholic Church has had to create a new form of family unity. On Sundays after mass, there is time for recreation and for communal projects. The pulpits of the Maya are their mountains; their worship is to discover God's love in a basic survival situation. There is no architecture to separate the people from God and themselves. But there is a human community which is ratifying God's presence. The actors are living witness who express their desires, dreams, frustrations, and confessions, as well as their thanksgiving. Their Covenant is to discuss and practice their affairs from the community and on behalf of the community.

A liberating practice of democracy

A number of Maya women are working towards a real democracy, within a base community movement. Even at the cost of their lives, Maya women are willing to take the risk to preserve their communitarian culture and values. Rigoberta Menchú, the 1992 Nobel Peace Laureate, represents one of the many thousands of women who have undergone oppression and exploitation, but who are also a symbol of resistance. Her family had been living in the highlands but were thrown out from their land by the "owners." She spent her early childhood in the "fincas", one of the many agro-export plantations with highest DDT levels in the Western world. In 1979, along with her mother and father, she saw her closest friend and her 16 year old brother, kidnapped and tortured. Later on, her father was imprisoned and crippled for joining the peasant land movement. Some time later he died, along with forty other protesting Maya, in the fire that consumed the Spanish Embassy that they had taken to dramatize their protest. Seven weeks later, her mother was kidnapped, raped, and tortured. Out of a family of nine, only three have managed to survive.

At present, Maya women are joining efforts with the "ladino" women to demand water rights. They see this as working towards "developing democracy". Today, Maya women are beginning to assume key roles in their society. Some women achieve important positions in their local governments in the heartland of the ancient Maya empire. But they do so by playing along with the political system. More significantly, Maya women have been at the forefront of the struggles for cultural cohesion and justice in the Guatemalan highlands. Rigoberta Menchú, while in exile, worked hard for Maya indigenous rights. She has become a potent symbol of women's liberation for the poor. In Latin America, "sirvienta", is used as a socially degrading term. But recently, in Nicaragua, 10th December was decreed "día de las sirvientas" (servants day) in honor of Rigoberta.[17]

Still, Maya women are a long way from obtaining justice and rights. But they are on their way. And above all they have hope on their side.

A liberating enjoyment of life

The lives of Maya women and men may be filled with doubt, but they do not allow themselves to be overcome by the fear of an uncertain future. They approach life with a keen sense of humor. The Maya especially enjoy playing practical jokes on each other. One of the earliest anthropologists to get to know them observed, "The Maya are a cheerful, joking, fun-loving lot, whose friendly, sunny dispositions have been admired by all foreigners

---

[17] La Voz del Maya Quiché, vol. lix, no. 2 (April-June, 93), 1.

who come in contact with them".[18]   Their creativity is evident in the
Maya's sense of humor, as well as in their approach to real life situations.
Even in what for many would be a "sad" experience or death itself, they
say, "life comes and goes, and it must continue".   They live life to its
fullness, each day as it comes. Tomorrow is only in God's plan.

Conclusion

As the Syrophoenician woman did with Jesus, Maya women are re-orienting
the perceptions of Christians. They are helping us see Christ among those
that we call "idolaters" and to value the struggle of marginalized peoples for
a place at the non-Christian table of the Kingdom of God".[19]   They have
a theological contribution to make to our concepts of development.

Many social workers have come to the Maya and to other peasant
peoples with "liberating solutions," yet without understanding their holistic
spirituality and their concept of time.   So the Maya have had to make
choices in favor of "their own way," and they've done so at the expense of
being seen as "odd," "backward," and even "pagan."   It is here that we
can see the contribution of the Maya—women in particular—to a profound
spirituality. They might not know such terms as "solidarity" and "ecumenical sharing," yet their practice often goes far beyond what technical terms
express. Perhaps if we learn to link the energies of Christian faith to the
energy for justice and peace, we can hope that the "underdeveloped"
countries and peoples will begin to experience genuine social transformation. What we need is a genuine dialogue between development and a
living and dynamic spirituality. This is the only way out of the dilemma of
the modern world.

The Maya experience, particularly as lived by women, can point the way
to our fulfillment of common obligations reinforced by individual responsibility. It could result in a sense of well being that could be transforming.
This is what is called, in development terms, mutual help for collective
benefit. In conclusion, Maya women are, indeed, the main bearers of
spiritual values and the maintainers of social relations in their communities.

---

[18] Sir Eric Thompson, *The Rise and Fall of Maya Civilization* (Norman:
University of Oklahoma Press), 31.

[19] *International Review of Mission*, vol. 82, no. 315, 21-28.

CHAPTER SEVEN

ANCHORED COMMUNITIES: SOURCES OF PAN-MAYA IDENTITY IN THE MAYA-Q'EQCHI'

Richard A. Wilson

"Religious conversions, armed insurrection, and state repression have transformed previous forms of imagining the community... they created new possibilities of rethinking the... ethnic group. A pan-Maya identity is forming through bilingual education, Catholic and Protestant churches, radio stations, and national indigenous groups". Anthropologist Richard Wilson lectures in the School of African and Asian Studies, University of Sussex, Brighton, England.[1]

Identity: Essential or Relational?

This chapter represents an attempt to move away from analyses of identity which emphasise the synchronic signs of boundary closure and overlook the historical reconstructions of conceptions of ethnicity and community. The context is the development of an ethnic revivalist movement among the Q'eqchi' of Guatemala, among whom I lived for 18 months in 1987-8.

In the literature on Mayan ethnicity and community, there have been two main approaches: essentialist historicism and Barth's relational boundary method. Carmack writes that analysts have paid attention either to the form or to the content of ethnicity; i.e, either indian identity is formed in opposition to the Spanish or "ladinos" ("mestizos"), or there is a genuinely nativistic thread of tradition linking modern Mayas with pre-Hispanic society.[2] Watanabe identifies these same two approaches to Mayan communities, which he refers to as "cultural essentialism" (community as

---

[1] This article first appeared as "Anchored Communities: Identity and History of the Maya Q'eqchi', in the *Journal of the Royal Anthropological Institute of Great Britain and Ireland*, Vol. 28, No. 1 (March 1993), 121-138. It is used with the permission of the RAI and of the author, Richard A. Wilson, whose doctoral research has been published as *Maya Resurgence in Guatemala: Q'eqchi' Experiences*, London & Norman, University of Oklahoma Press, 1995.

[2] Robert Carmack, "State and community in nineteenth-century Guatemala: the Momostenango case," in C. Smith (ed) *Guatemalan Indians and the State, 1540-1988* (Austin: University of Texas Press, 1990), 129.

primordial Mayan survival) or "historical contextualism" (community as the result of opposition to colonial oppression).[3]

These observations have wider import for anthropological approaches to identity, which have been dominated by Barth's boundary perspective. This paradigm emphasizes the relational attributes of categorization, which can be studied by looking at the boundaries between ethnic groups.[4] Barth, and Leach[5] before him, asserted that the signs of ethnicity are arbitrary, so they can flux and change. In this view, identity is a structure of difference; an organizational vessel which is static even though its elements change. It is a form, whose content is ultimately arbitrary and undeserving of attention. According to Barth: "The critical focus of investigation from this point of view becomes the ethnic boundary that defines the group, *not the cultural stuff* that it encloses"[6] (my emphasis).

This chapter argues that both paradigms, Barthian and essentialist, are limited in scope and it seeks a contextualized synthesis between structure and process. Certainly any study should concentrate on community boundaries, which are exactly as Barth conceptualises them—ultimately unfixed, temporal, and contextually renegotiated. Yet the elements of ethnicity are not simply arbitrary. They are linked to historical meanings, "the cultural stuff" Barth so highhandedly dismissed. There is now more concern in social anthropology with the historical transformations of "the cultural stuff" within ethnic boundaries.[7] Barth himself, to give him his due, seems to be trying to make amends, writing that ethnicity is not only a matter of structure but of life experience as well.[8]

As I hope to show with my ethnography, change occurs within a

---

[3] J. Watanabe, "Enduring but ineffable community in the western periphery of Guatemala", in C. Smith (ed) *Guatemalan Indians and the State, 1540-1988* (Austin: University of Texas Press, 1990), 183.

[4] F. Barth, *Ethnic Groups and Boundaries* (Boston: Little, Brown, 1969). Cp. "Problems in Conceptualising Cultural Pluralism with Illustrations from Somar, Oman," *Proceedings of the American Ethnological Society*, 1982; and D. Maybury-Lewis (ed), *The Prospects for Plural Societies*, 1982.

[5] Edmund Leach, *Political Systems of Highland Burma* (London: Athlone, 1954). Cp. "Tribal Ethnography: past, present and future," in E. Tonkin, M. McDonald and M. Chapman (eds) *History and Ethnicity*, ASA Monographs 27 (London: Routledge, 1989).

[6] Barth, *Ethnic Groups*, p. 15.

[7] E. Tonkin, M. McDonald and M. Chapman (eds) *History and Ethnicity*, ASA Monographs 27 (London: Routledge, 1989). Cp. T.H. Eriksen, "The Cultural Contexts of Ethnic Differences", in *Man*, 26(1), 1991, 127-144.

[8] Barth, "Problems", 1984, 83.

constrained and processual framework of meaning. New criteria of identity gravitate around the traditional signs, even though they may at times shun them. The concept of ethnicity needs a "polythetic definition" which explores its history of use.[9] Ethnic categories have a complex history which must be investigated, instead of painting a static portrait of each constituent element ("Q'eqchi' language", "Q'eqchi' religion", etc.). Like the floor of an old car, the symbols of ethnicity carry littered traces of their previous occupants.

Anderson's ideas on the "imagined community" furnish a more grounded, historical and discursive approach to identity.[10] They are particularly valuable in transcending sterile dualisms and focussing on the role of the state in shaping indigenous identities. Ethnicity is formed over time by historical processes based on pre-existing elements of community and culture; it is tied to an "imagined community" of a shared past and common future. A historical perspective is vital to understanding new identities, since ideas of history and tradition play such an important part in their construction.

For a new imagined community to be established, there need to be fundamental changes in prior modes of apprehending the world which make it possible to "think" the nation. Anderson argues that the nation arose out of the dissolution of the political power of the sacred imagined community (Christendom) and the demise of the dynastic realm. The themes of this paper—religious conversions, armed insurrection, and state repression—all

---

[9] R. Fardon, "African Ethnogenesis: Limits to the comparability of ethnic phenomena", in L. Holy (ed) *Comparative Anthropology* (London: Basil Blackwell, 1987), 170.

[10] B. Anderson (*Imagined Communities: Reflections on the Origin and Spread of Nationalism*, London: Verso, 1991) has written mainly about nationalism, yet his approach can just as easily be applied to other types of community (cf. J. Nash, *In the Eyes of the Ancestors: Belief and Behavior in a Maya Community*, New Haven: Yale University Press, 1970; see also *We Eat the Mines and the Mines Eat Us: Dependency and Exploitation in the Bolivian Tin Mines*, New York: Columbia University Press, 1989, 127). Is a theory of nationalism applicable to ethnicity? E. Hobsbawm ("Ethnicity and nationalism in Europe today", *Anthropology Today* Vol.8 No.1, February, 1992, 3-8) has recently argued that one should not place these two forms of identity on the same level of analysis. I agree with P. Worsley who writes, "Nationalism is also a form of ethnicity, but it is a special form. It is the institutionalization of one particular ethnic identity by attaching it to the state... When those interests are to obtain a State of its own the group becomes a nationality" (*The Three Worlds: Culture and World Development*, London: Weidenfeld and Nicholson, 1984, 247).

transformed previous forms of imagining the community. Yet they created new possibilities of rethinking the community and ethnic group. This chapter explores how radical "indigenist" catechists recreate Q'eqchi' ethnicity, and base their imaginings on the tenets of past sacred communities. Just as nationalism filled the gaps left by the demise of the dynastic realm and sacred religious community, the demise of the traditional Q'eqchi' community makes it possible to think the ethnic group as never before.[11]

Religion and identity

How does a fieldworker actually study historical transformations of identity and culture? Strangely enough, I could never phrase in Q'eqchi', much less get an answer to a question such as, "Uh... gee... how would you say your cultural identity has changed in the last ten years?" But people have their own idiom to discuss change, in this case, the religious symbolism of the mountain spirits, which is a central image of traditional identities. To begin to understand how different groups of Q'eqchi's perceive the recent changes, I follow their reflective discourse for making and remaking community.

As Weber argued, there is no objective existence of ethnicity, so it is not possible to have a general theory, just a "grounded theory" of ethnicity. In Q'eqchi' communities, different identities are grounded in relation to the mountain cult.[12] Ethnicity, then, is an ultimately subjective phenomenon. Its coherence is more local and contextual than systemic. Q'eqchi' ethnicity draws upon many dimensions of culture, but none so strongly as religion. Fardon writes:

> Ethnic discriminations are elements of more general classifications which identify relations of similarity and difference within social universes. As such they are always "adjacent" to other elements of these classifications which we choose to treat as non-ethnic. Ethnic idioms draw sustenance from and plagiarize these other idioms.[13]

---

[11] Anderson, 22.

[12] L. Holy (ed) *Comparative Anthropology* (London: Basil Blackwell 1987), 8. A central assumption here is that there is no objective basis for ethnic classification, since, "Ethnic boundaries are between whoever people think they are between" (R. Fardon, "African Ethnogenesis: Limits to the comparability of ethnic phenomena," in Holy, 176.

[13] Fardon, 1987, 171.

Bruner has drawn attention to the fact that there is a disjunction between two bodies of anthropological literature—one dealing with symbolism and the other with ethnicity. He calls this, "a kind of self-induced scholarly schizophrenia".[14] One of the theoretical ambitions of this chapter is to bring these two bodies of literature closer together.

The mountain spirit is a symbolic pocket, containing the history of various local identities. By reaching into it we can we document the twisting path of an identity and what that trip has meant for the actors. Gramsci writes: "The starting point of critical elaboration is the consciousness of what one really is, and is 'knowing thyself' as a product of the historical process to date which has deposited in you an infinity of traces, without leaving an inventory".[15] In Q'eqchi' discourses on the mountain spirits, we can see Gramsci's "infinity of traces" left by the Maya, the colonial experience, the Catholic Church, war, the modern Guatemalan military and so on. All of these influences on Q'eqchi' identities are projected upon and contained within the collective figure of the mountain spirit.

This chapter begins in the present with a section on Q'eqchi' ethnic revivalism. In order to explain the development of a new ethnic identity, I present a sequence of paradigms of identities, in their order of appearance: traditional community (roughly 1970); Catholic base group (1975); class identity and civil war (1980-85). This sequence is only a description of higher order tendencies, since the different identities created out of these processes still co-exist in *Q'eqchi'* communities. There are no neat fault lines between different identities.

The order of presentation of these identities reflects a presentist bias, since history is reconstructed from various vantage points in the present, as different interest groups with a plurality of collective identities compete over an imagined past. The national military, Q'eqchi' traditionalists, and Catholic catechists from different epochs are all working on history, and contesting their diverging interpretations.

However, the past is not a complete free-for-all. History and tradition are inevitably reconstructed by the present, but not in total disregard for events. I would like to see my telling of the stories of Q'eqchi' identities as realist fiction.[16]

---

[14] Bruner, 64.

[15] A. Gramsci, *Selections from the Prison Notebooks of Antonio Gramsci*. Q. Hoare and G. Nowell-Smith (eds.) (London: Lawrence and Wishart, 1971), 419.

[16] Cf. Leach, 1989.

Ethnic Revival

As an anthropologist, perhaps it was to be expected that I would intially fall
in with ethnic revivalists, or indigenists. After all, we engage in a similar
project, the conscious reconstruction of "Q'eqchi' culture", mine on paper,
theirs in real communities.

Most ethnic revivalists are urban dwellers. Only about ten percent of
the roughly 360,000[17] Q'eqchi' speakers work as artisans or proletarians
in urban areas. The rest live in independent agricultural communities or as
"colonos"[18] on large exporting plantations in the mountainous hinterlands
of Alta Verapaz, the Petén, and in Belize. Many Q'eqchi' communities in
Guatemala have recently been re-organised by the military so they have a
uniform forty families in each.

The most radical expression of indigenist values is found among young
urban catechists. Catechists are Catholic lay activists who lead weekly
celebrations in their communities. During the "Word of God" meeting,
catechists read the Bible in the vernacular and reflect upon its message.

In the towns, catechists feel most acutely the attrition of their *Q'eqchi'*
culture by "ladinos", the state, evangelicals and national culture in general.
Perhaps a renovation of traditions and a radical stance on ethnicity is most
likely to come from those, such as urban *Q'eqchi's*, caught on the blurry
boundary between two ethnicities. Bricker's work revealed how colonial
and post-colonial religious revitalization movements were often led by
"ladinoized" indigenous people.[19] Wolf has expressed this idea in class
terms, writing that neither the most downtrodden, nor the well-off, but the
middle peasantry is most likely to rebel.[20]

Urban catechists have seized upon language as a marker of identity.

---

[17] The Q'eqchi' are the fourth largest of Guatemala's twenty-two Mayan
linguistic groups.

[18] Or "serfs" who exchange labour for usufruct to plant subsistence crops.

[19] V. Bricker, *The Indian Christ, The Indian King; The Historical Substrate of
Mayan Myth and Ritual* (Austin: University of Texas Press, 1981).

[20] E. Wolf, *Pesants* (Englewood Cliffs, N. J.: Prentice-Hall, 1966), 291.

They consciously emphasize the speaking of Q'eqchi' in their homes and communities, scolding those who talk in Castilian (Spanish). Seeking to "purify" Q'eqchi', they purge it of the many Iberian borrowings. Catechists have renovated dozens of archaic words, not used commonly for centuries to replace the Spanish or "Q'eqchi'-ized" Spanish. They urge the use of archaic greetings and partings, formally used towards elders by juniors. They invent new words for foreign concepts such as "aeroplane", or "television" that were previously communicated in Spanish. Catechists teach members of their communities to use the Mayan counting system, which had been largely forgotten. Catechists bring pressure to bear upon the youth of the communities to prevent them from becoming "ladinos". They tell the youth to be proud of their indigenous attributes. Adolescent girls are coerced most heavily of all.

Indigenist catechists pressure the Catholic Church to use Q'eqchi' on a par with Castilian during rituals. They also seek to renovate aspects of the traditional earth cult and so pressure priests to incorporate traditional symbols of community religion into the Catholic mass and other orthodox rituals.

Indigenists' interests are expressed primarily through two organisations, the Catholic radio literacy program and the anti-market organisation called *Qawa Quk'a*.

The catechists' emphasis on language is supported by the work of a Catholic radio education program. The radio station broadcasts in the vernacular across the whole of the Q'eqchi' linguistic area. The ethnic revivalist movement took hold early on in the literacy campaign, which has become a central promulgator of its doctrines. The radio literacy program is managed by Q'eqchi's who provide the materials and teacher-training for catechists. Catechists in rural villages then give literacy classes in Q'eqchi'. For the first time, Q'eqchi's are learning how to write in their own language.

Anderson emphasises the rise of print languages in the formation of new types of imagined communities. Until very recently, the Bible and religious publications were the only written documents in Q'eqchi'. These forged literary links between disparate members of a linguistic community. The Constitution of the Republic was printed in Q'eqchi' in 1987, as part of the nationalist project of the government. Once again a sacred community and the nation-state compete for the villagers' imagination.[21]

---

[21] Anderson, 44.

In 1988, indigenist catechists formed the group *Qawa Quk'a*, or "Our Sustenance", to further their ethnic program. This organisation has focussed its energies primarily on economic issues, in opposition to the market. They exalt all that is "traditional", linking their dependence on the market to the demise of their traditional culture.

Prices on basic foodstuffs increased by twenty-two percent in a five-month period during fieldwork. The price of cardamom, the main cash crop, has fallen to twenty-five percent of its 1980 value. Indigenist catechists now bemoan their dependence on cash crops for money and store-bought goods. They subject "ladino" middlemen to heavy criticism for paying low prices for cash crops and selling them in town at 100% profit.

Through *Qawa Quk'a*, catechists have organised a consumer boycott and made efforts to defend their position as producers. They exhort villagers to boycott factory-made market goods and replace them with autochthonous items. *Qawa Quk'a* has called for a complete re-assessment of agricultural practices. Formerly, villagers followed a strategy that mixed cash crops, such as coffee and cardamom and subsistence crops such as maize which retains a major religious and economic significance. Still, the catechists urge others to reduce cash-cropping and to diversify so as to minimize the dependence on any one crop (especially cardamom).

Qawa Quk'a discourages the use of fertilizers, insecticides and herbicides. This is a radical departure from catechists' earlier development mentality, which advocated using chemicals to increase cash crop harvests. Now such scientific techniques are perceived as a debt-trap. As Wolf writes, the peasant "favours production for sale only within the context of an assured production for subsistence".[22] This strategy was advantageous for a period, but has now become catastrophic, as commodity prices plummet. Production oriented towards the market is not flexible, since the cash-crops represent an investment of time, and money. At present, most rural communities perceive the market as highly unfavourable to their interests.

The present economic crisis is hardly an unique phenomenon, and is documented for subsistence economies the world over.[23] What needs explanation, however, is the strident ethnic identity concurrent with this

---

[22] Wolf, xiv.

[23] Wolf, 43-47. Cp. J.C. Scott, *The Moral Economy of the Peasant: Rebellion and Subsistence in Southeast Asia* (New Haven: Yale University Press, 1976).

reaction to the market and Western goods.[24]

Indigenist ideas have been common currency in Guatemala and Latin America since the colonial period, but why have they gained pre-eminence among the Q'eqchi' at this particular time? Specifically, why have the mountain spirits and their surrounding rituals been the focus of this renovation movement? Why would this ideology appeal to and unite Q'eqchi's with radically different positions in the relations of production, some rural cash-crop producers, others working class consumers?

To begin to understand the characteristics of Q'eqchi' ethnic revivalism, we must look at a past which has become very pertinent in the process of constructing an ethnic identity.

Traditional Sacred Communities

The earth cult is no longer hegemonic in Q'eqchi' communities. Yet although it is not the dominant way in which communities are imagined, its elements are still practised and believed by a substantial section of the population. Since it is a living tradition, I profile its principles in the present tense.

Historically, the community has been a more salient basis of identity than the ethnic group. In the past, a strong pan-Q'eqchi' identity did not exist as such; people would only refer to themselves or others as "Q'eqchi's" when commenting on language ability. The word "Q'eqchi'" does

---

[24] The Q'eqchi' indigenist movement has historical parallels in Perú, where a pan-indigenous identity formed in the Taki Onqoy uprising of 1560-70. This identity was based on the separation of the indigenous and Spanish worlds (see M. J. Sallnow, *Pilgrims of the Andes: Regional Cults in Cusco*. Washington D.C.: Smithsonian Institution, 1987, 58-60), involving a total rejection of Spanish food, clothes and names (cp. R. T. Zuidema, R.T., "Observaciones Sobre el Taqui Onqoy", *Historia y Cultura*. Lima, 1966, vol. i (1), 37; see also N. Wachtel, *The Vision of the Vanquished: The Spanish Conquest of Peru Through Indian Eyes*. Translated by Reynolds, Hassocks, U.K.: Harvester Press, 1973). Another parallel lies in the Huamanga revolt of 1613, which Stern argues led to the creation of the insulating institutions of the "closed corporate community" (S.J. Stern, "The Struggle for Solidarity: Class, culture and community in highland Indian America," in E. Archetti, P. Cammack and B. Roberts, eds., *Sociology of "Developing Societies" in Latin America*, London: Macmillan, 1987, 47) To give a more recent Andean parallel, the Kataristas in Bolivia share many of the cultural objectives of *Qawa Quk'a*. (cp. X. Albó, "From MNRistas to Kataristas to Katarí," in S. Stern, *Resistance, Rebellion and Consciousness in the Andean Peasant World, 18th to 20th Centuries*. Madison: University of Wisconsin Press, 1987).

not originally refer to an ethnic group, but to a language. Any person who speaks this Mayan language fluently can be called an *aj Q'eqchi'*, including members of the neighbouring Poqomchi' group.

More frequently, traditional identity is associated with a municipality or certain village. Many other writers have commented on how the municipality is the basis of Mayan identities.[25] Smith writes that, "..indian identity is rooted in community rather than in any general sense of 'indianness'".[26] Historically, ethnic identities was derived from and secondary to community identities.

The cornerstone of community identities is location, the local geography. Community identities are imagined through the relationship with the local sacred landscape. John Berger writes that the peasant "village is....a living portrait of itself", which is not constructed out of stones but out of words and legends, and "it is a continuous portrait, work on it never stops".[27] For traditionalists, the ongoing portrait of the community is the local mountain spirit, the *Tzuultaq'a*. The mountain spirit is a Durkheimian collective representation, a social fact of the cognitive life of the village.

The traditionalists say that the mountains are living (*yo'yo*). They have the quality of *wiinqilal*, or "personhood", a concept which applies only to mountains and people. The *Tzuultaq'as* are spirits which have a human form and live in a "house", the cave, deep inside the mountain. Yet the mountain is also the physical body of a mountain spirit. The physical structure of the mountain is anthropomorphized, with each mountain having a face, head, body, and a cave which is said to be either a mouth or a womb.

Only one *Tzuultaq'a* resides in each mountain, and is called the "owner" of that mountain. Each spirit owner has a sex, name and character. The *Tzuultaq'as* are unique in being both male and female: in most indigenous cultures in Latin America the particular features of mountains are usually male.[28] The *Tzuultaq'as* own the land and everything on its surface. They are sentinels; the guardians of the plants, people and the forest animals, which are held in a corral inside the mountain. They are the original

---

[25] Cf. S. Tax, *Penny Capitalism: A Guatemalan Indian Economy* (Chicago: University of Chicago Press, 1963).

[26] C. A. Smith, (ed.) *Guatemalan Indians and the State, 1540-1988* (Austin: University of Texas Press. 1990), 18.

[27] J. Berger, *Pig Earth* (London: Writers and Readers, 1979), 9.

[28] Cf. Carmack, 382; B. J. Isbell, *To Defend Ourselves: Ecology and Ritual in an Andean Village* (Austin: University of Texas, 1978), 59; Nash, 1979, 122.

owners of the corn. People only hold corn on an extended loan with high interest rates. This is part of the explanation for sacrifice during the agricultural calendar—it allows access to continued use of land and corn.

Traditionalists say that the *Tzuultaq'as* are kin or "afines" to one another. The kin hierarchy of the mountains reflects the internal power differentials between locales. It is not a coincidence that *Xukaneb'*, who dominates the pre-Colombian and colonial capital, Cobán, is the father and king of the mountains. The relations between traditionalists and the mountain spirits are highly localized. This is not a generalized earth cult such as that of Pacha Mama in the Andes, the elements of which can be taken from one area to another. Villagers interact primarily with the mountain spirits who dwell in the caves around their communities. Villages are "owned" by individual mountains and they are often named after the closest sacred mountain to them.[29]

The elders, be they male or female, know their *Tzuultaq'as* through their dreams. In this way, Q'eqchi' communities are dreamed as much as they are imagined. In the past, the dreams helped elders to counsel village leaders on the setting of dates for events or appointments to religious office. In the nocturnal encounters, the *Tzuultaq'as* appear in human form as tall, with white skin and hair and if male, beards.[30] People repeatedly told me, "The *Tzuultaq'as* look like the Germans". The Germans, were the first major landowners in the area. They came to Alta Verapaz after the Liberal reforms of 1871 and bought, robbed and violently seized *Q'eqchi'* land. The experience of serf-like slavery to the German landlords significantly affected

---

[29] Writing about the Tzeltal-Maya, June Nash (*In the Eyes of the Ancestors: Belief and Behavior in a Maya Community*, New Haven: Yale University Press, 1970, 19) records that lineage patronyms are usually the same as the name of the most important sacred hill in the locale.

[30] In other parts of Guatemala, Mexico, and most of the Andes, mountain spirits appear as rich "ladinos" - often as plantation owners (cf. R. Adams, *Creencias y Prácticas del Indigena*, Guatemala, Instituto Indigenista Nacional, 1952, 31; M. Oakes, *The Two Crosses of Todos Santos: Survivals Of Mayan Religious Ritual*, New York, Bollingen Foundation, 1951, 93; M. Siegel, "Religion in Western Guatemala: A product of acculturation," *American Anthropologist* 43, 1941, 62-76; J. Ingham, *Mary, Michael and Lucifer: Folk Catholicism in Central Mexico*, Austin, University of Texas Press, 1986, 105; E. Vogt, *Zinacantán: A Maya community in the highlands of Chiapas*, Cambridge, Belknap Press of Harvard University Press, 1969, 302; A. Villa Rojas, *Los Elegidos de Dios; Etnografía de los Mayas de Quintana Roo*, México D.F., Instituto Nacional Indigenista, 1978, 288,289; and M. J. Sallnow, *Pilgrims of the Andes: Regional Cults in Cusco*, Washington D.C., Smithsonian Institution, 1987, 209).

the character of the *Tzuultaq'a*. Both the *Tzuultaq'as* and Germans are called "patrones" (or bosses). Elders recount many histories about German landowners who ate their workers, another similarity with the mountain spirits. Since both are authority figures and owners of the land, the personas of the mountain spirits and plantation landlords are merged to a degree.

The *Tzuultaq'a* is an historical figure and ideas of community are partly the product of colonial and post-colonial experiences. *Q'eqchi'* communities are not some ahistorical legacy of the Maya. It is fundamental to my argument that we see the *Tzuultaq'a* as being sensitively influenced by historical developments.

In elders' dreams, the *Tzuultaq'as* demand more food in the form of copious amounts of sticky resinous incense, candles, fermented maize drink, turkey blood and raw cacao beans. The relationship with the mountains is reciprocal. People and mountains must feed each other, not just consume without recompense.

Elders dream about the *Tzuultaq'as* frequently before the maize planting, and these dreams act as a justification for sacrifices in the caves. Each spring, traditionalists go to the caves which perforate the mountains and petition the spirits. In the past, the sacrifice for the planting was carried out first of all by the whole community and then by men individually. Now, few community sacrifices are carried out, although individual performances are common.

The community sacrifice grants usufruct to the community as a whole, whereas the individual sacrifice gives households specific rights. In the individual sacrifice, households register their intentions to one another, and document their relationships to particular sections of the landscape. Sacrifice inscribes local land tenure into the landscape, that of the whole village, and of the household. The community sacrifice expresses the shared image of the community, which is partly constructed in opposition to surrounding communities.

Traditionalist identity is not just bound to the community, but has an ethnic dimension as well. The mountain cult positively affirms Q'eqchi' identity with respect to the "ladinos", or non-indigenous peoples. During the cave sacrifice, the pilgrim speaks an ancient, archaic form of Q'eqchi'. The petitioner gives only autochthonous foods to the tellurian deities, not items which come from the Spanish or "ladinos". Before entering a cave, traditionalists remove any Western clothes they are wearing and don their traditional dress. Inside, pilgrims do not mention Jesus Christ, the standard bearer of orthodox catholicism. Only in this setting is God's son absent from Q'eqchi' prayers.[31]   Taken together, these elements underscore a valuing of the indigenous, whether it is in the realm of food, language, dress or religion.[32]

Traditionalist ideas relating to the landscape are more prevalent among women than among men. Women interact with the mountain spirit in the domain of health care and human fertility. One paradigm of fertility encompasses reproduction of children and production of the maize crop. Both involve a progressive increase in level of heat until growth is complete. Whereas male cave sacrifices involve "hot" items such as incense, candles, pine torches and turkey blood, pregnant women consume specific foods which maintain their raised heat levels.

Illness in children is generally caused by two things; either an insufficient or excessive degree of heat during pregnancy, or the mountain spirit has seized the child's soul because of the parents' moral transgressions. In order to retrieve the child's soul and restore him/her to health, the mother goes to a river or stream, which are specific expressions of the mountain spirit. Here she will call to the *Tzuultaq'a*, offer a sacrifice, hope that the mountain will free the child, and then call the errant soul back to its body.

As with agricultural production, the symbolism of human reproduction is involved in the construction of traditional identities. Only members of a particular community can lose their spirits to the one or two local mountains to whom they belong. These categories of illness derive from an ongoing moral relationship with the mountains. Q'eqchi' women have their own concepts of fertility which are not shared by "ladino" outsiders. The symbolism of reproduction defines itself as autonomous from Western medicine; no antibiotics could cure spirit loss.

The cult of the mountain spirits does not only express the traditional imagination of the community, but also concepts of health, welfare and fertility of humans and maize. For followers of the earth cult, the mountains reach right down inside them, moulding their concept of

---

[31] M. Taussig (*The Devil and Commodity Fetishism in South America*, Chapel Hill, University of North Carolina Press, 1980, 147) points out that across Latin America, Jesus is not mentioned in petitions to mountain spirits.

[32] There is a parallel here with mountain cults in eighteenth century Arequipa, as documented by F. Salomon. In this part of highland Perú, the mummies in cave shrines were seen as the "true owners" of the land, and functioned to define the "collective 'self' and 'other' within rigid boundaries". ("Ancestor Cults and Resistance in the State of Arequipa, ca. 1748-1754", in S. Stern, *Resistance, Rebellion and Consciousness in the Andean Peasant World 18th to 20th Centuries*, Madison, University of Wisconsin Press, 1987, 160, 161).

personhood. This involvement of the *Tzuultaq'as* inside the boundaries of the individual psyche is one of the factors that makes the traditional cosmology and sense of community so tenacious and persistent.

The Catholic Catechists

Traditional images of community came under attack in the mid 1970s, when the Catholic Church began to organise Catholic base communities in each village. The clergy used local Q'eqchi's to re-evangelize their idolatrous brethren. Clergy readily refer to this process as the "second evangelization".

In each community, a cabal of young male villagers, excluded by the gerontocratic basis of the traditional religion, embraced the new religious orthodoxy. These lay activists, or "catechists", set about teaching the catechism, or Catholic doctrine, in their villages. By the late 1970s the catechist program had taken root in nearly every Q'eqchi' community.

It is hard to over-emphasise the impact on identity of translating Catholic rituals and doctrine into Q'eqchi'. Anderson writes how it is only possible to imagine the nation once particular conceptions lose their grip on peoples' minds, especially the idea that a particular language (eg. Latin) offers a privileged access to truth, because *it is part* of that ontological truth.[33] Before the catechist program, the only languages suitable for interactions with God were Castilian and Latin. If a Mayan language could also be a language of truth, then it was possible to think of Q'eqchi' as a unifying basis for identities beyond that of the village.

With the external legitimacy of the Catholic Church behind them, the catechists challenged the elders' authority. Up to that point, gerontocratic power had been exercised through the Catholic brotherhoods, or "cofradías". These had been the main social institution in Mayan communities since the sixteenth century. The religious brotherhoods were the platforms for all intra-communal juridical decisions, organisation of land tenure, the celebration of the saint image of the community and representations to local and national government. The catechists undermined the "cofradías" from within, quickly rendered them hollow shells, and replicated their community functions. Some elders carried on with the "cofradías", but without the young men who made up the body of the organisations.

---

[33] Anderson, 36.

The Catholic Church introduced not only a new universal religious ethic to the communities but also a new economic ethic, that of development and the green revolution. Already economically mobile and entrepreneurial in outlook, the catechists were open to trying the new methods of the "ladinos" and foreigners. Importantly, they possessed the capital to invest in the formation of co-operatives and in fertilizers and insecticides.

Max Weber's (1930) analysis of protestantism is appropriate here; the catechists represented an emerging status group in their hitherto relatively unstratified communities. They became the principal advocates of an ideology which promoted an individualistic, market-oriented agriculture over a subsistence based economy. Economic trends and religious conversion enhanced the latent possibilities in each other. Studies on orthodox Catholic and Protestant conversion across highland Guatemala have emphasised the same relationship between economic development and spiritual conversion.[34]

Many young men become lay activists, since this role meant immediate access to village authority and prestige. Traditional holders of political power had fulfilled a lifetime of obligations in the "cofradía" and as local representatives to the municipality. Becoming a catechist meant avoiding the financially crippling expenditure in the "cofradía". This money could then serve as capital for cash-cropping. The catechist program was part of a general drift towards greater economic differentiation within Q'eqchi' villages. Like Calvinism three centuries before, one could now work hard, reinvest profits, and gain religious prestige and political power.

The catechists were hostile to the traditional image of community. The mountain spirits were anathema to their universalising, orthodox current. The first catechists did not completely suppress the *Tzuultaq'as*, but they obstructed collective rituals and those which involved blood sacrifice. Agricultural "development" represented not only an attempt at economic betterment, but also an attack on the *Tzuultaq'as* at another, technical level. The cult of the tellurian divinity is based on subsistence agriculture and is represented in myths and taboos as antithetical to cash-cropping.

However, many individual communications with the sacred landscape continued, especially in the realm of illness and human pregnancy.

---

[34] Cf. D. Brintnall, *Revolt Against the Dead: the modernization of a Maya community in the Highlands of Guatemala*, New York, Gordon And Breach, 1979, 4; K. Warren, *The Symbolism of Subordination: Indian Identity in a Guatemalan Community*, Austin, University of Texas Press, 174,1978; S. Annis, *God and Production in a Guatemalan Town*, Austin, University of Texas Press, 1987.

Catechists accept many traditional ideas concerning illness and pregnancy as legitimate. As stated earlier, these see fertility and illness as resulting from interactions with the landscape. Catechists often take their own families to see curers to be diagnosed and cured through prayer, rituals and herbs. So although the mountain spirits were uprooted from agricultural practice, they survived in health care and human fertility. Perhaps this is because these areas are mostly female-dominated. As with the first evangelization, Catholic doctrine was primarily aimed at men. Women became the principal carriers of the traditional community culture.

Overall, the catechist program unravelled traditional conceptions of the community. Most catechists scoffed at the elders' dreams, and the ties linking all villagers to one or two mountains became frayed. The collapse of the gerontocracy and its replacement with an externally legitimated source of political power meant that Q'eqchi's looked more than ever to the outside world for the creation of a community leadership.

The old ways of thinking about the community gave way to new ones, based, for instance, on the Bible as the "centre-pole" of the village. The base group could not, however, claim to represent the whole community in all instances, as the "cofradía" did. Instead, it competed with ascendent secular state institutions, eg. the "development committees" and other religious groupings such as the evangelicals and remnants of the "cofradía".

The rise of the catechists wreaked a fundamental change in the previous model of apprehending the world, which made it possible for catechists to imagine wider frames of reference, to think of class identification and later the "pan-Q'eqchi" community.' The catechists' meetings in Cobán set a precedent in being the first ever assemblies of village representatives from all over the Q'eqchi' area. The catechists became the pilgrims of a new type of sacred community.[35] As the catechists discussed issues of common interest, they constituted a parliament of deputies, the first modern Q'eqchi' intelligentsia.

Catechists replaced one insular sacred community, the "cofradía", with a more universal one, the Catholic base group. Community identity thus ceased to be a closed shop, but incorporated principles of universality and accepted a wider basis of association than just the community itself. This would later have implications for the development of a class-based identity.

---

[35] Cf. Sallnow (1987) and Anderson (1991, 115) discuss how pilgrimage is a characteristic of sacred, communal and national identities.

Civil War[36]

The Guatemalan guerrilla movement began to garner local support from about the late 1970s. At first, the guerrillas won support from the catechists who could be seen as corresponding to Wolf's "middle peasantry". Wolf writes that rural rebellion is most likely during the transformation from subsistence peasant to capitalist farmer.[37] This fits with the situation in Central America in the mid to late 1970s. The 1973 oil price rises led to a worldwide recession, an increase in price of fertilisers and a drop in commodity prices. Many "middle peasants" lost their capital built up from previous years, went deep into debt, and as Arias writes, they experienced "sudden unexpected misery".[38]

Rural poverty combined with spiritual tumult and raised expectations through cash-cropping led to a politicization of many communities. In some parishes, the clergy actively espoused liberation theology, focussing on the book of Exodus. Catechists began to undermine the foundations of all the traditional authority figures: the mountain spirits, village elders, saints, plantation owners and the government. By 1981, the guerrillas controlled a third of the country and were on the verge of announcing a provisional government.

In order to re-instate control over rural areas, the army ran amok, spreading generalised terror. In all, roughly one hundred Q'eqchi' villages were destroyed between 1980 and 1983. Tens of thousands were massacred. Selective repression against individuals, especially catechists, occurred in hundreds more villages. Bishop Flores estimates that 20,000 *Q'eqchi's* fled into the mountainous rainforest.[39] Army repression achieved the opposite of its stated intent, driving villages into the arms of the guerrillas, even ones which previously had no relation with the rebels.

---

[36] On Q'eqchi' experiences of war, see another article by the author, R.A. Wilson, 1991, 33-61.

[37] Cf. Wolf, xv, 291.

[38] A. Arias, "Changing Indian Identity: Guatemala's Violent Transition to Modernity," in C. Smith (ed) *Guatemalan Indians and the State, 1540-1988* (Austin: University of Texas Press, 1990), 240.

[39] Cf. America's Watch, "Closing the Space: Human Rights in Guatemala, May 1987-October 1988". Washington D.C., 1988, 96.

War and icons of community

The catechists' religion survived the civil war more intact than traditional conceptions of religion and community. The refugees' nomadic life precluded many mountain cult rituals. Many elders died from army attacks and exposure to the elements. As mentioned earlier, the earth cult is localised, and so could not be transported to new landscapes. Without sacrifice, reciprocal ties to the landscape withered. All the catechists needed for their celebrations was a Bible. Being less grounded in the local landscape, the catechists' religion was more transportable and flexible to social upheaval.

Civil war did not destroy all elements of traditional culture. In response to their crisis, certain communities gave even more emphasis to symbols of community. They prayed often to the *Tzuultaq'as* and God to shield them from adversity. The mountain spirits watched over the refugees, appearing in dreams to tell the group where to find wild animals and edible plants, and where to hide from army patrols.

In a situation where people from many different communities were jumbled together, and usually far from their place of origin, it is not surprising that the traditional images of the community, the mountain spirits, began to fade. The catechists, with their universal ideology which transcended the narrow confines of place, could then step into this identity gap and unfurl the banner of universal catholicism.

The soldier mountain spirit

The army resettled thousands of refugees in over 100 new communities, some on their original lands, others in new villages. The army planned the location and physical organisation of the new villages. Before the war, villages contained anything up to one hundred households, but the army model fixed an ideal size of forty families. The reconstituted villages are highly concentrated, with all the houses close to one another.

The army has replaced traditional community institutions with its own para-military structures: the Civil Defense Patrols, or PACs. These vigilante patrols are comprised of the civilian population itself and directed by the military. Local men are given a gun and told to "hunt communists", and so provide a vital surveillance function. Once again, village-based institutions have been replaced by those linked to an external source of power.

The military's system of social control has sought to have a resonance in indigenous culture itself. A militarization of indigenous symbolism got underway during the war. In particular, the army has strived to commandeer the authoritarian aspect of the *Tzuultaq'as*. For instance, the training program for new recruits is called, "The Soldier *Tzuultaq'a* Training Program". The Guatemalan crack commando troops are called the *Kaibiles*, or, in Mayan, "Jaguars". The "ladino" head of the Army's Information Department, told me, "We compare ourselves to the mountain spirits because like them, we dominate the land, we command over all who are in our territory". The army is the Guatemalan state institution with the most profound understanding of indigenous culture, borne out of centuries of exercising domination.

For these reasons, I thoroughly disagree with Watanabe when he writes, "Despite its ubiquity, state authority remains intrinsically foreign" to the indigenous community.[40] To the contrary, the military is right inside the indigenous community, having long since insinuated itself into levels of local social meaning. Once the army had physically imposed its control over a territory and exacted its brutal punishment, it moved to a new mode of exercising repression, surveillance. Foucault has drawn our attention to this same succession from punishment to surveillance by eighteenth century European states. The state's increasingly sophisticated understanding of the mechanisms of repression means that it invents what Foucault calls "a synaptic regime of power, a regime of its exercise within the social body, rather than from above it".[41]

Religion and resistance

In the reorganised communities, the mountain spirit is only an after-image in agricultural production. Collective and individual sacrifices are much less frequent than before the war. However, the political violence did not affect traditional healing methods to the same extent.[42] Infant sicknesses

---

[40] J. Watanabe, "Enduring but ineffable community in the western periphery of Guatemala," in C. Smith (ed) *Guatemalan Indians and the State, 1540-1988* (Austin: University of Texas Press, 1990), 195.

[41] M. Foucault, *Michel Foucault: Power/Knowledge: Selected Interviews and Other Writings, 1972-1977*. C. Gordon, ed (Brighton: Harvester, 1980), 38,39.

[42] Cf. M. Taussig, *Shamanism, Colonialism and the Wild Man: a study in terror and healing* (Chicago: University of Chicago Press, 1986). See also N. Whitten, *Sacha Runa: Ethnicity and Adaptation of Ecuadorian Jungle Quichua* (Urbana:

and spirit loss continue to be treated as before.

As for the catechists, they are closely monitored by the army and civil patrols and still face charges of supporting the guerrillas. The suppression of religious practice is a counter-insurgency tactic designed to stifle all independent community organization. Indeed, the Catholic base community and evangelical groups are the only village institutions which lie outside the military's command structure. Religion is all that is left of civil society. The other organizations, the civil patrol and betterment committees, compliantly collaborate with military policy. Religion is the only rural supra-community social organization which is autonomous from the state. For such reasons, Bruneau, writing about Brazil, says that Christian base communities are "the seed bed for popular initiatives under authoritarian regimes".[43]

Although indigenous peoples were on the whole unconverted to the guerrillas' class analysis, they were exposed to ideas which posited a wider basis for identity than just the community. Smith rightly argues that up until the 1970s, traditional Mayan conceptions of community blocked the possibility of a pan-indian struggle against the state. The indigenous imaginings of community through the mountain spirits and the "cofradías" needed to be transcended for any real development of a widespread insurrection to take place.[44] This is exactly what happened, when the catechists brought a supra-communal world view which stressed class association and universal ideas of Catholic brotherhood. Those on the side of the army went through a similar process. One patroller in a tiny, isolated mountain village announced to me "we Guatemalans must fight the outsiders!" expressing the over-defensive paranoia that is an essential building block of nationalism.

Throughout the war, the military exerted its own imagining of the communities; that they are ruled by soldier *Tzuultaq'as*, each a local representative of the national Guatemalan army. The army imposed new community political institutions, the civil patrols. These translate army messages down to the local level, and send representatives to the military base in Cobán, making Q'eqchi's "inner pilgrims" of the state, a crucial

---

University of Illinois Press), 1976.

[43] T. Bruneau, "Basic Christian Communities in Latin America: Their nature and significance (especially in Brazil)," in D. Levine (ed) *Churches and Politics in Latin America* (London: Sage, 1980), 225.

[44] C. A. Smith,, 1990, 20.

process in nation-building.[45] By speaking Mayan languages and manipulating their religious symbolism, the army is the chief vehicle of Guatemalan national identity.

As Smith has noted, the military is now trying to create a wide cultural consensus, to incorporate indigenous peoples into national society. This means it must obliterate traditional divisions in society, by destroying the primary bases of community and ethnic identities. He speculates on the indigenous response to the military state and predicts either the development of a pan-Maya identity or the "fragmentation" of communities, making it harder for the state to control them.[46] Both processes are already occurring in Mayan communities of Guatemala.

Revivalism Reconsidered

The civil war and catechist program undermined successive bases of identity and so carried within them the seeds of "ethnogenesis"[47] presently being sewn by the indigenist catechists. The attenuation of traditional bases of identity has necessitated the creation of new cultural formations. Though ethnogenesis purports to be the unearthing of previous customs, it is in part innovative. Indigenist catechists forge new cultural forms (eg. "indigenised" Catholic rituals) out of past customs, but they are to some extent distinct from the traditions. Indigenist catechists are now renovating rituals belonging to the mountain cult, according to their still rather orthodox tendencies.[48]

The rituals could not be exact replicas of ancient practice. Only some villagers still live in the conditions under which the mountain cult traditionally thrived. Those affected by landlessness, political violence, orthodox catholicism and cash-cropping must invent a new relationship with the

---

[45] Cf. Anderson, 1983, 115.

[46] Smith, 1990, 273, 282.

[47] Cf. Whitten, 1976. See also J. Murra, "The Cultural Future of the Andean Majority", in D. Maybury-Lewis (ed) *The Prospects for Plural Societies.* Proceedings of the American Ethnological Society, 1982.

[48] Barth (1969, 35) writes well about this process, saying that, "much of the activity of political innovators is concerned with the codification of idioms: the selection of signals for identity and the assertion of value for these cultural diacritica, and the suppression or denial of relevance for other differentiae. The issue as to which new cultural forms are compatible with the native ethnic identity is often hotly contended, but is generally settled in favour of syncretism...."

landscape, a new image of community.

If ethnic revivalists identify the market as the fount of their economic oppression, then it is not surprising that they hark back to a golden age of subsistence agriculture when there was less dependence on the international market. Resistance to the market serves as the spark for the revival of ancestral ways. When the market threatens the source of livelihood, there is a resurgence of the traditional cult of the earth deities. This comes hand-in-hand with a valuation of traditional agricultural practices and an idyllic isolationism.

Yet ethnic revivalism does not merely follow changes in material conditions. After all, the collapse of the rural economy in the late 1970s did not lead to a stronger ethnic identity. The present ethnic revival has been made possible through the pan-Q'eqchi' dissemination of catechists' ideas and the unfolding of a capacity to imagine identity in terms of a community wider than that of a person's immediate circle of kith and kin. By embracing "ladino" values, the catechists of the 1970s internalised principles of universality, which allowed them to transcend the narrow boundaries of the community. This laid the groundwork for a re-emergence of an ethnic identity with enough general features to forge meaningful links between communities which were not possible before. To use Anderson's phrase, a new mode of apprehending the world was established.

The first catechists broke the old template of imagining the community, but their revolutionary and developmental models failed. Now revivalist catechists look around for a new basis for the community, and end up re-using old criteria which preceded the catechist movement. In their search for elements of the past in the present, they encounter strands of ancient practice in the realm of health care and agricultural production. The indigenist catechists create a new identity, basing it on a revamped and Mayanised mountain spirit. The indigenists' mountain spirit is not the "German" of the traditionalists, but a dark-skinned "Maya". The Mayas in the mountains are their only link to a past which itself has to be reconstructed according to the needs of a new image of community. The Mayas link all Q'eqchi's to their past and redefine their relationship to the landscape.

The youth of the ethnic revivalists is also of significance, since these are the sons of the first catechists of the 1970s. They are identifying with the symbols of their grandfathers. New icons of community are therefore not just about changing collective representations, but are also part of an inter-generational psychological drama.

Finally, it must be recognised that groups based on Mayan identities are forming all over Guatemala. A pan-Maya identity is forming through bilingual education, Catholic and Protestant churches, radio stations, and national indigenous groups such as CONAVIGUA and CERJ. Such groups have flourished throughout Latin America in recent years, campaigning around the Quincentenary in 1992 and the UN Year of Indigenous Peoples in 1993. The processes which I am describing are not new, they are only a twenty year segment of a long history of countervailing processes of attrition and regeneration of indigenous identities.

Mayan Identities and Tradition

The most widespread approach to Mayan collective identities is the "relational view" which sees indigenous cultural patterns as a response to state and "ladino" hegemony. For example, Smith argues that indigenous identity is "not fixed in 'tradition'", but that it is renewed each generation and is created dialectically in opposition to the "ladino" world. Local belief emphasises the continuity of their tradition, but according to Smith "all tradition could disappear" tomorrow and indigenous identity would remain.[49]

This approach, adopted by Smith among many others, is in my view profoundly one-sided. The point that the indigenous community is partially the product of external relations, particularly with "ladinos"and the state, is wholly acceptable. Yet it is misguided to overlook the way in which indigenous identities are chained to images of tradition. Religious tradition serves as an unremitting anchor to identities, providing the idiom and limitations to the way community is portrayed. Q'eqchi' experiences have shown how, even under cataclysmic circumstances, tradition will never just "disappear". Instead, tradition is continually re-adjusted to the circumstances, but within a monumental matrix carried forward from the past. The mountains still loom over Q'eqchi' communities, casting their shadows on all present reformulations of the community. There is an immense inertia in Q'eqchi' experiences of shifting ethnic boundaries, even though change is wrought by events of epic scale such as civil war and Catholic re-evangelization. This is one reason why, in 1992, there were still indigenous peoples in the Americas to oppose the official celebrations of the quincentenary of Columbus's arrival in "Hispaniola".

---

[49] Smith, 1990, 220-222.

Social scientists, unlike their informants, are too ready to dismiss this past. In exalting form over content, they apply structural paradigms too insensitively. This has been the legacy of approaches to ethnicity informed by structuralism, structural-marxism and post-modernism. The social is never "in the last instance groundless", as Laclau argues,[50] since its possibilities of expression are limited by its own past. And like Marxism, one never arrives at the postulated post-modern "last instance" anyway.

Relational views of identity tend to neglect indigenous agency, and deny the autonomy of nativistic cultural constructions consciously developed by indigenous peoples. As Carmack argues, indigenous cultural forms are not dialectical reflections of "ladino" culture.[51] However, I am not making a sentimental argument for undefiled traditional communities. A romanticised essentialist view has little framework to cope with the impact of modernity, other than bemoaning its savaging of the "pure" indigenous community. Watanabe counsels against the naive reification of traditional indigenous communities which represents them as "fragile mosaics of 'shared poverty', political insularity and cultural inscrutability that then shatter irrevocably under the impact of global modernity".[52]

This chapter has sought to show how the symbolism of the landscape and icons of the community provide continuity to the past under the impact of modernity. Cultural reconstruction is going on, and Q'eqchi' identities and communities are patently not what they were. Yet indigenous peoples are the active agents in this reconstruction, drawing upon their cultural legacy. What I am proposing is a synthetic approach; that we see both the legacy of past content without distilling any essence, and recognise the influence of interactions with "ladinos" and their state without losing sight of how history mediates these interactions.

---

[50] E. Laclau, "New Social Movements and the Plurality of the Social," in D. Slater (ed) *New Social Movements and the State in Latin America* (Dordrecht, Holland: FORIS, 1985), 37.

[51] Carmack, 1990, 130.

[52] Watanabe, 1990, 201.

PART THREE
THE RISE OF INDIGENOUS THEOLOGY

CHAPTER EIGHT

TEUTLATOLLI: SPEAKING ABOUT GOD - INDIGENOUS THEOLOGY AND ROMAN CATHOLICISM

Fr. Eleazar López Hernández

"Indigenous theology is not the fruit of intellectual minds who spend their time writing books. Our approach is reflexive. We express ourselves in mythical-symbolic language: a culturally appropriate expression of the vital experience that our peoples have of God". The author of this chapter is a Zapotec priest-theologian who works in the diocese of Tehuantepec, México and with the Roman Catholic Centro Nacional de Ayuda a Misiones Indígenas (CENAMI).[1]

Introduction

To speak of indigenous theology, or of a theology of the native peoples of this continent, is to raise issues that are as controversial for indigenous communities as they are in the predominant society. First of all, so called "indigenous theology" would seem to many to go beyond the established canons of general academic reflection and specifically of church controlled theological endeavour. In other words, the very term "indigenous theology" raises questions that challenge previously and generally accepted parameters. Can we apply the term "theology" to a popular way of thinking that can neither boast of great exponents nor of highly literate publications and theoretical expositions? Aren't we in danger of making a branch of human knowledge meaningless, the critics argue, when we apply the term "theology" without further ado to rudimentary thinking and empirical approximations of indigenous beliefs, a subject matter that has, if anything, been overworked by experts? For their part, indigenous intellectuals are asking: do we not do violence to popular reflection when we try to fit it into molds and forms that are alien to our people?

---

[1] This paper was presented at the First Encounter on Indigenous Theology of the Mayan Region, in San Cristóbal de las Casas, Chiapas, 14-18 October, 1991. It is an updated version of Appendix II of the proceedings of that encounter: *Teología India Mayense*, CENAMI (Mexico), CCD (Honduras) and Abia Yala (Ecuador), 1993. It is used with permission.

In order to try to respond to these questions it is important to take into account that today's indigenous theology is part and parcel of the phenomenon which is known as the emergence of the poor of the world. The rise of indigenous theology is taking place precisely at a moment in history when modern thinkers have decreed the disappearance or exclusion of the poor from future projects. Thus, indigenous theology should be understood as the voice of *protest* of those who have been excluded from the system and from the church. But it is also a voice of *promise* as the poor offer to build a better world and a new way of being the church.

What is indigenous theology?

Although there is not a total consensus on this point, those of us who speak out for our peoples inside the church define it thus: *Indigenous theology is the body of millenia-old religious knowledge that our indigenous peoples possess and by means of which we explain our faith experience.* We do our theology within the context of our overall perception of the world, and of how others perceive us. In sum, indigenous theology is for us a *store-house of popular theological wisdom from which we draw the resources to face the new and ancient challenges of life.* In this sense, we are not talking about something new, nor of some churchly product. This is a very ancient reality that has survived the vicissitudes of time and even the various restrictions that have been placed upon it by the churches.

Now, in order to better understand the phenomenon of indigenous theology, we need to remember that, through centuries of persecution, this theology maintained itself clandestinely under the protective guise of the "popular religiosity" or "religion of the people" that is practised by the indigenous communities, as well as by marginalized "mestizo" peasants.

The historical role of indigenous theology

Ancestral indigenous theology has been the matrix and support of the way of life of our peoples during the long process of development before it clashed with the European worldview.

Indigenous theology is pastoral. Our theology sustained our peoples' faith during the aggression of the conquest. It provided encouragement in the struggle and resistance to oppression.

Indigenous theology became apocalyptic when we were faced with the fact of our subjection. During the colonial period, our theology became a refuge, haven and comfort revitalizing the faith of a vanquished people, in order to keep alive the hopes and utopias of the people.

Indigenous theology is, today, a prophetic theology of the oppressed. Our theology makes every effort today to maintain a critical awareness of forces of domination that are constantly being updated.

Indigenous theology is quite dynamic, in each case. It not only repeats the ancestral texts, but inspired by them, it creates new materials that are needed by the people.

The emergence of indigenous theology

The religious worldview of our native peoples—and of the related indigenous theology—that has surfaced in recent years is self generating. It demands to be respected by society and the churches. What is new and different from the remote and recent past is that the ecclesiastical sector that is committed to the indigenous peoples (bishops, priests, pastors, and indigenous nuns, pastoral agents and other personnel) are seriously attempting to provide ecclesial responses to indigenous demands. We desire to make space available pastorally where indigenous theology can express its fears; where we—pastors and representatives of indigenous religion—can together find appropriate and fruitful ways to dialogue.

"You are sending me to where I have never walked nor have I ever stood." This is what the indian Juan Diego is reputed to have said when the Virgin of Guadalupe sent him to relate his vision to bishop Juan de Zumárraga.[2] It is how we feel today. We are standing on totally new ground. In the process of developing our own theology, we cannot gloss over the fact that the worldview and theology of the indigenous peoples have been marginalized by the church. During the past five centuries, indigenous peoples were harshly persecuted by the "campaigns to extirpate idolatry" which were sponsored by the church. This was one of the characteristics of the church's evangelization of indigenous peoples. But because our people were never convinced that their beliefs were "diabolical and idolatrous" they continued to maintain them clandestinely beyond ecclesiastical control, i.e. hidden beneath Christian practices. This is to say that indigenous culture, religion and theology are products of the people. They do no proceed from

---

[2] Editor's note. Indigenous and liberation theologians have attached considerable importance to the fact that the Virgin appeared to an indigenous peasant man.

the dominant structures against which they are reacting when they insist on maintaining beliefs that have been negated by the structures.

Our passive resistance to imposition could perhaps have lasted many more years—as a kind of social schizophrenia—were it not that a new awareness of our dignity and of our rights in every way, including religious, has taken place among the indigenous peoples of this continent. We are no longer willing to let anyone step on us. We don't want any more to be the "excrement of the powerful," words again of the indian Juan Diego. We refuse any longer to wear masks in order to be accepted by the church; we want to be true to ourselves, to be open faced and true hearted. We who are christianized indians indeed desire to remain in the church, but without having to mask our culture, spirituality and theology. We want to be ourselves, sharing with all Christians our response to the call to conversion and to growth that is implicit in the Gospel. The great challenge that the church faced in Santo Domingo was how to "be Christian without ceasing to be indian".

Hostility toward christianity

Certainly there is a group of indigenous brothers and sisters who have become very critical and even hostile toward the churches, especially to the Roman Church—in the light of a history of 500 years of being "the vanquished ones". During the quincentenary of the arrival of the Europeans to our continent, some of these brethren went so far as to demand—in 1985, at a United Nations meeting where the Holy See was represented—"a condemnation of the Catholic Church for having supported and justified the invasion and illegal occupation of indigenous territories". The same year, during the first visit of John Paul II to Perú, several of our brethren handed back the Bible that the pope gave them because "they considered it an ideological arm of the domination that was imposed upon the inhabitants of this continent".

This quite visceral reaction is explainable and can be attributed to the pain that church members have caused our people during centuries of offensive attitudes toward our own dignity and human rights, as well as to the rights of specific peoples. But not all of us have reacted in such a visceral manner, blaming the churches of today for the crimes of the past. Instead, most of us have forgiven the churches for what happened 500 years ago and are seeking to dialogue with them, from within. This is why we struggle within the ecclesiastical structures for the word of indigenous peoples to be heard and taken into account. We want to take an active part in the institution in order for our people and our culture to be taken seriously. This is why we are looking to be accepted as partners in dialogue, on an equal footing with our pastors. We want to be seen as first class Christians, and not as second or third ranking citizens, tolerated though not fully accepted. In sum, we christianized indians no longer want to be permanently treated as children, as the property of the church, but as adults who are part of the church and who, furthermore, *are* the church.

Indigenous theology: Challenge or threat?

What we have said makes clear the degree to which the eruption of indigenous peoples into today's world, besides being a complex reality, constitutes a challenge of enormous proportions to national societies and to the churches. It demands profound changes in the way in which we understand what is taking place so that we can find solutions. It is no longer possible that indigenous peoples continue to be seen with yesterday's perceptions—either as objects for ethnological study or as people who must be integrated into the dominant society. We must be accepted as fellow pilgrims in a common humanity, as subjects and protagonists of our own development and evangelization. But this is precisely what fills some people in the dominant society and in the church with terror. It is why the conflicts have increased.

We know that the national churches, to which our indigenous peoples belong, are the first ones to be affected today by the indigenous eruption. For this reason, we must act at this moment with audacity of spirit and pastoral prudence, and always keeping before us the Gospel of Christ. We who are at the same time members of national churches and of the indigenous peoples ask ourselves with some anguish mixed with hope: under these circumstances, how can we remain true to the whole Gospel and at the same time faithful to our peoples and to their legitimate aspirations? How to keep evangelization from becoming the "spiritual conquest or reconquest" of our peoples which seeks to tie them to a particular social model that is deemed explicitly or implicitly Christian? How can our indigeneity become the fulfilment in Christ of our collective human aspirations?

The commitment of christianized indians

The large number of christianized indians who are working to build the Kingdom of God together with our peoples, fulfil various ninistries within the Christian faith. We are prayers, stewards, brotherhood members, standard bearers, catechists, delegates of the Word, celebrants, sisters, deacons, presbyters, pastors and bishops. We believe that it is possible today to create spaces within the churches where indigenous theology can be taken seriously, enabling it to emerge without interference. We believe that indigenous theology can demonstrate its profound wisdom as it engages in a mutually enriching dialogue with other theologies.

Based upon this premise—with prophetic audacity and pastoral prudence—we have launched upon the task of preparing the way for the indigenous peoples. We are fully aware that we, unfortunately, have not been prepared for this task: the theological premises in which we were formed are not enough. So we have turned to the deposit of faith where the church keeps its age old wisdom. Sometimes we find it necessary to update traditional theological tools or create new ones in order to facilitate dialogue with our brethren. According to the perceptive words of a much revered pastor to the indians, our indigenous sisters and brothers

> have begun to open their eyes. Their tongues are being loosened; they are beginning to speak and to do it courageously. They are rising to their feet and are beginning to walk, to organize themselves, and to initiate actions that can become significantly important for them, for the countries of Latin America and of the world.[3]

Signs of hope in the church

Churches that work among indigenous peoples are experiencig an internal shakeup. This is a challenge, as well as a kairos of grace. It is a call to the churches, once and for all, to turn the pages of yesterday, with their dark history of colonialism, slavery and destruction of entire peoples. Our churches are being asked to begin a fresh chapter in which a new story can be written of life for all. The new voice and presence of the indians, afroamericans and poor is like a breath of spring that is blowing at the doors of

---

[3] The late Bishop Leonidas Proaño, Río Bamba, Ecuador, 1987. No documentary source given.

the churches and civil society. Allow me to highlight some encouraging signs within my own Roman Catholic Church.

Vatican Council II, thirty years ago, opened the doors of the church to springtime. It various documents[4] have made it possible for the church to go forth to meet men and women, including our indigenous peoples, with renewed hearts and open minds.

The Pope's guidance. In numerous meetings with the native peoples of the world, John Paul II has spoken positively to the indigenous leaders and to their pastor-servants, the priests. We feel encouraged as we attempt to reply to the criticisms that are being levelled at the church by our indigenous brethren. With considerable eloquence, the pope has suggested many of the doors through which both indigenous peoples and missionaries are penetrating in search of life-giving solutions to the questions of our people. During the commemoration of the 500 years of evangelization—at the Fourth General Assembly of the Latin American Episcopate (CELAM IV) and the meeting in Yucatán with indigenous representatives from throughout the Continent—the Holy Father aroused yearnings for reconciliation and re-union of the church with native peoples.

The Latin American Bishop's Conference (CELAM) has been another source of support to indigenous theology and pastoral ministry—the documents of Medellín (1968) and Puebla (1979), and Santo Domingo (1992). In each of them the challenge of the indigenous peoples has been faced and specific guidelines for action have been set down which have been a source of inspiration for evangelization among indigenous peoples in recent years. CELAM's department of mission (DEMIS) has been particularly helpful in this regard. The Bogotá (Colombia, 1985) meeting was the beginning of a new stage in pastoral ministry among indigenous peoples. We moved from an "indigenist" to an indigenous pastoral ministry.[5] We began to speak about a specifically indigenous theology as a fundamental part of the growth of autochthonous churches.

Other DEMIS documents, produced for regional bishops' conferences, continued to contribute new elements to the discussion. But it was the Central American Bishops' meeting, in México in 1989, on Indigenous Pastoral ministry that tackled the specific topic of cultural and religious dialogue between the church and the indigenous peoples. At that time, we

---

[4] Lumen Gentium, Gaudium et Spes, Ad Gentes, Unitatis Redintegra-tio, Nosta Aetate, and other Vatican II documents.

[5] See the DEMIS quote in the chapter by Pop Cal.

indigenous priests presented the idea of a consultation on indigenous theology where we could set out the guidelines for interreligious dialogue with our peoples. The bishops endorsed the idea and then sponsored a consultation in 1990.

Insights from National Episcopal Conferences. The Mexican Bishops' Conference, through its Episcopal Commission for Indigenous Affairs, has worked on indigenous concerns for some time. It has been developing theological and pastoral guidelines that propose to "take on board, empower, and open up channels of communication for the concerns of indigenous people". In 1988 these episcopal efforts were further refined in a publication entitled T*he Theological Foundations of an Indigenous Pastoral Ministry of the Mexican Church.* In it the bishops expressed their willingness to "face up, Gospel in hand, to the challenges old and new which indigenous reality presents".

Other Bishops' Conferences in Latin America—e.g. Panamá, Argentina, Bolivia, Ecuador, Guatemala, and Brazil—have made various pronouncements that point the way toward Indigenous Pastoral Ministry and Theology. Those documents are also important sources to which we can go to clarify our own pastoral ministry.

We can affirm, without fear of equivocation, that at the level of words, the church's magisterium, both universal and Latin American has taken gigantic steps in the direction of the indigenous people of our continent. Actions, however, have fallen very far behind. We indigenous Christians must continue to insist on this matter, as St. Paul recommended to Timothy, "in season and out of season", even though our voices may seem inopportune and irritating to some members of the church.

From words to actions

More than twenty years ago, the Guatemalan Bishop's Conference began one of the most significant processes in Indigenous Pastoral Ministry on the continent. In 1992, through its Episcopal Commission on Indigenous Pastoral Ministry, it convened the Second Meeting and Workshop on Indigenous Theology in the Maya Region (Guatemala, México, Honduras and El Salvador). Later, several other bishops' conferences convened their own regional or national meetings on the same subject. The Panamanian Bishops' Conference brought together the Second Latin American Meeting on Indigenous Theology which took place in El Tabor, diocese of Colón, at the end of 1993.

The southern portion of the Pacific Region of México has the largest indigenous population in the entire country. The Pastoral Magisterium of this region is another bastion of doctrinal support for Indigenous Theology. A meeting of Central American clergy, in 1991, in Tehuantepec, to celebrate the first centennial of that diocese, gave bishops the opportunity to share their pastoral experience and their methodological insights concerning the development of an indigenous theology. The results of this experience were encouraging.

Many pastors of local diocese in México and elsewhere throughout the continent have been concerned to provide episcopal support to the theological pilgrimage of the indigenous peoples. Each one has contributed the best of his gifts and experience. But some have been particularly notable. On occasion of the annual pilgrimage of his church to the Basilica of Guadalupe, bishop Bartolomé Carrasco, now emeritus archbishop of Oaxaca, in a number of his homilies, focused upon a wide spectrum of topics that relate to indigenous theology. The bishop has engaged in a profound dialogue with the identity of his own people the Tlazcaltecas. He has made some amazing discoveries, pertaining to the Virgin of Ocotlán, which are supportive of indigenous theology.

Several studies of popular religiosity, particularly in relation to the appearance of the Virgin of Guadalupe to the indian Juan Diego, have provided the opportunity to penetrate more systematically in the vast religious worldview of our people. The book by Fr. Clodomiro Siller, "Understanding the Message of Guadalupe", has been very helpful to us in this process.

What we have stated thus far is evidence that we find ourselves at a new moment in history. We are seeing a church that has ceased to be the first enemy of our indigenous religious worldview and which is starting to become one of our principal allies. Some indigenous critics, however, warn that this is not the time to cry victory. They remain doubtful about the substance of these ecclesiastical changes. They point out that, side by side with the interest and enthusiasm in the indigenous cause by some bishops' conferences and of important members of the hierarchy, there are conferences and hierarchies that are expressing their concerns and their understandable fears, while others evidence prejudiced rejection of our cause. We know that virtually every episcopal delegation that has gone from Latin America to Rome in recent years has been questioned closely about their knowledge and involvement in indigenous theology. And we have been told by some of those present that several of our bishops have demonstrated a much more favourable attitude toward indigenous theology than the members of the Roman curia.

The Latin American Bishops' Conference, CELAM, has recently initiated a "Project concerning Indigenous Theology for teachers, seminary professors and information centres". The object of this project is to study the indigenous religious phenomenon from an academic perspective, that is, with "experts", in order to introduce it into the church within classical concepts that are officially accepted. This methodology requires that we indians hand over the wisdom of our peoples as prime material to be worked over by theological specialists. These theologians will produce the only "authentic indigenous theology", in the words of Mons. Javier Lozano Barragán, bishop of Zacatecas, México.

The role of a committed magisterium

Let us state that we indians are deeply concerned about indigenous theology and the unknown risks that are implicit in it. And we don't overlook nor reject the insights of other sectors of the church—in particular our bishops who have been placed by God to instruct us in the church's faith. The decisive contribution of those who have been appointed to the Magisterium is highly valued by Christian indigenous theology. However, we insist that they must first get to know our peoples by involving themselves in our vital processes of theological production. This will enable our bishops to speak knowledgeably and to avoid making value judgments that are alien to our idiosyncrasies and to our customs and beliefs. We ask them to help us reestablish the dialogue between our faith in Christ and the religious world of our ancestors that has been too often interrupted. We want them to act without intolerance and judgmentalism, avoiding shameful demonizing of indigenous beliefs, anachronistic stereotypes and idealistic theorizing. Let everything be done on the basis of truth, because "the truth shall set you free".

Reflections on Theological Methodology

Characteristics of indigenous theology

Indigenous theology cannot be attributed to any person in particular from among our peoples, and certainly not to any member of the church.

Indigenous theology is the most recent evidence of the long and ample resistance that native peoples of our continent have maintained vis a vis forms of society and faith that were imposed upon us without our consent.

Indigenous theology is not the fruit of intellectual minds who spend their time writing books. The approach is reflexive—it expresses itself in mythical-symbolic language: a culturally appropriate expression of the vital experience that our indian peoples have of God. This experience is only understandable to strangers if they affectively draw near to share our life and faith. A detached analysis of a handful of writings which only reflect a part of this experience can hardly produce a fair evaluation of indigenous theology. We recommend to our observers and critics what the Lord asked of his disciples: "Come and see" (Jn. 1:39).

Indigenous vs classical theology

The religious voice of indians is a recognized fact. Under the rubric of "indigenous theology", it is being taken more seriously than ever before. This first affirmation can be deduced from the theological discussions that are taking place within the larger context of the upsurge of native peoples throughout the continent.

Some sceptics, however, ask if it is valid to apply without qualifications the category of "theology" to the religious expression of indigenous peoples. What then is the meaning of theology? Admittedly, the generally accepted definitions of theology do not exist in the indigenous worldview.

The intellectual and scholarly definitions of "theology" were borrowed by Western christianity from hellenism. Medieval Christians defined "theology" as "the believers' search for an understanding of their faith... an attempt to explain christianity rationally to those who want to understand it". Or yet again, the effort "to make the teaching of revelation clear to the rational mind... in an organized and systematic way".[6]

From this perspective, theology is "understanding faith" (*intellectio fidei*). In other words, theology is the application of reason to the mysteries of faith (*"fides quarens intellectum"*: faith seeks knowledge, San Anselmo). This is why theology is defined as the act of "giving a reason for our hope", according to the very ancient expression of St. Peter (1 Pe. 3:15). In more technical language, theology is defined as *a reflective discourse that*

---

[6] Cp. the Instruction of the Congregation for the Doctrine of Faith (Concerning the theological vocation, 1.5.21).

attempts to explain the faith that we have in God—the One whom we experience in a vital way when we enter into communion with him and his life-giving project.

Therefore, theology is also the *word that accompanies and guides our commitment to live out God's project.* Theology is not faith, but rather a rational understanding of faith. For this reason, it does not focus only upon trying to understand God, but encompasses every aspect of human and cosmic reality.

Theology is a way of understanding ourselves and our world from the perspective of our faith in God. We do not do theology in order to believe in God. Faith comes before we attempt to rationalize our faith. To believe is the result of a theological act by which we launch upon the adventure of accepting with mind and heart the divine proposition. We do theology because we believe in Him. We do theology to explain to ourselves and for others in whom we believe and why we believe. We do theology (second act) because we believe (first act), and because we desire to understand, with our faith, the totality of human existence; because we want to explain, to ourselves and to others, the rationality of our beliefs and of human existence, as seen through the eyes of faith. Our interlocutors may be Christians as we are, or people of other faiths, or simply non-believers. In each case, theology is garbed in the most appropriate clothing.

Theology is also *the human word that seeks to demonstrate the rationale of divine faith.* This is based upon the conviction that faith does not contradict logic nor the scientific dictums of reason. In theology, faith and reason go hand in hand. Therefore,

> the proper task of theology—which is to understand the meaning of revel-
> ation—requires the use of philosophical knowledge... the historical sciences,
> in order to better understand the revealed truth about men and concerning the
> moral norms that govern their work. Theology should be collated with the
> valid results of science.[7]

Unlike faith, which is a gift of God, theology is a human product which makes use of the tools of knowledge that have been created by cultures and peoples—multiform jars in which we try to capture something of that immense ocean that is God. We know that there is no receptacle that is capable of containing God. So when theology speaks about God, we are conscious that we don't have more than a dim image of his presence—an

---

[7] Ibid, p. 10.

approximation or analogy of his person, based upon the best attempts at knowledge that are available from our human experience. What we don't know about God far exceeds what we do know about Him.

Every theology is limited, because it is a path that we humans are building toward understanding the divine purpose. This road is deeply scored by our particular history and cultures. This obligates us to always remain critical of the tools that we use, else we may fall into the blasphemy of believing that we can encapsulate God in our human concepts. Yet, at the same time, it is impossible to do anything theological without cultural tools. For this reason, theologians, Christian or not, will find that "the use of elements from our own cultures is certainly difficult; it implies risks, even while the effort is legitimate and worthy of encouragement".[8]

Theology, like culture, is a collective happening, it takes place within a believing community. Theologians receive their faith and share it in communities. Doing theology within their own communities, and on behalf of their communities enables theologians to give a reason for their faith. It is the community as a whole that validates, supports, or questions our theology. A community support service, usually done by people who have been set aside by the community, is what the church calls the Magisterium. Its role is "to conserve with holy intent and to faithfully expound the deposit of divine revelation... to watch that the people of God remain in the truth that sets us free".[9]   In other words, the Magisterium takes care that theological explanations that members of the church elaborate do not contradict nor fundamentally harm the faith of the community.

Levels of Christian Theology

Before moving on, it is important to remember that there are at least three levels of Christian theology:

Basic theology is the spontaneous theology of life. It is what we do when we know God experientially, and makes his plan of salvation our own. It is expressed also in ritual. It is living faith, or as others might put it, experienced faith. Without this fundamental theology the following levels are inoperative.

Reflective theology is that which becomes an explicit word about the faith that we live. It is the word that is shared with sisters and brothers of the

---

[8] Ibid.
[9] Ibid, pp. 16,20.

same faith, of other faiths or who do not profess any faith. The language differs in each case. This is the theology that we are taught in seminaries and convents.

Theological awareness is the word that illuminates, guides and accompanies believing action in history. It is the content of faith which is lived out and reflected upon. It is also the motor which energizes and transforms or converts our reality. At the first level, theology is life, ritual and witness. At the second level it is explanation, rationality, written word. The third level is prophecy, commitment and praxis.

Application to the indigenous world

Those of us who are both Christian and belong to indigenous groups have found the above theological reasoning to be useful when we address the mythical and symbolic world of our peoples and their religious beliefs and practices. When we have been asked for information by the Magisterium, we have given the following response:

> Indigenous theology is the complex of religious experience and knowledge that indigenous peoples possess and by means of which they explain, starting from thousands of years ago until now, their faith experience, within the context of their worldview and of the way other people perceive them. Indigenous theology is thus that common heritage of religious practices and popular theological wisdom that indigenous people draw upon in order to explain life's mysteries, both ancient and new. This is not, therefore, something new, nor strictly church related; it is a very ancient reality that has survived the vicissitudes of time.[10]

We understand the problematical nature of our use of the term "theology" when we speak of the religious beliefs of our peoples. On the one hand, within the church the belief still prevails that the word of the poor about God is too "imperfect" and too "contaminated" to merit consideration as genuine theological knowledge. On the other hand, indigenous intellectuals have serious reservations about applying to the intellectual production of our people the categories of Western thought, where "theology" originated. There is on the one side a fundamental prejudice regarding the value of popular tools of knowledge. On the other side there is fear of using thought patterns that, from the very start, look down upon indigenous people and their knowledge.

---

[10] Letter to the Congregation for the Doctrine of the Faith, 1992, p. 7.

Nonetheless, in order to overcome this impasse, an important sector of the indigenous peoples have dared to re-initiate the theological dialogue which it was not possible to engage in directly within the church 500 years ago. At that time, the theology of the vanquished was disqualified and roundly condemned as "diabolical" by the victors, in spite of the first attempts at communication in which our people gave evidence of their profound knowledge of God.[11]

We optimistically believe that conditions are favourable today for our people to bring the wealth of our age-old indigenous wisdom out from the caves, where it has maintained a clandestine and existence, and into the bright light of day. At the risk of being mistaken, we believe that it is worthwhile to attempt this dialogue between theologies. To act in secret is no longer the best survival strategy. We need to open up and seek useful alliances. Indigenous cultures are capable of being recreated and reformulated in dialogue with other cultures, not only for their own survival, but to help them become more dynamic. At this point some may ask questions such as the following: Do indigenous people really have the human and intellectual resources to engage in this dialogue? Is not dialogue too much to ask of two interlocutors who stand at such opposite extremes and are so unevenly matched? While one side in the debate have honed their skills over centuries, the other side are neophytes. We shall address these questions immediately.

The Nature of Indigenous Theology

The belief that the indigenous peoples of yesteryear lacked any real understanding of God was a very common mistake among scholars and missionaries during our colonial past. We continue to suffer the consequences of this today. Those scholars and missionaries took for granted that abstract ideas that derived from a Greek worldview were universal. The fact that they were not present among the indigenous peoples whom they encountered was taken as evidence that indians were simply not capable of understanding them. The perception was that if the indigenous world lacked adequate scientific theological tools, that theology itself was absent. At best, there could be only glimmerings and imprecise approximations of theology.

---

[11] Cp. "The Dialogue of the Twelve" in the writings of Fr. Bernardino de Sahagún.

This prejudice was based upon second or third hand information, and also on superficial ethnocentric observations. But a serious study of the ancient sources and of the present expressions of indigenous religiosity demonstrate the enormous theological understanding of our people which overflows into an impressive amount of theological production that is worthy of the best libraries. What happened was that the shortsightedness and closed mindedness of the colonizers found the religious symbols and ritual language of the people totally incomprehensible.

The original inhabitants of this continent—and their descendants today—were first of all theological agents and then expert stone-carvers, architects, mathematicians, astronomers, politicians and military strategists. In everything that they do or did the indigenous people emphasize the theological meaning that they perceive in life. Let us consider some examples from the geographical area that I know best, Mesoamérica, the region which reaches from the south of the United States to the north of Panamá.

Over a long period of material and spiritual development, the original peoples of this continent attained at every level, including their religion, admirable heights of knowledge. In fact, they gave evidences of having very refined tastes. We recognize, of course, that during the period of their greatest splendour there was a very great gap between the lucubrations of the priestly cast and the simple folk who found the high-flown language of the priests virtually unintelligibly. Still, we need to recognize that these lucubrations undergirded the entire belief system and that there existed specialized interpreters into the peoples' idiom.

The books of Chilam Balam of the Maya are part of that cryptic reading of history which, both in their time and today require translation into a more understandable idiom. When the supreme religious leaders—the *Halach Huinic* of the Maya and the *Tlatoanime* of the Aztecs—spoke of God to their people they always relied upon interpreters on behalf of the common folk, the *Macehualme*. This way of doing theology had its rationale, which ensured its continuance even after the priestly caste was destroyed. In fact, even outside of the Mesoamerican region the same scheme obtains. For example, among the Kunas of Panamá, the *Sailas* sing the traditions, even until now, and they are continuously being translated for the people by the *Argamar*.

In ancient times, and enduring somehow until today, there was a "polished" or "refined" theology and a "popular" theology which were not totally unrelated. Popular theology was nourished by refined theology which, in turn, borrowed the vital themes for its pedantic lucubrations from popular theology. Refined theology and its practitioners were very much appreciated in those days because they were the protectors of the community's secrets, which they also passed down to the community. Through the sacred songs of the *Halach Huinic, Tlatoani, Siriame*, and *Chagola* (their religious titles among different peoples), the common folk received—in cryptic language—the priestly message. Their utopian hopes were thus preserved, even while they were constantly being updated and applied to specific situations through the services of the interpreters. Through this form of theological exercise, their faith was transmitted in myths and sacred narrations that were chanted and ritualized in the great religious feasts.

When European christendom was imposed upon our peoples five hundred years ago, it took upon itself the task of eradicating institutional indigenous theology. This was done by waging outright war against the priests and wise-men, the sacred texts and places of our ancestors. Once the wise men have disappeared, reasoned the missionaries, the mass of common folk will no longer be able to resort to these "diabolical superstitions and practices."

The other side of this warfare was the strategy of hammering into the minds of the new generations a loathing for the beliefs of their parents and grandparents, thus predisposing them to a total acceptance of christianity. This is why the early missionaries were concerned to separate children from parents, in order to educate them into the new Christian worldview. The indigenous children were housed in dormitories, a very efficient way, indeed, of achieving cultural and religious penetration. This strategy very soon produced children and young people who were identified with christendom to the point of being willing to confront their elders in order to eradicate the ancient faith and implant a new one. This is what happened with the "child martyrs of Tlaxcala (México)". Inflamed with the fanatical teachings of the friars, they denounced the "idolatry" of their parents, going so far as to kill a representative of the indigenous religion, whom they identified as "the devil".[12]

Admittedly, this strategy was successful to the degree that it demolished the visible symbols of institutional theology—the temples, "idols," codices, priests, and ceremonies. However, it failed to significantly affect the common folk's beliefs and religiosity, which were not so easily recognizable

---

[12] Cp. the writings of Fr. Toribio de Benavente.

because they were so identified with the general culture of the people. Theological frameworks were privately maintained at personal and family levels. Ancient rites were secretly practised on the hill-tops and at night, or were allowed to interact with elements of christianity. The end result was the phenomenon which we now call "popular religion" or "religion of the people". There were, in fact, illustrious missionaries who, directly or indirectly, supported this kind of appropriation of christianity by the vanquished peoples.[13]

We can deduce from the above that, prior to the European conquest, there were among the peoples of this continent a variety of functions and categories that were used to express the varied theological activity of its members. Many of those categories and functions, although diminished or reformulated in a Christian context, hold today. From them we can, perhaps, catch a glimpse of their original meaning. For the sake of argument, allow me to suggest a few of these categories.

Indigenous Theological Categories

1. *Teutlatolli* is a Nahuatl (Aztec) term that can be translated both as "the God that speaks" and "speaking about God". It is the most abstract term in indigenous theology, and the most explicit vis a vis Christian theology. The term, and its equivalents in other mesoamerican languages, came into common usage during the time when the various ethnic groups in the region had achieved their highest level of economic development, enabling them to sustain a priestly caste that was totally dedicated to theology. This was the classic period (A.D. 300 to 800) of the empires of the Toltecs, of Tula and Teotihuacán, and of the Huastecs, Totonacs, Mayas, Zapotecs, and Mixtecs. Among each of these peoples, the concept of "speaking about God" flowered with a whole range of polished theological colours and shades. Much of this colouring and shading is no longer evident to us because of the destruction wrought by colonialism. Unfortunately, we can only speculate today concerning the fuller meaning of the concept. In the practice of priestly theology, which in essence was handling

---

[13] Editors's note. Other missioners, such as the Franciscan Diego de Landa, went to extremes of brutality to exterminate any lapse into the ancient religion. Cp. Inga Clendinnen, *Ambivalent Conquests: Maya and Spaniard in Yucatán - 1517-1570*. Cambridge University Press, 1987, pp. 72-92.

the word of God—the creative word of life—other theological expressions were used.

2. "Singing (*cuicoa*) the tradition", or the age-old wisdom of a people, is what the Nahuatl or Aztecs called *neltlamachiliztli* and *tlaneltoquilis*. Sacred singing is both an act of worship of the divinity and a very effective teaching tool for transmitting the oral tradition to the people. This task is assigned to the *Siríames* (among the Coras, Huicholes, Tepehuanes and Tarahumaras) and the *Sailas* (among the Kunas of Panamá). It is where the word, shared communally, nourishes the life of the people, and it is preserved largely in the songs of the poor.

3. "Dancing the myths" to awaken the life of God and of Mother Earth. Ritual dancing is a form of indigenous pedagogy which transmits the content of the faith. But as a ritual enactment of the myths, it is also the strongest way to bring to life and into practice what our peoples believe. It is both "god-speak" and "god-think". All of the native peoples have developed it fully, but in particular the nomadic, tribal and jungle peoples. It has a special place in popular religiosity. Processions and pilgrimages are kinds of ritual dances that activate popular beliefs.

4. "Rezadores" and "rezadoras" (men and women prayers) continue the tradition of the priests of old. Based upon their particular theology, they chanted elaborate prayers for every kind of need, as in the Biblical psalms. Today's "rezadores" use Christian prayers or creat new ones as needed.

We need to keep in mind that not all of the indigenous peoples achieved—or sustained—the same hights of theological development. Many of them did not enjoy, or at least were not able to maintain over the long term, the services of priests who were exclusively dedicated to the service of God. This meant that, in most cases, priests had to work at other tasks while they carried on their theological endeavours. This ensured that indigenous theology was profoundly involved in every aspect of the lives of the people. However, even though there may not always have been theologians, strictly speaking, there were theological functions and perspectives that were always present even as the people went about their everyday activities. I shall mention a few of these functions by way of example.

5. "Throwing the corn" symbolically expresses the ministry of discerning the future. In the early myths, the rite of *Oxomoco* was illustrated by a gourd full of corn in one hand and grains being cast to the wind by the other. It was a task equivalent to that of today's father confessor, personal counsellor, or spiritual director. The people turned to these ministers for discovering the will of God in the face of particular problems. There was

a secret to reading the scattered grains of corn which only the much sought after specialists knew. Colonial society, however, called them "sorcerers" and persecuted them tenaciously. They nonetheless continue to operate in many communities because the people trust them.

6. "Reading the calendar" is another form of divining the future, from one's date of birth. That task was attributed to *Cipactonal* in the myths of origin, where he is represented with a ritual knife in his hand and a flowered serpent in the other. To read the calendar is not only to be aware of a chronological date but to discover its theological meaning. This required expert men and women who were cognizant of the general and particular history of their people. This continues to have a strong theological relevance, particularly among the Mayan peoples. Mestizos have turned to the horoscope and such like in place of the ancient wise-men and women.

7. "Being a torch" (*ócutl*) that lights the pathway and doesn't smoke. This is the task of the wise-men, who dress in red and black, the colours of East and West—symbolical of God. They are the people's counsellors at every moment. In Mesoamerican legend, the wise-man par excellence was the mythological *Ketzalcoatl*, a wise Toltec ruler. Those who identify with him are called *Keketzalcoatl*.

8. "Being a mirror" (*tézcatl*) in which others can see their own faces and hearts. Not faces and hearts as other see them, but the faces and hearts that God has made for each of us. This is also the task of the wise-men, particularly with respect to the training of children and young people. The ancients developed elevated pedagogical concepts and methods which should be restudied as valid educational ideals for today.

9. Counselling is another form of theological activity. Counsel is offered for every occasion in life: at birth, puberty, marriage, investiture for a new task, and at death. It is everyone's responsibility, but in particular of the elders and leaders of the people. They dispense to each new generation the mature word (which the Nahuas call *huhuetlatolli* and the Zapotecs *didxagó-la*). Although counselling served civic and political needs, for the ancients it signified primarily pointing people toward the Sun—toward God. The Maya call this theological function "climbing up the ceiba tree" (their sacred symbol) to bring down its flowers—the fruits of life—to the people. The tree that sustains the heavens fulfills is function when counselling is performed by priests. The Aztecs associated this function with *Ketzalcoatl*.

10. "Guerra florida"—the blooms of war—was the most common Nahuatl (Aztec) expression for doing theology. Redefining warware, they addressed conflict positively in both the sacred and social spheres of life

because they considered human life to be a constant struggle between the bi-polar elements of reality: day-night, heaven-earth, man-woman, health-disease, etc. A theologian is one who understands, from God's perspective, the logic of these contradictions. He is able to decipher, by faith, the dialectic of life. This very dynamic theological concept eventually came to understand God as *Huitzilopochtli*, the warrior god. Human beings were part of this warfare—not necessarily in bloody fratricidal wars, but in the struggle for existence.[14]

11. To soar to the heavens as eagles, to stalk the earth like jaguars, or to glide serpent-like under earth and water, these were theological qualities that were very much appreciated by the ancients. They stemmed from the Mesoamerican worldview that conceives of total reality as a thirteen story edifice—four below earth and nine above. The true theologian is one who learns how to move upward and downward through all of these levels of human, divine and cosmic existence. Whoever can explain this reality to others understands the nature of the "Heart of Heaven and the Heart of Earth".[15]

12. Scanning the horizon to discover the signs of the times. Indigenous people believe that God speaks through nature. To be able to observe and understand nature, for the good of all the people, is a theological service of the first magnitude, because it is tied to agriculture and to the production of human sustenance. The Maya were very expert observers of nature—they had people who were exclusively dedicated to this service. Its is for this purpose that they constructed numerous observatories and developed astronomy and meteorology in relation to theology.

13. Deciphering dreams. The interpretation of dreams is a very special form of doing theology, not only in Abia Yala, but in other regions of the

---

[14] Editor's note. "Guerra florida"—flowery warfare—joins together the opposite concepts of death and life. For the lords of the Toltecs and their Yukateko Maya and Aztec successors, warfare was life-giving because the blood of the captives, sacrificed by the thousands in battle and on giant pyramids, fed the exacting deities who maintained the cosmic order and gave life to their people. Among the Aztecs, the memory of *Ketzacoatl*, the mythical peace-loving teacher-king of the ancient Toltecs who was ousted by a warrior cult, was gradually overshadowed by *Huitzilopochtli*, their sanguinary titular divinity. Not all Nahuatl, however, were comfortable with this spirituality of conquest; they worshipped a supreme Creator God for whose just rule they yearned (cp. Miguel León-Portilla, *Native Mesoamerican spirituality*. London, SPCK, 1980, p. 29, 241-247ff).

[15] Editor's note. *Corazón del Cielo y Corazón de la Tierra* (Heart of Heaven and Heart of Earth) is one of the Maya names for God.

world as well. Dreams relate both explicitly and implicitly to what goes on around us. Many peoples today make use of this mechanism to verify the divine word. Dreams, shared and analyzed collectively, are key factors in the theological analysis and critique of reality. They also motivate community commitment and action. Such is the case today with the Tarahumar people.

14. Keeping alive the historical memory. Perhaps the most dynamic and, at the same time, most traditional way of doing theology was the "recordación florida". This is the ongoing "blossoming of rememberance", i.e. the people' history of salvation as retold and reworked in each new context. This continues to be the most frequent theological resource of people who are keenly aware of their cultural and religious identity.

These are some of the variety of ancient theological tools that in many cases continue to be used by our peoples. It is merely a sampling from a small area of the Mesoamerican region. The Amazonian, Caribbean and Andean peoples could doubtless add many more elements to this list. It should be quite clear from the above that there is no such thing as mental categories and though patterns that are shared by all peoples. Each culture and race follows a unique process which conform to particular historical and cultural factors.

Stages in Indigenous Theology

Before we can proceed to a more detailed description of indigenous theology, we need to remember that there have three distinct "moments" in the theological development of our peoples:

"Native" or "original" theology

Prior to contact with christianity, indigenous sages were able to develop on their own and without interferences from other continents, the content and forms of expressing their faith. This theology, developed over a very long period of time, bears the marks of the history of each people and cultural region.

"Teología india", strictly speaking

During the 500 years of colonialism, native theology was harassed into resistance or forced into dialogue. It took refuge in mountain fastness, continuing to develop wherever possible, or became "syncretic", hiding behind a Christian mask.

After five hundred years: reawakening

In recent times, indigenous theology has been coming out from its caves and becoming a live option for many native people. This is the moment when there are new conditions for an enriching dialogue, because the world is turning its eyes to indigenous peoples as a "human reserve", from which societies and churches can be revitalized. Perhaps the term *teología india* or "indigenous theology" is no longer adequate and new expressions need to be found or created.

Unity and Diversity in Indigenous Theology

The expression "indigenous theology", in the singular, has been deliberately accepted as a generalization in order to simplify matters. It serves as a device to focus attention upon the prostrate condition of the native peoples of this continent, the common ground on which all indigenous peoples in our region can stand up against adversity, the source of which is singular, not plural. Having said this, we must recognize that there are numerous theologies that can be subsumed under the terminology of *teología india*. It is necessary to analyze the reasons for this diversity, while avoiding the trap of a pluralism that would divide us.

Indigenous plurality and historical diversity

Under the general category of "indios" or indigenous, enormous differences can be found even today. This is the result of the different degrees of development that were experienced before and during the colonial period. Starting with the Innuits or Eskimos of the northern polar regions and ending with the Mapuches and Patagonians in the extreme south there are more than 500 distinct peoples with their own languages and cultures, who when they speak of God, do it in very different ways. Consequently, might not one suppose that the same number of distinct theologies exist as well? This is certainly the case, but in appearance only. There are common thought patterns and ways of talking about God which allow us to discover large and well defined cultural blocks, although they can be variously defined, having developed in accordance with their environment.

Geographical location defines cultural groups

Cultural groups are defined primarily by geography. So we can speak of people who inhabit Polar, Prairie and Desert regions, in the North; the regions of Mesoamérica, the Caribbean, the Andes and the Amazon; the Southern Cone and the Extreme Southern region of the continent. Each cultural block has different material and spiritual characteristics.

Different histories—different cultures

Nomadic peoples develop cultural traits that are different from sedentary peoples; nor are purely agricultural peoples similar to urban cultures. To be for centuries the dominant culture in a region is not the same as being emigrants and refugees who are periodically on the move. Each of these situations conditions the development of peoples and makes for differences in culture and theology.

Different ways of relating to tradition — various approaches to theology

People who know and consciously act within a given indigenous tradition are different from those who are unable to verbalize their tradition; and they are even more distinct from those who neither know their tradition nor are bound by it. And there are still others who know their tradition and use it for their own benefit.

Relative contact with christianity - varying theological nuances

Convinced indigenous Christians who know what they believe are not the same as superficial and nominal Christians. These, in turn, are unlike the indigenous who have never been christianized, or who have turned their backs on christianity, or have become secularized over time. Each grouping will have different theological perspectives.

Various attitudes toward dialogue — different theological understandings

There are christianized indians who do not wish to dialogue with their indigenous past, while others will allow their Christian faith to be challenged by indigenous beliefs. There are non-christianized indigenous—or those who have been de-christianized by circumstances—that have not closed themselves to talking to Christians. Others in the same circumstances refuse any sort of dialogue with alien religions. All of this eventuates in a wide spread of different approaches to theology.

Intellectual formation divides indigenous theology

Some indigenous have been formed only in the traditions of their people, while others are also conversant in the alien tradition. A foreign tradition may be the only training that some indigenous persons have received; while others are lacking in any kind of intellectual stimulation.

Variations in theological language

Certain peoples communicate almost exclusively in the language of myth and ritual. Others express themselves in colloquial or experiential ways; while some use graphs, pictures and representations. Still others feel comfortable in the world of books.

Various Typologies

There are various ways of grouping indigenous theologies from a religious perspective.

A typology of indigenous identity

If we take into account the identity of the active subjects of theology the following typology emerges.

There is an indigenous theology that does not have a well defined source because it is a generic product of the people. It identifies itself to a large measure with *popular religious cultures* which function anonymously. But when the communities are organized and reflect upon their faith together, they produce a more defined theology which we could call *indigenous theology in community*. And when traditional religious leaders, usually illiterate, guide their communities, they produce an *indigenous theology for internal consumption only* which cannot be easily comprehended outside the community. But when new indigenous religious leaders, well educated, decide to do theology, they often do so with a wider public in mind. We might call this *export indigenous theology*.

Indigenous theology and ideology

Indigenous theologies of liberation. There is a tendency in "for export" indigenous theology to develop an indigenous theology with a liberationist motivation This approach is quite recent and we are only now discovering the mechanisms for dialogue, mutual support and shared approaches. The earlier presuppositions of liberation theology made it difficult for its theologians to perceive the liberating dimensions of culture. Today the situation is different and the Ecumenical Association of Third World Theologians (EATWOT) now includes indigenous theologians, and also fosters theological dialogue with indigenous communities.

Official indigenous theology. The recognition that the Latin American bishops granted to indigenous theology in Santo Domingo (1992) has opened new avenues for introducing it officially within the church. This seems to be the intention of those who are directing the Pastoral Theological Institute for Latin America (ITEPAL), if we are to judge from the recent projects and workshops on indigenous theology which are imparted to teachers and professors of seminaries and training centres.

Radical Protestant theologies. A somewhat more radical approach to recovering their indigenous past is practice by a handful of evangelical pastors. They encourage the use of indigenous sacred texts and traditional liturgy, making an effort to adapt them to the present context. They also foster the restoration of ancestral religions in their pure state without alien adulterations. This necessarily implies a process of de-christianization of the religiosity and theological expression of our peoples. Because of this, they do not speak of indigenous theology but of "native" or "original" theology. While the idea excites some indigenous protestant leaders, one wonders whether theirs is a genuine response to what is happening in their churches and communities or whether it is the concern of only a small elite who are attracted to millenarian ideologies.

Indigenous Catholic theology. Finally, for years there has been a movement of priests, nuns and Christian pastors who have taken upon ourselves the task of rediscovering our religious roots and to open spaces in the churches for dialogue with the Gospel. In this context we speak not so much concerning a pure theology from the past, but of an "indigenous Christian theology", that is to say, a reworking of the indigenous worldview in a Christian setting. We see this as part of the struggle to reconcile—through a new and vital synthesis of the different forms of God and their religious expressions—the two loves that have converted our hearts into a battlefield of gods and religions. Which is to say that we do not renounce either love but rather lift up and empower both of our identities, indigenous and Christian.

In this exhausting and difficult task we have been joined by grassroots indigenous ministers (stewards, brotherhood members, overseers, catechists, celebrants, etc.), non-indigenous pastoral agents, bishops and advisors from the church. So we move ahead on the strength of their support. At the same time, we are quite aware of the fact that by dialoguing we run the risk of loosing our indigenous perspective—of becoming entrapped in a Western Christian rationale. We need to be alert to these dangers and able to discern when dialogue is proceeding apace, and under what conditions, and when to insist upon respect for divergent positions. This autonomy must be upheld irrespective of the stand of the church.

Roman Catholic Indigenous Theology

At the risk of oversimplifying I suggest the following typology of indigenous theologies vis a vis the Catholic Church. The purpose of this recapitulation is to relate the various theological contributions to each other.

Christianized indians with a traditional Christian worldview

This group of indigenous Catholics does not want to have anything to do with the mythical and symbolic world of their ancestors. They became members of Catholic Action and were taught to turn against their indigenous identity as catechists around the time of Vatican II. Their conversion was for them a total renunciation of the "witch-craft of their ancestors", so they have no desire to return the past. Their self-identity and image of God is

totally Western without any concession to the indigenous world which, as
far as they are concerned, is completely dead and should remain that way.

Christianized indians and indigenized christianity

There are Christian indians who are dedicated to indigenizing their faith.
These are the new catechists and pastoral servants who have been recently
trained to become more open to the indigenous worldview. Aware of their
own basic Christian identity, they are trying to fit their ancestral beliefs into
Christian molds.

Indigenous Christian apologetics

Some christianized indigenous interact with Christian beliefs in order to
demonstrate that their recently discovered indigenous faith is indeed
Christian. They are the more aware members of the indigenous peoples,
community activists who have added indigenous religiosity to their cause.
These are also indigenous religious leaders who are convinced that Christ
became indian and has been with the indigenous and other peoples throughout their history. They believe that pre-Christian indigenous values were
seeds of the saving presence of God among us that need to be cultivated
today to produce fruit in our midst.

Non-christian indians in dialogue with christianity

Some indians, while not Christian, want to dialogue with christianity in
order to broaden their knowledge of God. They are the traditional religious
leaders in our communities who do not see christianity as a threat to their
ancient faith, but as a possible strategic ally and contributor to their survival
today. They do not see the Christian God as an enemy but as a different
manifestation of the only true God. For this reason, they desire to dialogue
with Christians for the good of all of humanity.

Total rejection of Christianity

In order to maintain their religious autonomy, some indigenous who were
never christianized or who have turned their backs upon christianity, are
refusing to have any dialogue with Christians. They are usually persons who
have had negative experiences with the church. They consider christianity

to be essentially colonialist, because of its proselitistic and missionary zeal. For this reason they are convinced that christianity will never cease to be the enemy of the indigenous religions. A corollary of this is their conviction that we indigenous will never be truly at liberty to rebuild our destiny until we free ourselves from our harmful dependence upon the church. Liberation, then, means to reject christianity and free one's self from the churches, whatever their denomination. This is clearly an extreme position which testifies to the bitterness that they feel at the abuses that our ancestors suffered at the hands of the church. Although it is a minority view, it has won the support of a few indigenous intellectuals among our people.

Risks for Indigenous Theology

The same as with any theology, indigenous theology, faces many risks.

1. *Escapism.* There is always the risk that indigenous theologies will become nothing more than an escape from reality—mere refuges from life's intractable problems. It is a risk that is inherent in all religions.

2. *Isolation.* Similarly, indigenous theologies run the risk of enclosing themselves within a ghetto or island—of isolating themselves from other ethnic groups or other disadvantaged sectors of society.

3. *Messianism.* The above attitude implies a degree of messianic pretension which may lead certain indigenous peoples to believe that they have a mission to save humanity. This is particularly a temptation for the larger indigenous groups, who have always looked upon themselves as a cut above the rest.

4. *Fundamentalism.* There is the further risk that indigenous theologies may be caught up in a kind of "archeological idealism", i.e. a fundamentalistic reading of our sacred texts and religious traditions by our leaders. They are tempted to live in the past rather than face up to a present time that has changed us radically from the self-contained peoples that we were long ago to indigenous groups who survive in a profoundly asymmetric relationship with the whole of society.

5. *Ritualism* is another risk for indigenous theology—and for christianity as well. It is a cyclical approach to theology and liturgy that overlooks the changing historical reality which is lineal. This kind of theology serves only to explain a symbolic world, but is not helpful in interacting with the real world.

6. *Disintegration*. There is real risk that indigenous theologies, having come out of hiding may fall apart. They could disintegrate when they become part of the mainstream of history, when they modernise, or are dressed up in non-symbolical language in response to their dialogue with other, stronger theologies. When things that have been hidden or buried for a very long time are suddenly exposed to sunlight they are in danger of disintegrating. They require a prior preparation stage to immunize them against alien matter in the atmosphere. The same thing must happen to indigenous theologies.

7. *Ideological manipulation*. Finally, there is the risk of indigenous theologies—their sources and documents—being used for ideological purposes that are totally alien to their original objectives. This could happen in a supposedly "pure" indigenous milieu or under the impact of the vested interests of the dominant society and of the Christian churches.

Challenges for Indigenous Theology

This closing section will be brief because it awaits further development during future meetings on indigenous theology. Our theology needs to be challenged in the following areas:

1. *The challenge of identity*. It is inconceivable that indigenous theology could be produced by persons and communities that are not sure of their identity.

2. *The challenge to be specific*. We must be more precise in defining our theology and expressing its content. We need to define what is specifically theological in our reflection and awareness.

3. *The challenge to be relevant*, i.e. to provide answers for the problems of today. Ours is a theology of life which addresses the lives of people—a daily search for adequate responses to historical problems. However elegantly formulated, when indigenous theology becomes too elaborate—too much debating on matters that bear no relation to the peoples' everyday struggles—it says nothing to the indigenous communities.

4. *The challenge of linking past and present*. We need to make the ancient sources accessible to our people who, for the most part, have lost direct contact with their ancient religious traditions. They must be helped, systematically and seriously, to link directly to these primary sources of their identity.

5. *The challenge and threat of modernity*; with its strong dose of secularism and individualism modernity is doing much harm to our people. While it is impossible to avoid its influence any longer, how can we learn from the positive contributions of modernity while avoiding being destroyed by it?

6. *The challenge of comunication.* We need to master the tools of "scientific" language. Our people need to know how to use the non-symbolic language of modern society so that we can dialogue with the rest of the world. How do we hold our own in discussions with non-indigenous peoples without doing violence to our own theological language?

7. *The challenge of intercultural dialogue.* Given the inevitable process of the mixing of peoples and cultures on a worldwide scale, we need to learn how to dialogue, not only with peoples like ourselves, but with persons from more technically developed cultures.

8. *The challenge of interreligious dialogue.* Our peoples have always been ready to dialogue with those of other religions. The proof of this is the synthesis that we have created with christianity over the past five hundred years. The dominant religions, however, have never been open to dialogue. But there are signs that this is beginning to change. How can we foster interreligious dialogue in favourable conditions for our peoples? We shall need to prepare the way for it.

9. *The challenge of ecclesial identity.* Those of us who are committed to indigenous theology while we remain loyal to the church—as persons and as members of the ecclesiastical institution—need to walk alongside our church in this process. This implies that we must accept the church as both a restraint and a support for our actions. How do we act as church people without allowing this to be a stumbling block and hindrance to the walk of our peoples?

These are some of the challenges that we can foresee as we move ahead with encouraging the theological pilgrimage of our indigenous peoples. Some of these challenges are on the way to being worked out by indigenous Christians who remain in the service of the people. Others will have to be confronted with audacity and a creative spirit. Our accumulated experience in the past will, of necessity, be the point of reference as we search for new avenues for expressing our age old theology.

By Way of Conclusion

The fruits of our consultations on indigenous theology in Latin America are being widely diseminated. They have been collected, and then distributed through various means, first to the participants, and then to all other indigenous brothers and sisters and to friends of the indigenous cause in church and the wider society. There can be no doubt that the indigenous theologies of today are opening new paths for now and for the future. But our efforts can be much more effective if we join forces with other sectors of Latin American society so as to bring about, for all the peoples of the world, God's plan—the "Big house", *Xochitlalpan* or *Tierra sin males*[16] that our ancestors dreamed about.

---

[16] "Xochitlalpan" (Nahuatl, Aztec) or "tierra sin males" (Spanish) signifies "land without ills".

CHAPTER NINE

BIRTH OF LATIN AMERICAN INDIGENOUS THEOLOGY

Edward L. Cleary

"Indians cultivate a great respect for life, for persons, for other living things, for what exists. Everything has life, a spirit, sentiments. Taking possession of things is not a goal since a person is not the owner of them, but their servant". The author, a Dominican priest from the United States who has served in Bolivia, is known for his numerous books and articles on the Latin American churches.[1] Fr. Cleary currently lectures in the Latin American Studies Program at Providence College in Rhode Island. This unpublished essay is used with the author's permission.

Introduction

Diego Irarrázaval attended St. George College in Santiago, Chile, as a member of the privileged classes in Chile, and later the School of Divinity at the University of Chicago, as a member of the Holy Cross order. Irarrázaval gained the attention of his professors at Chicago, returned in the early 1970s to Chile to become a participant in the left wing of the liberation theology movement (with Pablo Richard, Sergio Torres, and others), and shifted focus to working with Aymara indians at what seems like the end of the world, near Puno, Perú.

His presence and his writings help to explain the expansion of Latin American, if not liberation, theology to the indians of Latin America. Whether or not theology of liberation will diminish with the social and ecclesial changes which are taking place in Latin America or because of the advanced age of its founders, liberation theology has another life. It opened doors to other forms of theology in Latin America. A major expression of

---

[1] *Crisis and Change: The Church in Latin America Today* (Maryknoll, N.Y.: Orbis Books, 1984); co-edited with Hannah Stewart-Gambino, *Conflict and Competition: The Latin American Church in a Changing Invironment* (Boulder: Lynne Rienner, 1992) and *Power, Politics and Pentecostals in Latin America* (Boulder, CO., Westview Pres, 1996).

this influence is indigenous theology, or better, Maya, Andean, or other theologies which rest upon distinct cosmologies which are not European.

This chapter fulfills two purposes. It examines briefly a major set of religions of Latin America, religions which express christianity in a manner distinct from mainline European or North American religion. In contrast to dominant christianity which has lost touch with the earth, healing, and, to some extent, connectedness with one's ancestors, these religions offer an alternative which millions of practitioners consider superior. In addition to Christian versions, indigenous religions are also be non-Christian. Telling the difference has been one of the tasks of Diego Irarrázaval.

A second purpose of this chapter is to mark the birth of Latin American indigenous theology. Liberation theology set the example in modern times of contextualizing theology, making theology rest clearly on foundations which not primarily European. The initiative of liberation theologians has influenced theologians and activists in various regions and has helped to spawn other Latin American theologies.

In Latin America a second generation of contextual theology is beginning to appear, slowly, only in outline, but definitely taking shape, and in time for the 21st century. This theology is being midwifed by theologians and anthropologists steeped in the spirit of Vatican II, slowly and carefully nurturing theology done at the grassroots in indian communities. These outsiders are listening and expressing what they hear. And they are awaiting the emergence of theologians who are indian. These indian religions are strong and have been around a long time. What is new is, first, the present-day forms of indian religion; second, our perceptions of these distinct forms of religion; and third, efforts to express the beliefs of the people in a reflective form.

Seeking a comprehensive view of indian religion and theology is an extraordinarily difficult task for many reasons. Indians have had to shield their religion: the sacred should be guarded from the gaze of outsiders. This hooded quality bred further misunderstandings, as outsiders pointed to such practices, as drinking associated with rituals. Further, indian languages are many and not typically learned in schools.

Indian Magnitude and Awakening

The Fifth Centenary of Columbus's encounter with Latin America and the Caribbean caught the attention of a great many persons in and out of the region. Many voices were speaking during the centenary. A new voice from the grassroots was heard during the centenary. Previously mute or pushed to the margins of society, indians of Latin America spoke up and were heard.[2] No, they did not want a celebration, but penance for the devastation of the Spaniards. They gained a hearing in Europe to the extent that the Swedish Nobel committee granted its Peace award to Rigoberta Menchú Tum, a Guatemalan indian. John Paul II in his address on October 12, 1992, emphasized the human-rights violations 500 years ago and the present pitiable situation of indians today.[3] But Menchú and other leaders speaking for an indian movement do not solicit pity. They wish to be seen for what they are: moving spirits of their own destiny, protagonists of memory and resistance.

Latin American indians, by and large, do not live on reservations. They number more than 40 million, many more than the two million indians in Canada and the United States. They form about half or more of the population of four countries, mostly in highland regions, of Guatemala in Central America, and Perú, Bolivia, and Ecuador in South America. This remoteness has a lot to do with their survival through the last centuries because the indians, in closest contact with Spaniards and Portuguese, largely disappeared. Despite imported diseases, abuse, and the rigors of their characteristic dry land and mountainous environments, indians in these countries have been gradually building up their numbers to reach a high level in modern times. The indians of these four countries have traveled widely and have migrated in great numbers, helping to reshape the structures and tone of cities like La Paz, Lima, and Guatemala City.[4] They ride the subways and work on construction in Buenos Aires and have come in the last twenty years by the hundreds of thousands to the United States. They give further lie to the stereotype that Latinos or Hispanics are all one

---

[2] See, for example, the indigenous response at a consultation for CELAM (Latin American Bishops Council) in Mexico by CENAMI (Centro de Ayuda a Misiones Indígenas) in *Misiones Extranjeras* 116 (March-April 1991), pp. 169-175; "Indigenous Declaration", *LADOC New Keyhole Series* 3, 5 (Oct. 1988), pp. 49-50.

[3] Many organizations have documented human rights violations to indigenous peoples. See, for example: Amnesty International, *The Americas: Human Rights Violations against Indigenous Peoples* (New York: Amnesty International, 1992).

[4] For La Paz, see: Xavier Albó, Thomas Greaves, and Godofredo Sandoval, *Chukiyawu: La cara aymara de La Paz* (La Paz, Cuadernos de Investigación CIPCA; Centro de Investigación y Promoción del Campesinado, Nos. 20, 22, 24, 29, 1981-1987). A number of authors deal with the indigenization of cities in *América indígena*, esp. 51, Nos.2-3 (combined issue) and No. 4, 1991.

people.

Indoamericans, who are not Latinos or Hispanics in origin, are making their presence felt. Indians occupied México City's Zócalo, the central plaza, on October 12, 1992, to the embarrassment of ruling-party politicians who prefer to decide how indians will demonstrate. But indian political activity was growing in México and elsewhere before the quincentennial year. In June 1990, the movement gained enough power to convulse national life in Ecuador where conflicts had been controlled by the ruling elite and indians have been compliant. Thousands of indians paralyzed a large part of the country for more than a week.[5] In October 1990 Bolivian indians transversed a large part of the country, starting in the tropics and ending with thousands joining them for the entrance to La Paz. Indians made clear that they want power and politics to serve them.

Close observers can point to processes beginning well before the Centenary by which indigenous movements: 1) have gained strength in numbers and organization; 2) are non-violent but determined; 3) are increasingly aware of native religion; and 4) are speaking for themselves and not through non-native anthropologists or others.

Darcy Ribeiro, a Brazilian and a "great man" in anthropological circles, furnished the right phrase for the movement when he labelled indian groups as "pueblos testimonio" (witness peoples),[6] those who managed to maintain to the present day the most profound roots of the region. Stephen Judd characterizes the groups as giving witness to other values than those of the modern world in the survival of ancient and often clandestine cultures".[7] Many in the indian movements prefer to speak of themselves as "pueblos de resistencia". The degree and mechanisms of resistance are seldom assessed.

The nightmares of comfortable residents of La Paz or Quito that indians are on the edge of the city waiting to take over have been fueled by history in which blood was let flow to maintain the hegemony of the city over the

---

[5] For issues involved, see: Les Field, "Ecuador's Pan-Indian Uprising", *Report on the Americas*, 25, 3 (Dec. 1991), pp. 39-44.

[6] Darcy Ribeiro, "Introducción: La cultura", in Roberto Segre, ed., *América Latina en su arquitectura*, 2nd ed. (México: Unesco and Siglo XXI, 1978), p. 13.

[7] Stephen Judd, in Alfred T. Hennelly, "From Lamentation to Project: The Emergence of an Indigenous Theological Movement in Latin America", *Santo Domingo and Beyond* (Maryknoll, N.Y.: Orbis, 1993), pp. 226-227.

countryside.[8] The Quito daily, *El Comercio*, wrote that the 1990 event was the sixth indian "insurrection". CONAIE, a large-scale indian organization of Ecuador, by contrast, recounted a history with 145 insurrections. The view that the indians of Latin America had been peacefully put in their places after the conquest clearly was faulty.

Forty million indians are not waiting to take over. While their numbers have been sufficient to have an impact on provincial and national politics, there has not been, until recently, the conditions sufficient for indian movements, not even within cultural groups nor within Pan-indian movements. In a word, a great deal of life for indians in the last five centuries has been concentrated in local communities. Indians, it used to be said, did not even know they were indians; rather they were from Otovalo or Yura.[9] The oppression inflicted on the indian populations worked well to concentrate their energies on survival. This meant focusing on the local community and extended family structure for getting along, hoping for a small surplus to trade. But neither were the indians passive peasants. As changes took place in world systems, they also responded to changes in global economic and stratification systems. The sixfold increase in schools in Bolivia,[10] many of which Bolivian indians help build with their own hands, in the years immediately after the 1952 Revolution, was a response to these changes.

Although able to mobilize thousands for specific events or issues, indian movements are small in numbers, relatively new in national prominence,[11]

---

[8] Catholic bishops have called this dominance "internal colonialism". Second General Conference of Latin American Bishops, (Medellín), *Document on Peace* (Bogotá: General Secretariat of CELAM, 1970), nos 2-7.

[9] However, indians even in very remote areas had many ties with a larger world. See, for example: Roger Neil Rasnake, *Domination and Cultural Resistance: Authority and Power among an Andean People* (Durham, N.C.: Duke University Press, 1988), esp. pp. 260-276.

[10] For the effect of the Revolution on education, see, for example: Jonathan Kelley and Herbert S, Klein, *Revolution and the Rebirth of Inequality: A Theory Applied to the National Revolution in Bolivia* (Berkeley: University of California Press, 1981), pp. 131-135.

[11] But not in terms of movements and rebellions largely overlooked by historians. See, for example: Víctor Hugo Cárdenas, "La lucha de un pueblo", in Xavier Albó, comp., *Raices de América: El mundo Aymara* (Madrid: Unesco, 1988), pp. 495-534.

and sometimes fragile in unifying factors.[12]   As Carol Smith says of
Guatemala: "A 'Maya nationalist movement' is so young that it is difficult
to know exactly what it is and where it is going. But it will likely play a
major role in the future of this country".[13] The reason for this surge is
found in the rediscovery of what Smith calls "their proper identity" in
recent years. Key to understanding the groups is *memory* of their struggle,
especially since colonial times. This resurgence also affects indigenous
theology.

Indigenous Religion

Changes in Catholic theology expressed in Vatican II opened a new way for
approaching Latin American native religion. Theologians began to see that
God also was working in civilizations before the arrival of christianity to a
region. The "seeds of the Word of God" were there. Further, the native
cosmovision had to be one of the starting points for theology and a different
approach to ministry to the indigenous was called for. In the Suthern Andes
region of Perú, Maryknoll priests and sisters from various congregations:
1) abandoned the customary practice of living in rectories and convents to
live in ordinary houses as part of the indigenous community; 2) went to
listen to Aymara explanations for life and faith, of their ceremonies and
their motivations for entering into ritual; and 3) fit in with the indigenous
rhythm of life, for example, accepting the role of the native *yatiri* (priest-
healer) in seeking healing.[14]

Religion has been a major element in indian identity. Here an extraordi-

---

[12] For an account of the transition from paternalism to "indianismo", see: José
Alcina Franch, cp. *Indianismo e indigenismo en América* (Madrid: Alianza
Editorial/Quinto Centenario), 1990.

[13] Smith, "Maya Nationalism", *Report on the Americas*, 25, 3, (Dec. 1991), p.
29. See earlier accounts: Arturo Arias, "El movimiento indígena en Guatemala:
1970-1983", in Daniel Camacho and Rafael Menjívar, eds., *Movimientos populares
en Centroamérica* (San José, C.R.: Editorial Universitaria Centroamericana, 1985),
pp. 62-119; and "Changing Indian Identity: Guatemala's Violent Transition to
Modernity", in Carol Smith, ed., *Guatemalan Indians and the State: 1540 to 1998*
(Austin: University of Texas Press, 1990, pp. 258-286. See also Ricardo Falla, "El
movimiento indígena", *ECA - Estudios Centroamericanos* 33, (June-July 1978), pp.
437-461.

[14] Esteban Judd, "La inculturación en el contexto andino: Rasgos de una
presencia pastoral distinta", *Misiones Extranjeras* 116 (March-April, 1990), pp. 105-
121.

narily sensitive judgement is called for to avoid the stereotypes of indian religion. One convention, poetically embellished by Ted Lewellen, is: "Thus the religion is fading in bits, like a great Cheshire cat, its body—the theological system—gone; its stripes—the spirits—fading; so that only the grin of ritual will endure. But ritual, too, shows at least incipient signs of dissolving".[15] Other stereotypes have been invented by anthropologists and missionaries and been repeated by Catholics and protestants, as Jacques Monast and Quentin Nordyke.[16]

While indian religion has been diluted or has disappeared in some individuals, especially those in contact with cities, indian religion also flourishes. It has many practitioners and many forms. There are commonalities enough to allow for generalizations about the religion of large cultural groups, as Aymara, Quechua, and Maya but even the characterizing of these groupings is tentative, as those familiar with the warrior tone of the Ki Che' Maya as contrasted to the more pacifist proclivity of the Q'eqchi' Maya will attest.

Christian indian religion exists alongside non-Christian. So in Mesoamérica there are Maya Maya and Maya Católicos.[17] Telling the difference between them is a patient process of listening and evaluation.[18] In practice Diego Irarrázaval tends to accept as person as Christian who is baptized and identifies himself or herself as Christian. Non-Christian or "Aymara

---

[15] Ted Lewellen, *Peasants in Transition: The Changing Economy of the Peruvian Aymara: A General Systems Approach* (Boulder: Westview, 1978), p. 93.

[16] Jacquest Monast, *Los indios aimaras: Evangelizados o solamente bautizados?* (Buenos Aires: Carlos Lohlé), 1972; cp. Quentin Nordyke, *Animistic Aymaras and Church Growth* (Newberg, Ore.: Barclay Press, 1972).

[17] Many persons of Mayan background are pentecostal. Given the apparent pentecostal rejection of key elements of Mayan culture, as "los antepasados", the question arises of whether they retain Mayan identity. Richard N. Adams maintains that they do, in "Strategies of Ethnic Survival in Central America", in Greg Urban and Joel Sherzer, eds., *Nation-States and Indians in Latin America* (Austin: University of Texas Press, 1991), p. 200.

[18] Peter Schineller, S.J., suggests a "hermeneutical circle" in which three poles - the Christian message, the cultural situation, and the pastoral agents - are used in evaluation. See his "Inculturation and Syncretism: What Is the Real Issue?", *International Bulletin of Missionary Research* 16, 2 (April, 1992), pp. 49-53.

religious thought", for him, would be a theology which is based on Aymara ceremonial, leadership, or wisdom, with scant or no Christian component.[19]

Maintenance and change

Searching out and systematizing Aymara, Quechua, or Maya religious thought before Spanish influence has entailed a great effort but may help only marginally in describing indian religious thought which flourishes today. Within indian communities religion is a living enterprise which has changed over time, subject to the influence of other cultures (transistor radios have been common for 30 years) and to social and economic changes. But observers believe there is an identifiable Aymara or Q'eqchi' Maya cosmovision existing today which gives distinctive shape to a particular religion, its beliefs and practices. How is it that many ethnic groups have maintained a way of life, "or more specifically, symbolic configurations and complex modes of organization—which is derived from their... past and which distinguishes them from the hispanicized world of the 'modern' classes inhabiting the towns and cities?", as Roger Rasnake asks.[20] It would be strange if this religion did not bear similarity to the views of the Inca or Maya religion before Columbus because many of the same symbols and realities are there: mountains, sky, animals are still there and survival, then as now, is still problematic.

At the heart of indian cultures in Latin America, and one of the bases of theology, are distinct cosmologies. These views of the world persist through time and help to explain why, as Robert V. H. Dover states: "Andean indigenous communities remain recognizably Andean even after half a millennium of forced exposure to Western systems of thought".[21] Indian culture has persisted and emerged. The study of the mechanisms by which this is accomplished have led to intriguing studies, as those of Dover and colleagues, Rasnake, Nancy Farriss, Richard N. Adams, Inga

---

[19] Diego Irarrázaval, "Teología Aymara: Implicaciones para otras teologías", *Revista Latinoamericana de Teología* 9, 25 (Jan.- Apr., 1992), p. 100.

[20] Robert Rasnake, *Domination*, p. 4.

[21] Robert V.H. Dover, "Introduction", in Dover, et al, eds., *Andean Cosmologies through Time: Persistence and Emergence* (Bloomington, Ind.: Indiana University Press, 1992), p. 1.

Clendinnen, and Steve J. Stern.[22] The cosmologies are fundamental in explaining differences between the theologies which are emerging from Indoamerica.

These cosmologies also help explain why indian theology differs from "mestizo" theologies, like theology of liberation, and from European theologies, medieval or modern. *Indigenous theology is not western christianity to which Andean or Mesoamerican elements have been added.* Rather, as Dover says: "There is a structural and processural continuity in Andean cosmological thought through which non-Andean cultural features become systematically Andean".[23] So Christian concepts are reworked and assimilated as Andean. (Among Andean religions, one presumes differences between Aymara and Quechua, as a minimum.)

In a central debate of the Latin American church during the process leading up to the CELAM conference at Santo Domingo, a question was raised about the presumption made by many bishops (and many academics in the United States) of "Catholic substratum" in Latin America, giving Latin America a distinctive identity.[24] Many Catholic bishops and John Paul II, as well, assume that Latin America has a special unity, owing to "una alma católica". Pedro Morandé, has been a major figure among sociologists, and in the forefront of Catholics on the right, attempting to demonstrate a Latin American Catholic cultural synthesis.[25] This perspective is also used to paint protestants

---

[22] Dover, et al, eds., *Andean Cosmologies*; Rasnake (above); Nancy Farriss, *Maya Society under Colonial Rule: The Collective Enterprise of Survival* (Princeton, N.J., Princeton University Press, 1984); Adams, "Strategies", pp. 181-206; Inga Clendinnen, *Ambivalent Conquests: Maya and Spaniard in Yucatan, 1517-1570* (New York, Cambridge University Press, 1987); Steve J. Stern, *Perú's Indian Peoples and the Challenge of Spanish Conquests: Huamanga to 1640* (Madison, Wis., University of Wisconsin Press, 1982).

[23] Dover, "Introduction", in Dover, et al, eds. *Andean Cosmologies*, p. 2.

[24] Prominent examples include: Glen Dealy, "Prologomena on the Spanish American Political Tradition", *Hispanic American Historical Review* 48 (Feb. 1968), pp. 37-58 and *The Latin Americans: Spirit and Ethos* (Boulder: Westview, 1992); Howard Wiarda, "Toward a Framework for the Study of the Ibero-Latin Tradition: The Corporative Model", *World Politics* 25 (Jan. 1973), pp. 206-235.; and Richard Morse, "The Heritage of Latin America", in Louis Hartz, ed., *The Founding of New Societies* (New York: Harcourt, Brace, and World, 1964), pp. 123-172. Claudio Véliz and Lawrence Harrison have written in the same vein.

[25] Pedro Morandé, *Cultura y modernización en América Latina Ensayo sociológico acerca de la crisis del desarrollismo y su superación* (Madrid: Ediciones Encuentro, 1987) and "La síntesis cultural hispánica indígena", *Teología y Vida* 32:1-2 (1991), pp. 43-59.

as outsiders disrupting the soul of Latin America. In the debate, though, the indigenist point of view was heard clearly, perhaps for the first time in the main chambers of the Latin American Catholic Church. As Stephen Judd points out: "One's Catholic identity, they affirmed, owes as much to an encounter between the gospel and the Maya, Quechua, or Ayamara culture and religious worldview as it does to an evangelization from a European centered worldview".[26]

Popular religion, the world of rosaries, devotions, and statues, also was presumed to be largely one world, that or peasants and other ordinary persons in Hispanic America. Liberation theologians at first ignored this world and later discovered it. None have been mined this area as a starting-point of theologizing more ardently than Hispanic theologians in the United States. The presumption of unity of popular or traditional religion breaks down, though, in examining indigenous religion. Again, those with indigenous sensitivities feel obliged to say, this is not hispanicized religion but a distinct form of christianity, resting on a cosmology which differs from Iberian. No wonder, then, that: "In Yucatán there was almost complete lack of the apparatus of popular piety—the rosaries, the shrines, the images—so abundant in México".[27]

Lack of acknowledgement of the distinctness of indian worldview has hindered the recruitment of indians for leadership in the Catholic Church. Not only the cosmologies but the structures of thought also differ. Curt Cadorette describes this as difference in gestalt, a totality of objects and patterns of thought which make Aymara religious views differ from Mayan or European.[28] Frank Salomon speaks of the "cultural doubleness" of the Andean and European worlds which confronted one another and could not be integrated as long as both modes of discourse retained their essential integrity.[29]

One does not have to define well the differences to understand that they exist and may explain, in part, why in 500 years so few indians have become priests and today many do not persevere in seminaries. Carlos Berganza believes that in the case of the Mayan students, "The structures

---

[26] Judd, in Hennelly, *Santo Domingo*, p. 229.

[27] Clendinnen, *Ambivalent*, p. 191.

[28] Cadorette, interview, phone, Oct. 26, 1993.

[29] Frank Salomon, "Chronicles of the Impossible: Notes on Three Peruvian Indigenous Historians" in Rolena Adorno, ed., *From Oral to Written Expression: Native Andean Chronicles of the Early Colonial Period* (Syracuse, N.Y.: Maxwell School of Citizenship and Public Affairs, Syracuse University, 1982), pp. 9-39.

of their thought are entirely unsuited for 'Western' philosophy and theology of the seminary. They cannot persevere as Maya. Mayan Catholic priests who seem to last are the ones who turn their backs on their culture".[30]

Death and Resurrection

An extended parallel may aid in understanding differences in theological outlooks. Nothing is more fundamental to christianity than death and resurrection. When first viewed by outsiders the celebrations of Holy Week, as in the Andes, appear to be highly weighted toward Good Friday with an emphasis on suffering. (This alarmed Protestants, as John Mackay, many years ago and contemporary Catholics after the reforms of Vatican II.) After the build-up of processions and emotions centered on the cross, Easter seems to be an afterthought, or a gradual deflation from the emotional high of Good Friday. The question persists that perhaps the Aymaras do not have an understanding of Easter.

They would have to have a sense of resurrection to be Christian. And they do. Death and resurrection for many Aymaras means reincorporation of themselves in the community, signified for them especially in the Good Friday ceremonies. Aymaras do not have a highly developed sense of self, as Westerners do. For Europeans and Americans, resurrection may mean an exaltation of self. It may be that Ayamara indians not only have a defensible, but a commendable view of christianity, one of inclusion and incorporation, rather than raising up or glorifying self.

Moreover, as Cadorette, Judd, and others have suggested, many Andean indians have a vivid sense of the future, a future in which they will have a part through death and resurrection. Contemporary Perúvian Catholic intellectuals translate this as "utopia". Steve Stern describes this persistent view as it seized indians in the mid-1500s: "the desparate vision of an imminent, totally comprehensive transformation which, by power of super-natural forces and the insurgents' own moral purification, will soon destroy an evil social order and regenerate a new perfect world in its place".[31]

The Maya in the Yucatán held a similar forceful view of their future, as Inga Clendinnen describes: "When the Lord Jesus descends in the 'Province of the Yucatan,' then at last there will be an end to the domination of foreigners and of submission to their extractions. Then the rule of the Lord

---

[30] Interview, Guatemala City, Feb. 16, 1993.

[31] Stern, *Peru's*, p. 67.

Jesus, and of Maya Lords, will begin".[32]

These strong views of a reconstruction of the world in the future contribute some force to the heroic effort of maintaining a subordinate culture over a long period of time. These indian visions also foreshadow a theology which would be constructed from this culture, elements for a thisworldly view with a strong social justice orientation.

It is premature, though, to categorize Latin American indigenous theology as liberation theology, as has been attempted,[33] when the theology is not yet expressed systematically, when liberation praxis may not exist in the communities from which the theology arises, and when the theology rests on different fonts than "classic" liberation theology. Indigenous culture and religion has a highly conservative bent and its own imprint (in the Skinnerian sense). It will develop on its own.

But, beyond maintenance of traditional visions, a new world has to be assimilated as well. Indian religion in the "altiplano" (high Andean plateau) or in marginal settlements of Lima has been affected by massive changes in the world and the nation, changes which Irarrázaval, writing from Chucuito deep in the Perúvian "altiplano", calls "true social earthquakes: vast migrations to cities, forging of new identities among the masses,... multifaceted grassroots political activity, emergence of women's interests, and in the midst of all this, the anonymous citizen reconstructing his existence".[34] With the magnitude of these changes, Irarrázaval believes, indian (in his case, Aymara) theology is in an inaugural stage where one can only mark out the basic lines of Aymara theology.

Thus changes in indian culture, and their religion have come in response to larger social changes in Latin America, especially in the last twenty years. In describing the emergence of an indigenous theological movement in Latin America, Judd sees: "Vast social transformations across Latin America coupled with rapid urbanization have... fostered a new expression for them".[35] Judd who observed changes in Perú and indian America while at Instituto Pastoral Andina, has seen "remarkable growth of historical awareness of indigenous identity". So have many others in México, Central America, and South America.

---

[32] Clendinnen, *Ambivalent*, p. 192.

[33] See, for example: Enrique Jorda, *La cosmovisión aymara en el diálogo de la fe: Teología desde el Titicaca* (Lima, Pontificia Universidad Católica, 1980).

[34] Irarrázaval, "Teología," pp. 99-100.

[35] Judd, in Hennelly, *Santo Domingo*, p. 226.

The beginnings of systematized indian theology as it is emerging are the result of long and patient efforts by extraordinarily gifted and sensitive theologians and anthropologists,[36] as Irarrázaval, Miguel Briggs, Judd, and Cadorette on the Perúvian altiplano; Juan Hugues and Henrique Urbano, Cuzco; Xavier Albó, La Paz; Manuel Marzal, Perúvian altiplano and Lima; Berganza and other Dominicans, Cobán, Guatemala; and Clodimiro Siller, México.[37] Typically they have advanced degrees from Chicago, Cornell, Berkeley, and other universities; careful and extensive publishing records; and are making mature reflections on years of research.[38]

One of the marks of these persons is their self-conscious effort is to set the stage so that native-born will be the main theologians of indian religion. They see themselves as midwives of indians giving birth to systematic theology (theology already exists in the people) or mentors, advising as needed but stepping aside. Xavier Albó, S.J., a Cornell Ph.D. in anthropology, working with for many years with Quechua and Guaraní groups, as well as his principal work with Aymaras in Bolivia, has strenuously fought off suggestions of a study center to which outsiders would come and go, doing their studies of the Aymara. Instead he immersed himself in Aymara circles, helping them to create a sense of an Aymara "nation". Indians who are theologians are beginning to appear. They may have the training and capacity for theological understanding but, as yet, lack the special aptitude for the delineation of a fully expressed theology. One may point to Eleazar

---

[36] Their works are too extensive to list completely. Especially recommended are: Diego Irarrázaval, *Rito y pensar cristiano* (Lima, Centro de Estudios y Publicaciones, 1993) and *Tradición y porvenir andino* (Puno, Perú, Instituto de Estudios Aymaras, 1992); Manuel Marzal, *Transformación religiosa peruana*, Lima, Pontificia Universidad Católica del Perú, 1988); (with Marzal as coordinator) *El rostro indio de Dios* (Lima, Pontifica Universidad del Perú, Fondo Editorial, 1991); *Caminos religiosos de los inmigrantes en la Gran Lima: El caso de El Agostino* (Lima, Fondo Editorial, Pontifica Universidad Católica del Perú, 1986); *Estudios sobre religión campesina* (Lima, Fondo Editorial, Pontificia Universidad Católica del Perú, 1977); *El mundo religioso de Urcos: Un estudio de antropología religiosa y de pastoral campesina de los Andes*, Cusco, Instituto de Pastoral Andina, 1971); *El sincretismo iberoamericano: Un estudio comparativo sobre los quechuas (Cusco), los mayas (Chiapas) y los africanos (Bahia)* (Lima, Fondo Editorial, Pontifica Universidad del Perú, 1988) 2nd ed.

[37] Cf. M. Marzal, E. Maurer, X. Albó, B. Schreiter, *The Indian Face of God* (Maryknoll, Orbis Books, 1996).

[38] Besides works by individual authors, the work of these persons and their research centers can be found especially in: *Pastoral Andina, Allphanchis, Aymar Yatiyawi, Revista Andina*, and publications of CIPCA (Centro de Investigación y Promoción del Campesinado).

López Hernández in México and Domingo Llanque in Perú as offering indian perspectives on theology.

López Hernández's most forceful position statement was made in a letter addressed to the papal representative in México, Archbishop Girolamo Prigione, in June 1992.[39] John Paul II[40] and the bishops were preparing then for the Fourth General Conference of CELAM at Santo Domingo. López links the current emergence of indigenous theology to the openings of Vatican II and to the heightened awareness of indigenous peoples of their distinct identity and their movements for respect of their cultures and for increased respect for human rights (see chapter 8).

The events surrounding the Santo Domingo meeting—the choice of date, place of celebrations, honoring a Spanish missionary—offered few images to suggest that the church was prepared to deal adequately with indigenous traditions or movements.[41] These poorly chosen public images masked the leadership by progressive national churches which have arisen quietly to take the place of (or along side of) those of Brazil and Chile. The Guatemalan and Bolivian bishops are in the eyes of close observers the continuing force of Vatican II in Latin America. One need not accept that assessment to appreciate the leadership of Guatemalan and Bolivian bishops for the limited task of highlighting the place of indigenous culture and religion in the Latin American church. They began at home to foster in their countries and in neighboring areas (indians and nations are not coterminous). And they represent as well as themselves the pioneering efforts of bishops in other countries who conspicuously promoted indigenous interests (religion and human rights being most prominent). These include: Samuel Ruíz García of Chiapas, México; Leónidas Proaño of Riobamba, Ecuador; Jesús Calderón Barrueto of Puno, Perú; and Erwin Krautler of Xingú, Brazil.

The Guatemalan and Bolivian bishops reacted strongly to the documents circulating for comment in preparation for the Santo Domingo meeting. They published salient pastoral letters, "500 años sembrando el Evangelio"

---

[39] López Hernández, "Carta a Monseñor Girolamo Prigione," Mexico City, June 25, 1992.

[40] A description without analysis is provided of discourses of John Paul II before 1990 is provided by José J. Vera Blanco, "Las culturas indígenas en los discursos de Joan Pablo II," *Misiones Extranjeras* 116 (March-April 1990), pp. 142-151.

[41] See, esp. Stephen Judd's description of the events surrounding Santo Domingo, in Hennelly, *Santo Domingo*, pp. 224-226.

in Guatemala and "Aporte a la IV Conferencia" in Bolivia.[42] Their leadership continued into the Santo Domingo meeting. The final document furnishes further steps in the emancipation of indigenous culture within the Catholic church, creating à sense of anticipation for a fully developed indigenous theology.[43]

A Contemporary Theology

The indigenous theologies of Latin America addresses many contemporary concerns. This theology is based on contact with the earth and incorporates deeply felt concerns, as justice in this life and life after death, as well. Mayan religion, practiced by several millions in Guatemala and México, offers an example, in terms of awareness of limited resources, of health, human connectedness, and issues of masculinity-femininity. Its appeal, as based on one strain of Mayan religion (the Q'eqchi'), also rests on its proclivity for attracting adherents rather than coercing them.[44]

In this religion God is not nature, but a separate person. But he enters the earth as a force. He (masculine features on images) is especially to be found in the mountains (an idea given conspicuous place in the Old Testament in the Spanish mysticism of John of the Cross). The self is viewed as part of the historical world. Through their ancestors, humans are securely connected to the past but they are also connected to people in the future. (For Mayan and Andean indians, self alone makes no sense. Human personality, for them, includes masculine and feminine characteristics, as does God.)

The Q'eqchi' Mayan religious and cultural vision embraces the whole

---

[42] In addition to the documents, see also: Bishop Julio Cabrera Ovalle, El Quiché, "Desafíos de la pastoral indígena en Guatemala," and Bishop Gerard Flores Reyes, "Una experiencia concreta: La Verapaz," *Misiones Extranjeras* 116 (March-April 1990), pp. 122-129 and 152-156, respectively.

[43] *Conclusions, Fourth General Conference of Latin American Bishops, Santo Domingo, October12-28, 1993*, nos. 243-251. An English-language version is found in Hennelly, ed., *Santo Domingo*.

[44] The depiction of Mayan religion in this section is based in part on interviews with Dominican members of the Las Casas Center, Cobán, Guatemala, especially with Carlos Berganza. See: Carlos Rafael Cabarrus, *La cosmovisión k'ekchí en proceso de cambio* (San Salvador, UCA Editores, 1979); Luis Pacheco, *Religiosidad Maya-kekchí alrededor del maíz* (San José, C.R., Edicíon Escuela para Todos, 1985); and Pacheco, *Tradiciones y costumbres del pueblo Maya-K'ekchí* (San José, C.R., Ediciones Amba, 1988).

world as an integrated whole, with all men and women participating in the
same process of living and being. God has placed a harmony in creation
which one has to love and respect. The universe is an authentic manifestation of the divine and the transcendent. Every created thing is necessary for
unity and integration. Therefore, men and women have to give "justo valor
a cada cosa", not undervaluing anything created.

Healing and natural medicine are practiced with some connections to
religion, many native healers also being priests. This may owe more to an
indigenous vision of religion as life than religion seeking a hold over the
health field. Alternative medicine is becoming increasing less controversial
for educated indians and for readers at Barnes and Noble through contributions, as those of Libbet Crandon-Malamud and Joseph Bastien,[45] building
on a growing body of work of Margaret Lock, Jean Comaroff, and others.
Christian indians, out on the Andean altiplano and unawares of health-care
controversies, seek the care of "yatiris" on a pragmatic basis: healers work
better than nurses or paramedics for some symptoms. Berganza has
experienced cures from native healers for tropical ailments which baffle
medical doctors.

Indians cultivate a great respect for life, for persons, for other living
things, for what exists. Everything has life, a spirit, sentiments. Taking
possession of things is not a goal since a person is not the owner of them,
but their servant. To use them he or she has to ask the permission of the
Supreme Being. To make bad use of things, to abuse the equilibrium
established by God, or not to ask the proper permission is to break the
established order of the universe—to be a sin—and recompense and
restitution is called for, to recover lost harmony. The philosophy of the
Q'eqchi' aims at creating a great community where men and women feel
united among themselves. This ideal expresses itself as a fundamental
commitment: the sacred duty of protecting and loving life, of sharing it, and
of celebrating it.

In summary, theology developed along these lines leads to a deepened
awareness of the sacredness of the world, of the transcendence of God, of
God as male and female and of humans with both masculine and feminine

---

[45] Libbet Crandon-Malamud, *From the Fat of Our Souls: Social Change,
Political Process, and Medical Pluralism in Bolivia* (Berkeley, Calif., University of
California Press, 1991) and Joseph W. Bastien, "Shaman versus Nurse in an
Aymara Village: Traditional and Modern Medicine in Conflict," in Dover et al,
eds., *Andean*, pp. 137-165.

qualities, of identity only through community, and of connectedness with past and future.

Interreligious Relations

Berganza, a Spanish Dominican, has spent many years in Guatemala, especially in the Cobán area, listening to Mayan indians of the region. He believes that "los antepasados" (ancestors) are key to entering into this expression of christianity. When interviewed by José Parra Novo about the meaning and role of "antepasados", practitioners of the religion responded: "They lived before us. They are the ones who began our journey here in this world. They are our 'grandfathers' and 'grandmothers' and they are the ones who organized or began to organize life in this world".[46]

Berganza has experienced in the special way of the Maya a connection to his own ancestors, a religious experience which enhanced his sense of being grounded in the past, connected to others, and looking forward to communion with them. Catholic theology has a place for reverence of ancestors but catholicism, as experienced by the Maya, Berganza believes, sometimes "has damaged Mayan culture by breaking connections to the "antepasados". Berganza is thinking here of contemporary efforts, as those of Catholic Action and Delegados de la Palabra. They stress doing away with "la costumbre". Even worse, in his and others's view, are Protestants, especially Pentecostals, "who have snatched the souls away from the indians. They do not allow attention to "antepasados" and anything like praying to them. They turn their back on all customary beliefs. Their object is to convert indians to something different, without an indian identity".

Thus, Berganza was not surprised by the first meeting of Maya Maya priests with Maya Catholic priests. The meeting was "violent", in that the Maya Maya expressed pent-up resentment about the damage done their culture by outsiders, by attempts to steal the soul of indians by cutting the connection to ancestors. Mayan Catholics, in response, point to incorporation of respect for ancestors in what goes on in Mayan Catholic communities, as during the days of November 1-2, when All Saints and "antepasa-

---

[46] José Parra Novo conducted numerous interviews over a period of eighteen months in 1990. Parra Novo was interviewed by the author in Guatemala City, Feb. 20-21, 1993. See also his "Aproximación cultural a la comunidad Q'eqchi' de Santa María Cahalión: Reflexiones en torno al desafío de la inculturación", licenciatura thesis, Facultad de Teología, Universidad Francisco Marroquín, 1992.

dos" receive attention, like separate grains of rice melding into the flavor of one dish.

The Maya Maya priests present for the theological encounters were both men and women and included in their number "curanderos/as". These healers often employ natural medicines and techniques for healing. During the encounters Berganza presumed that those Maya, favoring influence through dialogue, were being patient with him, hoping for his enlightenment.

Conclusion

A measured view is called for in the assessment of the clash of dominant and subordinate cultures. Nowhere is that balanced view more important than in assessing indian theology, as contrasted to Latin American (for example, liberation theology) or Hispanic-mestizo (as confected in the United States) theology. Indigenous theologians are grateful to liberation and other Latin American theologians for the leadership they have given but the time has come for the development of indigenous theology, for indians to speak for themselves.

One sure sign of this vitality is organizational activity by those involved in the creation of indigenous theology. They have held Interamerican meetings (Talleres de la Teología Indígena) in 1989, 1991, and 1992. They have set up working groups for six areas: México, Central America, Caribbean, Andes, Amazon, and Southern Cone. Latin American theologians are reaching out in new and promising directions.

CHAPTER TEN

TOWARDS AN INDIGENOUS THEOLOGY:
A REFORMED PROTESTANT APPROACH

Facundo Ku Canché and team

"Mayas have a right to discover the One God in their own culture and to follow Jesus Christ in their own way. Every people has unique frames of reference from which to discover the One God. As the Church Fathers used the categories of Greek philosophy to explain christianity to the Hellenistic world, Maya thinkers wish today to develop Christian theology within their own worldview". Facundo Ku Canché is a Presbyterian minister in Yucatán, México and a leader of CEPAMEX, an evangelical Maya group that is engaged in pastoral reflection and action on indigenous issues.[1]

Long before christianity arrived in the Yucatán Peninsula, God—the Lord of nations—had already come and had revealed himself. The ancient Mayas (the Ancestors), in fact, had a deep faith (a theology) and a particular way of expressing it (a liturgy).

When the first "christians" arrived in our lands, they did not dialogue with our faith. Instead, they looked upon it with mistrust. Motivated by their own religious fanaticism—their zeal for "evangelism"—and by a need to justify before Charles the V of Spain the atrocities committed against the Maya people, they accused our religion of being idolatrous and demonic. They persecuted Mayan beliefs and went to great lengths to uproot it.

Of course there were idolatrous practices, but not everybody was an idolater. There were certainly human sacrifices, but not everyone agreed with this. These were specific cases upon which "christians" built their generalizations about us. This gave rise to the Maya stereotype: they are all a totally idolatrous people who once practiced human sacrifice.

Despite their best efforts, the conquistadores were unable to eradicate Mayan beliefs. From 1511, when Gerónimo Aguilar and Gonzalo Guerrero (two shipwrecked sailors) crawled unto a beach in Western Yucatán, the Mayas and their descendants have bravely resisted every depredation. They

---

[1] This chapter is adapted, with permission, from a paper presented, June 6-9, 1994, at an ecumenical "encuentro" on christology and indigenous theology, in the Totonaca village of Huhuetla, Puebla, México.

have managed to preserve until now much of their pre-Hispanic beliefs and their liturgy. They have been kept alive by various means: oral tradition, public and private liturgical celebrations, synchretism with christianity, the silent witness of the ancient cities of Chichén Itzá, Uxmal, Palenque, in the Yucatán peninsula, and ancient writings and documents which have come down to us.

Elements of the religion of our ancestors which, in God's sovereignty, managed to survive until today, had an "evangelical" side to it—it was good news to the Maya people. In this essay, we would like to discover (in the sense of *un*covering), in the light of the sacred traditions of the Mayas and the biblical record, the evangelical face of indigenous theology, with a view to providing some clues for a synthesis between indigenous beliefs and the gospel. Gamaliel's advice to the Sanhedrin continues to be valid: "In the present case I advise you: Leave these people alone!... For if their purpose or activity is of human origin, it will fail. But if it is from God, you will not be able to stop them; you will only find yourselves fighting against God" (Ac. 5:38,39).

The Evangelical Face of Indigenous Theology

We would like to suggest some premises on which to base a Protestant Christian dialogue with indigenous theology.

God reveals himself to all peoples and cultures

> What may be known about God is plain to them, because God has made it plain to them (Ro. 1:19).

God is the source of life for all peoples (cp. Jn. 1:1-4; cp. v.9); it is the basic tenet of indigenous theology. He has granted to every person, and to every race and people, the right to be creative and unique (cp. Ac. 17:24-27). God reveals himself to all peoples and communicates to them through their consciences (cp. Ro. 2:14-16 and 1:20). God liberates the oppressed: other nations and peoples besides Israel have experienced God's liberation and his judgment for disobedience (cp. Am. 9:7,9). He takes pleasure in the worship of all peoples who follow him in truth (cp. Mal. 1:11). God has charged all peoples to administer his creation (cp. Ps. 8:6).

Both Israel and the ancient Mayas rebelled against God

> The more I called Israel, the more they went from me; they sacrificed to their baals and they burned incense to images (Hos. 11:2).

As Israel was rejected for not following in God's way, the Maya peoples, their monotheistic faith distorted by a warrior cult, were told by their prophets of the coming of an alien people and religion. The Maya peoples were not always idolatrous. They worshipped One God. Although he was associated with the sun, there is no evidence of an image or painting being made to the supreme Maya deity *Hunab Ku'*.[2] The idolatrous elements, Maya sources suggest, were imposed by Toltec/Itzá invaders from central México.[3] Traditions recorded during the Spanish invasion period a few centuries later speak of this fact.

> For a time, they knew about One God who surveyed heaven and earth and everything, from his heavenly seat. They had dedicated a temple to him, with priests who received presents and alms from the people to be offered unto God. This was their way of worship until a great lord came from afar who, with his people, were idolaters and whom the whole land began to follow in their idolatry... having idols for everything (Relación de Motul).[4]

The ancient wise men of Yucatán "relate that some eight hundred years ago there was no idolatry in this land". But after the Mexicas "conquered us,[5] a captain who called himself Quetzacoatl (feathered serpent)... introduced... the idolatrous worship of gods made of wood and mud", to whom they even

---

[2] *Hunab ku'* is a composite name, somewhat akin to Yaweh, which denotes oneness (*hu*), being (*nab*) and divinity (*ku'*).

[3] Editor's note: See the Introductory chapter for an historical interpretation of the history of the Maya and related Mesoamerican peoples.

[4] Editor's note: During the early years of the Spanish colony in Yucatán, a series of "relaciones" related the historical memory of the Mayas, in their own words or as interpreted by Spanish chroniclers. Each narration bears either the author's name or a place name.

[5] Editor's note: In the eight century C.E., the *Mexicas* or *Chichimecas*, fierce warriors from the central plains of North America, displaced the Maya related *Toltecs* from central México. The alien religiosity and bloodthirstiness of the toltecs, when they later invaded the peninsula and founded an empire at Chichén Itzá-Maya, merited them the epithet of "mexica" by their Yucatec cousins. Centuries later, another "mexica" incursion from the north—the Aztecs— settled on the high plateau of central México, conquered a vast empire and were in turn conquered by the Spanish invaders.

offered human blood (Relación de don Martín de Palomar).

Although many Mayas became idolaters, there were also those who preserved their monotheistic faith. There were poets and rulers, and above all prophets, who like the Old Testament Elijah, called their people back to the worship of the One True God. Their pronunciations, known collectively as the "Chilam Balames", after the best known of several prophets,[6] are collections of predictions which were compiled shortly before the coming of the Europeans, and later transcribed into Latin script. Erroneously described as "prophecies of a new religion", Mayas insist that they are, in fact, prophecies concerning the resurgence of the ancient monotheistic faith which had been distorted by northern tribes. They announced the imminent destruction of the oppressive religious system of the Itzá rulers.

> Bow before the true God, omnipotent above all things... Creator of heaven and earth... My words shall be painful to you O Maya Itzá, water witch of the Mayas; you who refuse to hear about another God, who believe that your deities are worthy. But you shall come to acknowledge the truth of my preaching! (Prophecy of Natzín Yabún Chan).

When *Hunab Ku'*, the only deity, is manifest he shall bring peace to his peoples, including to the Itzás who are called to adore Him. It shall be the dawn of a new monotheistic faith, the beginning of a new humanity (the Prophecy of Chilam Balam). Mayas today understand these to be valid prophecies upon which to base a renewed indigenous theology in which there is ample room for Christian incarnational revelation.

Christianity failed to fulfill the prophecies. According to Franciscan missionary Diego de Landa:

> Cortés preached unto them the vanity of their idols and persuaded them to worship the cross, which he placed in their temples with the image of Our Lady. And this was to be the end of public idolatry.[7]

Little has changed, even among Protestants. The following is a summary of many Protestant sermons that Mayas hear today:

---

[6] Chilam Balam, in his own words, was "a priest who travels to every province on earth explaining the word of the Lord Kú, the only true deity" (Chilam Balaam de Chumayel).

[7] Fr. Diego de Landa, *Relación de las cosas de Yucatán*, Edición de Miguel Rivera. Madrid: Historia 16. Serie Crónicas de América, 1985, p. 7.

> As a proof of your authentic conversion to Jesus Christ as your Lord and Saviour, you must renounce your custom of offering food and drink according to the manner of your Maya ancestors, because this is not approved in God's Word.

The Europeans came at the time announced by the prophets, bringing a new religion of one supreme God, his Son Jesus Christ, and his mother, the Virgin Mary. For the Maya, these were implacable deities, in whose name every Maya representation of God had to be destroyed. Had the dedicated, and often fanatical, friars who learned the indigenous languages been able to understand the monotheistic undercurrent in Maya theology, would they have acted differently? Probably not. The Catholic monarchs and their armies had, after all, expelled monotheistic Jews and Muslims from their newly unified kingdom, on the same year of Columbus' "discovery" of Abia Yala. In the end, popular catholicism fused with indigenous religiosity; but it was the cult of *Hunab Ku'* that in fact prevailed and has survived over time. The priests of *Hunab Ku'* went underground while the official religion was being smashed. They continued to resist and to await the fulfillment of the prophecies.

Protestants began to arrive at the end of the nineteenth century. They proclaimed a one true God and his Son Jesus Christ, but in Western terms. Today, Maya Protestants are beginning to think through their relationship to Jesus Christ—and to make him more relevant—in the context of their own culture and spirituality.

Jesus Christ, God incarnate, is the Only Mediator

> For there is One God and one mediator between God and men, the man Christ Jesus, who gave himself as a ransom for all men (1 Tim. 2:5).

If Christ is being rejected by indigenous leaders it is because his mediation was announced to them with a hidden agenda: they were invited to accept Jesus as their Lord and Savior, and *then* told to reject their cultural identity. But this was not the intent of the original Christian message. Jesus became a Jew and did not require his followers to become Jews; he challenged them to discover and proclaim Christ within their own culture. God, therefore, is not limited in his revelation. Might he not have revealed himself as the "non-incarnate Word" to people of other races and cultures (cp. Gn. 16:7-16; 21:8-21) as He did on a number of occasions to proto-Israelites. This fact is, perhaps, hinted at in Micah 5:2: "the goings out" (*yatso*, sudden manifestations) of him who was to be born in Bethlehem Ephratah "are from old, from ancient times". Fr. Diego de Landa recorded in his memoirs that the Yucatan Maya celebrated an event which they called *em ku* -- "the descent of God".[8]

Even after falling into idolatry, the Mayas retained a notion of the Supreme Being. They built the temple of Chichén Itzá, in Yucatán, so that the supreme god *Kukulcán* (Quetzacoatl) could descend from heaven once a year, the rising sun rippling down the 360 steps, to be with his people—and with countless tourists who continue to observe the phenomenon yearly at the March 21 solstice.

Mayas have a right to discover the One God in their own culture...
...to follow Jesus Christ in their own way.

> Only Thee do I trust entirely, here where one dwells. For thou, O great Kin, providest that which is good, here where one dwells, to all living beings. Since Thou abidest to give reality to the earth, where all men live. And Thou art the true helper who grants that which is good.[9]

Every people has unique frames of reference from which to discover the One God. As the Church Fathers used the categories of Greek philosophy to explain christianity to the Helenistic world, Maya thinkers wish today to develop Christian theology within their own worldview. But it is not sufficient for theologians to develop culturally coherent christological statements. True christology is always substantiated by its fruits. The fruits of Western christianity have become bitterly apparent to indigenous peoples in the Americas. What are the fruits of indigenous spirituality?

Maya Names for God

Over many millennia of developing their theology and liturgy, the Maya people have called upon God under different names. Some have lost their original meaning; others continue to be sacred among the Maya. Although the names that we will mention are mostly of Yucatec origin, their counterparts can be found among the score or so of Maya languages.

---

[8] Ibid.

[9] *Book of Songs of Dzitbalche*, p. 80, quoted in "Yucatec-Maya Songs", *Native Mesoamerican Spirituality*, Miguel León-Portilla, ed., London, SPCK, 1980, p. 230.

Ku': Origin and First Cause

The name *Ku'* means God. It is a very sacred name for Yucatec Mayas. They frequently say *Ku' botic*, meaning "may God repay you, or recompense you for what you have done for me". Mayas have a very sacred day called *Kin Ku'*, "God's day". The particle *ku'* signifies origin, cause, reason for being or source—as in *Ku' uk che*, a bud on a plant; or *Ku' kum*, the downy feathers on a newborn chick.[10]

Hahal Ku': The Life-giver, the True God

God is the giver of life who sends rain upon the corn that sustains our people. The title may also have been used to distinguish the true God from the Mexica idols that were made of wood, mud and stone. *Ha'* means truth or water and *hahal*, rainy season, time to sow, the best time of the year. *Hahal ku'* then seems to signify "the God of good weather" who gives life to his people.[11]

Hunab ku': The Only Divine Being

This significant title is ascribed to God in contrast to the idols that the Itzá king Quetzalcoatl imposed upon the Mayas. The name was used before the coming of the Spaniards by the Chilam Balam prophets to call the Itzás to renounce their idols. *Hun* (sound, unique role), *ab* (being), *ku'*, God, signifies "the only being". This is strongly suggests that the Mayas were not originally polytheistic idolaters, but monotheists.

Itzamna': The One Who dwells at home in the temple

The name can be translated, "the One who knows everything that is in the house, or temple". This title was given to God as represented by the sun that daily shines upon the Maya people and comes down on a certain date as a ray of sunshine to feed upon the offerings of food that were given to

---

[10] Editor's note: As can be readily appreciated, Yucatec Maya is made up largely of one syllable words.

[11] Editor's note: Like "lord" in English or *kurios* in Greek, *ahal* or *kahal* is also a title which was used to address nobles and kings, perhaps because they controlled - liturgically as well as physically - the access to life-giving water.

him. The name is a composite of *itz* (wise), *a* (water), *am* (to be, location), *na* (house). A possible meaning of the name is, therefore: "The wiseman of the water", the vital element which can always be found in homes and temples. Only a vestige of this name exists in the city of Izamal, and as the dimly remembered deity *Zamna'* or *Itz*. This is no longer a significant element in the peoples' beliefs.

Kinichkakmo': The One with a face like the sun and the macaw

The legends about this deity and its counterpart *Itzamna'* are not easy to disentangle. *Kinichkakmo'* means, in the Yucatec tongue, the sun's (*kin*) face (*ich*) like the fiery (*kak*) feathers of the macaw (*mo'*). People turned to this deity for advice in times of storm, sickness, pestilence, and other tragedies of life. Originally an expression of one attribute of the One God, his worship eventually became and idol totally identified with the sun and was eventually wiped out. There is an image of *Kinichkakmo'* on the ruins of a temple in Izamal.

Kukumcán (Kukulcán): The Feathered Serpent God

According to the *Pop Vuh*, the Ancient Book of the Mayas, the feathered serpent antecedes creation, but historians date the beginings of the cult in 1000 B.C. *Kukum*, as we have already mentioned, means feathers or beginning. *Can*[12] signifies serpent, more specifically the rattlesnake which abounds in Yucatán.[13] After they were conquered by the Toltec prince Quetzalcoatl, the Nahuatl (Mexica) word for Kukulcán, the latent idolatrous elements seem to have become institutionalized, in association with human

---

[12] Editor's note: The highland Maya pronounce the word as "chan". It now seems clear that *Chan* is the name by which the ancient Maya's called themselves. It continues to be a fairly common Maya surname.

[13] Editor's note: While the Hebrew-Christian tradition considers serpents to be symbols of evil, the indigenous Mesoamericans perceived in the serpent a living symbol of several divine attributes. It moves at ease on the surface of the earth, underground and in the water; and in a hybrid shape with the beautiful feathered quetzal bird, the mythical feathered serpent reputedly flew above the earth. Its undulating movement symbolizes the unity of heaven and earth. The serpent symbolizes endless time: its body is capable of forming a perfect circle, spirals and undulating waves (cycles of time) and a straight line (advancing time). According to some interpretations, the rattles on its tail, signify infinity, and are perhaps reproduced in the Maya symbol for zero, which was one of their most stupendous scientific discoveries.

sacrifices. Although this deity is no longer venerated, he is remembered in various ways. At the 21 March solstice, Kukulcán's rays descend serpent-like down the steps of the Chichen Itzá temple, to fertilize the earth for good crops. There is a sports club in Mérida, Yucatán that is dedicated to this deity.

Yumtzil: The Father of All

This name is given to the One Creator God from whom everything and everyone without exception proceeds—the wind, rain, sun, fire, life, absolutely everything. *Yum* means good father, lord, and owner; *tzil*, signifies all, without any exception whatsoever. Mayas today pray fervently to this God for everything. They worship, love, and believe in Him. The same as *Ku'*, *Hahal ku'* and *Hunab ku'*, he has no representation. He is the beloved and Unknown God.

CHAPTER ELEVEN

IS CHRIST BEING RESURRECTED AMONG THE INDIGENOUS PEOPLE?

Moisés Colop

"If we reply that Christ is *not* being resurrected in our culture and people in Abia Yala, we simply mean that he has never left us ... Today he is allowing us to understand him with greater intensity". Pastor Colop is a K'iche' Maya a minister and a one-time Moderator of the National Evangelical Presbyterian Church of Guatemala. After several years of exile, he now directs the Guatemalan office of the Christian Reformed World Relief Commission.[1]

Introduction

In order to immerse oneself in the difficult, yet fascinating, theological world of the indians,[2] the following aspects need to be taken into consideration:

1. Accept from the outset that it is another theology about the same God of Abraham, but with a different understanding. This in itself should not be difficult to accept, since their are a great variety of theological approaches within Christian theology.

2. Understand that indigenous theology is not a distortion of Christian theology, but rather a proximate theological expression in a language which is not ours (Spanish), and using methods that are not our own.

3. Receive indigenous theology with respect and equality, instead of prejudice and misunderstanding. One cannot do indigenous theology from a superior vantage point.

---

[1] This article first appeared in the Nicaraguan journal *Xilotl: Revista nicaragüense de teología*, no. 12/13, 1994. Used with permission.

[2] The author uses the pejorative word "indio" with a new-found sense of pride. At one time, the Guatemalan Mayas preferred to be addressed as "indígenas" or "naturales", they now proudly adopt their tribal names.

Keeping these three facts in mind I would like to share a few insights that perhaps can help us to develop familiarity and understanding regarding indigenous theology.

A brief history of our theology

Prior to the Spanish invasion, more or less five hundred years ago, indigenous peoples worshipped the Supreme Being publicly, in a liturgy which invited people to participate in this relationship. When it met face to face with Christian theology, indigenous theology was forced to find new forms of survival. The altars and places of worship were moved to the highest mountains, while at the same time the signs and symbols were buried in the thick walls of the cathedrals and even placed within Catholic altars and symbols. Many indigenous who today bow before a cross, are not paying homage to the Christian cross, but to the age old cross of the Mayas, which symbolizes the unity of all creation.

When protestantism reached the Maya lands, it was even more intent upon annihilating any vestige of an indigenous God. However, the "Heart of Heaven and Earth" did not succumb to the strong Protestant winds. Many missionaries died with the mistaken conviction that they had wiped out *U Cux Caj Ulew*, but it was not so. We Mayas, honest and sincerely recognize that our God is alive, because we talk to him every day. Who is this God?

He is U Cux Caj Ulew

There is not a literal translation for this name of the Supreme Creator of the K'iche' Maya - *U Cux Caj Ulew*. The closest approximation is "Heart (or Spirit) of Heaven and Earth." It conveys the idea of a "living epicentre," of God being "the generator of life," the "absolute master" and "overseer of Heaven and Earth".

To be precise, we are not speaking here of heaven and earth in the non-indigenous worldview. Together, the terms include everything that is within them, as well as all of the influences that flow out of them. In other words, we are speaking of a total and unified universe - of universality and complementarity. As the Psalmist would say, "Herein is wisdom," or as the indigenous peoples would put it, "this is the guts of indigenous theology". "Heart of Heaven" is the expression and manifestation of the male side of

God, which is perfect, complete, and absolute. "Heart of Earth" is the complete and absolute perfection of the female side of God. This unity is shown in the phenomenon of day and night. There can be no night without day and vice versa. The God of the Maya is never apart from this account, nor can anything about God be hidden that cannot also be seen.

We can only sense the presence of the "Heart of Heaven and of Earth" when there is no hatred in our lives, nor rejection, prejudice, and haughtiness - that is, when there is brotherhood and justice between every one of God's creatures. Insight into the totality of creation is not a human ability. It is a gift of God to all of humanity to enable us to perceive the evidences of the Supreme Being throughout the whole of creation.

We come at this point to a great breach between Christian and indigenous theology. Christian doctrine teaches that all of creation is subject to humankind, and should therefore be exploited and extract profit from it. Meanwhile, in the understanding of indigenous theology, the earth is alive because it causes all plants to germinate in order to give life to human beings. This is why we always ask permission before touching mother earth. Our worldview is thus very practical and not very theoretical. Creation is where God is permanently manifested, and this includes our fellow human beings.

We can also note a certain difference in approach when we look at the foundation text of Christian redemption, John 3:16: "For God so loved the world". Christians do their theology from a different angle seeking to demonstrate without a shadow of doubt God's love to humanity. However, I have heard no one attempt to relate the "world" to God's purpose of redemption for "the whole universe." By which we mean the redemption of the earth, the heavens, the moon, sun, and everything that influences the lives of human beings. Furthermore, redemption makes us responsible for all of God's creation. The Supreme Being, the "Heart of Heaven and of Earth," not only asks our commitment, as indigenous peoples, to the whole of creation, but he has also empowered everything that surrounds us to give us more life, in order that we might grow in understanding of the Supreme Being. Indigenous people believe that the divine commitment to humanity and human commitment to God are both incomplete if they do not encompass every aspect of their existence. This is why an indigenous farmer will kiss the earth when he goes out to sow; he will look toward the sun and the heavens to request permission from the "Heart of Earth" to break the sod with his hoe.

Various approaches to indigenous theology

Even as there is variety in Christian theology, there is also variety in the exercise and practice of indigenous theology.

1. We must first recognize with sadness and resignation that there are indigenous people that have forgotten their cultural and theological roots. They are tying their identity, however awkwardly, to Christian theological dogmatism and fundamentalism.

2. A second current adapts the folklore, native languages, and some indigenous customs in order to foster the same fundamentalist protestantism. We call it "Christian indian theology."

3. At a third level, indigenous people are becoming aware of their worldview with a commitment to the Supreme Being, one and the same as the Trinitarian God of christianity, who is manifested in every culture of the world. This God requires harmony, fraternity, and respect, both between human beings and for the whole of creation. We experience a deepening in our faith and spirituality. We call this "indian Christian theology."[3]

4. The fourth stream is the total practice of indigenous theology, without any reference whatsoever to christianity. We call this "indian indian theology."

Conclusion

Now to answer our initial question. If we say that Christ is *not* being resurrected in our culture and people in Abia Yala, we simply mean that he has never left us—although many people have marginalized, vilified, and forgotten him. I believe that because we have also experienced alienation,

---

[3] Editor's note. There are, however, indigenous theologians that fit Colop's descriptive category of "indian christian", who think of themselves, nonetheless, as being "christian indian", though they are not by any means "fundamentalist". Cp. the typologies in chapters 10 and 14 by Frs. López and Zapeta.

indigenous Christians can understand Christ to be the fulfillment of the "Heart of Heaven and of Earth". Today he is allowing us to understand him with greater intensity.

PART FOUR
ISSUES IN DIALOGUE AND EVANGELIZATION

CHAPTER TWELVE

INCULTURATION AND INDIGENOUS THEOLOGY

coordinated by
Fr. Jesús Espeja

"Indigenous peoples have their own way of feeling, perceiving, acting and interpreting reality out of a strong experience of total and vital union with the cosmos and of communion with a personal God... On the basis of the Incarnation, every word that has to do with God must forever cease to be abstract and non-temporal. Words about God must henceforth spring from the contexts in which human beings express themselves and their own world".[1]

Introduction

1. The indigenous peoples are making their presence known today as never before in society and in the Church.[2]

Something new is happening in the region.

The subject of indigenous theology, which the indigenous peoples themselves have brought to light, is one of the most eloquent signs of the depth of their historical memory.

We are aware of how important this is for the life of these peoples and for the mission of the church, in which we are involved. Faithfulness to the persons and cultures of these peoples is required of us, as well as to our Dominican charisma.

We thus join all those who are reflecting upon indigenous theology, not only among the indigenous peoples of our Continent, but also in local churches throughout the Third World. We are particularly indebted to those black Christian communities in Africa whose theological reflection within

---

[1] This is Part 2, on indigenous theology, of a two-part statement prepared in 1993 by Dominican missioners. Permission to use was requested but unanswered by the publishers, Editorial San Esteban, of Salamanca.

[2] Cp. *Manifiesto de los indígenas participantes en la 2ª consulta ecuménica de Pastoral Indígena de América Latina*, Quito, 30 June to 06 July, 1986. *La Iglesia y los Indios: ¿500 años de diálogo o de agresión?*, Quito, Ecuador, Editorial Abya-Yala, 1989. Eleazar López, ed. "Aportes de los indígenas a las iglesias con ocasión del V Centenario", in *500 años de resistencia y de lucha de los pueblos de América contra la opresión*, México, CENAMI , 1991.

their own cultural milieu has given us a major stimulus and is a source of hope. Not only do we want to participate joyfully of the fruits that these our brethren are sharing with us, but we humbly offer them what we ourselves are observing, so that we might be mutually enriched and may profit from these attainments for the common good.

2. While we have in mind all indigenous peoples when we write, we want to make clear that our own pastoral experience   with indigenes—working toward the formation of an autochthonous church—is mainly within local churches where a process of real inculturation and theological reflection has already begun.

Revelation as dialogue

3. God and his plan of salvation are revealed in the cultures of every people. "God is and was with our people; he evangelized them first and gave them very peculiar traits and ways through which they might be found. He used our clothing, our arrows, our gourds full of maize brew, and has not repented of giving us this way of life. God is with us, with our elders; he helps us to work out a history of salvation which is very much our own".[3] Among these cultures we can discover and admire the seeds, the fruits and the very face of the Word.[4]

4. Indigenous peoples have their own way of feeling, perceiving, acting and interpreting reality out of a strong experience of total and vital union with the cosmos and of communion with a personal God.

In the words of an indigenous Catholic priest: "This faith in the God of life, the result of his love and purposes which he revealed throughout the history and cultures of our peoples, and which our grandfathers and grandmothers have carefully preserved in their ancestral traditions, is the root of our indigenous theology today".[5]

5. Every revelation is a dialogue between God and humanity. The indigenous religions and worldviews, as well as their history, contain and express this dialogue of revelation.[6]

---

[3] Aiban Wagua, an indigenous Kuna (Panamá) priest.
[4] Vatican II: GS, 57; AG, 6; DP, 401; DP,i(1), ii(2),2.2.
[5] Eleazar López, a Mexican Zapoteca priest who is the author of chapter 10.
[6] Vatican II: DV, 2,3.

A Theology of Accompaniment

6. If we can accept that indigenous theology is their comprehension that the totality of their lives is under God's guiding hand, we can recognize how decisive is their theology for them. It is a source of wisdom that accompanies, guides and explains the indigenous sojourn throughout their history.[7]

7. Before the Invasion, indigenous theology guided the native peoples of these lands. It helped them to maintain a creative tension with transcendence, in spite of the difficulties which they met along the way. At the same time, their theology guided them in their struggle to be fully human, providing them with a genuine cultural presence and an unique identity.

8. During the past 500 years, indigenous theology has been oppressed, and has responded with resistance. Throughout, it has not ceased to accompany and guide the people, providing them with an interpretation of history which is uniquely theirs. It has done this in a variety of ways, drawing upon the resources of the land which they have inhabited for thousands of years. Indigenous theology has transmitted its moral and cultural values through myths, while denouncing, ridiculing and condemning the invader's persona and world in drama and dance, using symbolic masks and ornate costumes. In short, indigenous theology has created mechanisms of protest against the injuries done against them and celebrated life and death situations with their own symbols. The indigenous peoples are upheld by the knowledge that they are always loved, protected and guided by the God of their ancestors who is symbolically with them as Mother Earth—*Pachamama, Tzuultaq'a, Corazón del Cielo y de la Tierra* (Heart of Heaven and of Earth).

There can be no doubt that it was from their traditional religions that the indigenous peoples derived the strength to maintain their identity, and to resist the aggressor of their lands and consciences.

9. All of the above presents us—Dominican missioners—with a tremendous challenge: we must create an awareness that the whole rich field of indigenous theology should be recognized by the church. But, first, this recognition must impact our own lives, and then recreate the life of our Dominican communities. It should make a difference at every level and place where the Order is present.

---

[7] *Teología india. Encuentro taller Latinoamericano*, México, 1991, pp. 5-16.

Characteristics of Indigenous Theology[8]

10. *Indigenous theology is specific*. It does not get lost in abstract lucubrations and postulates. Its point of departure is life, rejoicing in it. It defends, contemplates and loves life. The source of the peoples' wisdom is their very long history and experience of life.

11. *Indigenous theology is holistic*. It always encompasses the totality of the peoples' lives and their whole life project, in which God himself is involved. No aspect of life is too small to be appreciated by them. Everything that concerns their lives as a people is the object of their theology.

This is why their religious practice is centered totally upon human life and their reason for being—their life sustenance, food and drink, sickness and health, birth and death, survival, life beyond the grave, fate and tragedy, fecundity and children, family and community, success and failure, solidarity among community members and harmony between human beings and the cosmos. This explains the importance of ritual; it is the cosmic celebration of their religious experience.

12. *Indigenous people have channelled their theological discourse largely within the religious sphere* in order to maintain and recreate the inherited values and hopes of an oppressed people. If we keep in mind the marginalization of the indigenous peoples, the indignities that the dominant national structures force upon them, we can understand why.

This also explains why indigenous theology uses a decidedly ritual language. With notable frequency, the indigenous respond to conflictive situations in ritual silence. They find this kind of ritual communication to be more profound and more meaningful. "It is not because we don't have words to speak, but because words are not capable of expressing everything that we experience".[9]

13. *Indigenous theology is expressed in mythical and symbolic language*, as the people are developing it. They prefer this idiom because of its great capacity to express and interpret the profound and radical meaning which indigenous people attach to life.

---

[8] Adapted from A.G. Matibuena, *Fuentes de la teología indígena*, "Encuentro Centroamericano de la Orden Dominicana sobre inculturación". Guatemala, January, 1995.

[9] Fr. Eleazar López, the author of chapter 10.

Myths explain the totality of the meaning of life. They become religion and faith when they provide a transcendent explanation—when they attempt to explain history as God in action.

Specific Aspects and Goals

Indigenous anthropology

In the hope of raising awareness in others about the significance of this theology, we want to highlight the most important values and characteristics of the indigenous cultures in our Continent.

14. The loci of indigenous theology is, first and foremost, life and the way in which it is perceived. At the root of everything, it is perceived as the positive pole of the life-death tension. Human existence is the object of the wisdom, the religion, and the cultural institutions of the native peoples.

15. The following indigenous values resonate with Gospel values.
The transcendence of God the creator, and at the same time his life-giving immanence in every created being.

The potent symbol of God who protects us with his love and who gives us life is holy Mother Earth.

The integration and involvement of every being in one and the same process.

The harmony of nature and the unity of every person (body and soul).

The material, spiritual and historical dimensions are integrated into one indivisible reality.

The profound recognition of the intersexual, communitarian and cosmic dimensions of human beings. The role of the senses in religious experience.

The experience of gratuity, reciprocity and solidarity; a pervading sense of moderation and harmony in interpersonal relations.

Community awareness. A profound ethic of work and hospitality. Festivity. Authority based upon service to the community. Fellowship with the ancestors.

16. Particularly relevant to these cultures are the myths of light: light-darkness, good-evil, life-death-resurrection. Light is victorious over darkness.

A theology of the people

17. Indigenous theology is being built upon the genuine values of indigenous anthropology. It is nourished by their heritage—the ethics and wisdom of the people. They themselves develop a theology in assemblies where they come together under the guidance and motivation of leaders of recognized authority. This means that indigenous theology will always be rooted in their own historical reality and social structures and not in the cultures and beliefs of alien peoples. The indigenous worldview and religiosity provide answers to their basic questions, fortifying their identity and keeping them from being overwhelmed by the dominant cultures.

18. Indigenous communities are open to receiving everyone who, on an equal footing with them and with an attitude of service, are willing to become committed to their cause—so long as they don't attempt to take over or manipulate the indigenous identity.

A theology of inculturation

19. From the moment in which the Incarnate Word took on all of our humanities, with their commonalities and differences, every human culture has been called to develop a specific language of faith. God cannot communicate with people through a borrowed humanity. Rather, he did it on the basis of his unique existence as source and condition of every word. On the basis of the Incarnation, every word that has to do with God must forever cease to be abstract and non-temporal. Words about God must henceforth spring from the contexts in which human beings express themselves and their own world.[10]

20. Indigenous Christians are making their voices heard in the church, keeping in mind the right of every people to be recognized as different. The challenges that are surfacing within indigenous communities have a lot to offer to the future of our faith.[11]

21. How can indigenous people accept as Good News the Gospel that the church preaches, if it threatens to take away that which is essential to their profound sense of life, as well as to annul the spiritual and cultural heritage that they have received from their ancestors?

---

[10] Ro. 1:18-20; Vatican II: DV, n.6; LG, n.16; EN, no.53; DPI, i, ii (2), n.2.2, 2.7.

[11] Cp. Vatican II, GS, N. 62.

22. After 500 years, those indigenous that remained faithful, within the church, to their own religious worldview still have to put up with the tension between faith and customs. Their customs are looked down upon and continues to be viewed with suspicion by the institutional churches. In many places and sectors of the church it would seem that the principle of recognizing the uniqueness of persons different from us is not too clearly defined. Indigenous societies feel that they are being forcibly squeezed into a unified model of culture and religion.

23. Christianity, as it is lived within indigenous communities, needs to find its own language. The indigenous need to re-tell the Gospel in a new way, with respect for all the richness of indigenous culture. Expressions of the message that doe not take into account the indigenous practices and customs are insufficient. A new autochthonous humanity cannot flower within christianity without a due appreciation for the traditional indigenous religions in matters of faith.

In order to find a credible idiom, our faith must consider the fundamental experience of the kechua, aymara, kuna, maya, yanomani, and other indigenous peoples, as one of the constituent poles of Revelation. This is the fundamental challenge that our churches face in the present status of in-depth evangelization in our Continent.

24. The same can be said about the way we celebrate our salvation. It has to sink its roots deep into a symbolic experience that is respectful of the creativity of indigenous men and women. A church that promotes a spirituality that is alien to—or uprooted from—the symbols that express the peoples' understanding of life and death is depriving these Christians of a fundamental dimension of their identity. Along these same lines, we need to recover certain typical forms of addressing divinity, such as dances, certain types of fasting, continence, etc.

25. The questions that arise out of the land and from traditional religions need urgent answers, keeping in mind that they were overlooked during the first evangelization. These responses will not happen so long as church models and structures from the past, continue to exist on the Continent.

26. In order for new churches to be born, a whole new kind of mobilization will be needed, intent upon developing a future oriented creativity. The demands of inculturation require that the local churches invent new models of evangelization. We are talking about allowing the people themselves to develop, with creativity, a faith language that is appropriate to their small communities.

27. In other words, all that we have said about indigenous theology and the emergence of autochthonous churches (a kind of "treasure" hidden in the depths of the institutional church) invites our commitment to responsible actions pursuant to the church's acceptance. We hope that this theological contribution will be perceived and admired as Good News that God offers to his Universal Church.

28. Inculturation presupposes a holistic understanding of culture. It implies a complex of ideas, values and conducts; a coherent worldview which is linked to religious expectations and hopes.

All the dimensions of the social structures have to be understood within the dynamic framework of inculturation. This is why some indigenous theologians consider that inculturation signifies first and foremost power sharing. Political power is very important for defending and strengthening a peoples' identity. Their historical project can stagnate when they lack effective power to bring about their ideals and values. Without political power, identity can only be preserved at a very high human cost and with an incredible amount of collective effort. Seen from this perspective, one can understand why it is indispensable to bring about a democratic society in order for inculturation to be successful.

A theology of liberation

29. Indigenous theology of liberation has been called to support and guide all of the processes that are directed toward the search for identity and liberation.

30. The marginalization of an entire race of people places a question mark over the actions of the church and upon christianity's credibility.

31. Theological discourse must focus upon Jesus the liberator and his opposition to the subjugation of any people. What has happened to the word of God that offers freedom to the captives? Jesus' actions constantly remind us that mission is directed primarily to the prisoners and the oppressed, to those that are hungry and thirsty for righteousness (Lk. 4:16-21).

32. In the social and historical context of exploitation and unconcern for the lives and cultures of the indigenous peoples, the principal problem is not the culture of modernity nor even secularism, but the grave situation of poverty and oppression in which they are forced to live.

33. After a long history of slavery, colonization and massacre, indigenous people today are drowning in a sea of disrespect for human rights. This is happening everywhere: among our own people, in churches

and states. The challenges are multiple: political, economic, cultural and religious.

34. In this context, we understand theology to mean a process and a mobilization toward liberation. Christian faith has to resist everything that denies the right of indigenous peoples to their rightful status in history.[12]

35. For the same reason that we dare not separate incarnation and salvation, we cannot divorce inculturation and liberation. Salvation began the moment in which the Word became flesh. Liberation is already implicit in inculturation. It is not a distant goal but a process and a permanent struggle. Inculturation is oriented toward liberating the poor and liberation can only be radical if its roots are planted in the cultural context of particular peoples.[13]

Because of the depth of the indigenous peoples' plight, both economically and anthropologically, liberation cannot be understood in partial categories and levels, but in its totality. It should start with the best of the anthropologies of the various peoples. This is how theologians in the African churches understand the problem when they affirm that liberation theology is a theology of fraternity, solidarity, reciprocity and of human dignity.

---

[12] Medellín, *Pobreza* (Poverty), n. 5; Vatican II, DP, n. 847; ED, n. 31; *Sollicitudo Rei Socialis*, 41,42.

[13] Vatican II, LG, n. 16; EN, n. 31,63.

CHAPTER THIRTEEN

'THE OLD FACE OF THE NEW EVANGELIZATION

Antonio Pop Cal

"Christianity has exercised an alienating function which has brought about the destruction of our personality and ethnic consciousness. It has made us renounce our unique perception of the universe, forcing us to accept a semitic and exotic conception of human existence..." Antonio Pop Cal is a Q'eqchi' Maya lawyer who is also trained in theology and philosophy.[1]

The Christian religion bears the indelible mark of proselytism, which is essential its nature. Nor has it desisted from the missionary activity in the Americas which it began five hundred years ago. The supreme hierarchies of the Christian churches persist in carrying out their intense evangelizing activity. They persist in seeing our Indigenous Peoples as essentially pagan. The merciless fanatical war which the Christian religion initiated against the indigenous population, back in the beginning of the colonization period, now disguises its infiltration methods in sophisticated ways. The execution methods (the stake, guillotine, noose, and maledictions) of old have been transformed today into subtle techniques of penetration. Take for example, the extraordinary phenomenon of the communication media which, while it does not exterminate the body, is annihilating the personality of our peoples.

The problem of evangelization

The problem of the evangelization of indigenous peoples remains the fundamental topic of the christianizers in our region. It has forced them to set aside their controversies and to sit down together to evaluate the fruits of their efforts during five centuries of evangelization. For some, "indios"

---

[1] This is the final part of a booklet entitled *Judeo Cristianismo y Colonización (Li Juliisil Kirisyaanil ut li Minok ib')*, published in Guatemala by Editora Cholsamaj for the Seminario Permanente de Estudios Mayas, No. 2, 1992. It is used with permission. In the first part of his paper Pop Cal has analyzed biblical texts and the historical experience of the Indigenous Peoples and concluded that judeo-christianity is innately expansionist and violent.

are fervent Christians who, having recognized the absolute value of christianity have embraced it. For others, "indians," in spite of their seeming faithfulness to the colonizers' religion, are, in fact, practicing religious synchretism. The religiosity of the autochthonous peoples, they discern, contains more of indigenous principles than of Christian dogmas. Their involvement in Catholic ritual or at evangelical services is, they c conclude, merely a façade that covers up their ancestral religion.

Five hundred years have passed and the christianizers are escalating their efforts to convert us. We are being told now about a "new evangelization", an "indian Christ", "an autochthonous church"; it is as if they were trying to convince us that the violent gospel of the past had become somehow converted today to the "Good News of love" rooted in our very own culture.

The hierarchy of the Catholic Church—the Latin American Episcopal Conference (CELAM)—has recently made a pronouncement to underline their strategies for a definitive and total christianizing of the Indigenous Peoples. They call it the "New Evangelization." This is what they have said:

> As Bishops here gathered in the face of the urgent challenges of evangelization in the present historical juncture, we share our reflection and our commitment to remain firm in our purpose to move from an indigenist pastoral ministry to and indigenous pastoral ministry so that autochthonous churches may spring up in our region. A necessary condition during this lengthy process is genuine love for our Indigenous Communities who reflect the image of Christ in all its diversity. They are like abundant leaves and branches that have sprouted from one trunk—the history of human salvation. In this reflection, which we now share with other pastoral agents, we explored indigenous reality in depth and their own evangelization process, hoping to discover what the Lord demands of us as pastors of these Peoples. We are looking, as well, for the components of that New Evangelization that the Pope has asked of us in the present historical juncture.[2]

Euphemisms

The flagrant acts of history can never be changed int something else with euphemisms such as these. Nor will the fundamental principles of the

---

[2] Department of Missions (DEMIS) of the Latin American Conference of Bishops (CELAM), 1989. For a different perspective on the role of DEMIS se chapter ten, by another indigenous author.

Christian religion, which are at the heart of its intolerant proselyting, be modified. These attitudes amply explain why, despite the new methods of indoctrination, "indios" have not yet been christianized: because they have been able to preserve, at the heart of their being, the resistance mechanisms which their christianizers have tried in vain to annihilate.

Going back even farther, it is clear that if we have seemed to be faithful to catholicism during four hundred years of colonization, it has been by the gracious acts of a supra-state organization which was called the "Supreme Tribunal of the Holy Office of the Inquisition". For four centuries, its brutal repression of indigenous rebellions and schisms in the Spanish colonies saturated our towns with horror and fear. It was only with the advent of Political Liberalism in our lands, in the nineteenth century, that we were allowed a brief respite from these barbarities.

A bitter battle between churches

The freedom of worship that, at the beginning of the last century, liberal governments decreed, made it possible for evangelical churches to enter our countries from the United States. This fortuitous event spelled the end for ever of the monolithic unity of the Catholic Church. Ever since, these Christian churches have become embroiled in horrendous squabbles among themselves over the percentage of members that each claims as its own. We have now become the object of their heated debates. A bitter battle, bloodless but nonetheless full of resentment, is being fought among these churches, in an attempt to win over the "indians". We have become spectators in this fratricidal feud among Christians.

The Christian religion was part of the superstructure of colonial society. Today, it continues to actively support the system by means of dangerous methods of attraction, absorption, and gospel inculturation affecting the minutest aspect of indigenous culture. The Latin American Episcopal Conference (CELAM) had this to say on the subject: "The word of God is a hidden seed in the heart of every culture which is often oppressed by external structures. But God remains in the heart of each culture, loving the community in an all-encompassing salvation project. The poor and crucified Christ within these communities desires to show himself, to grow, and to resurrect".[3] What this statement implies is that christianity—Catholic or

---

[3] Ibid, DEMIS-CELAM, 1987.

Protestant—has an alienating hold upon us. It keeps us weak against our oppressors, and turns us all into abject servility.

In order to keep themselves in a dominant position, our oppressors have always needed two fundamental power components: the State and the Church. The one suffocates the protests of the oppressed with the repressive arm of government. The other helps alleviate the misfortunes of the oppressed with false promises. The Church convinces us to forgive, to love our enemies, and induces us to become resigned to our fate. We are urged to imitate the crucified Christ who was humiliated and cruelly assassinated by the Jews. Then, as a further incentive to forbearance, the Church offers us a rosy and promising future. We are told that, however cruel the calamities we suffer in this life, much greater still will be our consolations after death. Indigenous Christians accepted the veracity of these doctrines, while allowing themselves to be robbed of their possessions. With hands clasped, they looked toward heaven where they hoped to find the eternal joy of revenge—the weeping and gnashing of teeth of their enemies.

The real function of christianity

With the above in mind, we need to ask ourselves now, what is the role that the Christian religion has fulfilled and continues to fulfill over us? A truthful answer, one that is clearly in line with the deadly effects upon our own self-awareness, is that christianity, from the moment it appeared among us until today, has exercised an alienating function, which has brought about the destruction of our personality and ethnic consciousness. Christianity has made us renounce our unique perception of the universe, forcing us to accept a semitic and exotic conception of human existence which sees sin as the stumbling block that, presumably, has provoked the devastation of the harmony of the universe.

The real function of christianity when it evangelized our awareness was to force us into obedience and submission. It has signified the end of our revindications; evangelization tells us to show clemency, mercy, and pardon to our enemies, whose hidden agenda is to hang on to power. The purpose of Christian evangelization is to snuff out any impetus toward rebellion. It means to dissolve, once and for all, our dreams of vindication so that we might become assimilated into the Christian body. Its objective is "to bring all things in heaven and on earth together under one head, even Christ" (Eph. 1:10). To this end Christians must become Jews unto the Jews, gentiles to the gentiles, and "indios" to the "indians."

If this were not the case, why is it that the christianizers cannot accept with equanimity our ancient religiosity and its practices? Why do they feel such a profound aversion to every manifestation of our religiosity? How else to explain this eagerness to inculturate us and infiltrate christianity, even to the most secret depths of our religion? This constant concern of the christianizers is a function of their conviction that "indians," so long as they remain fully christianized, will not become rebellious. The evangelizers, then, can continue to maintain their spiritual and social hegemony.

Here we have the real reason for the animosity of friars, priests, and pastors toward our religion: they have understood all too well that indigenous religion, as long as it remains alive, will protect "indios" from falling into the snare of spiritual colonization. Christian missionaries know full well from long experience that wherever the pre-hispanic religion remained strong there were foci of rebellion, mutiny, and sedition; it was there where opposition to indoctrination was fiercest. Missionaries are perfectly aware that "indios" that stubbornly adhered to their own beliefs remained outside of the spiritual "conquista".[4]

Christian intolerance and absolutism

The response of the indoctrinators has been perfectly clear: to attack unto the death the threat of indigenous religion; to destroy and exterminate for ever from the minds of our people the memory of their beliefs. Because, they realize, wherever the religion of the "indios" survives, awareness of their own identity will remain, and consequently the potential for rebellion. Like bloodhounds, the christianizers have pounced upon any evidence of our religiosity. They have resolved to persecute systematically the priestly institution of our religion. This is why, from the very first, the main focus and fury of the Christian attacks has been directed against our priests. It seemed obvious that once our spiritual leaders disappeared, our religious manifestations would automatically vanish. Christ, the jealous god that permits no rival, could not tolerate at his side another god who was different from him. His followers, his accomplices have resolved to persecute, destroy and, annihilate our spiritual directors.

---

[4] Severo Martínez Peláez, *Racismo y Análisis histórico en la definición del indio guatemalteco*. Faculty paper No. 1. San Carlos University of Guatemala, 1987, p. 209.

The religious intolerance of christianity is founded upon the inescapable evangelical mandate to "Go and preach the gospel to every creature; whosoever believes and is baptized shall be saved; but whosoever does not believe shall be condemned" (Mark 16:15; Matthew 28:19). Proselytism, which is inherent to the Christian religion, constitutes an assault upon human freedom, because it deprives human beings from the right to search for God on their own, by imposing upon them a particular understanding of "their" God, "their" welfare, "their" truth. This Christian intolerance is the result of the fundamentalism of their doctrine—its conviction that at its heart it contains "absolute truth", permanent and immutable. Its religion is the "only one" revealed by God. All the other religions of the world are nothing more than a "preamble," an "old testament" to the unique and unfailing revelation of God to the world, in the person of his son Jesus Christ. This is clearly stated in the CELAM document:

> From the creation of the world, God is present within the human community, which he has made in his image and likeness. This presence of the Lord is mediated by the Word that unifies the human community through the development of culture—this Word that is a seed hidden in the heart of every culture, which often is oppressed and deformed by sin. Within this human community, not only can the seed of the Word be found, but the presence of Christ poor and crucified, who desires to show himself, to grow, and to resurrect.[5]

Consequently, Jesus Christ the son of God and son of Man, impetuous and triumphant, looms above humanity as the only and inescapable mediator between God and men. This reasoning of the Christian doctrine check mates the freedom of free conscience because human beings are left with no alternative way to draw nigh to God, but within the church of Christ. The Christian religion has been so seduced by its own self esteem and proprietary attitude toward truth that it has come to believe that it is the only one that can rightfully suppress the freedom of conscience and religion of humanity. In defense of this "absolute and immutable" truth, christianity has committed the most horrendous crimes, when it has imposed its own religious convictions, whether directly through proselytism, or indirectly by means of spiritual discrimination.

Events in recent times have forced christianity, in contradiction of its own dogmas, to recognize freedom of conscience and of religion, because these are an inescapable corollary of human dignity. This despite the fact

---

[5] Ibid, DEMIS, CELAM.

that it quite clearly upsets and fractures the absolutism of this religion. No human institution, no matter how divine it may claim to be, can take upon itself the authority to intervene in the conscience of human beings without threatening the essential nature of human rights. The characteristic of human beings is to act in freedom, particularly as they search for good and truth, and reject evil and error. God himself has given human beings the extraordinary gift of freedom, and it would be a contradiction that he should go against this very same freedom.

CHAPTER FOURTEEN

THE EVANGELIZATION OF CULTURE

Pablo Richard

"Evangelization is an act of discernment that requires humility, silence, vulnerability. Above all, it demands faith in the presence of the God of history in the life and culture of peoples". Fr. Pablo Richard is a well-known Bible biblicist and pastoral theologian who is associated with the Departamento Ecuménico de Investigación (DEI) in Costa Rica. Born in Chile and the descendant of French Huguenots who settled in Ireland, he is dedicated to ministering to base ecclesial communities and the indigenous peoples of Abia Yala. This unpublished reflection is used with his permission.

In this short article I should like to reflect upon a concrete experience of evangelization of culture, after which I shall comment briefly upon several fundamental theological principles that guide and illuminate the subject.

A Concrete Experience in Kuna-Yala

In August of 1989 we put together a workshop on evangelization with the Kuna-Yala people who live in the San Blas archipelago, off the Atlantic coast of Panamá (within the Apostolic Vicariate of Darien). It was the third workshop of this kind. The participants were some fifty Kuna pastoral agents, about ten leaders of the Kina tradition (the name of their tribal religion), along with a handful of Claretian missioners that are working at a liberating evangelization in the region during the past ten years. The theme of the workshop was "The History of Salvation among the Kuna people and in the Bible".

We began by discussing together two hermeneutical principles—discussed by Carlos Mesters in his book, *Defenseless Flower*,[1] and based upon an ancient teaching of St. Augustine.

---

[1] Carlos Mesters, *Defenseless Flower, A New Reading of the Bible*, Maryknoll, Orbis, 1989.

First principle

God wrote two books—the book of life and the Bible. The Bible, God's second book, was written to help us decipher God's first book, the book of life. The Bible was written to give us back a faith understanding concerning the world and to transform all of reality into one great revelation of God. In this particular context, we said to them, God's first book was the cosmos of Kuna Yala and all of the life and culture of the Kuna peoples. It is there that God first revealed himself. This is God's first book. The Bible is the instrument to discern the Word of God in that first book.

In our role as Christian evangelizers we were offering them the Bible toward this end. If the Bible was useful to them as a means of discernment, then we could give them the Bible. But if the Bible, God's second book, did not help them to read God's Revelation en his first book—that is the life and culture of the Kunas—they were then free to reject the Bible. If they, within their culture and religion, were able to discern the presence of God and know him in his power and divinity, without recourse to the Bible, then they could, if they so desired, set it aside.

Second principle

If they accepted the Bible as the instrument for discernment of the Word of God in their own Kuna life and culture, they had to own the interpretation of the Bible. They themselves, within their culture and tradition, needed to appropriate the Bible and its interpretation. The first hermeneutical principle would be nullified if we were the ones to impose a predetermined biblical interpretation. Our task was simply to make the biblical text available to them, share its history and the tradition of interpretation, as well as create the ecclesial, community, and faith context that are necessary to interpret the Bible. Nonetheless, they had to be the authentic and real subjects of the hermeneutical process.

We must admit that at the beginning of the workshop, when we presented these hermeneutical principles, we were quite literally risking our mission and reason for being, as Christians and as evangelizers. We risked being put aside as just another matter for future discussion.

The results

We shall go ahead and state that the results were amply positive. After they had discussed and fully understood the two hermeneutical principles, they opened wide their hearts and their culture to our offer of evangelization. They accepted the Bible, as the second book of God which would enable them to read God's first book which they already possessed. They also agreed to take ownership of the Bible in order for themselves to become active and creative subjects of the process of biblical interpretation, and of the process of discernment of the Word of God in their own lives, culture and Kuna religion.

Over two days I expounded the great themes of the biblical history of Salvation: the Exodus, the Alliance (Covenant), the Land, the Confederation of 12 tribes; the struggle between the memory and identity of the people of God and the monarchy; oral tradition and its passage to written tradition, the appearance of the historical and wisdom books; the struggle of the prophets to maintain the memory and identity of the people against the political and religious forces of domination; the confrontation between true and false prophets; the resistance of God's people and their centuries old confrontation with empires (Babylon, Persia, Hellenism, Rome); apocalyptic literature as popular theology and liberating politics, etc. And in the New Testament we discussed the historical memory of Jesus and the early church.

At the same time they shared their tradition, stories and historical myths, their laws, wisdom, etc. The dialogue between the two "books" moved from unpretentious and spontaneous confrontation to systematic depth.

The workshop awakened unexpected enthusiasm, as much because of the knowledge and discernment of the Kuna tradition itself, as from getting to know and interpreting the Bible. The experience convinced us that an evangelization process was really possible—one that did not destroy the indigenous culture and religion, but to the contrary held it in high esteem. There was a total consensus that the Bible had led them to a better knowledge of their own Kuna tradition and that their own tradition was helping them to better their comprehension of the Bible. The Bible led them to rediscover and appreciate their Kuna tradition in a new way, and their tradition opened the way for a new understanding of the Bible.

The evangelization process not only contributed to the discernment and liberation of the Kuna religion, but the Kunas themselves were freeing us from an oppressive and colonialist understanding of the Bible. To the same degree in which they were discovering the presence of God in their own religious environment, they were teaching us to better understand the presence of Yahweh in our own past and present history. The Kuna truth and the biblical truth were mutually and marvellously enriched, and the fruit was a liberation of the Kuna culture or of the cultural appropriation by the Kunas of the gospel. The more we understood the Kuna tradition, the more we were able to understand the biblical tradition. And the more we understood the Bible, the more we understood the Kuna tradition.

The success of this experience of evangelization was due basically to the hermeneutical principles that have been stated. These were consciously taken on board by us, and we honestly explained them to the Kuna community. The two hermeneutical principles implied, of course, a new way of living and understanding our faith—a new kind of spirituality, a new attitude toward ethics and the church, a new concept of mission and evangelization.

But in addition to this, we must give recognition to the the Catholic mission practice in Kuna Yala during the past decade or so. The attitude of the missionaries, and of the presiding bishop, has been one of total and unselfish giving of themselves for the indigenous people. They have risked all, not only for the cause of explicit evangelization, but on behalf of the material and cultural life of the Kunas. Another fruit of this liberating Christian witness has also been the number of indigenous pastoral agents—including several Kuna priests—who are truly Catholic priests without ever ceasing to be wholly Kuna.

We have, thus underlined the hermeneutical principles of our experience. It now becomes necessary to also analyze the ongoing ecclesial and spiritual aspects of mission.

Theological Principles: Gospel and Cultures

To evangelize is to discover, discern, and listen

To evangelize is, above all, to discover the presence of God, to discern God's Word and to listen to it. God does not arrive with the evangelizer. God did not arrive in America in 1492, but was already here a long time before. Evangelization is not imposition nor convincing arguments. It does not imply conquest and dogmatism. Evangelization is an act of discernment that requires humility, silence, vulnerability. Above all, it demands faith in the presence of the God of history in the life and culture of peoples.

The Bible: our criterium for evangelization

The Bible is not a file full of truths, dogmas, histories, and laws. The Bible is first and foremost the Revelation of God in history, and us such it is the criterium for discernment of the Word of God in our history. The Bible is the canon of the Word of God—the legitimate and accepted "ruler" in order to "measure" the Word of God in history. The Bible has the authority to read in the history of peoples the Word of God. It is not enough to know the History of the Bible; we must also know the history of peoples in order to read in them the Word of God in the light of Biblical History. The Bible is the instrument that enables us to read the Word of God in the history and culture of peoples. In order for the Bible to have the spiritual force for discernment, its is necessary that those who are being evangelized appropriate the Bible and interpret it from their own reality and culture.

Culture: the identity of flesh and blood people

When we speak of Latin American culture, of peasant, indigenous, or Afroamerican cultures, etc. we are referring to the cultural identity of flesh and blood people that see themselves as unique and different. The Latin American cultures are living cultures. We cannot, therefore, speak of them in the same way as we refer to ancient cultures, such as the Hittites, Hebrews, and Greeks. Culture is not something abstract or dead. Culture is always the culture of a people, which within their own milieu are affirming their life and their identity.

Nor is culture something supra-structural. This might apply to the dominant culture, but certainly not to the culture of peoples that are struggling for their liberation. As an indigenous Guatemalan said: "culture is agriculture," by which he was affirming the relationship of his culture to the land, with life. To speak of the culture of a people while ignoring their life and death problems (problems of land, work, housing, food, education, etc.) is to engage in abstract and false discourse. Therefore, the evangelization of culture is always the evangelization of a specific people who are fighting for their land, for work opportunities, their homes and their health, etc. These flesh and blood human beings find their identity as a people, and affirm by defending and constructing their own lives.

Culture: a specific dimension of the practice of liberation

Culture is not an asset that is safely hidden away. It is a dimension of our practice. For this reason, we must relate culture to every other dimension human practice—with awareness, with an historical project, with theory, with organization. Consequently, the evangelization of culture is not done in museums, in laboratories, nor in universities, but it happens at a specific moment within the liberation process. The evangelization of culture should be an integral part of the liberation of a people.

By the same token, cultures always have histories. When a culture becomes free, so does the history of its people; above all, the history of its struggles, its moments of heroism, its resistance.

The evangelization of culture and the BECs

The BECs are the privileged space for the participation of the people in the church. I am not speaking solely of the involvement of the laity, but also of the people as people, above all the people who are poor and marginalized. For the rich and influential laity it is somewhat easier to participate in the Church. But how difficult is it for peasants, Amerindians, Afroamericans, and women to take part in the life of the church! Furthermore, these groups do not participate individually, as "personalities," but as a people, as groups within the Church.

This involvement in the Church of groups which have traditionally been marginalized is only possible through a significant mass movement of BECs. In the BECs the people can participate creatively; by means of the BECs the poor and oppressed can begin to develop a new language, new symbols, new songs and prayers—a new way of reading the Bible, that is to reflect upon their faith. They can create new ministries, new services, and new forms of commitment in their communities.

This creative participation of the people in the BECs takes place within the context of their own culture, that is, of their own religious and cultural identity. This certainly doesn't take place in a day. At the beginning the people only repeat what they have heard. But if the method of creative involvement in the BECs is maintained over the years, then the people will begin to create out of their own cultural reality.

When this happens in the Church, there is the opportunity for a new language and symbolism to be born—a new rhythm and liturgy which is authentically Amerindian, Afro-American, peasant. It is in this sense that I believe that the BECs, or similar structures, are today in Latin America the most appropriate and efficient structure for the evangelization of culture or the cultural appropriation of the gospel.

CHAPTER FIFTEEN

POLITICAL ASPECTS OF GUATEMALAN REALITY:
MAYAN WIDOWS SPEAK OUT

Rosalina Tuyuc

"It is not enough to sign accords; they must be implemented without delay, and decisively... We Mayan widows of Guatemala feel that what happens after the accords is more important than what takes place before and during the negotiations around the table". The author is a Ki'Che' Maya and a coordinator of CONAVIGUA, the pressure group that represents the interests of the women who have been widowed because of the army violence in the highlands of Guatemala. Ms Tuyuc is one of four indigenous women who were recently elected to the Guatemalan parliament. This chapter brings together two short statements on the role of the military in Guatemalan life. They are used with permission.

Life has both taught and forced us to put up a fight. The age old repression, and especially today's counterinsurgency measures by the Guatemalan military, have brought about a lot of suffering. Despite it all, we have been able to draw from the depths of our dignity—of our history—and find a source of strength and resistance. We have been able to survive as persons and families, as communities and a people. We have also survived as grassroots organizations and, to a certain degree, as a vital element in the life of our nation.

A time of formation and participation

More than anything else, what has enabled us to work together has been the mutual supportiveness of our widows and children, of our displaced persons and refugees. The families of those that have been detained and the communities of resistance, our youth, organizations of peasants and mayas, labor unions and religious groups—all have contributed their share. It has been a process of discovering and of understanding our own situation and that of our country. This has been a time of learning and sharing, of getting our act together in spite of our diversity, and never forgetting our underlying unity of purpose.

We have had to overcome every kind of difficulty. Yet, it can be said today of the Guatemalan Mayas, that because we have taken some decisive steps, new avenues have opened up for us, and that we are now moving forward. In short, we have become organized and have achieved a consensus. We are now an active and creative component of an incipient Guatemalan civil society. In fact, through our "compañera" Rigoberta Menchú—the 1992 Nobel Peace Prize winner, the struggle for human rights and the rights of indigenous peoples has gained world wide attention.

But we move forward day by day in the face of tremendous obstacles, fighting every inch of the way. We women and our families confront defamation, intimidation, and persecution. Our dignity as women and as mothers has been threatened by the authorities. We have been assaulted by the military and its paramilitary groups, particularly the PAC[1] who have been placed to control us.

Human rights violations

We suffer all of this on behalf of an elemental right which is enshrined in our constitution: the universal rights of individuals and of peoples. However, claiming ones's rights takes a gigantic effort in Guatemala. And to stand up for the rights of others is a task for very great and worthy men and women. It requires a constant struggle, and daily risk taking to act fully upon these rights—in spite of the fact that Guatemala recently signed the Global Accord on Human Rights. So, as part of our ongoing struggle, and undeterred by our plight, we are claiming this accord as our own. We hope to God that it will not turn out to be just another empty document that our government has signed.

Yet recent events are not at all encouraging. The following are some of the violations to which we have been subjected. The forceful military induction of hundreds of our young men under the age of eighteen (in May and June of 1994); repression and intimidation in Colotenango (Huhuetenango department); and the repressive actions, in several locations, of PAC and the military commissioners (the virtual rulers in most highland villages). In addition, the relatives of persons whose bodies were dug up in Chuchipac, Río Negro, and Plan de Sánchez who have been intimidated. In fact, psychological warfare and intimidation is being waged against various grassroots indigenous organizations including our own CONAVIGUA—against displaced persons, Christian groups, working women, and against me and my family. The list of violations is endless.

---

[1] PAC, "Patrullas de Autodefensa Civil", civil self-defense patrols, forcibly conscripted from among the Mayan males by the army.

Militarization of the environment

Our main obstacle is the militarization of our environment. The army acts like an army of occupation, as strangers in their own land (they are, in fact, strangers to the indigenous peoples!) Their conduct is almost fascist. They have forcibly turned thousands of indigenous peasants against the civilian population, with armed violence and repression against their sisters and brothers. Thousands of pages of denunciation fill the files of national and international organizations, making Guatemala's record the most despicable in all of Latin America. The responsibility for the greater part of these acts falls squarely on the shoulders of the Military Chiefs.

In recent years, the government has acquired a civilian façade, but the military are still in command. The weight of the military's political power lays heavily upon every aspect of national, regional, and local life in Guatemala. Nothing escapes their attention. This inhibits the possibilities for civil society, particularly in the rural areas where the repression and control is most severe and criminal. The military acts with impunity. They capriciously twist and distort the laws. However much they try to hide it, this society is still militarized into its farthermost corners and at every level of human endeavor. The image change that the government and military are attempting does not hide what is the true reality.

In this situation of discrimination, of repeated violations, we widows continue to carry on a tireless fight against the forced military service of our menfolks. After all, we are engaged in other forms of service to our beloved Guatemala. In this way we are contributing, with all of society, to demilitarization and to the democratization of the entire country. We are fighting for our very lives.

It would seem that everything is upside down in Guatemala. Today, we who are concerned that the law be obeyed and are demanding respect for the dignity and rights of persons, are the ones who are accused of being "instigators", "destabilizers", "subversives", and many other epithets. But, thank God for the intelligence, reason, and eloquence that we have been given. Thanks to our ancestors' teachings, we also have the qualities of wisdom and equanimity. This allows us to present our case instead of resorting to calumnies and threats against those that do not see things precisely as we do.

Forced military service

It is very interesting to note that in Guatemala state matters are defined by the army. There are many examples about which we could say a lot of things. But I shall only mention the problems that have arisen as a result of the petition from CONAVIGUA that obligatory military service be abolished. Instead, we ask that it be a well-regulated voluntary patriotic service, that freedom of conscience be respected, and that a civilian social service be set up.

The Constitution of Guatemala, which I have before me as I write, is the highest Law that should govern our nation. Under the section dealing with "the Army, sub-heading, Prohibitions,[2] the Constitution states that members of the Army of Guatemala cannot exercise the right of suffrage, they are not allowed to petition on political matters, nor can they exercise the right of collective petitioning. I read this, then I remember that every day it is the army spokespersons who determine the official position on various national issues. Moving back a few pages to the section on Civic and Political Rights and Duties, I notice the following sub-heading: "to do military and social service, in accordance with the law."[3]   I then remember that only the military service is enforced in Guatemala, and not the social service, and that the first is done in violation of numerous laws and many human rights.

The law is clear. Military service must be carried out "in accordance with the law." But forced military recruitment is openly illegal. This is what we are denouncing and petitioning to be changed. It is against the law of freedom of movement[4] for young men to be dragged to the barracks against their will. It is the same as kidnapping or illegal detention. There are hundreds of open files on cases such as these in Guatemala, in national and international human rights organizations.

On the other hand, voluntary service is reasonable, legitimate, just, and above all, completely within the law. CONAVIGUA is not asking for the disappearance of the army, nor of military service. What we are petitioning is the elimination of forced military recruitment, which is in total violation of the Constitution.

---

[2] Chapter 5, article 248 (Prohibitions) of the *Political Constitution of the Republic of Guatemala*.

[3] Ibid, Chapter 3, article 135, paragraph (g).

[4] Ibid, Article 26.

Defense of human rights

Our Constitution goes even further. It says:

> Any judicial action against human rights violators must be public and can be undertaken by simple denouncement, without any legal formalities. The resistance of the people in protection and defense of the rights and guarantees that are in the Constitution is legitimate.[5]

Going even farther, CONAVIGUA and other groups with whom we are talking and working together in this struggle, are making use of our right to propose constitutional reforms. We want to broaden the Constitution to incorporate our main petitions. These are: the explicit prohibition of forced military recruitment, altogether voluntary military service, recognition of freedom of conscience, and the establishment of a civilian social service. The Constitution states that a minimum of five thousand duly registered citizens can propose constitutional reforms.[6] CONAVIGUA alone has gathered more than twice the necessary number. However we intend for the petition to be presented by every possible sector of society, whether organized or not. To date we have receive a considerable number of positive responses.

The privilege of social service

We are demonstrating in this way just who are the ones who are truly on the side of the law and who are those who violate it. The distinguished army leaders do not have to remind us that they are doing social service. We know this full well. We realize that they have a tremendous infrastructure at their disposal, with equipment, personnel, and a budget which other civilian ministries are lacking. In a democratic nation, the task of the army is to protect our territorial sovereignty and integrity. It is not their responsibility to take part in matters of internal policy nor in the administration of social services. That burden corresponds to other state ministries. In other words, instead of the army's social service being meritorious, it is just another example of the things that the army should not be doing in Guatemala!

We repeat once more that if they are convinced, as they say, that the

---

[5] Ibid, Article 45.
[6] Ibid, Article 277.

conscripted young people present themselves to the barracks voluntarily, they should not feel threatened nor concerned about our fight for a voluntary military service. When one is sure of something, one does not see threats coming from every side. If the army is convinced of this, they should look upon our struggle with a lot of sympathy, and help us. And if they are truly respectful of the law, they should stop confronting virtually every sector of society with threats and vilification.

Unfortunately, the ministry of defense and spokespersons for the military find it easy to avoid the issue by defining this struggle as political and ideological. But one cannot blot out the sun with one finger. The majority of the people sense that these are the signs of the times. This is the preeminent moment for Guatemalan civil society. The consensus of the majority will sooner or later have to be heeded. And it will be echoed at the international level.

Hope against hope

Despite this harsh reality, our country seems to be looking at this moment for a political solution to the crisis that we are living, as the government, the army, and the URNG[7] sit down to negotiate around the table. Beginning with the Cerezo administration, with (president) Serrano, then (president) Ramiro de León Carpio,and more recently (president) Alvaro Arzú, there have been several attempts to find a political solution to the economic, social, political, and military problems of the country. Some gains have been made, which allows us to hope. This in itself is a great, history making fact for our people. The worse thing that could happen is for this hope to be defeated and forever annihilated. Nonetheless, from our perspective, this should not only be a hope for the future, and for future generations, but we would like for our own present to improve as well.

For this to happen, it is not enough to sign accords; they must be implemented without delay, and decisively. What is at stake here is not whether this or that item gets on the agenda, however important these may be to achieving the ultimate peace. What is endangered, if the accords are not implemented, is dialogue, which is the way to achieve democracy. For this reason, we Mayan widows of Guatemala feel that what happens after the accords is more important than what takes place before and during the

---

[7] URNG: Unidad Revolucionaria Nacional Guatemalteca, the United guerrila front.

negotiations around the table.

The first trial by fire, which will prove whether there is a will for peace, is the implementation of the Global Agreement on Human Rights. Next comes the accord on Resettlement of the Uprooted Population. Unfortunately, the administration is not passing the test. And it is all too probable that there will be no decisive implementation unless the International Verification Mission makes it here soon, and the Truth Commission gets down to work quickly, with additional pressure from the international community and of all civil society. Otherwise, our hopes will be dashed.

It must be said quite frankly that if the Guatemalan government and army are left to their own designs, we will have no guarantees. Confrontation will increase, and reconstruction of this beautiful multiethnic Guatemalan nation will be postponed with all the social costs that this implies. In the same way that the gains that other generations of patriots in Guatemala and Latin America dreamt about fifty years ago (in the Revolution of 1944) had to be postponed.

We mothers and widows, a portion of civil society that is committed to the struggles of the Maya peoples to achieve their rights—in the name of all women and men in our motherland[8]— call upon the uprooted, upon the whole of society, and upon our friends who stand beside us during these birth pangs, to intensify their efforts, and not permit them to be put away in some anonymous file, or even worse, buried along with our hopes.

Let us expedite the implementation of the signed accords. We ask for the immediate installation of the International Verification Committee, and of the Truth Committee. We *must* continue fighting for a New Guatemala, where Peace, Justice, and the respect for our human and Maya rights, shall soon become a reality. LET THE SUN RISE! LET THE DAWN ARRIVE!

---

[8] Editor's note: The expression "madre tierra"—which the author substitutes for the universal Spanish term "patria" or "fatherland"—has the double sense of mother earth and motherland.

CHAPTER SIXTEEN

CHRISTIAN AND MAYAN SPIRITUALITY: A DIALOGUE

Wuqub' Iq'

"We must be quite clear about the foundations upon which we can start building a dialogue... that will help each of us to face up to our own reality in all of its harshness. We must be crystal clear about the root causes of the particular ills that need to be set right". Wuqub' Iq', nee José Angel Zapeta, is a former K'iche' Catholic priest and an associate of Nobel Laureate Rigoberta Menchú. Having returned to the spirituality of his forefathers—as are a growing number of his indigenous colleagues—he actively encourages dialogue between Maya and Christian religionists.[1]

Introduction

What is the meaning of life, both personal and collective, here in Central America? This is an important question. It is particularly so for those of us who must justify our actions and life commitments, at this moment in time when all kinds of social models are being put forward. Our problems are economic (the imposition of a global market economy), social (acute poverty), and political (crisis in government), as well as ethical (changing values, permissiveness, moral collapse, and growing conflict).

In this context we dare to contribute our word of encouragement, hope, and solidarity for all those who defend the sacredness of life, the worth of the poor, and who desire a better tomorrow for all of our peoples. In short, we are grateful to everyone who is staking a claim to space for reflection and struggle on behalf of an alternative society. Our own point of reference are the countless centuries of experience that the Maya have; as well as the decades of struggle for justice by progressive and democratic groups. People are hungry for answers to unresolved questions. The paths that the

---

[1] "Presupuestos teórico-metodológicos para un diálogo interteológico" was originally presented at an Anabaptist Consultation on Christ and Culture (Nicaragua, July, 1994). It has been published by CIEETS of Managua, Nicaragua in *Xilotl: Espiritualidad Indígena*, vol. 9, no. 16, 1996, 51-79.
This summary is used with permission of the author and publisher.

powerful sectors of society have imposed upon us have not often been helpful in discerning the "divine will". How many people are trying to relate to God, to feel God, to please God, to praise God! But we always are left with the nagging doubt whether our actions and worship, our sacrifices and rites are really pleasing God. The very fact that we feel these doubts is in itself positive, because, as someone has said, "even when we are convinced that we are doing God's will we might be totally mistaken".

This essay reflects a search for guidelines that while taking our daily reality into account, can throw light upon the future, and guide our pastoral planning. Believers need help in defining their attitudes toward their present situation, and in discerning where the Creator and Former of Life (both personal and collective) is at work—the one who Christians call "the Lord of history". We indigenous find ourselves, however, seeking understanding by way of negation rather than affirmation, because the latter can all too easily be manipulated. Our critical sense of what is evil can be lulled to sleep even by our personal and collective religious practices.

The thesis of this essay is that any dialogue between Christian and Mayan theologies will necessarily require its own frame of reference; it will also need to determine who is to take part in the dialogue. Once this is done, we can arrive at guidelines to orient respectful and peaceful relations between the practitioners of both faiths in our indigenous communities. This means that we shall be touching upon topics in this paper that Christians may deem to be controversial, and which are even new to the "first nations" of Abia Yala.

The History of the Native Peoples

Some five hundred years have passed since our lands were invaded and colonized by the Spaniards. The COPMAGUA document[2] points out that, during their more recent history, the Maya peoples of Guatemala have experienced three holocausts: the war of conquest and occupation; the thousands that were subsequently killed, tortured, displaced and forced into

---

[2] COPMAGUA (Coordinación de Organizaciones del Pueblo Maya de Guatemala), was founded on 11 May, 1994. At that time a consensus document, "Identity and Rights of the Maya People," was presented and approved as a contribution to the peace negotiations that are taking place between the Government, the Army, and the guerrilla movement (Unidad Revolucionaria Nacional Guatemalteca).

concentrated villages called "repartimientos" and "encomiendas", and in the 1970s and '80s, the massacre of thousands of innocent Maya by the army.

A necessary critique of christianity

The christianity that arrived with the "conquistadores" can be understood as christendom, which is to say that it was essentially unlike the fundamental human values which were set forth by the God of Jesus Christ. Christendom is more a culture of conquest and domination; a religious ideology for soldiers, adventurers and zealots. It is the foundation of power, privilege and wealth; and the source of false values that focus more upon quantifiable and superficial matters, than upon ethics. Christendom was thus able to justify the Right of Conquest, with all that this implies: misappropriation of lands, forced labor, destruction of existing political and economic structures, and the persecution of the wise men, scientists and religious leaders of the Maya nations.

To speak of an encounter between two worlds or two cultures is an euphemistic way of referring to the armed clash between a majority of indigenous peoples and the small bands of invaders under the Spanish crown. Instead of respect for the humanity of the original inhabitants of our lands, rather than resorting to dialogue and cooperation, the christians practiced imposition and caused deprivation. The aim was to procure more lands for the crown, more territories for christendom. The defeat of infidels and pagans, they were convinced, was a victory for the rule of Christ.

At the same time, there was another approach with implications for Christians today—the actions of friars like Bartolomé de las Casas, Antonio de Montesinos, and others like them. Yet, despite the positive aspect of their actions in favor of the indigenous peoples, their approach can be questioned in light of the spirituality and the best interests of the indigenous peoples. First, because, even in this model of mission, the right of the Crown to take possession of our people was never questioned. Secondly, indians had still to kneel and be baptized as Christians in order to save their lives; they had to learn the catechism and to faithfully practice the sacraments of the Church. Our people were told that their lives could be saved by becoming Christians and vassals of the Spanish King. In so doing, they were able to escape the worst excesses of imposition, domination and exploitation. Nonetheless, after all is said and done, a peaceful, spiritual conquest was not any less of a conquest and a domination of my people. At no time was there an opportunity for face to face negotiation and respectful dialogue among equals, despite our differences.

What other evidences do we have of the spirit of conquest in christendom as it was imposed upon the religion and spirituality of the indigenous peoples? (1) The Church owned great wealth—large and sumptuously adorned churches, houses, schools and lands. It was often the case that the religious orders—the same as all the other landlords—owned large "haciendas" with ill paid laborers. (2) The Church has always been politically allied to the powerful sectors of society. It was first tied into the vested interests of the Crown, and ever since has walked hand in hand with the conservative and liberal elite. (3) The Church is behind the culturally insensitive attempts to civilize and christianize the "poor, barbarian indians"—and is therefore the worst enemy of Maya spirituality.

The present situation: A tentative evaluation

Until recently, the religious crusade of the Catholic Church in the Maya communities took the form of persecution against the clandestine practices of the Maya religion. Its spirituality was written off as witchcraft and "things of the devil". To be converted to christianity meant abandoning these beliefs and practices.[3] Indigenous people needed to receive instruction in the catechism and practice frequent attendance at the sacraments.

More recently, Catholic Action (C.A.) has been gaining ground in the social conscience of the Maya, with considerable influence in our communities. In truth let it be said that there are different currents within the movement, the most consistent being the promotion of human, social, and labor rights, which has been labelled dangerous and subversive by the power structures and by international imperialism. Counterinsurgency measures, with threats, kidnapings and killings, are practiced against indigenous catechists and their communities. The fundamentalist sects which proliferate in the villages, accuse C.A. activists of being guerrillas, and go on to label the Catholic Church as idolatrous and to demean Maya spirituality. To become converted to these groups and enter into "the true

---

[3] Giving up their beliefs and practices requires the Mayas to throw sacred icons and ancient documents over the cliffs, not keeping the special days of the sacred Maya calendar, and to stop practicing the maize and rain rituals, and the special marriage and birth ceremonies, etc.

religion" one must abandon both the Catholic and indigenous practices. One is required to believe "only in the Bible", to concentrate on heavenly matters and not concern oneself about material things.

Another religious current, at present rather low key, is made up of indigenous that are beginning to perceive and understand the religious experiences of the Maya from a different perspective.[4] Our beliefs are taken seriously and given thoughtful consideration by increasing numbers of our people. Some among us are seeking for the revelation of the Christian God, "the Only God". in the spiritual experience of the indigenous peoples. This includes a variety of attitudes and methods which we shall later discuss. This has spun off a number of pastoral approaches variously called "indigenous", Maya", and "aboriginal", among others. What have they done and what have they accomplished? Actually, for us, it is more important to ask whether the goals that they express are the same as their planned objectives, that is what is behind their actions.

Meanwhile, the people who are the flesh and blood repositories of the spirituality of the ancestors of indigenous peoples, have not remained passive either. In this regard, we shall refer to several facts and actions on which we base the fundamental thesis of this paper. They are the necessary conditions for an "intertheological" dialogue between the Christian traditions and those of the indigenous peoples.

Theoretical and Methodological Presuppositions

Whatever the socioeconomic reality, it can usually be evaluated from several socioeconomic perspectives. Whenever a particular reality requires change, clarity of expression may help to bring together common concerns. So we shall state quite emphatically that we do not speak from the vantage point of comfort, business, and privilege; these are the values of the society

---

[4] The Indigenous Pastoral was guided with considerable wisdom in the '70s, but in the decade of the '80s had to be suspended because of the violence. It resumed in 1986 with a similar orientation. The Guatemalan Conference of Bishops was at first sympathetic to it, but gradually became uneasy with the approach of the Indigenous Pastoral team. So they withdrew their representative from the team and eventually set up their own official commission. Right now there are two approaches: the official Indigenous Pastoral of the Conference of Bishops and the Pastoral of the Maya People. They are distinguished primarily by their methods and particular objectives.

that has deprived us of everything. We approach the issue as people who have been disinherited and impoverished. So only those who truly share our feelings and who desire to build—together with us—a promising future for all of Guatemalan society, will be capable of understanding us and of entering into dialogue with us. Otherwise, we will be left with nothing more than a monologue about God which has been devised by the powerful of this earth, and which does not take into account those in whose name they profess to speak. This is why we must be quite clear about the foundations upon which we can start to build a dialogue that will help each of us to face up to our own reality in all of its harshness. We must be crystal clear about the root causes of the particular ills that need to be set right. As a first step, we shall need to rigorously apply a socioeconomic and anthropological analysis to our recent past.

The challenge to liberation theology

The methodology of liberation theology continues to be useful. The spiritual and intellectual leaders of Latin America have made a theological contribution to the Christian churches that has shaken the very foundations of North American imperialism and challenged the highest levels of the Catholic church to a veritable kairos. Yet, in spite of the seeds of hope that were sown, a certain stagnation—a process of involution—is evident. It is the result of the retrograde and conservative measures that are being implemented by the power structures of the church, in unholy alliance, one strongly suspects, with the powers of this world. Today, the privileged subjects of the Bible, the *Anawin*, the "Remnant of Israel", the little people and destitute ones of the Gospel—the poor that Latin American theology speaks about—have been pushed aside by a wealthy minority. These have now become the privileged subjects of the new Christian culture that the Catholic church is promoting—or if you wish, the "one nation under God" which Californian evangelicals are about.

When we say that it is important to recover and carry forward the Latin American methodology of a decade ago, we mean to challenge liberation theology to continue to be a "critical reflection on the praxis of liberation in the light of the word of God". The privileged subjects of this reflection are the poor. They are sacraments of God in history who, by their very presence, are living voices who cry out that the minimum requirement of charity is justice and solidarity. The poor are questioning the ethics of liberal economics and politics at both the institutional and personal levels.

The medium for this challenge is their grassroots religiosity—within the Church, their own spirituality, and their unique pastoral concerns.

At Puebla, we indigenous peoples were recognized by the Latin American bishops as the suffering face of Christ in the Americas. We were deprived of our lands, ignored and pushed aside in the juridical and political reordering of colonial society. It was part of a conscious effort to impoverish us socioeconomically and culturally. What today's bishops fail to recognize is that the practices of the conquest and of colonialism continue today: we are still being robbed of our own unique identity. *We are asked to desist from being ourselves*. Even though this policy has, admittedly, affected a large proportion of the population, there remains a substratum of self-identity harking back thousands of years. Nonetheless, the Maya people lack the room to develop and fully express themselves—in their music and art, spirituality and family relations, and oneness with nature. This condition is called "cultural poverty". It comes from being denied the right to be authentically ourselves; to be allowed to grow in the awareness of our alienation from our own political, cultural, and religious values.

Liberation theology, that is, critical reflection upon the praxis of liberation, in the light of the Word of God, will have to evaluate the various pastoral approaches, crusades, and campaigns that are pushed upon the poor, and in particular, the indigenous peoples by the many churches and sects in Guatemala.

A Challenge to the Faith and Culture Dialogue

We must move beyond the concept of dialogue between faith and culture. When Christian intellectuals discuss the relationship between these two dimensions, they tend to emphasize the rational aspects, being careful all the while not to modify Christian doctrine. By maintaining noetic purity they ensure that a dialogue will take place that benefits christianization. The logic goes something like this: "We must dialogue at all costs, because you need to be christianized in order to become civilized; and it will also guarantee you eternal life". This is a fundamental presupposition of the Christian faith which Pentecostal and apocalyptic groups over-exploit to the detriment of a liberation commitment to impoverished and undiscerning communities. Although some variants of this approach may, perhaps, decry cultural genocide, behind every kind of evangelization the same rationale remains. All the while, the roots of our authentic human and cultural values continue to be destroyed in the name of God. Our values, some of them admittedly acquired, have proven their worth to us for more than five centuries. In contrast, the values that so many Christian denominations now press upon us are not only unhelpful but hinder our potential for real development. We would be better off if we were not subjected to the powers of money, of military boots, and of Bible dispensers.

But Christian intellectuals, looking upon our culture theoretically, have concluded that, after more than five hundred years of systemic pressures, our culture—and above all our religion—is syncretic. Having decided that the culture of the indigenous peoples and its new emerging generation maintains a significant substratum of christianity, they call for a greater understanding of indigenous culture, and even its encouragement, while ensuring that it draws essentially closer to the fundamental principles of the Christian faith. So goes the reasoning.

We insist that dialogue requires that we go beyond this approach. From our point of view, this is little more than a dialogue of professionals who have taken on the task of purifying popular religiosity (the spirituality of my people), in the interests of orthodoxy. Whether or not this same process obtains within the churches is no concern of ours. But if it is applied to the indigenous peoples, we want to be the ones to defend two essential dimensions of human existence: Life and faith.

In a dialogue, both sides must take part as equals. There must be mutual respect, no predetermined outcome, and freedom of choice for all. The Christian faith speaks from a body of presuppositions[5] which, when they are fully lived out, can either attract or repulse.[6] The culture of the indigenous peoples is their way of life, in every dimension, spiritual and material. Therefore, when indigenous people speak about culture we are addressing a different understanding of reality which has as much right to exist as any other.

---

[5] I think we are growing weary of religious demagoguery, of words that aren't bolstered by actions, both personal and institutional. In a land where death, untruth and corruption reign with impunity, where the lives of individuals and groups are threatened, what we need are not obfuscating clouds. We require a clear and transparent light to illumine and encourage us.

[6] When people have worthy values which are their own, christianity's attraction may not necessarily ensue in belief and identification with institutional christianity. It may, however, bring about mutual appreciation of value, coordination of goals and meaningful community living, whether it be in a town or within an entire nation. The real and systematic rejecters of Christianity are the powerful, because it threatens their vested interests—their properties, employment practices, and killing the people with arms, drugs, and demeaning public spectacles.

The role of culture in pastoral theology

Perhaps we might consider some of the more recent efforts to understand culture and its relationship to the command to evangelize, which is of the very essence of the church and of christianity. A helpful typology discusses three different understandings of culture and respective approaches to inculturation.[7]

1. *Cognitive or aristocratic meaning*. Culture is a function of high education in arts, sciences, and letters. Inculturation is therefore tied to knowledge acquisition.

2. *Ethnic or "classist" meaning*. There are tribal cultures and there are "more civilized cultures". Thus one can speak of more or less cultured races. Inculturation is adaptation to certain life-styles and living together with this or that culture group.

3. *Anthropological meaning*. Culture is one of two vital contexts in which persons are born, grow, communicate and express their utopias. It is the framework within which every human phenomenon can be understood. Consequently, the author concludes that we shall only be capable of understanding the culture of a particular person or group, when we know how to explain in a coherent fashion their every action among a multiplicity of expressions. Inculturation, therefore, must take into account the totality of the life of a people, their symbolic world and their social organization. Evangelizers must recognize that it is necessary to learn before they can teach, begining with the values and virtues of a people in order to find their fulfillment in the gospel.

Our comments on this third definition of culture do not mean to diminish in any way the value of the dedicated work of a committed Christian who is looking for guidance from the different policy making levels of his church—Rome and the Latin American and Guatemalan Bishop's Conferences. Rejecting the first two definitions of culture out of hand, along with their implications for the church, he opts for the third which he sees as a

---

[7] Angel García Zamorano, "La inculturación: Problema antiguo con rostro nuevo" (inculturation, old problem with a new face). In *Voces del tiempo: Revista de religión y sociedad*. No. 10, Guatemala, 1994, 18-29.

more complete and necessary definition, as well as the right direction for the pastoral ministry of the church. Nonetheless, he is critical of two official church documents on the subject, finding them ambiguous and short on real life applications. The Christian faith, he insists, needs to be expressed through indigenous cultural patterns.

Anthropology also comes to the aid of the indigenous peoples. From their point of view, there will always be ambiguity and a not very satisfactory relationship between christianity and Mayan culture and religion for two fundamental reasons:

1. Christian presuppositions—the theory, theology and doctrine—are as alien to us as the missionaries. This last remark is not meant to undervalue the vocation, dedication and service that missionaries offer to their parishioners and to needy persons in general.

2. Dependence upon foreign personnel, as well as upon foreign finances and doctrine, theory and method, along with their institutional models, are clear signs of immaturity in a church that is now five hundred years old. Catholicism has been unable to train suitable indigenous personnel, nor has it been up to developing a theology, with accompanying institutions and structures, that fits our cultural forms. Profound changes will have to be initiated for this to happen in our time.

Key Elements in Maya Spirituality

I am keenly aware that I am not an authority on this subject. Which is why I shall discuss the profound reality of the daily lives and spirituality, as well as the essence of Maya religion in a very tentative way. I want to focus upon some of the fundamental and sustaining aspects of Maya spirituality, taking into account their values and attitudes toward life, human relations, and nature.

The cosmogony of the Maya

The cosmos is one of the principal referents of Maya spirituality which has to do with every aspect of human, animal and vegetable life. This is why the ancient sages, our "abuelos" (ancestors),[8] were acute observers of the heavenly bodies. And they continue to do so. Stars and planets are frequently mentioned in their rites and ceremonies. They are also the reference points of the flow of time, announcing warm and cool periods, rains and droughts, as well as other natural phenomena such as hurricanes, earthquakes, and rainstorms.[9]

The best known celestial bodies are the nine planets of the solar system. Three interlocking calendars were developed based upon the movements of the moon, the sun, and of Venus. Also, each of the constellations was given a name by the Maya. The principal elements of the cosmos are fire (heat and light), earth, water, and air. Each is capable of representation by a divinity who is ceremonially venerated in recognition of its usefulness in everyday life. Natural phenomena such as rain, the sun rays, tremors, and hurricanes are anthropomorphically represented.

Human beings stand not at the centre of nature, but are part of it. Perhaps they are the most responsible, most aware, and most dynamic of creatures, but they are certainly not alone in gratefully worshipping the *Rajawal Uwinaqil*, the Creator and Former of Everything, who is also called *Tzaqol B'itol, Alom Kajolom*, in Ki'Che' maya.[10]

---

[8] Editor's note. The Spanish word "abuelos", grandparents, rather than "ancestros", reflects the indigenous sense of the proximity and pertinence to their present lives of all the members of their race that have gone before them.

[9] Editor's note. The author plays upon the Spanish term "temporal", a derivative of "tiempo" (time). As an adjective it means "temporary", but as a noun it signifies "seasonal weather". In Central America, the term often refers to a phenomenon which coincides with the spring and fall solstices when drenching monsoon-like rains inaugurate and close the rainy season upon which much of Mesoamerican food production depends.

[10] Editor's note. Each of the four words in the second title refer to the cardinal points and symbolize the four ways in which the universe was created. Four is the number of creation and of universality. "*Tzaqol* signifies the divine will to become manifest and act in nature. *B'itol* is the formative force which is part of that will which acts in creation. *Alom* is an incomprehensible force, the omnipotent emanation of that germinal word of wisdom, of such immensity that it cannot be adequately expressed in any language, nor can any brain capture and understand it. *K'aholom* is the infinite space that germinal matrix constituted for the creation of the universe" (Vitalino Similox Salazar, *La expresión y Metodología del Pensami-*

The goodness of the *Rajawal Uwinaqil* is diversely expressed through anthropomorphic representations of the cosmos. Father Sun represents the daily and ritual recurrence of Maya spirituality. He announces the hope of another dawn, shines upon us by day and pours his warmth upon every human being. Without his largesse life would be impossible. Grandmother Moon is wise in the knowledge of the life cycles of the vegetable and animal worlds, and particularly the human realm. Her nine month cycle corresponds to the nine moths of human gestation. Understanding and right practice of the lunar sacred calendar corresponds to human psychology, with personal implications for spiritual development and the orientation of the psychological qualities needed for responding to the demands of family, work, and religion. From the depths of Mother earth, inseminated by the heat and rain that comes from Father Sun, life is born. At her breast we are nourished, and at the end of the road we rest in her arms.

Principal elements of Maya spirituality

The main components or guiding principles of the spirituality, rituals, and interpersonal relationships of the Maya are:
   Life, in all of its expressions, is sacred and is therefore venerated. Because it is, for us, hierarchically more important even than the category of truth, we have avoided the differences that arise between religious groups on the matter of truth that are so harmful to community, family, and personal life. Everything that has to do with life is very important to us and must be reverenced in our daily living and rituals. Human life—the quality of life of the elderly and adults, of young people and children of both sexes—is every bit of it essential. We need the experience, example and wisdom of older men and women. We need responsible adults to maintain the order of things. And because young people and children are our hope for the future, they are the objects of our care, from birth until initiation.
   Animal and vegetable life express the variety and marvelous colours of nature. This is why we associate the qualities of nature with plants and animals. Every plant and animal is useful to us when nature is allowed to maintain its harmony and interdependence. Before the use of pesticides and herbicides, we knew how to work our land, as well as to protect it with rites such as sexual abstinence and other religious ceremonies. There are

ento Maya Contemporáneo en Guatemala. Guatemala, Editorial Cholsamaj, 1992, p. 62).

many extant examples of this, some of them quite current, and others that are being displaced but can still be recovered.

Respect in the community. First the parents and then the entire community initiate children in the qualities of mutual respect. Every person learns how to fulfil their particular role, influencing and complementing each others character and personality. Our rituals are the maximum expression of this quality. Those who continue to uphold the values and principles which undergird the Maya thinking and conduct are exemplary in their respect to others; but they can become very angry when alien people or government officials show a lack of respect for them and their values. Such a thing happened in Santiago Atitlán in 1990, causing the village elders to demand respect of the military authorities for themselves and the way of life of their people.

Each of our ritual gestures are accompanied by verbal expressions, stated with great feeling. We usually kneel, after reverently addressing the four cardinal points, whenever we ask forgiveness, give thanks for our family meal of tortillas and beans, and when we implore good health for the family, our animals, and crops.

Respect is a quality that is evidenced by the Maya in other ways. Upon arising, children and young people great their parents and elders with clasped hands. Not to do so is to be not much better than a pig or any kind of animal except birds, who greet each other every morning when they awaken. In rites of initiation and passage one can observe how much value is placed upon respect in families, communities and among the Maya people in general. For example, during the several phases of marriage, each partner is evaluated by the families of both of them, because it is understood that the essence of one's personality shows in the degree of respect and real humility that is demonstrated in each of the ritual acts that are performed. The degree and quality of respect that is shown is related to the degree of confidence, obedience and training that parents have attained with their children. It is also a guarantee that any mistake can be corrected, because children will be respectfully attentive.

Balance and complementarity. This is a guiding principle in the thought and actions of the Maya. They have observed it at work in nature and seek to practice it in their social relations. Perhaps the most helpful way of understanding this is to think in terms of paired opposites in a dialectical relationship.

Everywhere in nature we find pairs of opposites—light/darkness, fire/water, east/west, hot/cold, etc.—which are indispensable to each other.

The Maya worldview conceives of the four corners of the universe in the sense of totality and balance. Human life—woman and man—is also created in equilibrium and complementarity, in understanding and experience, in wisdom and decision making. Balance and complementarity extends to the future, involving the children that are brought forth by women and men. Having said this, we must admit that this principle has been altered by recent conditions in the lives of the Maya people.

Many of our towns are built upon the principle of totality and equilibrium. This is why we have towns with four "cantones" (quarters), north, south, sunrise, and sunset. Some also have an additional central quarter. This arrangement helps us to understand the kind of relationship that human community must have with nature, because it is most important to maintain optimum life conditions—vegetable, animal, and human—on the planet. This latter day concern for our environment and for ecology was already present among our grandparents who taught us to work our lands and to keep them up. This practice was gradually set aside as the size of our plots, on which our livelihood depended, diminished and we were forced to find subsistence elsewhere.

Resistance. We cannot claim that this quality, as it relates to work, struggle, and hope, is unique to our people. At the other extreme, we are not totally passive or uncaring. Rather, over the past 500 years of deprivation and exploitation, oppression and discrimination, our seeming passivity has given us the opportunity to build up our energies for the moment when they can become a force for change. Change is expressed in two dimensions: 1) the present during which we are able to recover our roots in order to set down the foundations for a different and better future; 2) the future in which we shall work together to overcome the conditions of misery, hunger and need in which we presently find ourselves. Resistance is not mere words (demagoguery), but action that can be translated into lives and attainments.

The sacred lunar (maternal) calendar

Altogether, the day symbols of the sacred-maternal Maya calendar are 20, which together make up a Maya month. Thirteen months make up a lunar year of 260 days. We could also say that a Maya week consists of thirteen days.[11] These indicators have an influence upon persons. Personal character traits are more or less pronounced according to their location on the numerical scale. A desirable and well balanced temperament has an indicator of 7 or 8. Each day relates to some aspect of cosmic and human reality, as well as to the traits of animals, plants and human beings. Four examples will suffice.[12]

The first day, *Ajaw Batz'*, symbolizes time and space, the beginning and the end of everything that exists. Our ancestors represented time in the form of a spool of thread which unravels over time, so that, like native cloth, history is woven on the loom of time.[13] Persons who are born on this day are judicious defenders, skilful artisans, and have a strong character. Priests and priestesses are particularly gifted. *Ajaw E*, day two of the month, continues the historical process which began the day before. People who are born on this day are kind and teach others the right way. Subsequent days represent the triumph of good over evil, the regenerative power of nature and of human sexuality, the plumed serpent (Quetzacoatl).

Day nine, *Ajaw Kawoq*, is dedicated to women, our wives and mothers who bring happiness into the home. It also symbolizes the just arbiters and defenders of the people's rights. Those who are born on this day are noble and can forecast the future. The following day, *Ajaw Imox*, signifies the left arm which complements the work of the right arm. Two days are tied to natural phenomena, and others to life and death. Significant plants (maize), animals (birds, serpents, dears, dogs) and instruments for hunting and fishing also have their day and relate to natural phenomena and to human conduct. There is also a day dedicated to the concept of justice, peace, and equality.[14]

---

[11] Editor's note: See the Introduction and chapters 4 and 5 for fuller explanations of the Maya way of reckoning time.

[12] Editor's note: The following two paragraphs summarize a detailed explanation of the 20 Maya day names in Wuqub Iq's original article. The names, and sometimes the meanings, vary from language to language. They are here rendered in Ki'Che' Maya, The author prefixes each name with the title *Ajaw*, or lord. The lunar, or *Tzolkin* calendar, appears to be the only part of the ancient Mayas' incredibly complex and imcomparably exact computation of time that survives today in the Guatemalan highlands.

[13] The simile is drawn from the cone-shaped spools that are attached to the loom. The weaver's shuttle-cock draws the many colored threads to form the pattern of the beautiful Maya cloth.

[14] Editor's note: Here ends the summary.

From the above considerations we can now draw some conclusions. We must keep in mind that we Maya live within an all absorbing frame of reference whose cultural standards are being imposed upon every aspect of our lives. Despite these adverse circumstances, the Maya continue to maintain the authenticity and integrity of their calendar. The beauty of this calendar is the way it correlates astronomy—marvelous deductions concerning the movement of the sun, earth, and grandmother moon—to possible general tendencies in social psychology based on date of birth, all of which has positive implications for counselling. The implications for a spirituality that brings together personal, celestial and historical dimensions are clear.

Suggestions for Interreligious Dialogue

I would like to suggest four starting points for our discussion.

Recognize Maya spirituality and religion

From the outset I must make my own position clear. There cannot be true dialogue without a prior recognition of the "other" who is not merely the object of a charitable—even solidary—act, but is indeed another subject. And not just any subject but a collective subject who, over the centuries and millennia, have developed their own spirituality. What we have today is essentially what at one time was the religion of all the Maya peoples. This spirituality impacted the values, conduct, attitudes and actions of our race. Because religion and calendar are completely articulated, spirituality also structured time in our collective life—our festivals, periods of work and of rest, etc. This is why the rites of initiation and of passage which determine what a person is also affect the entire community.

But the balance between privilege, freedom, and obligation was upset with the Conquest. Our values were systematically opposed so as to totally eradicate them. Subsequently there were variations on the same theme: attempted destruction from within, in order to manipulate, absorb or subdue our spirituality. For over five centuries our religion has been persecuted and demeaned, subdued and assimilated.

Nonetheless, passive resistance has been effective and promises to be even more dynamic in the future. We are reaffirming our roots, our values and our principles. Meanwhile, a process of rebuilding our religious structures is underway, with altars, festivals, initiation and passage rites, along with the formation of councils of Maya priests and priestesses. They are the protagonists of a genuine and enriching interreligious dialogue and encounter with Catholic and Protestant grassroots leaders, often without the full knowledge of their respective hierarchies.

Mutual respect of lifestyles, integrity and cultural expressions

Respect is a necessary condition if we are to have any conversation that can be called dialogue. Its basic premise is to overcome theological and doctrinal stereotypes that demonise the religions of the indigenous people; which is what was done to us in Guatemala during the invasion and colonization, and after "independence" by both conservative and liberal governments. Consequently, the various churches and denominations will have to undergo an attitudinal sea change in this respect. We are living in a day when basic human rights and freedoms are being upheld and defended—including the specific rights of indigenous peoples which, as a result of their struggles, are now recognized and defended in international forums. No longer can we take for granted that persons, and least of all entire communities, can continue to be dominated and subjected indefinitely.

In my view, every authentic religion supports basic values and encourages their practice in every time and place. Authentic spiritualities do not encourage discrimination, oppression and exploitation, nor do they justify genocide and ethnocide (whether physical or cultural). This provides common ground for greater understanding among us. It gives us a common basis for cooperation with each other in conflict resolution and meeting needs, at every level of human intercourse.

Commonalities and differences

Distinguish between what we have in common and our real differences. The things that we have in common will make understanding and cooperation between us easier. Our differences, because they are by nature and practice more specific, are what divide us. As I understand it, there are certain principles which are shared by every human being, including ethical values. However, the specific content of these values in each culture is the result of historical processes and local customs such as social initiation, or social control, through various sanctions and stimuli. The real differences stand out when we ritualize our values, using gestures, exhortations, words, natural symbols (e.g. fire, water, incense, candles, chocolate), time, space, and persons, all of which are important to the Maya. So that what we might call liturgical action can exacerbate our differences. Liturgy condenses and intensifies the spiritual experience which is so difficult to understand. Liturgy takes into account foundational experiences, myths of origin, guiding theological principles, and those things—both material and human—which are essential to the structure of liturgy. Because of this, liturgy can hinder encounter and dialogue.

It is not here, then, that we should begin our encounter and dialogue. Liturgy touches upon the most intimate and sensitive aspects of our spiritualities, which is where the contrasts and differences stand out. So instead of helping us to understand each other, more often than not liturgy has produced friction and confrontation, as both universal and local experience has so amply demonstrated. Because it is so fraught with difficulties, liturgical sharing should be left for some future date, as the experience of the various Christian confessions has shown.

Peace and harmony between us

Encourage peace between the diverse religious groups within indigenous communities. This is the best place for a meeting of bodies and minds, because, at the local level, we share the same needs which are born of poverty and the structural imbalances of the so-called Third World. It is here also that we find men and women with deep religious principles and feelings—although unfortunately, all too often they are being manipulated by transnational religious enterprises. The various Christian denominations have contributed to the dismemberment of our community structures and practices. This is all the more reason for us to recover values such as mutual respect and responsibility for what we hold in common. Together we must regain our appreciation for our history and ethical and religious roots. The search for a "more realistic understanding of Scripture" by all the faithful in any given community should lead to a shared Christian language and practice. This could make it easier for us to work together in peaceful coexistence, as we grow in respect and understanding for the practitioners of the millenarian religion of the indigenous peoples.

Conclusions

What I have written on behalf of the indigenous peoples—exploited and marginalized as they are from the social benefits of their production, oppressed and subjected, both politically and culturally—is a very modest attempt at dealing with a topic as complex as religion and spirituality. Consequently, what I, an Indigenous Person, am about to affirm are but tentative suggestions presented for debate. At the very least this will commit me to pursuing the matter further and to systematize my own experience.

Yet, while these propositions may be provisional, I suggest that they have intrinsic value because of my personal experience in both Christian and Maya spirituality, along with training in both theology and anthropology. In other words, these are not haphazard remarks, but initial impressions, some of them, and more basic considerations, the rest, which will need more systematic treatment, such as working hypothesis and fundamental theses for further development.

So we are really talking less about conclusions than about points of departure for analysis, for discussion, debate and systematic study. These starting points are not arbitrary but responses to real questions and concerns. We seek to plumb the depths of human spirituality while at the same time responding to the real needs and problems which the impoverished and deprived indigenous peoples are trying to overcome.

In order to speak about an inter-theological dialogue between christianity and Maya spirituality we must state our motives (objectives and goals). Then together we can determine the framework for our dialogue, and who is to participate.

What is the reason for my insistence upon dialogue? As one of the indigenous peoples, of the Maya, I am concerned that the research, the literary production, and the initiatives are only being carried out by Christians. Furthermore, like it or nor, their objectives are still proselitistic—the evangelization of culture, the inculturation of the gospel, aboriginal pastoral ministry. What the Guatemalan Episcopal Conference (CEG) did is worth noting, as a case in point. They asked Maya Christians what they thought of "their church's" approach to gospel inculturation. Some of what came out of this was echoed in the Santo Domingo Bishop's Conference (1992). But what was left unsaid is that the bishops are bothered by the legitimate reappearance of an autonomous Mayan religion, which at its most radical is a direct confrontation with the Catholic church and with the Protestant groups that are following the same approach of a new spiritual "conquista". As for the latter, they are confusing and dividing the community structures. Their approach to conversion contributes to the passivity of the people when they offer naive, even fanatical, explanations of the indigenous' reality of misery, kidnappings, assassinations, and exploitation. Their message focusses the attention of our people upon "the sweet by and by" when they could be doing something together with their sisters and brothers in the struggle to resolve the root causes of our problems and needs.

I shall conclude with the following thesis: The Maya People and their various linguistic communities are heirs to a spirituality which is thousands of years old which has every right to continue its development. Furthermore, a new religion was forced upon us early on; today, other Christian denominations are urging us to opt for their spirituality. So why shouldn't the Maya be able to exercise their human right to choose their own religion. It is their right to reconvert and reappropriate what belongs to them, as a consequence of a new awareness of their own identity, roots, values, and spirituality. Consequently, no person or institution can stop the Maya from developing and practicing their renewed spirituality.

The Maya people at this moment have two spiritual fountains: christianity and their Maya religion. Some of our people know christianity better and are nourished by it, others are opting for Maya spirituality. A third, intermediate group is segmented into those who bring their "mayaness" to their Christian faith, and those whose christianity draws heavily upon the Maya tradition.

Only one option is open for purists, when considering the above responses. Either one religion or the other. To accept both can be seen in two ways: as syncretism (whatever the mix) or as ecumenism (with rationality and order). We can either respond with intolerance toward each other or we can try dialoguing, so long as each side understands its place. Unfortunately, there will always be those who find it hard to relate and to come to an understanding.

CHAPTER SEVENTEEN

TRADITIONAL VALUES AND CHRISTIAN ETHICS:
A MAYA PROTESTANT SPIRITUALITY

Antonio Otzoy

"We indigenous do not believe in lost causes. We patiently resist
pain, enduring the infringement of our rights and continuing
disrespect by others. In silence and hope, and love and compassion, we also await the manifestation of the children of God".
Pastor Antonio Otzoy is the General Secretary of the Herman-
dad de Presbiterios Mayas, which fosters ethnic identity, as well
as common ecclesial goals and strategies, for the numerous
Maya communities of the National Presbyterian Church of
Guatemala, of which he is an ordained minister.[1] This paper,
prepared in 1992 in the midst of growing tensions between
Presbyterian "mestizos" and their indigenous sisters and
brothers, has been translated with the author's permission.

Introduction

This has not been an easy essay to write. There has been all too little
fraternal dialogue between the values of the gospel and the values of that
distinct culture of Guatemala called Maya! With some hesitation I should
like to argue factually that we indigenous people have never been understood because no one has cared to listen to us. Instead, we have been
caricatured. Pejorative—even insulting—terms are constantly hurled at us,
exceeding, at times, the bounds of common decency. It is one thing to talk
about the gospel, it is another to experience it as a transforming force that
dignifies, redeems us, and affirms our equality before God.

If only those who interpose themselves between Jesus and the Maya—who label us pagans—would recognize that he[2] speaks to us, walks
with us, and shines upon our pathway. We feel somewhat like the blind man
who cried out to Jesus to have compassion upon him while the multitude

---

[1] Otzoy, a Kaqchikel Maya, is a graduate of the Faculty of Theology of the
Protestant Mariano Galvez University (Guatemala) who for seven years was
instructed in the mysteries of his ancestral religion.

[2] Editor's note: Mayan cosmology reveres one God who is both male and
female, Father and Mother. However, the Spanish language and a patriarchal
society predispose us to use male pronouns for the Supreme Being.

repressed him. Undeterred, he cried even louder; Jesus healed him and he went on his way singing. We Maya experience the same thing as the blind man. We have heard the voice that tells us that our faith is saving us. We follow him and glorify his name (Lk. 18:35-43). We want to deepen our knowledge of the Jesus who held people spellbound, who exalted the nobodies, welcomed the marginalized (lepers and others), and who condemned the proud and the sinners. Because he does the same today, we are eager to meet this Christ whose voice enthralls us and does not make us afraid.

Admittedly, we have no right to demand from any group of Christians attitudes that are outside the boundaries of their comprehension nor is it for us to label them. We do recognize that, in the providence of God, there are situations and conditions that, from our indigenous perspective, may seem inadmissible, if not to others. Keeping this in mind, we shall attempt to point out some elements that could help us to discover where we are in agreement and where we disagree with our "mestizo" sisters and brothers.

In the five sections of this essay we shall talk about God the Creator and the value of life; about how we relate to God in community, and toward each other. By way of conclusion, I shall suggest some challenges to the church. We want to discuss these matters, not in a theoretical way, but from an indigenous perspective, hoping to inspire an open and frank dialogue on the subject of the interface between Maya and Christian spirituality and values.

God the Creator

One way or another, every human being acknowledges the ultimate existence of one Creator God. We Presbyterians confess that:

> In the beginning it pleased God the Father, Son and Holy Spirit (Heb. 1:2; Jn. 1:2,3; Jb. 26:13; 33:4), to create the world out of nothing in order to reveal the glory of his eternal power, wisdom, and goodness (Ro. 1:20; Ps. 104:24). He made everything in the world, visible and invisible, in the space of six days, and it was very good (Gen. 1-2:3; Col. 1:16).[3]

---

[3] "Concerning Creation", The Westminster Confession, No. 4. Douglas Kelly, Hugh McClure, and Philip B. Rollinson, eds. Greenville, S.C., Attic Press, Inc., p. 9.

The significance of recognizing God as creator is highlighted in other confessions as well. Take for example Luther's confession in the Minor Catechism.

> I believe that God has made me and all creatures; that he has given me my body and soul, eyes, ears, and all my members, my reason and all my senses. He still preserves me and all creatures. He gives me clothing and shoes, meat and drink, house and home, wife and children, fields, cattle, and all my goods. He richly and daily provides me with all that I need to support this body and life. He defends me against all danger and guards and protects me from all evil. God does all this purely out of fatherly divine goodness and mercy, without any merit or worthiness within me. For all this it is my duty to thank and praise, to serve and obey him. Because all that I confess in this article is plainly taught in the Bible; therefore I firmly believe it.[4]

The Maya people have similar beliefs. Listen, if you will, to the following prayerful confession:

> That God is the *Tata Ixel* (Divine Father), that everything that is around us, animals and plants, are our sisters and brothers, because he cares for us equally. *Ri loq'olej Ahaf* (the Almighty God, in Kaqchikel) protects all of us; he feeds us, watches over our way, and grants us the gift of a joyous life.[5]

Note the coincidences and differences between the Reformation creeds and the Maya confession. In both, the supremacy of the one God is upheld, as well as human submission to the deity, which must be voluntary for the dialogue that has been promised not to be broken. Reformation theology indicates that the capacity to dialogue is an evidence of the supremacy that God has granted human beings above all other creatures (who, nonetheless, are equally cared for by God, according to the Maya invocation). In any case, human participation in dialogue is essential. Along these lines, Paul Tillich comments that

> Man occupies a preeminent position in ontology, not as an outstanding object among other objects, but as that being who asks the ontological question and in whose self-awareness the ontological answer can be found.[6]

---

[4] Luther's Shorter Catechism, Articles 115-120.

[5] A prayer by the indigenous "rezadores" who go from house to house praying for the needs of the people.

[6] Paul Tillich, *Systematic Theology*, vol. i, p. 168. Chicago, The University of Chicago Press, 1966. Tenth printing.

Reformed theology holds that the centre and source of human activity is God. But we must be careful not to generalize, nor to accept a theological criteria as uniquely valid, particularly when it comes to ascribing human activities to God. As Guatemalan Christians we need to broaden our criteria in order to understand why some practices should be considered bad or merely inadequate. The Maya and Reformers need to get to know each other in order to understand the contributions that each can make to the other's theology.

The value of life

To look at life with respect to its value allows us to broaden our understanding of what we can do with it. It is both necessary and urgent to recognize the value of life instead of following in the way of Cain. We must cease snuffing out life like a candle, enveloping peoples and communities in darkness. We must love life, protect it, care for it in order to enjoy it freely and unselfishly. Jesus comes so that people can have "life in abundance" (Jn. 10:10). It is not just a matter of being alive, as far as Jesus is concerned, but of nourishing life and enjoying it. When the Jewish people had wasted their lives and given them up for lost Jesus came to the rescue (Lk. 19:10).

For life to spring forth among the people, we need to take the sacred commandment—"You shall love your neighbour as yourself" (Matt. 22:38)—seriously. When we recognize the Old Testament truth that men and women are created in the image and likeness of God we dignify life and uphold the self-worth and respect of human beings. The New Testament teaching that life is a gift of God, that Jesus gave his life for the redemption of many, that he came that we might have abundant life, gives further s strength to this Christian conviction.

What is the Maya understanding of life? We Maya believe that not loving one's neighbour is tantamount to cursing God. When we fail to serve others we sin against God who is the foundation of community. These beliefs are based upon the two concepts of *xahan*—sin and sacredness—and *urtisanic*, curse and blessing. Both concepts are bipolar,[7] i.e. each opposite

---

[7] Maya reality always consists of two or more dimensions—heaven-hades, life-death, light-darkness, good-evil, above-below, east-west, north-south man-woman, youth-aged—which, while opposits in Western philosophical terms, are experienced by indigenous peoples as complementary.

compliments and gives meaning to the other. Because life is sacred, what does not bless life curses it. It is a sin. Human beings have the choice of being one or the other. We find the same message in God's dialogue with the Old Testament Patriarchs (Dt. 30:19,20).

Maya ethical values can be strengthened through the power of the gospel, based upon biblical principles and the promises of God. Let us look at the two sides of *xahan*. Understood as sinfulness it is comparable to St. Paul's list in Galatians 5:19-21. It is the opposite of good; thus the Maya require of each other that we abstain from evil so that God can become manifest in the realm of evil. When we practice evil we become accursed and God cannot come near us. *Xahan* is also "the holy other" (a reality which is not solely attributed to divinity).[8] One cannot play around with it because, as creatures of the divine, we cannot go against our source. The name *Ahaf* (Lord, *Ahau*, in several other dialects), which is equivalent to the Old Testament Yaweh, came rapidly into use as a profoundly respectful way of addressing God. *Ahaf* is the God that becomes human—he lives within us as individuals (his messengers) and a people (his creatures, expressions of his being). *Xahan* is to observe the divine commandments, its a correct attitude toward others, upholding life and human existence. Therefore, and because we are children of God, laws that preserve life and the commonwealth are important. At this point we have, of course, moved into the realm of the "thou shalt not kill" of the Ten Commandments (Ex. 20:13).

The *urtizanic* of the Maya is blessing, it is the very presence of God—his dominion in all and for all which culminates in Christ, according to St. Paul (Col. 1:16-17). The *xahan* and the *urtizanic* act as the Maya's compass in life—their mirror, point of reference and mandate. The dark side of *urtizanic* is to transgress life, which brings about a curse upon oneself and one's people.

How human beings relate to God

The Maya believe that God makes himself known. Men and women are called to know goodness and to do good. But we are incapable of doing anything good to God, except through his children with whom he is closely

---

[8] Editor's note. This belief seems to be akin to the Polynesian concept of *tapu* (taboo), in which good and evil in the spirit world are both "sacred" or out of bounds to mere mortals.

linked in community. We do good to God when we do good to our neighbours, to people in need, whether or not they ask for our help. Good is always a community activity: the community is where God expresses his divinity and humanity—it is therefore a place of good, where men and women encounter God. Because only in community does God show himself and can he be experienced. The gospel makes clear that it makes no sense to do good to someone that can return the favour (Lk. 6:33). It is very clear that doing good must be directed toward people in need.

God shows himself at every dawn, when we look at the stars, when we feel a breeze, enjoy the light, when raindrops fall. In all of these experiences we ask that *Loq'olej* (the Divine God) not remove himself from us. In rural areas, places of worship fill up because they bring to mind the experience of God who has drawn near and brought men and women together once more to work for the common good.

The oft repeated biblical statement, "I am Yaweh your God" speaks to the Maya in many ways. God has shown himself to us—and is recognized by us—as the *Ru k'ux* (the Centre-God) and *Q'a Tat'a* (Father). In this way, the Maya communities recognize the fact that God is our only God. This is why they cannot leave their homes without praying to him for permission. The religiosity of the Maya people is based upon the fact that anything that they do without God's permission is *xahan*. The most devout people in the churches of Guatemala are the Maya, because an intrinsic part of our being is to stay close to God.

Life in community

The cosmogony and religious life of the Maya is not isolated from the rest of their lives. Indeed, it is part of their whole environment. There are people in the world who find fulfilment only in church; others find it in politics, or in the exercise of their personal and civic rights and duties. Such people make a clear cut distinction between religious rights and privileges and everything else that they do in life. In stark contrast, spirituality is the totality of life for us Maya. Everything that we do and feel is constantly related to every aspect of our environment. If people could only learn that an isolated perception of reality fragments communities; that separation destroys active, creative, and productive involvement in the community. In the long view, whoever thinks that individualism is a shortcut to success is condemned to failure. Those who isolate themselves—physically, geographically or ecclesiastically—from the wider community, insisting that "there can only be problems when too many people are brought into the picture", will turn out to be mistaken.

Mayan culture has not yet lost its communitarian ethos. That is why, when you visit a rural area in Guatemala, a church "fiesta", no matter the reason, becomes a community celebration. Everybody shows up, invited or not. Religious events can turn into feasts that unite communities. The church building is jam-packed, everybody brings enough food to go around; everybody has a good time and shares what they have with everybody else. In sum, community is built on the goodwill of everyone. To live as the Maya do is what Jesus called being the salt and light of the world (Matt. 5:13,14).

Mutual respect in the community

Paul emphasizes over and over again the need for parental respect, drumming it into the hearts of the early church. He speaks about promises for those who obey and complications for those who don't. The Maya believe that we should respect all our elders, not only our parents. We are blessed when we respect the elderly—that is, when we do it out of good will, otherwise we receive no reward. Younger children should heed the reprimands and commands of their elders because they that have the benefit of a lifetime of experience and close walk with their Maker.

When it is directed Godward, respect is closely tied to worship and praise. Towards our elders it becomes veneration and gratefulness for their friendship and comradeship. Respect is a voluntary giving up of selfishness, allowing the Spirit of God to work deep in our lives. It is the incarnation of God, the real evidence—in humility, service and harmony—of the presence of the God that we worship and adore. Whomsoever is unable to live in community is incapable of praising and worshipping God (1 Jn. 2:6).

Challenges to the churches

Having made the point that there is no overt contradiction between the basic elements of the Maya worldview and the message of Jesus, we are left with the painful task of pointing out the error in which institutional christianity in our country has fallen with its continued lack of tolerance for Maya culture. It is a theological error because of its heavy burden of identity denial. Church leaders deny our identity when they, in effect, say to us that the way you express yourself is wrong because it is different; your feelings and worldview are wrong because they are outside the bounds of our comprehension. Your experience of God, because it is mediated by your natural environment, must be sinful. Therefore, you are not worthy of our respect. We are not equal, so we cannot live together as Christians.

Examples of this colossal error in basic human understanding abounded during the time of the Conquest. We have only to remember how shocked the Spanish were at the Maya symbol of the cross. But why be surprised at the coincidence of an astronomical cross that indicates the cardinal points in heaven and earth? When faced with this "revelation", could one not argue that God—the one and only Lord—has a right to reveal himself according to the worldview of each people? Can we not accept that transcendent knowledge by another people at some point may coincide with the Christian revelation of salvation by the incarnation and death of Jesus?

With all due respect, we need to ask the following questions of ourselves. How do we feel about people that are different from us? Do we see ourselves as sisters and brothers, worshipping the same Father God who sent us his Son? Even if the answers are negative, perhaps some good can come out of it. Can we not find parallels in our situation to what Paul writes to the Roman community about his people Israel? "They too have now become disobedient in order that they too may now receive mercy as a result of God's mercy to you?" (Ro. 11:31). Whatever the case, we indigenous do not believe in lost causes. We patiently resist pain, enduring the infringement of our rights and continuing disrespect by others. We reject the epithets of "satanic" and "idolaters" while in silence and hope, with love and compassion, we also await the manifestation of the children of God.

When churches require a particular kind of conduct from us, we feel impelled to suggest that they need to take a hard look at aspects of their religious culture which are not in harmony with gospel values. Take for example methods of evangelism which try to impose faith. The good news of Jesus is that "no one can come to me unless the Father who sent me draws him" (Jn. 6:44). In stark contrast to mournful crucifixes and dead Christs, God's gift is a free expression of joyfulness; it is fully affirming and respectful. The exchange, "Lord if you are willing... I am willing, Be clean!" (Matt. 8:2,3), expresses well God's free gift in Jesus.

It was not only christianity but alien values as well that were forced upon ancient peoples whose faith and cultures had existed for centuries. The Christian message, as proclaimed to us by Spain, imposed a language, an ideology, imported values, and a worldview that are alien to us. Foreign attitudes and cultural values were also taught to us by protestants. Today, new values are imposed upon us. By way of example, Maya believers are made to worship God to the tune of "spiritual" instruments[9] which are mainly suited to nourishing a kind of individualistic spirituality which fits a particular culture. It is characteristic of a certain type of quietest personality which values a solitary relationship with God.

For the Maya, faith is joyful celebration of God's blessings: of abundance, the *ajkik* (good). This is why we sing joyfully to the rhythm of the marimba; it is why the whole community shares in the food. They join together in one meal which signifies life for all. The source of blessing and of life is maize and the sacred tortilla; it gives us the strength to stand firm, trusting in a better tomorrow.

Lastly, we regret the imposition of anti-Christian practices, such as the "faith sales" which take advantage of the poverty and hunger of our people. They are being victimized by an evangelization which, with cavalier contempt, uses the transparency and simplicity of the Maya to gain followers.

The Church and the Maya People are not, as such, self-exclusive entities. Having pointed out that the gospel has contributions to make to the Maya heritage, we close with a question that might guide our future dialogue: Does the gospel merely contribute positive elements to the Maya heritage, or does it revitalize a faith that already existed?

---

[9] Editor's note. This is an alusion to pianos and pump organs, the only instruments that were deemed worthy of use in Protestant services while marimbas and other native instruments were considered "worldly".

CHAPTER EIGHTEEN

"A NATION WHERE EVERYONE HAS A PLACE"

Ofelia Ortega

"Since the sixteenth century, Chiapas has always been a region
of indigenous resistances... There were religious overtones to
the rebellion". In the early days, "Catholic priests of different
regions called for uprising and alliances were formed with the
lower clergy". In recent years, "a reign of terror was imposed
against evangelicals who live in Chiapas". Then the Maya of
Chiapas shouted "Enough!" on New Year's Day, 1994. The
Rev. Ofelia Ortega has, for a number of years, been the Latin
American Secretary for the WCC's Ecumenical Theological
Education, in which capacity she has been close to the reconciliation process in Chiapas. This article, translated from French,
is used with her permission.[1]

1 January 1994 is the day when the Ejército Zapatista de Liberación
Nacional (EZLN or Zapatista Army for National Liberation) became
publicly known through its occupation of five localities of the State of
Chiapas. The objective of the movement is to denounce the consequences
of NAFTA, the North American Free Trade Act between Canada, México
and the United States on the peasants, corruption in the political system
dominated by the PRI, the Institutional Revolutionary Party, that has been
in power since 1929. Thus, the "Zapatista" revolt of January 1994 has its
roots in the situation of unjust, flagrant inequality and oppression. The
intensified repression contributed in creating social upheaval and disapproval
of the government's policy of violence.

Today, it is said that violence that began in 1 January 1994, but in actual
fact, violence started in May 1974, and was not provoked by indigenous
communities. It was institutional violence, violence that has increasingly
become selective.

The movement bears the name of the national hero of the Mexican social
revolution, General Emiliano Zapata (1877-1919). The Zapatista Army for
National Liberation, or EZLN, became dramatically known at the time that

---

[1] Ms Ortega is an ordained minister in the Presbyterian Church of Cuba, her
homeland, where she will soon take up duties as the President of the Evangelical
Theological Seminary of Matanzas. She has recently completed her Doctor in
Ministry Degree at San Francisco Theological Seminary.

NAFTA was to come into effect. This uprising surprised only those who did not want to see, because it is the final conclusion of a protracted struggle. It is the latest stage in a progressive indigenous involvement in their own affairs, of the creation of religious, economic, educational and social organizations. In this regard, the exceptional role of Bishop Samuel Ruíz, who also encouraged the first indigenous congress in 1974, must be noted.

All this transformed the Indians from passive objects to active subjects in their history. Abiding by the community's decision and lead by the enigmatic "sub-commander Marcos" (a "ladino" who has been "adopted" by the Indians), a group of indigenous people shouted "Basta! We've had enough!" on the first day of January, 1994.

The Root Causes

The "discovery of the Americas", for the indigenous populations, meant conquest, genocide, cultural shock, slavery. This exploitation had atrocious consequences—short-term and long-term— the latter almost impossible to overcome. Todorov, explains this atrocious genocide:

> If the word genocide has ever been used with utmost precision, it is would be in this particular case. It seems to me that it was unprecedented-not only in relative, but also absolute terms—because we are speaking here of 90 per cent of a population of 80 million who were eliminated: one fifth of the world's population at that time. Not one of the most extensive massacres of the twentieth century can compare to this systematic slaughter. One understands how vain are the efforts of some authors to disclaim what is known as the "black legend", which establishes the responsibility of Spain in this genocide and tarnishing its reputation. The blackness is there, even though there is no legend.[2]

Friar Bartolomé de las Casas (1474-1566), one of rare men of the period to have criticized the Spanish invasion, described in a book that became famous, the monstrous violence of the invaders:

> The Spaniards came in like famished wolves, tigers and lions in the land of the tender sheep, endowed, like they were, by the Creator with qualities and gifts. For 40 years, they killed them in pieces, they afflicted them, they tormented them and they destroyed them through strange, cruel

---

[2] T. Todorov, *La conquête de l'Amerique: la question de l'autre* (Paris, Editions du Soleil, 1992), 139.

and varied new means which were never seen, heard of, and read about. This savagery was such that of the 3 million "naturales" of the Spanish island (Haiti) that we saw, there are not even 200 today.[3]

The "discovery" and the conquest of the Americas became a brutal extermination of the Indigenous tribes and peoples: through assassination, undernourishment, contagious diseases brought by the conquerors, and massive suicide to escape cruelty and the uncertainty of their future. The survivors had to confront a painful destiny: they were massively deported or had to escape to inhospitable areas. The remarkable Indian cultures were almost totally destroyed. The ancestral lands of the Indians were taken away from them. One can still be impressed by the Iberian virtues of honor: word of honor, respect for names, etc. These still exist and continue to be valid in some parts of the Iberian world. Nevertheless, the testimony of the Indians tells us that in most cases, these virtues were notably absent. Let's listen, for example, to the testimony of Chilam Balam de Chumayel, a Maya:

> On that day, dust possesses the earth,
> On that dy, a blight is on the face of the earth,
> On that day, a cloud rises,
> On that day, a mountain rises,
> On that day, a strong man seizes the land,
> On that day, things fall to ruin,
> On that day, the tender leaf is destroyed,
> On that day, the dying eyes are closed.

> With the true God, the true *Dios*,
> came the beginning of our misery.
> It was the beginning of tribute,
> the beginning of church dues...
> the beginning of strife by trampling on people,
> the beginning of robbery by violence,
> the beginning of forced debts,
> the beginning of debts enforced by false testimony,
> the beginning of individual strife.[4]

---

[3] C. Colomb, *La d'ecouverte de l'Amérique, Relations de voyages, 1493-1504* (Paris, La Découverte, 1089), 30.

[4] M. L. Portilla, *El reverso de la conquista, relaciones aztecas, mayas e incas* (México, Siglo XXI, 1980), 119. Translations from Ralph L. Roys, *The Book of Chilam Balam of Chumayel* (Norman, University of Oklahoma Press, 1967), 186 n, 77-79.

Unfortunately, this story cannot be tidied up. One must take responsibility for it. It is a common heritage that we inherited. But the good news is that indigenous peoples are not only victims. They survived five centuries of oppression, and have succeeded to a large extent in preserving their culture. Today they continue to resist repression, exploitation and cultural domination under extreme conditions.

The Indian Resistance: Survivors of Genocide

The recent history of México, that of the last 500 years, is a permanent story of those who pretend to be ruling a country but are stuck between two projects: that of western civilization, and the project of a society who resists, rooted in millenia old life forms—the indigenous population.

The first project arrived with European colonization, but was never abandoned when independence was declared. The new groups who came to power—first the creoles (Mexican-born Spaniards) and then the "mestizos" (mixed bloods)—have never given up western civilization. In fact, the western model of nationhood guided México's consolidation as an independent state (at least in appearance) throughout the nineteenth century. The Mexican nation was conceived from the beginning as culturally homogenous, following the prevailing European spirit which believed that the state was the expression of one people who have the same culture, the same language and a common history. From that time, the goal of all who have aspired for power in México was to consolidate the different majorities systematically into a cultural whole. "To consolidate the nation signified, then, the prospect of eliminating the real culture of almost everyone in order to enforce another culture to which only a handful belonged".[5]

The Mexican nation was unable to rise above the inherent contradiction in its nature: The principles of liberty, justice and equality were defended with the objective of transforming the Mexican society into a modern nation state. This imposed model was not, in any case, a superior phase in the development of the nation but a different model, another civilization. This western project has ever since been a project that excludes and denies the indigenous civilization—a "millennium" civilization, which is characterized by extraordinary cultural richness and diversity.

---

[5] G. Bonfil Batalla, *México profundo: Una civilización negada* (Editorial Grijalbo, México, 1990), 104.

If México was to become a homogeneous nation, there needed to be a convergence of civilizations, an eventual merging into one society, different but inspired by the two original models. What happened was a permanent standoff between the two groups who uphold the values of indigenous peoples and of the West. The opposition has sometimes been violent (e.g. the Chiapas civil war) as each side has tried to attain its own distinct objectives.

The starting point for the reconstruction the Mexican nation is a fundamental truth: what is known today as Mexican territory was inhabited for thousands of years by one of the earliest advanced civilizations on earth, the Mesoamerican civilization. From this fact emanates the Indian character of México. This is México's starting point and its deepest roots.

It is necessary to underline that the millennia long presence of human beings on present Mexican territory produced an extraordinary civilization.

> Without metal instruments, without plows, without the use of wheels nor the availability of draft animals, they practiced an intensive and highly productive agriculture with a relatively small work force. They constructed great earthworks to keep salt water from mingling with fresh. Their lakes served as communication routes that allowed for easy transportation of people and merchandise between the many population centers scattered around the basin. The constructed hydraulic projects of surprising magnitude, such as the irrigation system around Tezoutzingo, near Texcoco.[6]

The colonial vision was blind to the profound ancestral vision of the Indians. They made no effort to see and understand this land, and continue to ignored the indigenous experience and memory.

The Indian Presence Today

The name "Indian" is not a name of aboriginal peoples. Until the coming of the Spaniards in 1492, they were called Nahuas, Zapotecas, Mayas, Bribis, and by countless other names. The "conquistadores" who converted them into "Indians" when they started oppressing them. Eleazar López, a Zapotec theologian (cf. chapter 8), observes, "We did not choose to be 'indios', nor did other exploited people chose to be so called. It was evil

---

[6] Ibid, 31-33.

men who made us 'indios', and enslaved Blacks, and who have exploited the poor".[7]

It is not possible to give an exact figure for Mexicans who consider themselves indigenous. According to one source, the indigenous population in México numbers between 8 and 10 million people. This would represent 10 to 12.5% of the total population of 80 million. These are peoples who maintain close ties to a local society and who identify themselves as being different from others of the same class. Not included in this estimate are individuals and social groups that have lost their sense of ethnic identity, in spite of their indigenous way of life.[8]

Neither is it easy to define how many indigenous groups there are in México today. To begin with, the identification of Indian peoples on the basis of spoken language is not enough. In general, it is estimated that there are 65 surviving indigenous languages, but other studies suggest that there are more because some dialects are in fact considered as languages.

Furthermore, defining the number of spoken indigenous languages does not solve the question of how many indigenous groups exist in México. While a common language is one of the major definers of cultural (or ethnic) identity, not all who speak the same language belong to one ethnic unit. For example, the 700,000 Mayas who live in the Yucatán peninsula, occupy a continuous territory, speak the same language and share a large part of the same culture. One can speak then of the Maya people.

The "Zapotecas", however, are more than 300,000 but occupy non-contiguous territories. They speak different dialects, which are sometimes mutually unintelligible and evidence very sharp cultural differences.

And we must not overlook the many Indian peoples who are very small minorities in comparison with the major indigenous cultures of México. Some 20 ethnic groups have less than 10,000 inhabitants and half of them do not even reach 1,000 in their total population. They risk extinction from continual harassment from secular forces.[9]

---

[7] E. López, "Teología india hoy", in *Christus*, no. 7 (Septembre 1991), 22.

[8] "The Other Side of Mexico", no. 42 (September-October 1995), México, D.F., 33.

[9] The demographic statistics are taken from Bonfil Batalla, 50,51.

Fundamental Values of the Indigenous Cultures

1. The principal productive activity of Indian communities is agriculture. The instruments used are simple and to a large extent made in the communities itself. Yet, the agricultural activity is far from being "primitive". Indians can rely upon a rich range of knowledge that is a product of accumulated secular experience. This allows them to recognize the soil's characteristics, choose compatible species, cultivate each according to their particular needs, obey the dates of cultivation, combat the insects and plant diseases, that is, carry out the innumerable activities that are necessary for a good harvest.

2. In indigenous cultures, men and women are part of a cosmic order of things and the indigenous aspire to become integrated into this order. This can only be attained through a harmonious relationship with nature. This is one of the fundamental characteristics of indigenous culture. In this civilization, contrary to western civilization, nature is not perceived as an enemy but a way to adjust in a harmonious way to the cosmic order.

3. Indigenous cultures tend toward self-sufficiency. This is discernible at different levels: family, neighborhood, community and people. The indigenous economy provides, before anything else, for basic security. They unite in collecting, hunting, fishing and breeding of domestic animals, interspersed with different forms of local craftsmanship (pottery, textile, etc.) could be combined or alternated, according to their needs. Among the indigenous peoples, not one person assures the survival of the community but instead together they are able to provide for basic economic security. This question does not have an exact response either.

4. The family is the basis for the maintenance of indigenous cultures. Women play a fundamental role: rearing and educating children, as well as transmitting the cultural traits that will allow them to later fulfill their own roles in the community. To a large extent women are the principal link to the future: they guarantee language continuity and are the custodian of norms and values which are of prime importance in maintaining the indigenous cultures. Their role is recognized in society, family and community, which are the most propitious places for maintaining cultural norms. Women are more active participants and on a more equal basis with the than in Hispanic society, not only in domestic affairs but also in decisions affecting the community.

The attention of those who study the indigenous way of life is often drawn to the kind and respectful manner in which fathers treat their children. It is rare that physical violence is used. Children's participation is not limited to family discussions. There is considerable tolerance when it comes to premarital experience, which involves, in some cases, the acceptance of homosexual relations during adolescence. Relationships between grandparents and grandchildren are encouraged, allowing the elderly to maintain their social position and for the young to learn from their experience.

5. Land is not considered private property but rather as a communal property. It is not conceived as a piece of merchandise. There is a deeper meaning. Land is an indispensable productive resource, but more than that, it is a common property, which is a part of the cultural heritage which is handed down from generation to generation. It is the great land, where the community's ancestors lay in peace.

6. Many sicknesses are explained in indigenous cultures as the intervention of supernatural forces who are punishing unacceptable conduct and behavior. In addition, indigenous peoples possess traditional knowledge of the therapeutic properties of herbs and other products. Indigenous doctors are specialists who diagnose and prescribe on the basis of "natural" body symptoms; but they interpret the symptoms within a symbolic framework and treat them according to a wide range of cultural elements, whether to heal completely or to prepare the body for an eventual passage to the world beyond.

The greater portion of these indigenous values have managed to survive official attempts at "civilizing", domesticating and "bleaching" the Indian population. This "culture of resistance" availed itself of various mechanisms that anthropologists call a) conservation of cultural space, b) appropriation and control of foreign cultural elements (popular Catholicism), c) innovation (recycling of waste industrial products and creative social organization), and linguistic resistance (recent increase in number of ethnic speakers).

> The cultures of the Mesoamerican civilization that exist today have managed to survive thanks to the fierce will of the people. This fact is expressed in a stubborn commitment to maintaining their decision making capacity as part of their cultural heritage. This is demonstrated in their constant and selective appropriation of alien cultural elements that they find useful in resisting domination. It can be seen in their unceasing creativity, allowing them to shape new cultural elements as well as to modify the existing ones; thus subtly adjusting their own culture to the framework of the oppression and aggression in which they live.[10]

---

[10] Ibid, 199,200.

Chiapas and the Crisis in the Mexican State

The crisis in Chiapas which has made world headlines is a paradigm of the crisis in the Mexican state, which is itself a special case in the crisis of all of Latin America. Enormous and unpayable debts—institutional violence which provokes extensive social poverty.[11] México is often presented, thanks to subtle propaganda, as a democratic state, respectful of human rights. In reality, the situation is completely different, especially for the poorest of the population, the Indians.

For almost 70 years, México has been governed by the Institutional Revolutionary Party (PRI), a name that says a lot. This party have not only monopolized political party at all levels (México is a federal state), through fraudulent elections, but has also dominated all the wheels of socioeconomic life. Political assassinations, arbitrary arrests and detention, torture, disappearances—the principal victims of whom are poor farmers and defenders of justice—generalized corruption, all of which have been denounced for many years by international human rights organizations.

The economic crisis is not new to México. It has been going on for two decades, at least. What is new, and profoundly more unsettling for those in power, is the profound sociopolitical crisis that the country now faces. But now, México has been offered the opportunity to create conditions that will eventually satisfy the people's demands for democracy and justice. México needs to redefine the government's function, the private sector and organized civil society. And those that are forcing the nation to face up to its future are faceless indigenous peasants in the lowly state of Chiapas.

The days of "paternalistic" government control are past. The era of the one party system as the principal pillar of society is fast declining. The concept that the private sector can solve the problems of fair distribution of

---

[11] This debt must be reviewed. It cannot be paid in its totality and must be reevaluated. It is institutionalized violence. It marginalizes farmers, privileges capital and increases the burdens of workers, which mostly affects the poor-miners, Blacks, Indians, etc.-and leads to widespread violation of human rights. The debt can only be paid on the day when the domination of capital is curbed and the people can exercise genuine democratic participation. A group of poor countries, Latin America is kept at a distance from the global development process-locked into unsafe technologies, authoritarian social organization, cultures reduced to silence, and its unrecognized religions. We continue to be controlled by a caste of military men who can guarantee order within institutional disorder. The peoples of Latin America must become masters of their own destinies, create social relations and values that will express their own cultural roots.

wealth is only an ideological notion. But the idea that civil society can change the political direction of the country is still to be explored. In considering a viable model for the construction of a nation, the spirit of sovereignty and self-determination are critical factors.

Chiapas: a culture of civil resistance

Independence from Spain was not achieved in Central America through war but through a series of municipal rebellions. When colonial Chiapas found that it could not count on its mining resources, farming and stock breeding expanded, as well as the exploitation of the indigenous work force, which became the principal attraction of entrepreneurs to the region. This is at the root of today's conflicts.

Since the sixteenth century, Chiapas has always been a region where indigenous resistance led to virtually constant non-conformist movements in indigenous communities. The seventeenth century was one rebellion after another. In 1727, forty two communities revolted and formed their own "audencia" (jurisdiction) which they called New Spain. The municipal council which directed the rebellion was called the "Audencia de Guatemala". They justified their actions as a kind of inversion of the established order, because to be called "Indians" or "Jews" by the Spaniards was part of their oppression.

There were religious overtones to the rebellion. There are documents that prove that Catholic priests of different regions called for uprising and that alliances were formed with the lower clergy. Thus, there is a long tradition not only of indigenous resistance but also of the grassroots Catholic Church's denouncement of the oppressive situation and injustice of the colonial system.

At Independence, and through the plebiscite of 1824, Chiapas was annexed to México. But the culture of indigenous resistance has stayed alive. It gave birth to symbolic elements: the saints, who give daily counsel, and in situations of crisis, advise either to begin a revolt or to join ongoing battles in the region.

There was a widespread revolt in 1938 brought about by a conflict on land distribution, and then a period of calm from 1940 to 1973. In May 1974 a new revolt broke out, almost in the same territories as in 1938, and for the same reasons. In October 1974 the first indigenous congress was held in Chiapas, during which the four major issues were tackled: land, education, health, and trade.   As regards education, the indigenous peoples concluded that "education must be educated" because their education so far has been racist, and discriminates against Indians and their language. Regarding land, the demands were more forceful due to the injustice which in Chiapas is more extensive. This congress was the beginning of subsequent indigenous mobilizations. It was a very democratic process that encouraged the participation of the community in discussing their own affairs.

From 1978 to 1980, there was a climate of greater oppression in the Chiapas. The national army was used in an illegal manner as both political and agricultural police. Between 1980 and 1991, the federal army was withdrawn from the repressive actions, but, in its place, new forms of state police was created. Towards 1991, the "white guards", the killers hired by landowners, became institutionalized. It was a period during which indigenous communities were confronted with a formidable state apparatus, in which the hired killers do not belong anymore to the private armies but to the Mexican state.

Repression grew. It affected not only those who requested land but other members of the civil society like, for example, homosexuals, Catholic defenders of the theology of liberation, and the Protestant churches, and fundamentalist sects, because they were not orthodox Catholics. It was a war, an official intolerance against all types of dissidence. The essence of this repression is embodied in the Penal Code of 1927, in which being an Indian meant having limited rights.

In this climate of intolerance and absence of political liberties, racism and permanent violation of human rights in the State of Chiapas, the sole institution to denounce this situation is the Catholic church of Chiapas, Don Samuel Ruíz and the diocese of San Cristóbal.

The recent revolt of 1994 goes far beyond Chiapas. It has dramatically demonstrated the need for structural changes in the whole country, and the need to evolve towards a real democracy. The indigenous peoples of Chiapas end their supporters elsewhere are simply proposing an evolution towards a just society, wherein there is a legislative power and a judiciary power which are independent of the exclusive decisions of the executive and state powers.

The religious phenomenon

In Chiapas, as elsewhere in Indian México and throughout indigenous Latin America, evangelism took the form of transposing the symbols, concepts and moral rules of the European Christian culture to the "New World". It failed to take advantage of those points where faith and indigenous reality, the Gospel and indigenous cultures converged. What resulted was a Christian expression which was typically western. Only popular Catholicism, on the borderlines of official Catholicism, was created by the people within the dominated culture and society. This demonstrates the important of undertaking liberating evangelism within the cultural parameters, allow the people to organize themselves based upon their origins, which are often poor and deeply religious.

It is significant that social transformations took place within the existing disastrous social realities. Out of extremely unjust structures, more human and social relations sometimes spring that create justice and participation. Liberation was necessary for communion and participation in society and Church to take place. It is not only the content that must be new and liberating, the method must be so as well, whether it is to overcome to evangelist-evangelized dichotomy in order to enter into a process of evangelism that encompasses everyone, or whether it means to give up all cultural pressure in the name of the Gospel.

Evangelism, under the colonial flag, did not prevent genocide. If yesterday, Christianity accepted this death machine as an accomplice, then today, it must join itself to the victims of a certain model of development that excluded the larger majority, and bring about new life. The suffering of today is the consequence of what happened 500 years ago. It does not mean to continue the kind of traditional evangelism which was developed in Latin America, which emphasizes reforms and renewal processes that do not change structures. It means a new experience.

The evangelism which was practiced since the fifteenth century was and continues to be insufficient. It has not adapted to today's challenges in Latin America. This was made dramatically clear in a letter that was signed by Andean Indians and addressed to John Paul II when he visited Peru in 1985:

> We, the Indians of the Andes and of the Americas would like to take this opportunity of John Paul II's visit to give the Bible back to him , because, in five centuries, it has not given us love, nor peace nor justice. Please take back your Bible and hand it over to our oppressors because they need it more than we do. In fact, since Christopher Columbus set foot here, one culture, one language, one religion and values intrinsically European were imposed upon America by force.[12]

---

[12] Translated from L. Boff, La nouvelle évangélisation: perspective des opprimés (Editions du Cerf, Paris, 1992), 15.

The "new evangelism" must become new in its expressions. It must be the production of indigenous cultures and not only-as was the case during five hundred years—the reproduction of European culture for the use of indigenous peoples (the Tupí-Guaraní, Quechuas, Aymaras, Maya, or Aztec), who know nothing of Latin nor of any ceremonial liturgy punctuated by western cultural experience. The inalienable right to know, worship and serve the God of history with the instruments one's own culture and symbols of tradition, must be recognized. This right can not be exercised without full liberties. But what we have are not many faces of Catholicism that are sharing the Gospel meaningfully in diverse cultures, but one sole, official Catholicism, of Roman character. The fruit of the "new evangelism" must be a Latin American and ecumenical Christianity, whose face will reflect the diverse cultural forces that co-exist in the continent.

This new evangelism must be able to bring life to the large crowds, who shamefully do not have the means to live. To evangelize, in the context of Latin America, principally means to save the lives of the poor, marked by a liberating dimension.

The role of the churches

The Church has played an important role in the Chiapas conflict, most especially through the involvement of the Bishop of San Cristóbal de Las Casas, Don Samuel Ruíz, who has dedicated more 30 years of pastoral work to indigenous peoples. He helped them, with the support of the Vatican, to be "conscienticized", in spite of their differences, and to form one unique people. The Church played the role of an arbiter to stop the momentum of war, when negotiations failed. It sent communications to North America, South America, and Europe. A number of dioceses engaged in active campaigns and fasting. Eighteen Evangelical congregations in the United States became part of this movement. The movement also had repercussions within México, including Chiapas. A truce, an agreement, was eventually reached.

A number of persons were consulted in order to achieve a substantive proposal. The government stated that it wanted peace and, despite lengthy delays, the President of México continues to affirm that the dialogue has not been interrupted, but rather has stayed open. Both parties in the dialogue, the Zapatista army and the government, recognize that there are a series of new events, factors and interlocutors who have more or less justified claims. And along the way, they have realized that peace is not a given, not a conquest, but a process. In this regard, they all had to work for peace.

Turning ideology on its head

The Chiapas conflict contradicts a fundamental premise of marxist ideology: to change a system that concentrates economic and political power into the hands of a minority, one must focus upon production. The general idea is that the economic system will not change unless those who are in the productive system—i.e. the workers—act. A corollary of this dictum states that one must not develop Indian awareness in Indians because it will reinforce Indian submission to those who are at the center of productive and economic power. Instead, one must encourage in Indians and exploited awareness which will enable the indigenous peoples to join and support the workers who are the subjects of socio-economic transformation.

The revolt that took place on the first of January, 1994, right after the NAFTA was signed, caused widespread interest because, for the first time, it not only concerned the four coffee producing provinces of Chiapas, but the economic system of the entire country. The situation worsened because of the political situation in which emergency nationwide elections, held on 21 August, amidst widespread fraud and irregularities. The only exception was in Chiapas, where the EZLN, the Zapatista front, won, though their victory was not recognized.

The "rebel" government proposed three stages of peaceful action—urban protest, resistance, urban uprising—in order to put pressure upon the authorities and obtain recognition of their election. The urban protest gives an idea of the extent of the movement. The people blocked Chiapas for two days and cut off roads, occupied some land and took over several municipalities, thus showing that they had potential to act. The EZLN then announced that there was no more room for dialogue after fraudulent elections. The last opportunity to fulfill the minimum requirements for civic participation towards a transition government had been squandered.

The objective of the Zapatista movement is not, as it declares in its communiques, to take over power: it is a popular movement, well-structured, that aspires for a profound change to take place in Mexican society. It thus differentiates itself from previous movements.

The EZLN stresses in its communiques the need for new "actors in national and local life", meaning the civil society. It confirms that the social conflict that the EZLN has revealed is not a struggle of insurgents for power. They are calling for a level of dialogue for which the government does not seem to be prepared. The government statements are more or less a call for negotiation. Sub-commander Marcos is calling for another mode: a national agreement, composed of concrete commitments and new institutions. What the Zapatista army is about is not war—which would mean the destruction of the ethnic groups of México—but a new social base.

Indigenous participation in the uprising

The movement was indigenous in nature. But there were three types of reaction to the phenomenon: a) the limited reaction of communities who are opposed to the armed struggle and to its demands; b) the reaction of the majority of the communities which, while they do not agree with the means used, support the cause of the Zapatista movement; c) the reaction of two-thirds of the indigenous population was armed uprising.

A great deal of suffering has resulted from the power struggles that are implicit in the above positions and the realities of civil war. Entire peoples, like the Chamulas, have been expelled from their communities for a number of years. They have found support in the Center for Human rights of the Catholic diocese.

At the same time, a reconciliation process has been underway in the midst of the extreme tensions, divisions and political opportunism. There were people who left their communities, leaving their   Under such circumstances, several communities have had the good sense to dialogue and seek reconciliation.

Over the past twenty years there have been expulsions in the Chiapas region. The first one happened in 1974 and was directed against the Catholic communities. More than 200 persons became victims of arrest, robbery, insult, injury, death threats, destruction of house and property. This was the beginning of a new era of expulsions that were directed against anyone in any form whatsoever of dissidence against the "caciques" (chiefs) who ruled the region. In 1993, 600 Chamulas sought refuge in the office of the Coordination for Indigenous Affairs. Based upon the rule of law and the free exercise of their beliefs, they asked to be allowed to return to their communities, to receive reparations for the damages to their land and property, and demanded the punishment of the "caciques".

These expulsions have been branded by the authorities as "religious conflicts". They blame the "sects" and the church of Samuel Ruíz as the guilty parties, charging that pastoral activities are an "attack on indigenous customs and traditions". In this way, the government covers and justifies the action of the "caciques". Responses from the civil authorities to demands for justice are either ignored or stalled.

When the new, imposed, governor of the province came to power a new wave of expulsion began. This time, a reign of terror was imposed against evangelicals who live in Chiapas which brought about deaths, disease and other social evils. Meanwhile, the government is trying to oust Bishop Ruíz from the presidency of the National Commission of Mediation (CONAI) and replace him with a parliamentarian.

The New Awareness of Unity

On the basis of their millennial history and the recent history of México, the indigenous movement today affirms that its unity can not be obtained through the State nor through traditional political parties nor popular organizations, but through indigenous methods, through indigenous popular organizations who are the protagonists of the unification process.

One of the principal characteristics of the unification process is the exercise of the right to self-determination. This implies Indian self-government and control of their territories.

The second fundamental characteristic is respect for diversity, which signifies the recognition of problems specific to each people, ethnic group, sector, movement, as well as independence in their struggle.

The movement for indigenous unity moves along three axis:

1. Educational-cultural struggle, brought about through the awareness of the masses.

2. Political-juridical struggle, through the defense of human rights in national and international arenas.

3. Economic-ecological struggle, through research of alternative economic and ecological models to the current neo-liberal model.

The Declaration of Managua is an affirmation of this new awareness of unity; it is indignant, proud and rebellious.

> We have walked the paths of survival separated from our families, expelled into inhospitable regions and forced to till the unproductive lands of our continent. We have been always resisting, reacting, defending, refusing to submit, holding fast to our identities; we will not engender slaves for children; we have not surrendered, we have not given up, even

in those glorious moments when we have tasted the fruits of freedom which have been won by blood.[13]

Self-determination and the role of women

The indigenous population demands the recognition of the Mexican government in a entire series of rights: political, social, economic and cultural. The principles that must guide the State in relation with indigenous peoples are:

1. Right to self-determination; respect for the indigenous capacity for self-determination and development, respect of identities, cultures and all forms of social organizations.

2. Plurality; the recognition and respect for their presence on national territory; for the richness and diversity of indigenous cultures.

3. Participation; encourage the participation of indigenous peoples and respect their forms of social and community organizations, with a view to reinforcing their capacity for self-development.

4. Integration; uphold the integrated and ongoing actions of institutions and different levels of government, which have to do with indigenous peoples, avoiding partisan and divisive practices.

5. Transparency; encourage the honest and transparent use of resources for the benefit of indigenous peoples, and involving them in the decision-making process and the social control of expenditures.

6. Sustainable development of Indigenous resources, with respect for the cultural diversity of indigenous peoples.

This means:

a) satisfaction of basic human needs. A minimum social level for the indigenous population, so they will have access to well-being and subsistence, such as food, health, education, housing;

b) assured production and employment. This action must respect the economic base of indigenous communities, through a strategy of rural development that will generate employment;

c) assured education and training. This action must respect and enhance traditions and forms of organizations;

---

[13] "Documento de Managua", 12 Octubre, 1992, photocopy.

d) assured cultural enhancement. The plurality of cultures in the nation must be promoted and enhanced;

c) assure justice. This includes equal access to justice and unrestricted respect for individual and social guarantees;

d) guarantee of identity in cases of internal and external migration, whether it is from the countryside to the city, or to a foreign country (the United States, for example).

Self-determination, obviously must grant the same right to women, and perhaps more so. Women, are thrice oppressed: as poor, as indigenous, and women. Women are also more directly linked to the defense of life.

But more specific reasons for doing so come from the indigenous culture. Indigenous peoples believe that discrimination and submission of wives did not exist in the original cultures. These evils are a product of the European invasion and of the logic of the imposed socio-economic-political system throughout the long years of oppression. For this reason, there is a close connection between the movement of return to the original cultures and the reaffirmation of the preponderant role of women.

In the indigenous worldview, before western values, women occupied one-half of the cosmos. Thus, in order to exercise self-determination and liberation as oppressed peoples, women and men must participate equally, according to the traditional values of indigenous nations. Moreover, the role of women is fundamental in matters of environmental protection. There is, in fact, a special relationship between women and Mother Earth: they are united in the generation of life.

Yet women continue to be submitted to extreme forms of exploitation, authoritarianism and violence. Subordinated to men and in families and communities, under the Spanish system, women have less access to education, are the first to abandon school and obtain inferior salary levels. A large majority exercise activities that are not income-generating and which do not show in official statistics, in spite of their input not only in domestic work but also in the fields of maize, animal husbandry, craftsmanship, marketing and selling, etc. They are also subjected to conjugal violence, often raped and beaten. Men continue to make decisions concerning the number of children.

In October 1994, more than 150 indigenous women from nine communes of Chiapas, the majority craftswomen, met for the first time in San Cristóbal de las Casas to discuss the discrimination to which they are subjected every day. They demand: a) the right to start a new life (when husband is imprisoned or in cases of conjugal violence) and to ask for a divorce or separation; b) the right to equal pay; c) the right to determine the number and spacing of children, health centers, and nourishing food for pregnant women; d) the creation of schools in each community, the development and distribution of bilingual booklets and literacy programs for adults; e) the right to own land, access to agricultural credit once they start taking care of their children; f) the right to be elected to representative positions or popular offices, and to free participation.

Nationhood and the Indigenous movement

It is interesting to analyze the rejection of indigenous peoples of the term "ethnic" or "race" that anthropologists use, which, according to them, reduces them to objects of observation and study. "Indigenous peoples claim the word "people" for their communities, which also accords them the right, on the international level, to self-determination".[14] In their languages, "people" means a collective of persons, united in awareness of their original community, history, tradition, culture, religion. They are people who have their on cultural, political and economic rights.

The continental indigenous movement has two levels of struggles: ecological and economic, both being closely connected. Indigenous peoples thus lay claim on the dimension of life that bonds Mother Earth to Father Sun.

The indigenous peoples' search for their identity does not deny cultural diversity, but on the contrary recognizes and reaffirms it. The return to one's identity is not an obstacle to the recognition of others, but rather the surest path towards respect and valorization. The indigenous peoples of Chiapas are not against an historical meeting between cultures, within the boundaries of mutual respect and equality. What they are against is the imposition of one culture upon another, protected by economic, political and military power.

In their search for unity, there are a number of factors that indigenous peoples try to identify in order to consolidate nationhood:

1. Respect for the preponderant role of the grassroots communities. The political will and unity of the grassroots are necessary. They guarantee, at a high level, a true social movement.

---

[14] G. Girardi, *Los excluídos: ¿construirán la nueva historia?* (Madrid, Editorial Nueva Utopía, 1994), 60.

2. The value, in nation building, of the richness of the past: cultures, religions, indigenous experiences. It is indispensable knowledge in order to build an indigenous way to the future according to the needs and aspirations of indigenous peoples. The new confidence of the peoples in them themselves upholds a systematic return to their history, and assures them that this largely untapped patrimony can offer them an immense well of resources to construct a nation.

3. Encourage a "culture of respect", where people listen to each other without imposing their opinions, nor the opinions of others, while they consolidate the process of indigenous unity. A diverse world of peace and cooperation must be created, where there is harmony between human beings, people and nature. That is how one builds a nation.

The objective of the Zapatista Army for National Liberation (EZLN) is to build "a nation where everyone has a place". Thus, their demands are limited to the necessities to the indigenous population: land, housing, employment, food, health, education, culture, information, independence, democracy, liberty, justice and peace. These 13 demands implies a profound political reform that guarantees equality, urban participation, the right to vote, and the recognition of all political, regional and national forces.

A nation where every one has a place, implies accepting that a) indigenous peoples are equal to other peoples in terms of self-dignity and rights; b) we must urgently recognize the need to respect and promote the rights and intrinsic characteristics of indigenous peoples, especially their rights to land, territory and property, that spring from their political, economic and social structures, and from their cultures, traditions, spirituality, history and philosophies.

Conclusion

Unfortunately, the situation has not much changed since 1942 and the colonization process which we reviewed earlier in this essay. Nothing has happened in spite of the independence obtained, from the Spaniards and the Portuguese, in the nineteenth century by the colonies of Latin America; in spite of the abolition of slavery; and in spite of tentative undertakings since World War II to modernize—that is industrialize—the so-called developing countries.

The Indian tribes have not ceased to be hounded from their ancestral lands by gold seekers (the Yanomamis in the Amazon), government institutions wishing to construct multi-million projects or military bases, or by private companies (transnationals) wishing to exploit the rich raw materials.

The study of the history of colonization and its consequences challenges us on the ethical level: justice and solidarity demands that we repair the injustices of the past, within our individual, economic and political means, and so to lighten the more serious consequences of colonization and "modernization", in particular for the poor masses.

I wanted to show in this paper that México was a carrier of a civilization denied to her and which has a history of several millennia. During the last five centuries, the indigenous peoples have been subjected to a brutal oppressive system, which has affected all aspects of their lives and cultures.

I have tried to demonstrate that the crisis today is not the crisis of México, but only the failure of a model of development that created an "imaginary nation"; that this millennial civilization is still present in the "real México" that aspires to be a genuine nation.

This nation must be plural, incarnated in a wide diversity of cultures, looking at the west from México, which means taking into consideration other civilizations and learning from its successes, while maintaining a perspective of nation-building on Mexican soil, since antiquity; and knowing that this millennial civilization is not dead and gone, but rather inspires and lives on in the bowels of México.

To this end the indigenous peoples of México aspire: the adoption of a pluralist project drawn from its own objectives, which accepts the diversity of languages and looks back to the objectives of its history. That is to say, "a nation where every one has a place".

- translated by Diwata Olalia Hunziker

CONCLUSION

Guillermo Cook and Dalila Nayap-Pot

Indigenous women and men have shared with us some of their ongoing search for a relevant spirituality—one that is at the same time faithful to their rich heritage and responsive to the challenges of the world in which they live today. An important part of this heritage is Christianity which, for better or for worse, has irremediably altered the way in which they understand their past, interpret their present and look forward to the future. Whether or not the "outside voices"—those of the theologians and social scientists that have attempted to provide a background, sometimes an interpretation, of the indigenous context and worldview—has been helpful is for our readers to judge.

By Way of Review

In the General Introduction we attempted to situate indigenous spirituality and theological reflection in historical context. While we made use of scholarly research, we sought to be faithful to the way in which indigenous thinkers interpret their oral and written traditions and their most recent history. Our readers have the right to question this interpretation and to argue, if they wish, with any of the statements made by the indigenous contributors. We ask only that their statements be taken seriously and not discarded without thoroughly grappling with the implications of what they say. For their part, indigenous spokespersons have every reason to speak their own mind. They have a right, even, to be suspicious and critical of everything that is said and done on their behalf by all of us who, for whatever reason, have taken up the "white man's burden". This includes anthropologists, missionaries, evangelists, social workers, theologians (conservative and liberationist) and, first and foremost, the editor of this book!

It is not the purpose of this concluding chapter to interact critically with the book's contributors, but to encourage reflection on issues of import which have arisen in their documents. Let us first take the materials as they relate to each other in each section of the book, keeping in mind that a representative number of the thirty plus Maya language groups have been dealt with in this book.

Clash of cultures and religious worldviews

Two indigenous leaders have shared with us the results of their own serious
search to return to their roots. How much can we really understand of the
trauma that indigenous peoples still experience at the spoiling of their
advanced civilization and the destruction of their vibrant culture by
avaricious Europeans? Are world Christians able today to sense the
bewilderment of their indigenous sisters and brothers at the denaturing of
a very ancient religion by an arrogant deformation of Christianity? Is it
possible for us to understand the depth of meaning behind religious symbols
that are so foreign to many of us? This is what Guatemala Presbyterian
pastor and political activist Similox challenges us to do in chapter 1. In the
following chapter, the survey by Peruvian Quechua Cutimanco, another
Protestant—of the status of indigenous theology and of his honest assessment of the dangers it faces—situates these questions in very specific
contexts. In their questions and searchings we sense a genuine desire to
return to their ancestral roots without giving up on their commitment to
Jesus Christ. In an interesting juxtaposition, two ethnologists, Goldin and
Metz, show how, highland Maya are able to maintain a dynamic tension
between their Roman Catholic profession and Protestant beliefs, without
necessarily turning their backs completely on their Maya culture.

Maya culture and resistance strategies

The Maya are the only indigenous nation that have left us a written
tradition. Fortunately for posterity, their Scriptures, the *Pop Vuh* escaped
destruction by the invaders and large portions of it, at least, were transcribed from memory in Latin script. Numerous post Conquest records and
memories were written down in the same way, to eventually be translated
into Spanish and other languages. A total of six bark-paper documents have
survived in the original Maya glyphs and are gradually being deciphered.
Edgar Cabrera, a noted native scholar, shares the significance of this in
chapter 4—for his people and for world civilization. In the process, he
argues the hypothesis that the Maya civilization, in a variety of forms, has
been the source of Mesoamerican culture. While this theory continues to be
questioned, it should not be so easily dismissed, as we have tried to show
in our General Introduction. In chapter 5, Jesús García, another Central
American anthropologist, shows how one form of the unique Maya calendar
has survived for thousands of years in highland Guatemala. It is, he argues,

the integrating factor that continues to maintain the culture in the face of countless adversities.

Women—wives and mothers—play a key role in preserving the cultural and religious values of Maya people, in spite of civil war, genocide and the invasion of new religious movements from the North. They demonstrate their radicality, observes Dalila Nayap, the author of chapter 6, not by turning against men but in fighting alongside of them and by continuing to struggle even after their menfolks have been eliminated by evil forces. As part of their resistance, they are willing to experiment with new religious options, yet without loosing their cultural soul.

No more than three decades ago, the thirty or so Maya family groups had very little sense of a common identity. Today, Pan-Mayanism is a fact of life from the Mexican Yucatán to the western border of Honduras, and in between Guatemala. The research that Richard Wilson has done among one large but isolated Mayan group, the Keqchi', provides some clues as to how this phenomenon came about. Along the way, he makes the point that Spanish speaking catechists and guerilla hunting soldiers (as well as North American missionaries, as he argues in another article) confronted the indigenous people with conflicting messages—sometimes disguised in indigenous symbols—which virtually destroyed the homogeneity of their centuries old spirituality and culture. But it also made the Keqchi' aware of a world outside, of other Mayas with kindred experiences and of new religious symbols capable of coaptation into a resurgent Maya spirituality. From the ashes of their seeming destruction, a new sense of Pan-Maya identity is taking shape.

The rise of indigenous theology

Another group of four essays are more self-consciously theological. In chapter 8, Fr. López, a Zapotec Catholic theologian, offers an insiders analysis of indigenous theology which seeks to bridge the wide gap between the spirituality of his ancestors and the increasingly hardening position of the Roman hierarchy. He can be forgiven for being sometimes as optimistic about the chances that indigenous theology will be recognized by his church as Protestant indigenous theologians are pessimistic. Some of the most challenging concepts come from this essay, and we shall have occasion to come back to them.

Readers will have found quite helpful Fr. Cleary's survey of the growing volume of literature on Latin American indigenous theology, in Spanish,

English and Portuguese. He provides us also with a sympathetic "outsider's" perception of the phenomena as he builds links between the two main foci of indigenous theological reflection—Mesoamérica and the Andean region.

A group of Protestant Mayas demonstrate the seriousness in which they take their theological task. In chapter 10, a team of Maya Presbyterians have made a very conscious effort to relate indigenous theology to fundamental themes in the history of salvation, from a Reformed perspective. It may provide us with some useful entries into the discussion a little further along. The final chapter in this section, by Pastor Colop, is christological. This is a topic which is rarely addressed in the discussions by indigenous theologians. The reason for this avoidance, and the answers that derive from the question that becomes the title of his essay will need to be considered in some depth later on in this concluding chapter.

Issues in dialogue and evangelization

The style of the first chapter (12) in this final section is schematic and didactic. It is the distillation of the pastoral experience of priests who have spent years working with indigenous communities. It probably had an apologetic purpose, as well, given the resistance that there is in many Roman Catholic quarters to indigenous theology. We have included it because it provides missiological insights which must be taken into account as we assess our own response to the challenge of indigenous theology. The most polemical essay in this book is that of Pop Cal (chapter 13). His intimate knowledge of Protestant language and evangelistic preaching causes one to suspect that, at some time in his life, he was in close relationship with one of the large number of evangelical congregations in his native Guatemala. It is not our purpose to debate him, nor to reply to some of the most extreme remarks. The important thing is for us to understand how others perceive the "Christian message" that we so proudly proclaim. One cannot help but wonder how different indigenous Christianity—Protestant as well as Catholic—might have been if more missionaries, pastors and priests had used the methodology that Fr. Richard espouses in chapter 14.

A well known indigenous political leader, Ms Tuyuc, reminds us that culture has a political dimension, particularly if we are speaking about powerful forces that seek to destroy a culture and people. She writes about an issue which is still alive: the mortal threat to the constitution of Guatemala, as well as to the lives of the indigenous people that is posed by the ever powerful military. Representing the small but significant number of Catholic priests that are turning their back on their vocations and going back to their ancient spirituality, is Wuqub Iq. His essay (chapter 16) somewhat summarized in this book, challenges Christians and Mayas to leave the doors open for dialogue. His tone is measured and respectful. Using liberation theology as a platform provides background for his positions and proposes a minimum of conditions for dialogue to take place. As we noted in the Introduction, the uprising of Maya peasants in Chiapas, México, has attracted worldwide attention. In chapter 17, theologian and pastor Antonio Otzoy, appeals for respect and understanding on the part of the leaders of his church. He argues on the basis of Maya values, which he learned at the feet of Maya priests, and of the ethics of his own Reformed tradition. In the final essay, chapter 18, Dr. Ofelia Ortega places the "Zapatista" uprising in Chiapas in the context of national crisis and call to national renewal, and documents the role of Christians in the process.

The object of this book has not been to debate with any of the contributors. We have not set up straw men in order to knock them down. Instead, we want to seriously address the issues that they are raising and to ask what these have to say to our own faith and practice, and to the way in which we communicate the gospel of Jesus Christ. A discussion of such magnitude cannot hope to cover every issue nor in much detail. But, before we can understand the issues, we must first consider the key points of the Mesoamerican worldview, with special reference to Maya spirituality.)

Worldviews in Perspective

The God of the Judeo-Christian revelation is *One, total and harmonious*. In the Christian revelation, the one God is worshipped in three Persons—Father, Son and Holy Spirit—each of whom expresses the fullness of divinity and is at the same time complemented by the other. What is rejected as idolatry by the other two great monotheistic religions: Judaism and Islam, is fundamental doctrine of the Christian faith—a contradiction, a mystery, which must be accepted by faith. The respective and interdependent actions of the persons of the Trinity are implied in the gospels, more clearly stated in the Pauline epistles and fully defined in the early church creeds and councils—not in isolation from the worldview of each culture within which God was being revealed. Christians believe that God is One and Three, Three and One at the same time, whose attributes and actions are manifested in the creation, in spite of the imperfections brought on by sin. Good and evil, God and Satan are locked in a cosmic battle which Christ has, in fact won by his death on the cross. This is traditional Christianity at its best—and worst. In the name of Christ, the victorious Son, the course of history has been changed over and over again: countless lives have been transformed, thousands of minds and bodies have been healed—and untold primal cultures have been denatured and destroyed.

Maya spirituality is based upon the concepts of *unity*, *totality* and *complementarity*. Nothing is omitted in Maya religiosity wherein "unity is found in plurality or diversity and vice versa". There is only one God who is manifest in the cosmos in many ways, shapes and forms, both good and evil. That is, good and evil are complementary opposites of the same reality. The interrelationships and complementarity are not at the level of the godhead, as with Christianity, but between the Creator, human beings and the natural world. What Christians mistakenly take to be polytheism—the worship of many gods—is in fact the manifestation of the multiple interactions of the Creator with human beings and nature.

> The cosmos is the totality of the God-Human-Nature relationship. Totality is the cosmos in all of its magnitude and grandeur. Nothing and no one is unrelated from everything and everyone else, because in each can be found the essence of the Creator which holds things together and in balance. Human beings are both part of the natural world and of the immensity of the cosmos.[1]

Within this context, the Maya people, for countless centuries have related their daily lives with the cosmic and temporal dimensions. What is the reason for this unusual urge to predict time with such precision and their need to control it? To begin to answer this question, we need to look more closely at three interrelated aspects of the Mesoamerican world view: the meaning of time for the Mayas, its impact upon their survival, and the religious dimensions which are inextricably related. Three Maya words, *may* (to reckon time)[2], *ixiim*[3] (maize) and *tamoanchán*[4] (the place of

---

[1] Vitalino Similox, *La expresión y Metodología del Pensamiento Maya Contemporáneo en Guatemala* (Guatemala, Cholsamaj, 1992), 37.

[2] In the modified chronology that was instituted in northern Yucatán (ca. 900 C.E.), *may* denoted a full cycle of thirteen periods of twenty years. Hundreds of years earlier, it signified "to count" or "to divine". See Introduction, Nos. 11 and 33.

[3] *Ix-i'm* (eesh-ee'm) in reconstructed proto-Mayan is *ixim* or *ixiim* in the majority of highland Mayan tongues. Cf. Nora

creation) are paradigmatic of their holistic worldview, as well as totally different from the dominant view of the affluent world.

"May": reckoning with time

For the Maya time was everything and everything was time. In villages less affected by modernity this continues to be so today.[5] One cannot understand Maya culture, the amazing scientific discoveries of a stone age people, architectural achievements and social organization without digging deep into their understanding of time. The function of the gods was to maintain the unchanging cycle of time. A famous Maya relief depicts their deities following each other in an endless circle, their head-straps bearing the symbols of the divisions of time. Every aspect of time and of natural phenomena was studied by them in order to predict imbalances in the normal rhythm of nature, with their often disastrous results. In sum, for the traditional Maya today, as with their ancestors, religion is essentially the language of nature, of the totality of the cosmos, of which human beings are an integral part.

Even today, time has a different meaning for "undeveloped" indigenous people than it does for the "developed world". In the West, time is a commodity ("time is money") to be made and spent for profit ("make time", "spend time"). In the "civilized world", there is "time-sharing"—each one of us spends our leisure time more as individuals (one-at-at-a-time), and not in community as the indigenous people do. Time is rarely enjoyed for its own sake; instead, we "enjoy ourselves!" The values of the Christian work ethic are "time is money" and "in God we trust", which are two sides of the same idolatrous coin.

England, *Autonomía de los idiomas mayas: historia e identidad* (Guatemala, Cholsamaj, 1992, 158). Also by England (ed.) *Maya' Chii': Los idiomas mayas de Guatemala* (Cholsamaj, 1993, 82).

[4] *Tamoanchán*: "A mythical and paradisiacal place of origin" for the Toltecs and Aztecs. The word, which is, in fact, Mayan, is paraphrased by some as "place of the misty sky", which corresponds, according to some, with "the general [north] Gulf Coast region of the Huastec Maya". (Mary Miller and Karl Taube, *The God's and Symbols of Ancient Mexico and the Maya*. New York and London, Thames & Hudson 1993, 160). However, according to Girard (1966, 391) it signifies place ("ta") of the bird ("moan") serpent ("chan" or "kaan") and corresponds more closely to the cloud forest of western Guatemala where maize is said to have originated. The Cho'rti' of northern Chiapas still refer to themselves as "chan".

[5] Cf. the argument in the second part of chapter 5.

"Ixiim": in harmony with nature

So germane is maize, or corn to Maya culture that virtually the same word for it has been used in most of the highland Guatemalan languages, for thousands of years. If every aspect of Maya existence was ordered by its time centered worldview, their culture, religion and very existence are based, even until now, on the maize cycle.[6] Maize is, as it were, the earthly incarnation of time. The Maya calendar is based upon the conjunction, every 52 solar years (365 days), with the cycle of 73 lunar calendars (260 days). According to Girard, 52 and 73 correspond also to the number of days for the first and second corn crops to ripen.[7] Maize appears at the creation of humanity.[8] In some myths, it is also the tree of life that stands at the center of the world, pointing to the four corners of the universe. The stylized cornstalk or "foliated cross" at the ruins of Palenque (Chiapas) is the prime example. In sum, for the ancient Maya, maize was a potent symbol of the divine force which brought together heaven and earth, humanity and nature, family needs and social structures. For the Maya, order in the cosmos was not accidental or distant from human affairs. Like the great metaphor of Maya life—the life-cycle of maize—the continued well—being of the universe required the active participation of the human community through ritual. As maize cannot seed itself without the intervention of human beings, so the cosmos required sacrificial blood to maintain life. Maya life was filled with endless rituals which seem to us bizarre and shocking, but which to them embodied the highest concepts of their spiritual devotion.[9]

The ecological crisis that concerns world leaders today is in large measure the result of the radical divorce in Western culture between otherworldly religion and non-religious everyday life. "Give us this day our daily bread" of the Lord's prayer has absolutely nothing to do with cutting down forests to grow hybrid corn and leaving behind deserts where native

---

[6] As we have discussed in the Introduction maize was "discovered" and "engineered" by the Mesoamerican peoples.

[7] Rafael Girard, *Los mayas* (México, Libromex, 1966), 296.

[8] The creation myths of the ancient Mayas relate that the parents of the original peoples were created from yellow and white corn. *Popol Vuh: The Sacred Book of the Quiché Maya*. Goetz and Morley versions of the translation by Adrián Recinos. Norman and London, University of Oklahoma Press, 1950, 167).

[9] Linda Schele and David Freidel, *A Forest of Kings: The Untold Story of the Ancient Maya* (New York, William Morrow, 1990), 19.

maize cannot grow. The preeminent symbols of our Christian faith—the cross, bread and wine—have significance also for everyday life. For Christians, the cross on which Christ was died to redeem us joins heaven and earth and the four corners of the world in its embrace. The product of grain, native "tortillas" or English bread, signifies communion and the basic needs of the human race. The distillation of the vine keeps salvation—the blood of Jesus—ever present before us, even as it (or its cultural equivalent) gladdens or hearts and makes easier our load.

Tamoamnchán: creation and utopia

Every culture and every people on earth treasures a myth of its origins as "the people", chosen by the Creator with a special mission, and yearning for that earthly paradise from which they came. The legendary first home of the Maya, the "garden of Eden" of the Mesoamerican peoples-the utopia which drove the Ki'che' federation back to the misty highlands of Guatemala, was *Tamoanchán*. It is where their forefathers and mothers were created by *Hunab ku'* (the Only Divine Being) of the Yukatekos (see chapter 10), *U Cux Caj Ulew* (Heart of Heaven and Heart of Earth) of the Ki'che' (see chapter 11)—who is for all the Maya peoples the Former and Shaper of Life and *Alom Q'aholom*: Child-bearer and Engenderer (see chapter 16).[10] The fact that this God has many manifestations which seem abhorrent to Christianity—such as Kukulkán (Gukumatx, Quetzalcoatl) the serpent deity—and that they are depicted in forms which to us seem repulsive, should not obscure the fact of this underlying belief in one God, which is at the heart of the resurgent Maya spirituality.

Throughout the Maya highlands today, indigenous peoples speaking many languages and dialects, memorialize their worldview in rites, dances and ceremonies. They have never heard of the *Pop Vuh*, but they have maintained the traditions for centuries. There is, however, a major difference between the religiosity of the ancient Maya that archaeologists and epigraphers have uncovered. Today's Maya theology is both in continuity and discontinuity with their ancient beliefs. Maya religion is essentially the same today as before, but after five hundred years of

---

[10] *Tzakol*, Maker or builder; *Bitol*, Shaper of pottery. *Alom Q'aholom* (Child-bearer, feminine principle and Engenderer, male principle). Cf. León-Portilla, ed., p. 101, ns. 4,5, based on Munro Edmonson's annotated edition of the *Popol Vuh*, the Council Book ("the book of the man of the mat") of the Ki'Che'.

oppression and submission to a form of Christianity, their spirituality is quite different from that of the temples and stelae of the mighty warrior priests of old. As Ku Canche' observes (chapter 10), when the Spaniards began to hound the Maya religious hierarchy in Yucatán to death,

> in the end, popular catholicism fused with indigenous religiosity; but it was the cult of *Hunab Ku'* (the One Creator God) that in fact prevailed and has survived over time. The priests of *Hunab Ku'* went underground while the official religion was being smashed. They continued to resist and to await the fulfillment of the prophecies.

It is with today's indigenous spirituality, then, that Christians must dialogue, and not with a bygone and long forgotten—and often oppressive—religious system.

Beginning to Dialogue

Despite the profound differences between the theology of the Bible and Maya theology, bridges can be found between indigenous theology and the Old Testament. In both we find a "down-to-earth" and holistic value system that is Biblical and which we must regain today if the human race is to survive on this planet.

The spirituality of the ancestors

In the early chapters of Genesis we find the epic forefathers of the human race and of Middle Eastern civilization—Adam and Eve, Abel, Noah and his family, Enoch—who worshipped the One True God. Later we find seekers of Elohim, like Abram, and the patriarchs to whom God calls out from the culture of Babel to father a special people for the divine glory. Melchizedek, a "heathen" priest-king, comes out to meet Abraham with sacramental offerings. He too worships "the Most High" God and will become a paradigm in the New Testament of the pontifical (bridge-building, from "pontifex", priest) ministry of Christ the High Priest. Paul is not afraid to quote "pagan" poets in his address to Athenians and to use the categories of nature to proclaim the good news to the tribal people of Licaonia. These are bridges into the world of non-Christian religions.

Is there divine revelation outside of the Judeo-Christan tradition? Do the Biblical stories of the dawn of humanity exhaust the possibilities of divine revelation? As the human race spread around the globe, did God turn a blind eye and a deaf ear to the prayers of devout people in distant lands that "Christian" Europe would eventually "discover" in its thirst for empire and material gain? No, says a Kuna priest.

> God is and was with our people; he evangelized them first and gave them very peculiar traits and ways through which they might be found. He used our clothing, our arrows, our gourds full of maize brew, and has not repented of giving us this way of life. God is with us, with our elders; he helps us to work out a history of salvation which is very much our own (quoted in chapter 12).

"Elements of the religion of our ancestors which, in God's sovereignty, managed to survive until today, had an 'evangelical' side to it—it was good news to the Maya people' writes Ku Canche'. Examples of this can be found in some of the poetry of ancient Mesoamérica which has survived until today.

> Only Thee do I trust entirely, here where one dwells.
> For thou, O great Kin,[11] providest that which is good,
> here where one dwells, to all living beings. Since Thou abidest to give reality to the earth, where all men live.
> And thou art the true helper who grants that which is good (Yukatec-Maya songs).[12]

> There alone, in the interior of heaven You invent Your word,
> Giver of Life! What will you decide? Do you disdain us here?
> Do you conceal your fame and your glory on the earth?
> What will you decide? No one can be intimate
> with the Giver of Life... Then, where shall we go?
> Direct yourselves, we all go to the place of mystery.
> (Nezahualcoyotl, Aztec chieftain and sage, 1402-1472).[13]

Natural revelation

Classical theology speaks of two revelations, "natural" and "biblical". A traditional way of analyzing the issue would be: 1) Natural revelation is universal but not complete (Acts 14:15-17; 17:26-31; Ro 1:19,20).2) Prophetic revelation in the O.T. was unique but also incomplete (Heb. 1:1). 3) Christ came to fulfil the law and the prophets—he is the fullness of all

---

[11] *Kin*, Yukatek name for the sun who is the representation of the One God, *Ah Kin*. See chapter 10.
[12] León-Portilla, 230.
[13] Ibid, 244-246.

in all (Acts 17:30,31; Heb. 1:1,2). 4) But individual Christian conceptions and understandings of God are imperfect and incomplete; they require universal input (Am. 9:7). 5) Universal input can also be forthcoming from people who have learned about God through natural revelation (Mal 1:11; Ac. 17:29).

The ancients discovered God in Nature. "Since the creation of the world God's invisible qualities... have been clearly seen, being understood by what has been made, so that men are without excuse" (Ro. 1:20).

Natural revelation is God's Word in and through Creation. This is what Fr. Richard (chapter 14) calls "the book of life", which antecedes the Bible, God's written Word. Fr. López (quoted in chapter 10) explains this further:

> This faith in the God of life, the result of his loving purposes which he revealed throughout the history and cultures of our peoples, and which our grandfathers and grandmothers have carefully preserved in their ancestral traditions, is the root of our indigenous theology today.

Natural revelation is a bridge to God's revelation in Scripture and in Jesus Christ. The fact of God's self-revelation to a specific people, Israel, makes clear the divine intention to dwell among nations and peoples and confirms the key role of Creation in this process. Although will of God that Israel be a witness to the whole world was thwarted by that nation's ethnocentrism and religious pride, God has not been left without witnesses.

> From furthest east to furthest west my name is great among the nations. Everywhere fragrant sacrifice and pure gifts are offered in my name; for my name is great among the nations, says the Lord of Hosts (Mal. 1:11).

> In no place can be the house of He who invents Himself...
> But in all places he is venerated.
> His glory, his majesty is sought throughout the earth.
> (Nezahualcoyotl).[14]

---

[14] Ibid.

Our shared humanity

It has always been so, but we now need to recognize it even more: the oneness of the human race. This is a fact of natural law, a basic component of the order of Creation.

> From one ancestor he made all nations to inhabit the whole earth, and he allotted the times of their existence and the boundaries of the places where they would live, so that they would search for God and perhaps grope for him and find him—though indeed he is not far from each one of us. For, "In him we live and move and have our being"; as even some of your own poets have said, "For we too are his offspring" (Acts 17:26-28).

The love of God for the poor and oppressed

> I have indeed seen the misery of my people in Egypt. I have heard them crying out because of their slave drivers, and I am concerned about their suffering. So I have come down to rescue them from the hand of the Egyptians and to bring them up and out of that land into a good and spacious land flowing with milk and honey (Ex. 3:7,8).

"For God so loved the world... (Jn. 3:16). Is a key theme in God's "special revelation", Scripture. This love, which is manifest in Jesus Christ' redemptive work, was anticipated in the exodus event. Wuqub Iq observes that liberation is a valid theological paradigm for dialogue with the people of Abia Yala (chapter 16). Says Fr. Richard, "The evangelization of culture is always the evangelization of a specific people who are fighting for their land, for work opportunities, their homes and their health... The evangelization of culture should be an integral part of the liberation of a people" (chapter 14).

Somewhat to our surprise, we find that Israel did not have a monopoly on exodus and liberation. Other peoples and other cultures have also been favored by the Creator. "Are not you Israelites the same to me as the Cushites? declares the Lord. Did I not bring Israel up from Egypt, the Philistines from Caphtor and the Arameans from Kir?" (Am. 9:7). This is an amazing statement. God was directly involved in the liberations and migrations of ancient people, some of them enemies of Israel! Was the Creator present in the countless migrations of peoples from Asia down to the very southern tip of Abia Yala, the "American" land mass? Was the Only True God, the One that Maya peoples call *Hunab Ku'*, guiding that ancient race in its complex web of migrations throughout several centuries?

Was the Creator present when ancient tribes settled in the valley of Cuzco, the seeds of the great Quechua/Quichua nation?

The gospel in cultures

St. Paul encourages the people of Licaonia to abandon their idols and turn "to the living God, who made heaven and earth and sea and everything in them".

> In the past, God let all nations go their own way. Yet God has not been left without a witness. God has shown kindness by giving you rain from heaven and crops in their seasons. God provides you with plenty of food and fills your hearts with joy (Ac. 14:15-17).

The gospel in nature, the book of life! This is what the Maya peoples have studied for centuries, and continue to value and heed. If their own tradition means more to them than the Christian message, might it not be because the messages that they received have distorted the gospel?

Divine revelation in Jesus Christ

The God of Jesus Christ was revealed in a specific culture and historical context. The same Father/Mother God has been revealed to other cultures throughout history, through Creation, the book of life, and through prophets, the likes of Enoc, Noah, and Melchizedek—or the prophetic figures of Mesoamerican myth and history: Quetzalcoatl, Netzalcoyotl, Chilam Balaam, etc.

> In the past God spoke to our forefathers through the prophets at many times and in various ways, but in these last days he has spoken to us through his Son, who he appointed heir of all things and through whom he made the universe (He. 1:1,2).

The Christian Scriptures reveal that—through his incarnation, life, death and resurrection—Jesus Christ, the Son of the Living God, came to give meaning to all of God's actions in history, past, present and future. The following texts situate this theodicy in particular cultural contexts and provide a Christian basis for respectful dialogue.

> Out of you (Bethlehem Ephrata) will come for me one who will be a ruler over Israel, *whose origins are of old, from ancient times* (Mi. 5:2).

People will come from east and west and north and south, and will take
their places at the feast in the kingdom of God (Math. 13.29).

In the past God overlooked such ignorance, but now he commands all
people everywhere to repent. For he has set a day when he will judge the
world with justice by the man he has appointed. He has given proof of
this to all men by raising him from the dead (Ac. 17:30,31).

Issues in Dialogue

The above statements might seem to provide a Christian agenda for
dialogue. But from an indigenous perspective, this is not enough, because
it seems to take their own theology less than seriously (see Wuqub Iq,
chapter 16) and introduces a problematic figure, Jesus Christ (see Pop Cal,
chapter 13). For their part, Christians are prone to throw at least two
roadblocks in the path of dialogue—idolatry and syncretism—which need to
be seriously addressed before meaningful dialogue can take place: "idolatry"
and "syncretism".

The Bible and radical monotheism

The radical monotheism of the Old Testament, which is based upon the first
and second commandments in the Decalogue—no other gods, no graven
images—and the *Shema*—"The Lord our God, the Lord is one"—would
seem to place an insurmountable obstacle in the way of dialogue with
indigenous religions. God is a mystery; finite minds cannot fathom infinity,
eternity, perfection and all the other attributes that are ascribed to God.
Nevertheless, because we were created in the divine image, men and
women, since Eden, have always striven to understand God, to cut the deity
down to size, to imagine the Creator in images of the creation. Further,
while Scripture condemns our human obsession with packaging God in
manageable "bits", there is a recognition that human minds and spirits can
only grasp very small "pieces" of divine reality, and need to put names to
these perceptions.

Symbols of divine action in Scripture. There are symbols from nature,
such as the rainbow after the Deluge and the pillars of fire and cloud at the
Exodus; symbols taken from the mineral (water, rock) and plant worlds
(rose, seed, wheat, bread, wine, the cross); from the animal world (blood,
the serpent in the desert, lamb, blood, lion, dove, eagle); symbols from the
heavens (sun, morning star) and from the spirit world (angels); liturgical

symbols (ark, candlestick; and last but not least, human symbols/or paradigms of the divine presence (Adam, prophets, priests, kings, the "pagan" Melchizedek, Cyrus my servant).

Naming God in the Old Testament. To name something or someone in the Hebrew tradition was to establish proprietary rights over them.[15] In the Od Testament, God allows himself to be named and reveals himself through evocative names. Elohim, Yahweh, Adonai, El Shaddai, Yaveh Sabaoth. But, even the unpronounceable name of God, Yahweh, became an idol in popular religiosity. Recent archeological evidence suggests that, even under monarchs who were high monotheists, the general populace may have worshiped Yahweh in a mixture of "orthodox" and "pagan" cultic forms.[16]

Thus, mediations can easily become idols. The fine line that divides a sign or a symbol from an image or idol is often almost invisible. Yet we cannot do without symbols. They are essential to communication. But an important characteristic of symbols is their flexibility and adaptability. The moment they become static they loose their capacity to communicate, to free people up, to make them alive. In a word, they become idols—symbols of death. We have an interesting example of this in the Bible. When the Israelites were being bitten by vipers in punishment for their sin of rebellion against God, Moses interceded for his people and God ordered him to make a bronze serpent, to tell the people to gaze upon the image and they would be healed (Num. 21:4-9). This is, indeed, a strange passage, given the clear prohibition in Exodus (20:4) against making graven images and worshiping them. Several centuries later, a life-giving image had become an unclean idol[17] which needed to be destroyed (2 Ki. 18:4). But this is not the end of the story. Jesus uses the image of Nehushtan to teach Nicodemus, an idol hating Jew, about his own redeeming death (Jn. 3:14).

Idolatry and the capacity to imagine

---

[15] Enrique Dussel, *History and the Theology of Liberation* (Maryknoll, N.Y., Orbis, 1976), 78.

[16] J. Glen Taylor, "Was Yahweh Worshipped as the Sun?" in *Biblical Archeology Review* (May-June). 1994, 53-91. Archaeologists have uncovered a tenth century B.C.E. clay representation of the temple in which the invisible God (represented by an empty space, and also by the sun) is accompanied by his consort, flanked by royal horses and lions.

[17] The idol's name, "Nehushtan" is a double entendre in Hebrew which sounds both like bronze snake and unclean thing.

At the heart of the divine image in human beings is the gift of imagination. To be able to imagine the past, use our imagination creatively in the present, and imagine a better future for ourselves, our families and our peoples is what human communication and community is all about. But, when images grow static, when movements become monuments, when ideas (from gr. *eidos*) close in upon themselves and are imposed as ideologies (*eidologia*) or are made sacred and are idolized (from *eidolatria*), they take the place of God and are called an abomination. Obviously, political systems that we abhor and peoples whose cultures and religions that we find strange do not have a corner on making images to "strange gods".

Idolatry, according to Fromm, is not simply about worshipping many gods nor even alien gods. How many times, he asks, did not the veneration of God become the worship of an idol dressed up as the God of the Bible? What is the difference between the human sacrifices that the Aztecs offered to their gods and today's human sacrifices that are offered in war to the idols of nationalism and the sovereign state? Or, we might add, to the idols of the ideology of neo-liberalism and gods of consumerism and materialism?[18]

Every religion, including the christian religion, needs symbols to represent realities that go beyond the believers' comprehension. Every religious system, christendom not excepted, needs myths to justify its existence. Every form of religiosity, including that of christianity, has ways of manipulating its deities or idols. This is called magic. Whenever we offer our prayers, gifts and service to God out of fear or expecting to get something back in exchange, we are practicing magic. How many Protestant Christians use the Bible and its contents, Christian community and worship, the structures of the church and Christian conduct in magical and idolatrous ways?

John A. Mackay, a much respected Presbyterian missionary to Perú, an authority on hispanic culture and literature and one time president of Princeton Theological Seminary, highlights four essential facets of the Christian faith: divine revelation, the encounter of human beings with God, the community of God's people and human obedience to God. At each of these levels he found Latin American Protestant Christianity idolatrous. The idols were (and are even more so today), the worship of ideas, emotions, church structures and morality.

---

[18] Erich Fromm, *And You Shall be as Gods*. From the Spanish translation, *Y seréis como dioses* (Buenos Aires, Paidós, 1980), pp. 43,44,48,49.

> When theology, the role of which is to interpret reality, becomes an end in itself, christian doctrine, however orthodox, becomes an idol... loyalty to ideas... and not to God whom these ideas represent... An idol can also appear out of a real encounter with God... In this case an emotion or a feeling becomes an idol... The organized community, as well, the institution can become an end in itself... Even when the church takes the place of God it substitutes God in the loyalty of human beings... Finally, at the very moment when a specific precept, a scruple, or perhaps a high ideal is absolutized... it then becomes an idol.[19]

If Christianity has had trouble understanding God without making idols of divinity, can we expect otherwise from a pre-Christian religion that never knew the Jewish Decalogue and Shema, nor read the New Testament because it existed centuries before Judeo-Christian revelation? Furthermore, the versions of Christianity which they have received from the West have been plagued with idols—images, cultural baggage, dogmas and alien social organization.

In our present world where everyone, even God, is brought down to our own size, we forget that the ancients were overwhelmed with the concept of God. They thought about him, they bowed down to him, and they did everything in their power to appease him when they perceived that bountiful nature had become their enemy. The infinite facets of God have always been too much for human minds to grasp. So, indigenous peoples thousands of years ago, as we still do today, focused upon more manageable forms of God which they eventually came to idolize.

Indigenous leaders have readily admitted in their essays that there were, of course idolatrous practices in their ancient religion, but not everybody was an idolater. There were certainly human sacrifices, but not everyone agreed with this. These were specific cases upon which "christians" built their generalizations about "indians". This gave rise to the stereotype that the Mesoamerican peoples were all a totally idolatrous people who once practiced human sacrifice. There is evidence that the Maya peoples were not always idolatrous. They worshipped One God. Although he was associated with the sun, there is no evidence of an image or painting being made to the supreme Maya deity.

---

[19] Juan A. Mackay, *Realidad e idolatría en el cristianismo contemporáneo* (Buenos Aires, La Aurora, 1970) pp.9,10,19,20.

Syncretism and the capacity to adapt

Juan Sepúlveda, a Chilean Pentecostal missiologist wrote his doctoral dissertation on the subject of syncretism. He did so after he found himself and his spirituality dismissed as "alienating" by indigenous leaders. He began to question why the pentecostal movement—a sinchretistic form of the Christianity which came to Latin America from Europe and the United States, finds it so difficult contextualize or inculturate the gospel in other cultures? Students of the phenomenon of cultural interpenetration argue that to discover the meaning of the term "syncretism" it is to the history of the word (i.e. its usage over time), and not to its technical etymology, that we must turn.[20]   What follows is a summary of his research:

The ancient Greek historian, Plutarch, relates that the Cretans spent a lot of their time fighting among themselves. But when they were attacked by outside enemies, they put aside their differences to combat a common enemy. "And that," says Plutarch, "was it which they commonly called syncretism (*sugkretismós*). This first recorded usage of the term is a compound of *sug* (together), *cret* (Crete), and *ismos* ("ism" or system). Concludes Sepúlveda, "'together-Crete-system' means something like 'to unite or to federate, as did the Cretan'. Syncretism is here an act of fraternal love.[21]

In the sixteenth century, Erasmus picked up the theme in the process of introducing the writings of Plutarch and other classics to his contemporaries. Erasmus interprets "together-Crete-system" metaphorically to signify "common interest" even when "sincere love" is lacking. The Dutch philosopher, a Catholic, soon began to apply the proverb to concrete situations. He urged the reformer Melanchton to set aside their differences with each other and, "Cretan with Cretan stand against the foe". In another letter he described the way in which St. Paul adapted the Christian message to the Corinthian church as "syncretism" (*sugkretizein*).   Going even

---

[20] Juan Sepúlveda, *Gospel in Culture in Latin American Protestantism: Toward a New Theological Appreciation of Synchretism*. Th.D. disertation, University of Birmingham, UK, 1996 (second draft), 1. Cf. Charles Stewart and Rosalind Shaw (eds.). *Syncretism/Anti-Syncretism. The Politics of Religious Synthesis* (London and New York, Rutledge, 1994), pp. 2ff.

[21] Sepúlveda, 2, citing Plutarch, "On brotherly Love", No. 9, in *Plutarch's Morals*. Wm. W. Goodwin (ed.). (Boston, Little, Brown and Co., 188), p. 62, and Henry G. Burger, "Synchretism, An Acculturative Acceleration", in *Human Organization*: vol. 25 (1966), p. 104.

further, he argued that the Apostle was only following the method of his Master who "adjusted himself to those whom he wanted to pull over to himself".[22] This usage is very close to the technical term "contextualization" (used by Protestant evangelicals) and "inculturation" (used by the Catholic Church). Theologically, Sepúlveda suggests, "syncretism", as used metaphorically by Erasmus sounds very much like "incarnating oneself into the characteristics of those whom one wants to address".[23]

> Erasmus is applying the term to the necessary cultural mediation of the Gospel. If this interpretation is correct, here the understanding of "syncretism" is amazingly close to the modern "descriptive" use of the word, and therefore, Erasmus should be the first in suggesting that the Bible is, in this specific sense, a syncretistic document.[24]

A century later, a group of German Lutheran intellectuals became embroiled in a controversy over a proposed dialogue between all the Christian churches, including the Roman Catholicism. At this time, the original, harmonious, meaning of syncretism was turned on its head with the first recorded usage of the term in a negative way, to label Christians who wanted to achieve unity at the expense of truth. This derogatory connotation—as hybridization (*synkeranume*), rather than solidarity (*sugkretismós*)—was hardened in the fires of religious controversy, and has persisted until today in both conservative and early ecumenical circles. More recently, *sugkrêtos* or *sugkratos* ("mixed together") has been suggested as a possible source. One suspects that ideology, as well as theology, has had something to do with this negative exegesis. Racial and cultural hybridization has long had, in Northern Europe and North America, a negative connotation which in our present world of mass migrations can no longer be empirically defended.[25]

The social sciences use "syncretism" as shorthand for the phenomenon of hybridization or cultural interpenetration which is as old as the human race. Although missiologists use the social sciences as a useful tool of analysis, there is no agreement among them concerning the usage of the term when it is applied to the interface between culture and the Christian

---

[22] Sepúlveda, 7,8, quoting from *Collected Works of Erasmus*, Margaret Mann Phillips and R.A.B. Mynors (ed.) Toronto University Press, 1982, and other sources.

[23] Sepúlveda, 6.

[24] Sepúlveda, 8,9.

[25] Sepúlveda, p. 8-10ff?, 23f?.

faith. The semantic, rather than the metaphorical definition, is the basis for today's outright rejection of syncretism by conservative missiologists who rely on the social sciences for other insights. Sepúlveda makes a case for setting aside technical definitions of syncretism and imitate Erasmus' metaphorical usage of the term. "Syncretism refers, in a metaphorical fashion, to something which we know through experience that happens in human life. A metaphorical or "narrative" usage liberates the term from "the dichotomies of the abstract Western mind" and makes it capable of embracing the "inseparable unities of experience" and the "concrete mind of the common human being".[26]

Syncretism and incarnation

Applying this metaphorical meaning of syncretism to Christian witness we can affirm that wherever Christian incarnation takes places there is syncretism. The first syncretism took place when "the Word was made flesh and dwelt among us" (Jn. 1:14). Whether for the sake of solidarity with a world in crisis or for evangelistic witness, wherever the Holy Spirit is truly at work, there will be syncretism ("together-Christian-system"). If Jesus Christ the Son of God could bridge the infinite void between heaven and earth, we who profess to follow him should be capable of stepping across the gap between two very different cultures ("ours" and "theirs")—both by definition idolatrous—to receive and, at the same time offer the Good News of life. Much wisdom is therefore needed to discern between outright pollution of the Gospel—of which institutionalized Christianity is quite guilty—and incarnation. This is mission in Christ's way.

The opposite of "indigenous" in Spanish is "alienígena", an alien or extraterrestrial being. This is the Christ that has been presented to them. However, aboriginal peoples are looking for a Christ that is, indeed, an aborigine. One who is autochthonous, or indigenous to their cultures. Might not Quetzalcoatl, the wise Toltec chieftain who taught them to live in peace, that quase messianic figure who gave up his kingdom and promised some day to return to re-establish his kingdom?[27] Might not the "foliated cross",

---

[26] Sepúlveda, pp. 27-29?

[27] "It is said that [Quetzalcoatl] just lay covered, he just lay with his face covered. And it is said he did not look as a human. His face was like something monstrous, battered. And his beard was very long, very lengthy. He was heavily bearded". ("The Story of Quetzalcoatl" in *Native Mesoamerican Spirituality*, León-Portilla, ed. London, SPCK, 1980), 151.

the "tree of life" point to the indigenous Christ who died, was buried, like a grain of wheat (Jn. 12:24) and rose again to become the Lord of the four corners of the earth?

A Pause for Reflection

The announcement of the Good News of Jesus is not necessarily the same as the good news of christianity. The Good News was proclaimed within a specific socio-cultural context to his own people in a marginalized province. Thus, very quickly we can identify with it and apply the message to our own situations. What, we might ask, is the state of our own families and communities where we live? Is it Good News or good news? Before we can answer this question, we need urgently to evaluate the kind of image of Jesus that we have? Generally we associate him with "the Christian Jesus". But this raises another important question. If Jesus were with us here today, would he imagine Christianity in the same way as we do?

In search of an indigenous Jesus

We need to take a new look at the biblical Jesus. Can we see him as the "Jesús originario"-the indigenous or aboriginal[28] Jesus? According to Mark 1:14,15, in a very specific situation Jesus did not preach doctrine but acted to bring about life. He focused his attention upon others. We must therefore center our attention upon him in order to understand what he did and what he invites us to do.

Throughout his life, death and resurrection, Jesus sought to identify with his Father through the Holy Spirit-this is complementarity and totality. At least in the Synoptics, he did not affirm his divine origins, but through his humanity demonstrated his divinity. His life was an example of simplicity, honesty and of loyalty to his origins. Though he didn't try to exalt his origins, neither did he attempt to deny or hide his divine roots. He didn't have to make the effort tp become part of the Jewish culture because

---

A messianic prophecy: "He had no beauty, no majesty to draw our eyes, no grace to make us delight in him; his form, disfigured, lost all the likeness of a man, his beauty changed beyond human semblance. He was despised, he shrank from the sight of men, tormented and humbled by suffering; we despised him, we held him of no account, a thing from which men turn away their eyes" (Isa. 2a,3, NEB).

[28] Editor's note. "Originario": primal, related to ones origins or roots.

he himself, in his incarnation, had become that culture. It is this point that the gospel truly becomes Good News.

Throughout his life Jesus worked to free the oppressive elements in his culture, the same culture in which he proclaimed the gospel. While he affirmed his Jewish culture, he also affirmed the cultural identity of others. In Matthew 8:11 Jesus states that many would come from the East and the West to sit down at table with him. This is a promise of hope for all religions that have been excluded from christianity: Jesus does not exalt himself as a prerequisite for salvation. He leaves room for choice and invites us to take part in building his kingdom. He does not set aside the histories of pre-Christian peoples, like Abraham who is called the "father of the faithful". This is an invitation to affirm the faith of our ancestors and to not be ashamed of it. Jesus is the liberator of history and continues to take part in transforming our histories.

Jesus and the "mestizos"

The Samaritans were quite close to Jesus' race and culture, since they were partly Israelite and shared the faith of Abraham. Having been rejected by Zerubbabel (Ezr. 4), the only choice they had was to build their own holy place-the sacred mountain of the covenant (in memory of the sacrifice of Isaac and of Jacob's vision). This rejection of the Samaritans by the traditions of the Jewish elders, in effect kept them away from the faith of Abraham. So Jesus spoke to them about the God of Isaac and Jacob, who must be worshipped "in Spirit and in Truth". What or whom is this Spirit and this Truth? Might it not be the Spirit of Truth that cannot be possessed, but only shared by inviting other people into the kingdom of God. The attitude of arrogance mixed with shame that "mestizos" evidence and feel comes about when we fail to become acquainted with the spiritual traditions of our indigenous ancestors. In Jesus, the "mestizos" of his time found faith and hope-Spirit and Truth. They added to their own truth the hope of following the true God. These are complementary realities which should not be separated by their differences.

For "mestizos" and bicultural people everywhere, like the co-authors of this chapter, it is important to affirm our identity and origins. We need not deny them. We can affirm them even as we affirm the cultural roots of others. This process can be helped as we discover the divine reality within human reality which enables us to work toward a better humanity. This can only be achieved through Jesus Christ, who as a divine and human person transformed the universal way of perceiving-that we might become one while remaining different. Jesus is both an "originario" and a "mestizo". There is not contradiction in his identity and mission. There is hope for all: for those who are "inside" as well as for those who are "outside".

Beginning to Dialogue

> As Wuqub Iq has reminded us (chapter 16),
> any dialogue between Christian and Mayan theologies will necessarily require its own frame of reference; it will also need to determine who is to take part in the dialogue. Once this is done, we can arrive at guidelines to orient respectful and peaceful relations between the practitioners of both faiths in our indigenous communities.

The guidelines that he suggests are framed within a Roman Catholic (and liberationist) perspective which we need to understand and respect, within the framework of Protestant theology. A major difficulty with dialogue which has not been mentioned in any of the essays is the radically different self-understanding of the Christian faith (and indeed of most major religions) vis a vis that of indigenous spirituality. Christianity, Judaism and Islam are by their very nature missionary. Unlike the indigenous religions-and also the great eastern faiths,[29] they exist by proselytism or evangelism, however one may want to define it. Having been for millennia a fairly hegemonic religion in Mesoamerica, and for five centuries a supposed sub-product of Catholic Christianity (also hegemonic), the practitioners of a revitalized indigenous religion are more concerned at this point about protecting their beliefs than in propagating them. Many of them are, however, eager to share their values for the benefit of a world in crisis (Cf. the lists of indigenous values in chapter 18).

Maya values: a gift to the world

Mesoamerican peoples believe that human existence and the cosmos are interrelated. The fact that human health eventually deteriorates and comes to an end, to be reborn in the lives of their offspring is but a reflection of the universe. Maya sages are always reflecting on the most radical problems

---

[29] The spread of peoples of Hindu and Buddhist religions to the "West" or "North" has forced them to compete with Christianity and become "missionary" to varying degrees.

of humanity. "What is humanity? Where does it come from? How should human beings act towards themselves and others? What are the relationships between human beings and God?" These questions bring together science and religion which are, in the Maya worldview, indivisible.[30] Maya values govern every aspect of life. A few snippets of their wisdom should suffice to make this point.

"We have not received the Earth as an inheritance, but as a loan which we must return to our children as they also to their children".[31]

"Before we clear the land and pierce Mother Earth [with our tools], we fast and we offer gifts to the Earth. Each phase of the agricultural process is a ceremony which brings together intimately agriculture and religion".[32]

Music and silence are two sides of the same reality. At the moment of creation, according to the *Pop Wuh*, "There was only immobility and silence, in the darkness, in the night. Only the Creator, the Maker, Tepeu, Gucumatz, the Forefathers, were in the water surrounded with light... Then came the word... and Tepeu and Gukumatz talked together... discussing and deliberating, they agreed, they united their words and their thoughts".[33] It is out of their desire to understand sound and silence (nothingness) that the Mesoamerican peoples may have been the first race to discover the concept of zero.

The *Pop Wuh* relates the myth of a personage called Vucub Caquix (Seven Shames). He rebelled against the supreme God wrapped in mantles of pride, ambition, envy, untruth, ungratefulness, crime and ignorance-the "seven shames" in Maya culture. The elders teach that these "shames" can be found in every human being and that every effort must be made to overcome the individualism and egotism of which these are but symptoms.[34]

---

[30] Daniel Matul, *Somos un sólo corazón: cultura maya contemporánea* (San José, Costa Rica, Liga Maya Internacional, 1994), 19.

[31] Ibid, 42.

[32] Ibid, 49.

[33] "The Forefathers" translates *e Alom*, "those who conceive and give birth", *Qaholom*, "those who beget the children". D. Goetz and S. Morley, *Popol Vuh: The Sacred Book of the Ancient Quiché Maya* (Norman and London, University of Oklahoma Press, 1950), 81, n. 1, 82.

[34] Motul, 101,102.

The values that the Mayas uphold are, in contrast, those of freedom and responsibility in community: respect, solidarity, equality and justice. They can be summarized in the Maya proverb: "I am You and You are I".[35]

Despite having survived five centuries of injustice and oppression, the Maya people look toward the future with hope and optimism. "This is the present history of an ancient nation that is being rejuvenated even as it maintains its ancient values. The Mayas share the expectation of building a new society born out of diversity and concerned with unity".[36]

It can be asked, What has the Christian faith to offer a people who maintain such high values-values that correspond in most ways to the Judeo-Christian tradition? Christians who believe that the Good News of Jesus Christ is meant to be shared must ask themselves how they can do this without running rough-shod over indigenous values and beliefs.

The Christian faith: a gift to the Maya peoples?

Fr. Pablo Richard (chapter 14) relates one example of how this might be done and suggests several hermeneutical and theological principles to guide orient Christian witness in dialogue with other faiths. These might perhaps be brought together in just three principles of Christian communication.

The principle of the two revelations. The first principle goes to the heart of the sources of our faith. What Christians often forget when they overlook or downplay divine revelation in Creation in their eagerness to exalt biblical revelation is that the latter could not exist without the former. The Bible is, after all a book, which presupposes some form of created matter. Those who wrote it under inspiration and we who read it are said to be "the crown of God's creation". The Bible begins with Creation in Genesis and concludes with Re-creation in Revelation Everything in between is the story of how the Creator is bringing about the transformation of a natural world that is flawed by sin. The stories that are told and the images that are used are all about life, about the natural world. This is what Richard calls "the book of life".

> God wrote two books—the book of life and the Bible. The Bible, God's second book, was written to help us decipher God's first book, the book

---

[35] Ibid, 109.
[36] Ibid, 115,116.

of life. The Bible was written to give us back a faith understanding concerning the world and to transform all of reality into one great revelation of God.

St. Paul calls "the book of life"-natural revelation "the law" which is written on the hearts and consciences of the *ethne* or peoples, even when they do not have "the Law" of Scripture (Ro. 2:14,15). Richard goes on to argue to the Kuna peoples of Panamá that God first revealed himself in their life and culture. This is God's first book. The Bible is the instrument to discern the Word of God in that first book". St. Paul practices this principle in his address to the Lycaonians when he refers to natural phenomena as a fact of divine revelation and goes on from there to announce the Good News (Ac. 14:15-17).

The incarnational principle. The Dominican missioners who drafted chapter 12 have put it very well.

> From the moment in which the Incarnate Word took on all of our humanities, with their commonalities and differences, every human culture has been called to develop a specific language of faith. God cannot communicate with people through a borrowed humanity. Rather, he did it on the basis of his unique existence as source and condition of every word. On the basis of the Incarnation, every word that has to do with God must forever cease to be abstract and non-temporal. Words about God must henceforth spring from the contexts in which human beings express themselves and their own world.

Incarnation goes beyond what some Protestants call "contextualization" and what Catholics currently describe as "inculturation". While these last two terms seem to focus more upon the message than upon the messenger, the very essence of incarnation is the Word that "was made flesh and dwelt among us" (Jn. 1:14), i.e. upon the messenger who is also the message-the Living Word. We can ask questions about each of the three terms. "Contextualization" is a process that puts methods and message-and derivatively the people who wield them-in touch with a "context", a term which resonates more with literary and sociological nuances than with living and breathing human beings. "Inculturation" takes for granted that an alien message and messenger can penetrate a culture, but to what end? indigenous people ask. To undermine its foundations and destroy it? To so change a culture that it becomes alien and unrecognizable? Or to accept its greatest values as harbingers of the gospel and touchstones of cultural revitalization? In contrast to the above, the incarnation of the Son of God signifies taking on human flesh fully and with it a specific culture as a bridge to all cultures, while maintaining a critical distance from them. But what we must remember about incarnation is that none of us can truly become incarnate in a culture as did Jesus Christ. This fact does not, however, diminish our responsibility to do "mission in Christ's way".

The vulnerability principle. "He came unto his own and his own received him not" (Jn. 1:11). The incarnate Son of God was not given any guarantee of success. Even his "chosen people" rejected him. A divine law which is asserted in both Biblical and natural revelation is the right of people to make choices, including the rejection of the incarnation. In his report on the visit to the Kuna people, Fr. Richard comments:

> If they accepted the Bible as the instrument for discernment of the Word of God in their own Kuna life and culture, they had to own the interpretation of the Bible. They themselves, within their culture and tradition, needed to appropriate the Bible and its interpretation. The first hermeneutical principle would be nullified if we were the ones to impose a predetermined biblical interpretation.

The task of a follower of Jesus Christ is "simply to make the biblical text available" to flesh and blood people within their own cultures. Nonetheless, "they had to be the authentic and real subjects of the hermeneutical process". At one and the same time, Christian witnesses need to become open to learn, in this case from the peoples of Abia Yala, how to read "the book of life", the book of Creation. The writer admits that "when we presented these hermeneutical principles, we were quite literally risking our mission and reason for being, as Christians and as evangelizers." The happy ending-the creative response of the people and of the evangelizers to the role of Scripture in the Kuna culture, does not, by itself, validate the principle of vulnerability. We are not given any guarantee of success. We are only asked to be faithful to the message of Scripture and Creation, and to remain in attentive and respectful solidarity ("together-Christian-style") with the subjects of evangelization. The vulnerability principle implies the possibility of rejection and "failure". Might it also imply conversion to "their" way of life? This is the way of the cross. But, after the cross comes the resurrection. At this point, the "foliated cross" of the Maya, with its constantly dying and resurrecting seeds of maize, and the cross of Jesus Christ become joined into one life-giving and transforming symbol.

"Pontifex" not·"pontificate"

In closing, we return to an image that was used at the end of the Foreword to this book. Bridge-building. As we face the challenge of listening to aboriginal peoples, learning from them and sharing our faith experience with them, may we become both bridges and bridge-builders. Bridges only fulfill their purpose when they are firmly anchored on both sides of a deep divide-*the principle of the two revelations*. If we are unable to extend our bridges all the way to the "other side"—or to make the jump when the bridge is not complete, then we do not understand *the principle of the Incarnation*, nor the mission of Jesus the Son of God.

"Pontifex", the Latin word for bridge-builders (eng.: pontiff) as been assumed as a privileged title by some religious leaders, or derided as a dubious religious vocation by others. All the same, far too many of us today would rather "pontificate" than to build genuine bridges.

To complete the metaphor, bridges are made to be walked upon-*the vulnerability principle*. Whoever wants to be a bridge, must be willing to be trampled upon and misunderstood—a painful exercise for all of us and for most human institutions.

BRIDGES
Apartado 634-1150
San José, Costa Rica

INDEX

Abia Yala, xi, xii, xiii, 6, 29, 49,
Agriculture (see "milpa"), 46, 69
Ancestors, 187
Anthropology, 172, 249
Assimilation, 179
Astronomy, 3

Bartolomé de las Casas, 15, 43, 89,
    243, 272
Base Community, 104, 117, 128,
    132, 230
Bible, 38-39, 50, 56, 59, 103, 117,
    128, 130, 142, 156, 190, 226,
    227, 245, 246, 248, 317
Brotherhoods ("cofradías"), 47, 68,
    126

Calendar, 3, 4, 46, 92, 95-99, 254,
    256
Catholic, 259
    Action, 110, 244
    catechists, 118, 126
    church, 43, 47, 280
    cultural synthesis, 179
    pastoral, 242, 249
    priests, 271
    theology, 46, 165
Catholicism, 49, 250
    popular, 140, 147, 156, 164, 180,
    282
    progressive, 51
CELAM, 145, 146, 148, 184
Change agents, 110
Chiapas, xii, 1, 271, 279
Chilam Balam, 154, 273
Civil Defense Patrols, 130, 234
Christ, 58, 124, 199, 218-220, 222,
    247, 312
Christendom, 115, 155, 243
Christianity, 35, 40, 49, 69, 142,
    180, 189, 193, 194, 220, 243,
    267, 312
Christian theology,
    contextual, 172
    levels, 151
    vs indigenous, 152
    intolerance, 217

Colonialism, 219, 217
Community, 103, 109, 110, 267
    authority structures, 91, 92-
    95
    competition vs individualism,
    75, 266,
    goals, 109
    imagined, 115
    traditional, 117, 128
CONAI, 286
CONAVIGUA, 234, 236
Conquest, 49, 106, 259
"Conquistadores", 243, 275
Conversion, 63, 74, 217, 219, 260
    to Catholicism, 127, 241
    to indigenous religion, 241
    to Protestantism, 41, 61, 113,
    127, 244, 245
"Costumbre", 65
Creation, 37, 41, 201
Cross, 192, 200, 268
Culture, 225, 226, 247, 249, 250

Deity (see monotheism), 85, 192,
    197, 245, 252
Democracy, 110, 235
Development, 106, 287
Dialogue, 57, 143, 153, 163, 166,
    187, 190, 208, 227, 242, 246-
    248, 256, 257, 259, 319, 314

Ecology, 52,
Ethnic revival, 118, 119, 133
European invasion, 13,41
Evangelicals, 45, 190, 246, 271,
    283, 286, 306
Evangelization, 39, 49, 50, 141,
    143, 225, 247, 249, 268, 208,
    219, 281, 301
    New evangelization, 126, 217,
    218, 225, 283
Evangelical churches, 28, 132, 219,
    221, 282
EZLN (see Zapatistas), 284, 290

Family, xii, 41, 104, 175, 107,

children, 110, 107, 125, 233, 267, 277
    parental respect, 267, 277
    play, 111, 112
    marriage, 71, 101, 104, 253
    sex and fertility, 125, 277
Fifth Centenary, xii, 139, 161, 172, 173
Fundamentalism, 222, 244, 281

Genocide, 41, 129, 274, 282
Gospel, 212, 246, 269
Glyphs (see writing), 4
Guerrillas, 129, 244

Healing and wholeness, 94, 125, 186, 278
Hermeneutics, 225, 228, 318
Human rights, 173, 111, 214, 223, 237, 239

Identity, 113, 126, 129, 130, 176, 229, 267, 289
Ideology, 85
Idolatry, 35, 49, 141, 155, 189, 191, 192, 194, 244, 305-308
Incarnation, 267
Inculturation, 52, 58, 207, 214, 221, 249
Indigenous religion, 85, 172, 177, 308
Indigenous theology, 37, 39, 40, 148, 160, 199,
    aspects and goals, 202, 207
    biblical themes, 56
    categories, 156
    challenges, 143, 168
    characteristics, 148, 210
    contemporary concerns, 185
    definition, 140
    emergence, 141
    historical role, 140, 200
    nature, 153
    risks, 167
    rites, 96, 242, 253
    stages, 160
    unity and diversity, 127, 161
Indigenous Decade (UNO), xii
John Paul II, 145, 173, 178, 282

Kaqchikel peoples, 10, 14, 35, 85, 86

Ki'che' peoples, 14, 83, 86, 91

"Ladinos" (see "mestizos"), 70, 118
Land issues, xii, 211, 213, 278
Landa, Fr. Diego de, 17, 89
Languages, xi, xii, 35, 37, 74, 86, 88, 124, 126, 276
Las Casas (see Bartolomé de)
Liberation, 215, 227
    indigenous, 59, 190, 319
    theology, 39, 52, 54, 129, 164, 214, 246, 247, 294, 280, 314
    women, 102, 109, 111
Life,
    Maya understanding, 241, 262, 264
    respect for, 171, 186

Male domination (see paternalism), 103, 104, 105
Mam peoples, 10, 91
Managua Declaration, 286
Marcos, sub-commander, 271, 285
Marxism, 105, 136, 284
Maya cities, 88
Mesoamerican civilization, 3, 9, 297, 275
"Mestizos" (see "ladinos"), 54, 56, 58, 104, 179, 313
Military oppression, 25, 101, 130, 131, 233, 235, 244
"Milpa", 46, 69
Mission, 49, 52, 180, 243, 316
Missionaries, 94, 177, 217, 250
Modernity, 109, 136
Monotheism, 85, 192, 197
Montesinos, Fr. Antonio de, 15, 243
Mountain spirits (Tzuultaq'as), 116, 117, 122, 124, 130, 269
Mythology, 89

NAFTA, xii, 284
Names for God,
    Christian, 305, 306
    Indigenous, 15, 36, 107, 194-197, 200, 242, 251, 299
New World Order, 29

Oral traditions, 106, 190

Paganism, 49, 59, 261, 221

Pan-Mayanism, 113, 132, 135
Paternalism, 21, 52, 103
Pluralism, 53, 161
Politics and power, 174, 214, 233
Popular organizations, 286
Pop Vuh, 1, 83, 87, 91, 106
Priests,
    Catholic, 187, 272,
    Maya, 93, 187, 221, 257
Protestantism, 18, 36, 37, 39, 40,
    43, 47, 48, 193
    churches, 135, 269, 281
    ethics, 66
    missions, 19
    pentecostal, 247
    racism, 50,
    sects, 43, 244, 281
    theology, 164
Q'eqchi' peoples, 113, 128, 178,
    185
Quetzalcoatl, 12, 191, 194, 195

Racism, 235
Reconciliation process, 285
Redemption, 201
Reformation theology, 263
Religion
    identity, 130
    resistance, 116
Repression, 113
Resistance, 36, 45, 51, 91, 105,
    131, 142, 225 254, 256, 302
    assimilation, 179
    cultural affirmation, 86, 107
    defense mechanisms, 91f, 97,
    178, 209, 219
    miming (reenactment), 44, 55
    religion, 116
    strategies,173
    survival, 109, 173
Revelation, 40, 56, 26, 268, 317
Revolts, 113, 129, 280
Rigoberta Menchú, 111
Ruíz, bishop Samuel, 27, 272, 281,
    285

Salvation, 213, 215, 226, 268, 313
Santo Domingo document, 179, 184

Self-determination, 286-289
Sexuality, 103, 104, 109,125, 276
Socioeconomic, 246
    alternative, 241
    new class, 63, 117,
    128, 129
    new order, xii
    conditions, 67
    improvement, 64
    marginalization, 35, 37, 241
    refugees, 130
    structures, 214
    transformations, 282
Solidarity, 112
Spirituality, xii, 35, 48, 49, 56,
    106, 125, 228, 242, 244, 245,
    247, 248, 250, 252, 259, 260
Symbolism, 131, 136, 139, 201, 304
Synchretism, 40, 44, 45, 46, 55, 59,
    190, 218, 248, 260, 305, 309-312

Theological methodology, 148, 202
Time (see calendar)
Transculturation, 52
Trinity, 89, 295
Typologies, 53, 163, 260
Values, 92, 108, 241, 246-248, 256,
    257, 265, 277, 314
Vatican II, 145, 175

Widows, 109, 233, 239
Women, 102, 125, 182, 234, 276,
    286
    liberation, 109, 111
    reproduction and production,
    101
    resistance, 104, 131
    tradition, 128
Worldview,
    European, 180
    indigenous, 99, 113, 126,
    180, 253, 251, 264, 288
Worship, 110, 269
Writing (see glyphs), 4
Wycliff Translators (SIL), 50, 21-24
Zapatistas (see EZLN), xii, 271,
    284

ESSENTIAL BIBLIOGRAPHY

Amaro, N., *Guatemala: Historia despierta* (Guatemala: IDESAC, 1992).

Annis, S., *God and Production in a Guatemalan Town*. Austin, University of Texas Press, 1987).

Ariarajah, W., *The Bible and Peoples of Other Faiths* (Geneva, World Council of Churches, 1987). Risk Book Series.

—, *Gospel and Culture: An Ongoing Discussion With the Ecumenical Movement* (Geneva, WCC Publications, 1994).

Bediako, K., *Theology and Identity: The Impact of Culture Upon Christian Thought in the Second Century and Modern Africa* (Oxford: Regnum Books, 1992).

Benson, E. P., *The Maya World* (New York, Thomas Y. Crowell Co., 1967).

Bosch, D.J. *Transforming Mission: Paradigm Shifts in Theology of Mission* (Maryknoll: Orbis, 1992).

Bricker, V.R., *The Indian Christ, the Indian King: The Historical Substrate of Maya Myth and Ritual* (Austin, University of Texas Press, 1981).

Brintnall, D. 1979 *Revolt Against the Dead: The Modernization of a Maya Com munity in the Highlands of Guatemala*. New York, Gordon and Breach.

Burgos-Debray, E., ed., *I, Rigoberta Menchú: An Indian Woman in Guatemala* (London/New York, Verso Editions, 1984).

Cabarrús, C.R., *La cosmovisión Kékchí en proceso de cambio* (San Salvador: UCA Editores, 1979).

Cabrera, E., *La Cosmogonía Maya* (Costa Rica, Liga Maya Internacional, 1992).

Carmack, R.M., ed., *Harvest of Violence: The Maya Indians and the Guatemalan Crisis* (Norman and London, University of Oklahoma Press, 1988).

—, *Evolution of the Utatlan Quiché: An Ethnohistoric Study of a Highland Maya Kingdom*. (*Evolución del Reino Quiché*. Guatemala: Editorial Piedra Santa, 1979).

Carrasco, D., *Religions of Mesoamerica: Cosmovision and Ceremonial Centers* (San Francisco, Harper and Row, 1990).

Castañeda, Amilcar, *Búsqueda de espacios para la vida*. First Continental Meeting of Afro, Indigenous and Christian Theologies and Philosophies (Cayambe, Ecuador, Editorial Abya-Yala, 1994).

Chamberlain, R.S., *The Conquest and Colonization of Yucatán: 1517-1550*. (Washington, Carnegie Institution, 1948).

Clendinnen, I., *Ambivalent Conquests: Maya and Spaniard in Yucatán*, 1517-1570 (London and New York, Cambridge University Press, 1987).

Coe, M.D., *Breaking the Maya Code* (New York, Thames Hudson, 1992).

Costas, O.E., *Liberating News: A Theology of Contextual Evangelization* (Grand Rapids, Eerdmans, 1989).

Dussel, E. (ed.), *The Church in Latin America: 1492-1992* (Maryknoll, Orbis, 1992).

Edmonson, M.S., *The Book of Counsel: The Popol Vuh of the Quiche Maya of Guatemala* (New Orleans, Middle Amerian Research Institute, 1971).

Everton, M., *The Modern Maya: A Culture in Transition* (University of New Mexico Press, 1991).

Gaqurae, Joe, "Indigenisation as incarnation: The concept of a Melanesian Christ", in *Evangelical Review of Theology: Toward Integral Mission Theology*. Vol. xx, no. 3 (July 1996), pp. 240-247.

Garza, M. de la, *La Conciencia histórica de los antiguos Mayas* (University of

México, 1975).

Girard, Rafael, *Los mayas eternos* (México, Antigua Librería Robredo, 1962).

—, *Los Mayas: Su civilización, su historia, sus vínculos continentales* (México, Libromex, 1966).

Girard, René, *Violence and the Sacred* (Baltimore and London: John Hopkins University Press, 1977). Original French version, 1972.

Goetz, D. and Morley, S.G., *Popol Vuh: The Sacred Book of the Ancient Quiché-Maya* (Norman and London, University of Oklahoma Press, 1950).

Gossen, G.H., *The Chamulas in the World of the Sun: Time and pace in a Maya Oral Tradition* (Cambridge, MS, Harvard University Press, 1974).

—, "Mission Strategy and the Political Consequences of Evangelical Growth in Guatemala". Public Justice Report. Center for Public Justice, Washington, D.C., 1993.

—, *South and Meso-American Spirituality: From the Cult of the Feathered Serpent to the Theology of Liberation* (London, SCM Press, 1993).

Gutiérrez, G., *Las Casas: In Search of the Poor of Jesus Christ* (Maryknoll, Orbis, 1993).

Hill, R.M. II, *Colonial Cakchiqueles: Highland Maya Adaptation to Spanish Rule 1600-1700* (New York & London, Harcourt Brace Jovanovich, 1991).

Hill, R.M. and M.J., *Continuities in Highland Maya Social Organization* (Philadelphia, University of Pennsylvania Press, 1987).

Kampen, M.E., *The Religion of the Maya* (Leiden, E.J . Brill, 1981).

Landa, Friar D. de, *Relación de las cosas de Yucatán* (México, Editorial Porrúa, 1959).

León-Portilla, Miguel ed., *Native Mesoamerican Spirituality*, (London: SPCK, 1980).

Mackey, S. and Silman, J., *The First Nations: A Canadian Experience of the Gospel and Culture Encounter* (Geneva, WCC Publications, 1995).

Makensie, M.W., *The Book of the Jaguar Priest: A Translation of the Book of Chilam Balam of Tizimim with Commentary* (New York: Henry Schuman, 1951).

Manz, B., *Refugees of a Hidden War* (New York, State University of New York Press, 1988).

Marzal, M.M., *El Sincretismo Iberoamericano: Un estudio comparativo sobre los quechuas (Cusco), los mayas (Chiapas) y los africanos (Bahia)* (Lima, Perú, Pontificia Universidad Católica, 1988).

Marzal, M.M., Maurer, E., Albó, X., and Melià, B., *The Indian Face of God in Latin America* (Maryknoll: Orbis, 1996).

Matul, D., *Somos un solo corazón: cultura Maya contemporánea* (San José, C.R., Liga Maya Internacional, 1994).

McClear, M., *Popol Vuh: Structure and Meaning* (Madrid, Playor, S.A., 1973).

Morley, S. G., *An Introduction to the Study of Maya Hieroglyphs* (New York, Dover Publications, 1975).

Nelson, W.M., *Protestantism in Central America* (Grand Rapids, Eerdmans 1984).

Nicholson, I., *Mexican and Central American Mythology* (Feltham, Middlesex, England, Newnes Books, 1983).

Pacheco, L., *Religiosidad Maya-kékchí alrededor del maíz* (San José, C.R.: Edición Escuela para Todos, 1985).

—, *Tradiciones y costumbres del pueblo Maya-Kékchí* (San José, C.R.: Ediciones Amba, 1988).

Reina, R.E., *Shadows: A Mayan Way of Knowing* (New York, Horizon Press, 1984).

Rivera Pagán, L.N., *A Violent Evangelism: The Political and Religious Conquest of the Americas* (Westminster, John Knox Press, 1992).

Schele, L. and Freidel, D., *A Forest of Kings: The Untold Story of the Ancient Maya* (New York, Morrow, 1990).

Sepúlveda, J., *Gospel in Culture in Latin American Protestantism: Toward a New Theological Appreciation of Synchretism*. Th.D. disertation, University of Birmingham, UK, 1996.

Schineller, SJ, P., "Inculturation: A Difficult and Delicate Task", in *International Bulletin of Missionary Research*. Vol xx, no. 3 (July 1996), pp. 109-112.

Smith, C. A. (ed.) *Guatemalan Indians and the State, 1540-1988*. Austin, University of Texas Press, 1990.

Stevens, J.L., *Incidents of Travel in Yucatán*, vol ii (New York, Dover Publications, 1965).

Sullivan, P., *Unfinished Conversations: Mayas and Foreigners Between Two Wars* (New York, Knopf, 1989).

Taube, K.A., *The Major Gods of Ancient Yucatan* (Washington, D.C., Dumbarton Oaks Research Library and Collection, 1992).

Tedlock, B., *Time and the Highland Maya* (University of New Mexico Press, 1982).

Thornton, R., *Indian Holocaust and Survival* (Norman, University of Oklahoma Press, 1987).

Urban, G. and Sherzer, J., *Nation-States and Indians in Latin America* (Austin: University of Texas Press, 1991).

Van der Raaij, M., "An African Doctrine of God and Images of Christ" in *Evangelical Review of Theology: Toward Integral Mission Theology*. Vol xx, no. 3 (July 1996), pp. 233-239.

Watanabe, J., *Maya Saints and Souls in a Changing World* (Austin, University of Texas Press).

Warren, K.B., *The Symbolism of Subordination: Indian Identity in a Guatemalan Town* (Austin, University of Texas Press, 1978).

Wearne, P. and Calvert, P., *The Maya of Guatemala* (London, The Minority Rights Group, 1989).

Wilson, R., *Maya Resurgence in Guatemala: Q'eqchi' Experiences* (London & Norman, University of Oklahoma Press, 1995).

Wright, R., *Stolen Continents: The Indian Story* (London, John Murray, 1992).

Prayers of Protestant pastors and Maya baton of authority for Pentecostal leader in Chiapas, México. (I)

Prayers of Protestant pastors and Maya baton of authority for Pentecostal leader in Chiapas, México. (II)

STUDIES IN
CHRISTIAN MISSION

1. WILLIAMS, C.P. *The Ideal of the Self-Governing Church.* A Study in Victorian Missionary Strategy. 1990. ISBN 90 04 09188 2
2. STINE, P.C. (ed.). *Bible Translation and the Spread of the Church.* The Last 200 Years. 1990. Reprint 1992. ISBN 90 04 09331 1
3. OOSTHUIZEN, G.C. *The Healer-Prophet in Afro-Christian Churches.* 1992. ISBN 90 04 09468 7
4. CARMODY s.j., B.P. *Conversion and Jesuit Schooling in Zambia.* 1992. ISBN 90 04 09428 8
5. PIROTTE, J. & H. DERROITE (eds.). *Églises et santé dans le Tiers Monde.* Hier et Aujourd'hui — *Churches and Health Care in the Third World.* Past and Present. 1991. ISBN 90 04 09470 9
6. BRENT, A. *Cultural Episcopacy and Ecumenism.* Representative Ministry in Church History from the Age of Ignatius of Antioch to the Reformation, With Special Reference to Contemporary Ecumenism. 1992. ISBN 90 04 09432 6
7. RUOKANEN, M. *The Catholic Doctrine of Non-Christian Religions.* According to the Second Vatican Council. 1992. ISBN 90 04 09517 9
8. T'IEN JU-K'ANG. *Peaks of Faith.* Protestant Mission in Revolutionary China. 1993. ISBN 90 04 09723 6
9. WEBER, Ch.W. *International Influences and Baptist Mission in West Cameroon.* German-American Missionary Endeavor under International Mandate and British Colonialism. 1993. ISBN 90 04 09765 1
10. ARITONANG, J.S. *Mission Schools in Batakland (Indonesia), 1861-1940.* 1994. ISBN 90 04 09967 0
11. DOTI SANOU, B. *L'Émancipation des femmes Madare.* L'impact du projet administratif et missionnaire sur une société africaine, 1900-1960. 1994. ISBN 90 04 09852 6
12. LAPOINTE, E. (éd.). *Correspondance entre François Laydevant et Albert Perbal, 1927-1952.* Dialogue du Missionnaire et du Missiologue. Avec annotations et introduction. 1994. ISBN 90 04 10171 3
13. TOULLELAN, P.-Y. *Missionnaires au quotidien à Tahiti.* Les Picpuciens en Polynésie au XIXe siècle. 1995. ISBN 90 04 10100 4
14. JOHNSON BLACK, N. *The Frontier Mission and Social Transformation in Western Honduras.* The Order of Our Lady of Mercy, 1525-1773. 1995. ISBN 90 04 10219 1
15. THOMPSON, T.J. *Christianity in Northern Malaŵi.* Donald Fraser's Missionary Methods and Ngoni Culture. 1995. ISBN 90 04 10208 6
16. BENEDETTO, R. (ed.). Translations by WINIFRED K. VASS. *Presbyterian Reformers in Central Africa.* A Documentary Account of the American Presbyterian Congo Mission and the Human Rights Struggle in the Congo, 1890-1918. 1996. ISBN 90 04 10239 6
17. REED, C. *Pastors, Partners and Paternalists.* African Church Leaders and Western Missionaries in the Anglican Church inKenya, 1850-1900. 1997. ISBN 90 04 10639 1
18. COOK, Q. (ed.). *Crosscurrents in Indigenous Spirituality.* Interface of Maya, Catholic and Protestant Worldviews. 1997. ISBN 90 04 10622 7